DOROTHY WORDSWORTH

OXFORD UNIVERSITY PRESS
AMEN HOUSE, E.C. 4
London Edinburgh Glasgow New York Toronto
Melbourne Capetown Bombay Calcutta Madras
HUMPHREY MILFORD
PUBLISHER TO THE UNIVERSITY

First edition 1933
Reprinted photographically in Great Britain
at the University Press, Oxford, 1944
from sheets of the first edition

DOVE COTTAGE ABOUT 1805

DOROTHY WORDSWORTH

A BIOGRAPHY

BY

ERNEST DE SELINCOURT

OXFORD
AT THE CLARENDON PRESS

PRINTED IN GREAT BRITAIN

To

GORDON WORDSWORTH

PREFACE

THIS book will be found to bear more resemblance to the old-fashioned *Life and Letters* than to a biography in the approved modern manner. But since Dorothy Wordsworth was a writer with a rare gift of description and a transparent sincerity in speaking of herself, I have thought it best to let her tell her own story, leaving her *ipsissima verba* to stand out clear from the narrative that connects them. For some of the richest years of her life she kept a diary, and she was at all times a voluminous correspondent; and the revelation of both herself and her surroundings that she gives in her letters and journals tallies with what we can learn of her from other sources, and has everywhere the stamp of truth.

In writing her biography, therefore, I have relied almost entirely upon the original documents. Some of these have long been accessible, e.g. in the *Journals of Dorothy Wordsworth*, edited by William Knight, 2 vols., 1897, and in the *Letters of the Wordsworth Family*, collected and edited by William Knight, 3 vols., 1907; but neither of these works professes to be complete—from both of them interesting and highly significant personal details are frequently omitted—and when I have compared their text with the originals I have not always found the transcription to be accurate. Some of the letters, in particular, have been carelessly copied, and not seldom they are wrongly dated. The originals of the Clarkson correspondence are, with few exceptions, in the British Museum: other MSS. are for the most part in private hands; and many of them, including some important letters which passed between members of the Wordsworth family, Dorothy's letters to Lady Beaumont written before June 1806, her later diaries and her narrative of the tragedy of the Greens, the personal memoranda of Mary Wordsworth and Edward Quillinan, and Quillinan's correspondence with Dorothy and Dora Wordsworth and with Sara Hutchinson, have not previously been available.

With these resources to draw upon, I have been able to give a fuller and, I believe, a juster account than has hitherto been possible of the relations which existed between Dorothy, her brother William, and their friend Coleridge, both at the height of their intimacy and in the days of its lamentable decline. This new evidence lends no support to those who have looked on Dorothy as a pathetic figure and an object for commiseration. The tale of her last twenty years makes, indeed, pitiful reading, though it is throughout illumined by the love that she inspired; but this period of cruelly protracted illness should be regarded as a posthumous life. During the sixty years which preceded it, though her capacity for suffering was commensurate with her capacity for joy, and her instinct for entering into the lives of others intensified both, she was yet essentially happy. She had a genius for friendship, and many of her friendships brought her a lasting pleasure; but the dominant absorbing passion of her life was always for her brother, and in the return of that passion she was more than satisfied. Such a passion is rare indeed, and the incorrigible romanticism from which even the literary critic is not immune has often preferred to regard her as the victim of a tragic frustration. But Dorothy Wordsworth was no ordinary woman, and it is never safe to judge the exceptional by the commonplace. This single-minded devotion to her brother called from her the finest powers of her intellect and heart, and strengthened the growth of her spirit; through her knowledge of him and her power to draw upon the sources whence his poetic inspiration sprang, she kept an ever fresh contact with all that matters most.

Naturally enough, her brother William, seen through her eyes, appears in a more attractive light than that in which he is usually presented. But in estimating his character too much stress is often laid upon the impressions of casual and unsympathetic observers; and Dorothy's conception of him, though barely on this side idolatry, may help to adjust the balance. For, after all, she was a woman of acute and sensitive intelligence, she lived in intimate companionship with him for more than fifty years, and the survival of her love and admiration undimmed to the end is in itself a tribute to him hardly less than to her. This narrative may also serve to discount the theories of those modern critics who, allured by the simplifications of a crude psycho-analysis, see in Annette the chief inspiration of his poetic achievement, and in the ghost of Annette the chief, if not the sole cause of his poetic decline.

But Dorothy Wordsworth, in her letters and journals, has not merely given us portraits of herself and William, and of their inner circle: she has left behind her a faithful picture of the world in which they moved. No one, not even her brother, has captured with a more delicate perception the distinctive beauties of the countryside in which her days were passed, nor revealed with a more penetrating sympathy the daily goings-on of its lowly inhabitants. Less intimate, but hardly less vivid, is her account of the lands she visited, of Germany at the close of the eighteenth century, of Scotland, Switzerland, and France at the beginning of the nineteenth; whilst her lively descriptions of an England so different from ours—of the sights of London, of travel to and fro by coach and chaise, of the court of George III at Windsor, of the tense excitement of the Napoleonic wars and the lesser stirrings of a county election, give an authentic background of the life of her time.

It is a pleasure to acknowledge the generous help that I have received from many quarters in the making of this book. To Messrs. Macmillan & Co. I am greatly indebted for permission to quote from those portions of the Journals which have already been printed, and of which they hold the copyright: as the *Alfoxden Journal* is now untraceable their selection from it is the sole authority for its text. Miss Catherine Marshall placed at my disposal the MSS. of the Pollard-Marshall correspondence; the Misses Baird Smith allowed me to examine the MSS. of the letters to De Quincey. Miss Helen Darbishire has read my book both in MS. and proof, and made many valuable suggestions.

To Mr. Gordon Wordsworth I owe the deepest debt: he has not only given me free access to the mass of material in his possession, but has allowed me constantly to draw upon his unrivalled knowledge of the family history. My book was first undertaken at his suggestion, and without his aid and encouragement it could not have been written.

I have also to thank him for three of my illustrations—the reproductions of the water-colour of Dove Cottage, of Dora Wordsworth's pencil drawing of Whitwick Parsonage, and of two memorable pages from the *Grasmere Journal*. Edridge's portrait of the poet as he was in his best years I owe to the kindness of Mrs. Rawnsley; 'Rydal Water', from an oil painting by Fred Yates, and Dorothy's Letter to Mrs. Clarkson (June 29, 1803) are from originals in my possession; the beautiful drawings of Forncett Rectory and of the Wishing Gate were specially made for me by my friend and colleague Miss J. J. Milne.

Lastly, I would express my gratitude to Miss Freda Thompson who has compiled the Index and given me much help in transcription and in corrections of proofs, and to the Clarendon Press, for the interest and care they have taken in the production of the volume.

E. de S.

CONTENTS

LIST OF ILLUSTRATIONS

LIST OF ABBREVIATIONS USED IN FOOTNOTES

D. W., W. W., M. W., R. W., J. W., and C. W. = Dorothy, William, Mary, Richard, John, and Christopher Wordsworth.

M. H. = Mary Hutchinson (*later* M. W.).

S. H. = Sara Hutchinson.

S. T. C. = Samuel Taylor Coleridge.

J. P. and J. M. = Jane Pollard, *later* Mrs. John Marshall.

C. C. = Mrs. Thomas Clarkson *née* Catharine Buck).

H. C. R. = Henry Crabb Robinson.

E. Q. = Edward Quillinan.

K. = Professor William Knight.

Oxf. W. = Poetical Works of W. W. ed. by Thomas Hutchinson; Oxford University Press.

Memoirs = *Memoirs of W. W.* by Christopher W., 2 vols. 1851.

ERRATA

Page 10, line 1 : *for* Pollard's *read* Pollards'
„ 18, note : for *Reminiscenes* read *Reminiscences*
„ 65, line 12 : *for* here *read* have
„ 78, line 19 : *for* March *read* May
„ 107, note 2, and Index, page 423 : *for* Rayson *read* Raysor
„ 113, 6 lines from bottom : *for* John *read* Thomas
„ 179, 3 lines from bottom : *delete* the last
„ 267, note 1 : *for* Sadler, i. 203. *read* Sadler (3rd ed. 1872), i. 203.
„ 281, line 19 : *for* end of it. *read* end of it.'
„ 281, line 4 of note 3 ; *for* Michael *read* Daniel
„ 311–12, notes : *for* Samuel *read* William
„ 353, note 1 : *for* Michael *read* Daniel
„ 367, line 10 : *for* Marshall's *read* Marshalls
„ 408, line 21 : *for* K. ii. 47 *read* K. ii. 57

De Selincourt : *Dorothy Wordsworth.*

I
EARLY YEARS
(*1771–1788*)

FEW lovers of Wordsworth's poetry have failed to realize something of what he owed to his sister Dorothy; the more discerning have seen in her, not merely the alert companion of his creative hours, and their faithful chronicler, but the deepest and most permanent influence upon his life. Her diaries and private correspondence go far to explain that influence. If she had not his intellectual power, she had all his passionate intensity of feeling; if she had not that speculative turn of mind, which led Coleridge to speak of him[1] as 'a great poet by inspirations, and in the moments of revelation, but a thinking, feeling philosopher habitually', she had the same vibrant artistic sensibility, with an even quicker response than his to the sights and sounds of the world about her, and a still happier gift for the inevitable words to communicate what she saw and heard and felt. Alike by what she wrote and what she was, Dorothy Wordsworth illumined her brother's life and poetry.

She would have desired no fuller tribute. No thought can ever have strayed into her restless, eager mind that she would in herself have the least interest for posterity. Yet the spell that she cast over her brother and all who knew her is still potent, and she has taken an assured place among that company of women who by a rare beauty of person, or mind, or character have enduring life in the pages of history and romance.

There is no portrait of her as she was in her prime; but in default of a fitting frontispiece to this story we may recall the vivid word-picture in which De Quincey set down the impression she made upon him when, already in her thirty-sixth year, he first met her and became her friend: short and slight, stooping forward as she walked, with a glancing quickness in all her movements, with a warm, even ardent manner, and a speech that often suffered in clearness and steadiness from the agitation of her excessive organic sensibility; her face tanned to an

[1] S. T. C. to W. W., Aug. 6, 1803.

'Egyptian brown' by constant exposure to sun and wind and rain, her eyes not soft, but wild and startling, which seemed to glow with some subtle fire of intellect that burned within her. And yet his predominant impression was not of her intellect, but rather of 'the exceeding sympathy, always ready and always profound, by which she made all that one could tell her reverberate to one's own feelings by the manifest impression that it made on *hers*. The pulses of light are not more quick or more inevitable in their flow and undulation, than were the answering and echoing movements of her sympathizing attention'. 'I may sum up her character as a companion', he concludes, 'by saying that she was the very wildest (in the sense of the most natural) person I have ever known; and also the truest, most inevitable, and at the same time the quickest and readiest in her sympathy with either joy or sorrow, with laughter or with tears, with the realities of life, or the larger realities of the poets.'[1]

The fidelity of De Quincey's picture is borne out by the fuller record of her life.

The Wordsworths were of good Yorkshire stock; they are first heard of at Peniston in the fourteenth century, and seem to have come from the neighbouring village of Wadsworth.[2] Dorothy's grandfather, Richard Wordsworth, born in 1690, left his native county for Westmorland in 1723, to take up an appointment as steward of a leading family in Appleby, bought a small property at Sockbridge in the parish of Barton near Penrith, and in 1745 became Clerk of the Peace and Receiver General of the county of Westmorland. His wife bore him two daughters, Anne and Mary, and two sons; the elder of these, Richard, became Collector of Customs at the port of Whitehaven, whilst the younger, John, was educated for the law, settled down at Cockermouth, and like his father, entered the service of the Lowther family. On February 5, 1766, when he was just over twenty-four years old, he married Anne Cookson, daughter of William Cookson, the chief mercer of Penrith, and of Dorothy, sister and heiress of James Crackanthorpe of Newbiggin Hall. They had five children, Richard, born on May 19, 1768; William on April 7, 1770; Dorothy on December 25, 1771; John on December 4, 1772; and Christopher on June 9, 1774.

[1] De Quincey, *Works*, ed. Masson, ii. 239, 297.

[2] *The Wordsworths of Peniston*, by G. G. Wordsworth, privately printed, 1929.

In the summer of 1828, travelling to Cockermouth by the Keswick road, Dorothy 'had a good view of the many cloudy summits and swelling breastworks of Skiddaw, and was particularly struck with the amplitude of style and objects,—flat Italian foreground, large fields, and luxuriant hedges,—a perfect garden of Eden, with immense rose bushes garlanded with flowers—the white elder, rich as ivory and pearls',[1] so that when she approached the town the country seemed 'dull and barish', and Cockermouth itself surprised her 'with its poor aspect'. But that was only because she expected too much from a scene which in her imagination still shone with all the golden glamour of childhood. It was in reality a pleasant enough little market-town, and her father had occupied one of the best houses in it—a long red-brick building on the north side of the main street, close to the bridge over the Derwent. There was a garden at the back, bounded by a high terrace abutting on the river, with a view of the castle to the right. The house belonged to Sir James Lowther, and as there is no entry for rent in the careful accounts kept by John Wordsworth, it is probable that he lived in it rent free, in part payment for his professional services. But the fields on the far side of the river and towards the castle were his own property, and these he farmed himself, keeping on them his mare and a cow.

In addition to his other duties John Wordsworth was Bailiff and Recorder of the Borough of Cockermouth and Coroner of the Seignory of Millom. He was clearly a man of unflagging industry and good practical ability, intent on building up for himself a sound financial position. He was widely respected in the district for his high integrity, and his unusual mental vigour and eloquence; and the small library that he had collected bears witness to his literary taste and interests. To his wife he was passionately devoted, and he was on affectionate terms with his brother and brothers-in-law; but outside his family he seems to have had no intimate friends, and his position at Cockermouth as the representative of the tyrannical Sir James Lowther would not tend to ease his relations with his neighbours. On his sons and daughter he seems to have made no deep or lasting impression. Of a reserved nature, and preoccupied with affairs, which often took him far afield, he was not,

[1] D. W., *Diary of Tour in the Isle of Man*, 1828.

perhaps, the type of man who finds it easy to enter into the life of his children.

Anyhow, it is natural enough that in their early days their mother should count for more. She it was, says her son,

> who was the heart
> And hinge of all our learnings and our loves.

'I know', wrote Dorothy to Lady Beaumont in 1804, 'that I received much good that I can trace back to her', and she promises to give her friend fuller details of her mother's character. In no surviving letter was this promise fulfilled, yet the glowing tribute paid her in *The Prelude*[1] goes far to make good our loss. Anne Wordsworth was a fine example of the old type of motherhood. If not intellectual she was a woman of high character, and rich in common sense. Devoted to her children, and fully understanding them, she was not one of those mothers who expect their children to be prodigies, and in the desire to prove them so, turn them into prigs. She loved them for what they were rather than for what they might become. She was infected by none of the newfangled theories of education which had followed in the wake of Rousseau. She was not over-anxious or fussy, afraid to trust them out of her sight; but let them run wild in the open, disporting themselves at will in the garden and on the terrace walk, or in the fields of yellow ragwort by the river's edge; and when she read to them it was not from those improving moral tales that were just beginning to flood the market, but from stories of immemorial delight—Jack the Giant-Killer, Robin Hood, and the like, tales of romance and mystery which, instead of encouraging a morbid introspection, took them out of themselves. Thus their world lay

> justly balanced; partly at their feet,
> And part far from them.

From the first William and Dorothy were specially drawn to one another: in age little more than a year apart, in temperament alike, yet different, they were born to be companions. Both were affectionate, sensitive, excitable; but to the rougher and more passionate nature of the boy Dorothy brought tenderness and delicacy, and an even quicker perception. The few loving records of her childhood, preserved for us by William,

[1] *The Prelude* (1805), v. 256–90.

bear witness to that abnormal sensibility, that union of alert vision with instinctive sympathy, which only grew with the years. When she first heard the voice of the sea, and beheld it spread out before her, she burst into tears; when they chased the butterfly together, and he would rush like a hunter upon the prey, she feared to brush the dust from off its wings; when they visited the sparrow's nest in the holly at the foot of the garden, and saw its bright blue eggs lying close together:

> She looked at it and seemed to fear it;
> Dreading, tho' wishing, to be near it:
> Such heart was in her, being then
> A little Prattler among men.

But Dorothy's life at Cockermouth was brief as it was happy. When she was just six years old she went to her grandparents at Penrith whilst her mother was paying visits in the south. In the guest room of some friends in London Mrs. Wordsworth slept in damp sheets, and she returned to Penrith seriously ill. A rapid consumption developed, and on March 11 she was laid to rest in the Penrith Churchyard. At her dying request Dorothy was entrusted to the care of her cousin Elizabeth Threlkeld, and early in the following June the little orphan left Penrith in a postchaise with Miss Threlkeld, bound for her new home.

The Threlkelds were an old Cumberland family with a rich historic past, related to the Wordsworths through the marriage of Elizabeth's father Samuel to Elizabeth Cookson, Anne Wordsworth's aunt. Samuel Threlkeld (1701–67) after training at the University of Glasgow had settled down in 1732 at Penrith as a Unitarian minister. Ten years later he accepted a call to the more important pastorate of the Northgate-end Chapel at Halifax, a place of worship attended by some of the most prosperous and influential citizens of the town, and playing no small part in its social and intellectual life. But he had kept in close touch with his Cumberland relatives, and his daughter's intimacy with her cousin Anne is attested by the fact that when Anne married John Wordsworth, Elizabeth Threlkeld was one of the two witnesses who signed the register.

Not the least of the debts which Dorothy owed to her mother was this wise provision for her future. Elizabeth Threlkeld, as is clear from the testimony of all who knew her and from those of her letters that are still extant, was a woman of alert intelligence, wide culture, and a shrewd practical common sense, always busy, but devoted to her garden and to the simple pleasures of a country life. Of children and their ways she had already something of a mother's experience, for the death in 1773 of her sister Anne Ferguson, followed two years later by that of her brother-in-law, had left her the guardian of five little nephews and nieces, of ages ranging from eleven to five years old. She had, indeed, an instinctive understanding of young children, and succeeded, where the best of parents often fail, in combining a firm sense of discipline with due respect for the child's personality and inborn love of freedom. Thus she not only won their confidence and affection but kept it; so that the nephews and nieces who had looked up to her as children turned to her throughout their lives for sympathy and guidance.

To the acutely sensitive and affectionate Dorothy the loss of her mother and the separation from her playmate William must have been a passionate sorrow; but the tears of childhood, for all their bitterness, are quickly dried. It could not have been without some memory of her own experience that years later, in telling the tale of the Green family, whose parents were lost in the snow above Langdale, she recounted the agony of their grief at leaving the cottage that had been their home, and their speedy restoration to happiness under the kindly guardianship of the good dalesmen to whom they were entrusted. Certainly Dorothy's reminiscences of the nine years she passed at Halifax show no trace of melancholy or depression. 'Aunt' Threlkeld, as she always called her, won the affections of her new ward as surely as she had already gained that of the little Fergusons. Phrases from later letters, such as 'the loss of a mother can only be made up by such a friend as my dear Aunt', or 'my Aunt, you know, has been my Mother', bear ample witness to the warmth of Dorothy's attachment. She was, wrote Dorothy,[1] 'the very best tempered woman and the most thoroughly intent upon doing what is right of any person I ever knew, all without effort, from a blessed nature'. For fifty years after she left Halifax Dorothy kept in close touch with her, seeing her whenever opportunity offered, and until the happy time when she

[1] D. W. to C. C., July 19, 1807.

could set up house with William she always looked upon Halifax as her home.

It is clear that to the precept, and still more to the example, of her dear aunt, Dorothy owed the development of much that was best in her character—her strong sense of duty, her unselfishness, her ready delight in the service of those she loved. Her aunt was responsible too for the best part of her education. The careful accounts kept by John Wordsworth supply evidence of her passing six months, when she was ten years old, at a boarding school at Hipperholme, some two miles from Halifax, and when she was thirteen an entrance fee of five shillings was paid for her to a day-school, where she probably remained till she left her aunt's care. But her sole allusion to the time she spent there is not impressive. 'When I was a little girl like you', she told her god-daughter,[1] 'I wrote very neatly and also what was called a *very good hand*, but with making French exercises and scribbling long letters to one of my companions I fell into a careless way of making crooked lines and irregular words, and have never been able to get the better of it.' The school at Halifax, unlike the fashionable seminaries of the day, did not aim at perfecting its pupils in those elegant accomplishments which would impress the masculine world. Readers of Jane Austen will remember how over the mantelpiece of Miss Charlotte Jennings' room 'hung a landscape in coloured silks of her own performance, in proof of her having spent seven years at a great school in town to some effect'. Dorothy, indeed, may have worked her sampler, but the sewing on which, we may be sure, her aunt insisted was of a more homely kind; and the records of her later life say nothing of elaborate embroidery, but much of altering curtains and mending stockings, of making the household linen and shirts for her brothers. Of neither music nor drawing, those two other essentials in the equipment of a lady, did she learn even the rudiments. When it fell to her lot to amuse a baby, she wrote, 'Mary is delighted with my singing: you will wonder at her taste.' She had to confess to Lady Beaumont: 'I have not been taught to exercise the pencil. It is indeed, true that I scarcely ever take a walk without lamenting it'; and when she attempted to give her friend a rough idea of the exterior of Dove Cottage she found that the knowledge of

[1] D. W. to Elizabeth Hutchinson, July 16, 1830.

perspective required to delineate the 'out-jutting' lay entirely beyond her powers. 'My drawings', she wrote, 'will make you smile at my little skill.'[1] True, she was addressing the wife of a distinguished artist, but her draughtsmanship would hardly have passed muster with a less exacting critic.

But if, like her friend Bridget Elia, she 'missed all that female garniture which passeth by the name of accomplishments', like Bridget, 'she was early turned into the wholesome pasturage of good old English reading'. At the age of fourteen she devoured *Clarissa Harlowe*, a diet which the modern parent would hardly think digestible at such tender years, and before she was sixteen her small library contained the works of Shakespeare, Milton, and Fielding, Homer's *Iliad* and *Odyssey*, probably in Pope's translation, *Gil Blas*, *The Spectator*, and Goldsmith. Thus early she acquired a taste for the best things in literature and that easy mastery of language and happy sense for the right word which distinguish her own later writing. The letters which she wrote as a girl of sixteen are remarkable for their correctness and maturity of style. They betray, indeed, in places where she has nothing much to say, signs of her eighteenth-century models in a slight stiffness and formality of expression alien to her frank and impulsive nature, but when she is interested her pen runs easily and naturally, and her gift of language grew in strength and delicacy with the growth of her powers of sympathetic vision.

But books never came first with Dorothy. Halifax was a social place, and she had plenty of gay young companions with whom to play games, and dance, and go for country rambles. Her five Ferguson cousins, Samuel, Martha, Edward, Anne, and Elizabeth, who lived with her under her aunt's roof, and her other cousins, the two daughters of William Threlkeld who lived hard by, were all some years older than she, and though she was a favourite with them and retained through life a warm regard for them, they can hardly have been the companions of her childish games. But there were plenty of girls of her own age, either schoolfellows or daughters of her aunt's friends. Chief of these was Jane Pollard, eldest daughter of William Pollard, a prosperous mill-owner, and one of the staunchest supporters of the Northgate-end Chapel. With Jane, Dorothy struck up one of those passionate friendships which, though they may provoke

[1] D. W. to Lady B., Aug. 26, 1805 (misdated in K. 1806).

amusement or disapproval from the older world, are yet among the intensest and most educative of the experiences of girlhood. Dorothy's devotion to Jane differed from the common run of such attachments in that it lasted all their lives. To her letters to Jane Pollard, written after she left Halifax, we owe almost all our knowledge of her early life, for whilst recounting to her absent friend news of her latest doings she delighted to recall the happy days they had passed together, when they would steal away from their playfellows to enjoy the sweets of intimacy, and build their airy castles in the back kitchen or the croft; or in the summer would sally forth, their black porringers in their hands, to search for bilberries on the moors.

The castle that they built most persistently took the modest form of a cottage in which to pass a life of untiring companionship:

A cottage in a verdant dell
A pure unsullied household well,
A garden stored with fruit and flowers
And sunny seats and shady bowers
A file of hives for humming bees
Under a row of stately trees
And, sheltering all this faery ground,
A belt of hills must wrap it round
Not stern, or mountainous, or bare,
Nor lacking herbs to scent the air;
Besprinkled o'er with trees and rocks,
And pastured by the blameless flocks,
That leave their green tracks to invite
Our wanderings to the topmost height.
Such was the scene I fondly framed
When life was new and hope untamed—
—There with my one dear friend to dwell
Nor wish for aught beyond the dell.

So forty years afterwards, in a *Christmas Rhyme* written for Jane's daughter Julia, Dorothy described the dream of her youth. If it was not realized, the love, at least, that prompted it, was constant throughout her life.

Dorothy's early correspondence with Jane, with its eager inquiries about all that was happening in the circle she had just left, and its passing allusions to one person or another, gives glimpses of the company of lively young people which gathered round the fireside at the Pollard's or Aunt Threlkeld's, and met at the summer picnics and winter 'routs'. There were Jane's three younger sisters, of whom Harriot was the most charming, and the handsome Mary Grimshaw, and Peggy Taylor, whom Dorothy loved so well as to cause Jane some passing pangs of jealousy, 'though', protests Dorothy, 'she never had so large a share of my heart as you'. And some of Dorothy's comments are critical enough, as that on her untidy cousin Patty Ferguson, 'who curled her hair and put on her cap with less skill than any girl I know', and on Molly Waterhouse, the pretty little blue-stocking, who leaves in the spare bedroom, possibly not without thought of the effect to be produced on the male visitor, 'copies of Locke *On the Human Understanding*, *Euclid*, and other such books, with her name in them'.

It is clear that Dorothy was a great favourite at Halifax. Impulsive as she was in manner and movement, quick in response to all that was going on about her, with an inexhaustible fund of enjoyment and an impetuous way of talking, in which her words seemed to tumble over one another in her eagerness to share her feelings with others, she put life into the dullest company, and the affection she won on all sides she returned in full measure.

But in May 1787, when she was in her sixteenth year, she was summoned from Halifax to take up her abode with her grandparents at Penrith. Her father had died three years before and the little fortune that he had left behind him was nearly all in the hands of the despotic Lord Lowther, who refused to surrender it; doubtless her guardians thought it high time that Dorothy made herself useful. But it was a heavy change for her. To bid good-bye to Jane and her dear Aunt and all her kindly friends and cousins would have been a wrench whatever the future might have held in store for her; but though she could look forward eagerly enough to reunion with her brothers, Penrith had little else to invite her. Grandparents seldom prove the wisest companions for the young; if they remember their own childhood they wish to live again vicariously the thoughtless joys of youth, and they accept the pleasures of parenthood more readily than its responsibilities: if their memories are shorter, they are apt to resent the child's irrepressible vitality as a criticism on their own sobriety, and by persistent fault-finding persuade themselves that they are exercising a healthful discipline, when they are, in reality, avenging on the innocent their own inevitable loss. Such were the elderly Cooksons. There is no reason to doubt their good intentions, but theirs was a crabbed age. William Cookson was a well respected citizen of Penrith, and a pillar of the Church, but children had long ceased to enter into his scheme of life; and, moreover, the painful illness, soon to prove fatal, from which he was already suffering, did not tend to sweeten his temper. His wife held by a different system of education from that under which Dorothy had thriven at Cockermouth and Halifax. Not the only person who noted that Dorothy was 'intractable and wild', she saw in her high spirits the clear sign of original sin, and made it her pleasure as well as her duty to tame them. Her son Christopher Crackanthorpe shared her views. Naturally, then, Dorothy's first weeks at Penrith were lonely and miserable, only buoyed up by anticipation of her brothers' return from school, and when at last they arrived, though they proved all that she had hoped for, she still found much to repine at in her lot. In the first of her extant letters to Jane Pollard she pours out all her woes:

(Penrith: summer, 1787)
Sunday eve

Has not my dear Jane accused me of having forgotten already my promise? Has she not accused me of neglect? Believe me I am not deserving of these reproaches. However great may have been my dear friend's disappointment at not having heard from me, it cannot equal my distress at being prevented writing to her for I have had the mortification of thinking one I love reproaches me with ingratitude besides that of being deprived of the pleasure of writing to her, but if you have harboured any such suspicions of me let me entreat you, my dear Jane, to banish them. Believe me I am not deserving of them. Every night since the time I ought to have wrote to you I have gone to bed with an aching heart. I have thought there is one who perhaps at this moment is thinking of me as having forgotten our friendship, forgotten to love her; Ah! how have these thoughts affected me, but I will proceed to lay before you my excuses, I hope they are such as will insure my pardon. Sunday, was the day I fixt upon for writing to you, but I went out into the country at seven o'clock in the morning and did not return till it was too late to attempt beginning. On Monday my Grandmr was in a very bad humour and I could not get out of the room for a moment, on Tuesday I had fully intended writing both to my Aunt and you but as I had been longer in her debt I thought I ought to begin my letter to her the first, and I did not finish it till it was too late to attempt writing another, on Wednesday night I began one to you, but the shop was shut up and I could get no ink-stand but one which was quite dry. I desired my Br John to put a little water in it, and he filled it so full that it blotted all my paper and when I had finished half a sheet I found it was impossible for you to read it therefore I threw it aside; on Thursday night I began writing but my Br Wm. was sitting by me and I could not help talking with him till it was too late to finish, on Friday night *work* prevented me, and yesterday all my little preparations for Sunday—do you forgive me? or are you still inclined to accuse me of indolence? I hope you do not. I hope you say within yourself "She is equally as pardonable as I was, she has felt the same uneasiness, the same fears lest her friend should think she has forgotten her". Do, pray do forgive me and write to me at the appointed time. I might perhaps have employed an hour or two in writing to you but I have so few, so very few to pass with my Brothers that I could not leave them. You know not how happy I am in their company. I do not now want a friend who will share with me all my distresses. I do not now pass half my time alone. I can bear the illnature of all my relations, for the affection of my brothers consoles me in all my griefs, but how soon alas! shall I be deprived of this consolation! and how soon shall I become melancholy, even more melancholy than before. They are just the boys I could wish them, they are so affectionate and so kind to me as makes me love them more and more every day. Wm and Christopher are very clever boys, at least so they appear in the partial eyes of a sister. No doubt I am partial and see virtues in them that by everybody else will pass unnoticed. John, who is to be a sailor, has a most excellent heart, he is not so bright as either William or Christopher but he has very good commonsense and is very well calculated for the profession he has chosen. Richard (the eldest) I have seen. He is equally affectionate and good, but is far from being as clever as William, but I have no doubts of his succeeding in his business for he is very diligent and far from being dull, he only spent a night with us. Many a time have W., J, C, and myself shed tears together, tears of the bitterest sorrow; we all of us, each day, feel more sensibly the loss we sustained when we were deprived of our parents, and each day we receive fresh insults. You will wonder of what sort; believe me of the most mortifying kind, the insults of servants, but I will give you the particulars of our distresses as far as my paper will allow, but I cannot tell you half what I wish and I fear that when I have finished you will feel yourself almost as much in the dark as ever. I was for a whole week kept in expectation of my brothers, who staid at school all the time after the vacation began owing to the ill nature of my Uncle who would not send horses for them because when they wrote they did not happen to mention them, and only said when they should break up, which was always before sufficient. This was the beginning of my mortifications, for I felt that if they had had another home to go to, they would have been behaved to in a very different manner, and received with more chearful countenances, indeed nobody but myself expressed one wish to see them. At last however they were sent for, but not till my Brother Wm had hired a horse for himself and came over because he thought someone must be ill; the servants are every one of them so insolent to us as makes the kitchen as well as the parlour quite insupportable. James has even gone so far as to tell us we had nobody to depend upon but my Grandfr, for that our fortunes were very small; and my Brothers cannot even get a pair of shoes cleaned without James's telling them they require as much waiting upon as any "gentlemen", nor can I get a thing done for myself without absolutely entreating it as a favour. James happens to be a particular favorite with my Uncle Kit, who has taken a dislike to my Br and never takes any notice of us, so that he thinks while my Uncle behaves in this way to us he may do anything. We are found fault with every hour of the day both by the servants and my grandfr and grandmr, the former of whom never speaks to us but when he scolds, which is not seldom. I dare say our fortunes have been weighed thousands of times at the tea table in the kitchen and I have no doubt but they always conclude their conversations with 'they have nothing to be proud of'. Our fortunes will I fear be very small as Lord Lonsdale will most likely only pay a very small part of his debt which is 4700 pound. My uncle Kit (who is our guardian) having said many disrespectful things of him and having always espoused the cause of the Duke of Norfolk, has incensed him so much that I fear we shall feel through life the effects of his imprudence. We shall however have sufficient to educate my Brothers. John poor fellow! says he shall have occasion for very little, two hundred pounds will be enough to fit him out, and he should wish Wm to have the rest for his education, as he has a wish to be a Lawyer if his health will permit, and it will be very expensive. We shall have I believe about six hundred pound a piece if Lord Lonsdale does not pay. It is but very little, but it will be quite enough for my Brothers' education and after they are once put forward in the world there is little doubt of their succeeding, and for me, while they live I shall never want a friend. Oh Jane! when they have left me I shall be quite unhappy, I shall long more ardently than ever for you, my dearest dearest friend. We have been told thousands of times that we were liars but we treat such behaviour with the contempt it deserves. We always finish our conversations which generally take a melancholy turn, with wishing we had a father and a home. Oh! Jane, I hope it may be long ere you experience the loss of your parents, but till you know that loss you will never know how dear to you your sisters are; till you feel that loss! do I say? I almost wish you may never feel it, for 'tis the greatest misfortune that can befall one, but 'tis what in the course of nature one must expect: but I shall be making you as melancholy as myself and am distressing both you and myself with thinking of an event that I hope will not happen these many, many years, during which time I hope my dear Jane will never experience any of the mortifications to which her friend is continually subject, and that the domestic happiness which now reigns in your family may never once be interrupted.

I have read over my letter, and find it is only filled with my concerns; pardon me my dearest girl; what is uppermost in my mind I must write. Write pray do write on Sunday and depend upon an answer.

My love to each of your family.

When Dorothy complained that no one but herself had a wish to see her brothers she cannot have been far wrong. The incursion of three high-spirited boys, fresh from the school at Hawkshead where, out of lesson hours, they enjoyed a generous liberty, can hardly have made for peace in a well-ordered elderly household. The moody and headstrong William was in particular disfavour. Even his mother had felt some apprehensions about his future, and his grandparents and uncle cannot have forgotten how, some years before, in sheer devilry, he had flicked his whip through a treasured ancestral portrait. Small wonder, then, that when, on August 5, the holidays came to an end, William was sent back to Hawkshead with John and Christopher, though his school-days were over and he was bound for Cambridge in the autumn. But to Dorothy this was a new and unexpected sorrow, and her next letter is no more cheerful than the first. After the usual apologies for not writing sooner she runs on, the lightness of her punctuation being suggestive of her breathless haste:

'. . . Yesterday morning I parted with the kindest and most affectionate of Brothers, I cannot paint to you my distress at their departure, I can only tell you that for a few hours I was absolutely miserable, a thousand tormenting fears rushed upon me, the approaching winter, the illnature of my Grandfather and Uncle Chris. the little probability there is of my soon again seeing my younger Brother, and the still less likelihood of my revisiting my Halifax friends, in quick succession filled my mind. Could I write to you while I was in this situation? My dear Jane's feeling heart will I am sure at once tell her, "No." After dinner I began a letter of which I wrote one side before Church-time. As I was returning home in the afternoon two young ladies engaged me to walk with them; I was in low spirits; I thought a walk would perhaps put off for a while my melancholy reflections therefore I consented; I rose early this morning, and I should certainly have employed my time in addressing you my dear Jane if I had not had some work to finish before my Grandmother's coming downstairs, it was what I neglected doing while my Brothers were here, as when they were with me I could always employ my time much more agreeably than in mending an old shirt. She did not know that I had not finished it, and if I had not done it this morning she would have found me out, to-day I went out a visiting and when I came home it was too late for the post. My Grandmother is now gone to bed and I am quite alone. Imagine me sitting in my bed-gown, my hair out of curl and hanging about my face, with a small candle beside me, and my whole person the picture of poverty (as it always is in a bed-gown) and you will then see your friend Dorothy. It is after eleven o'clock. I begin to find myself very sleepy and I have my Hair to curl, so I must bid my very dear friend a good night.

'Tuesday evening. I have stolen a moment again to take up my pen to write to my dear Jane and I hope to be able to finish my Epistle before the post goes off, though I am sure I could not write in a dozen sheets all I have to say to her, and perhaps if I was to be able to tell her all I wish she would think I only troubled her with trifles—You know not how forlorn and dull I find myself now that my Brs are gone, neither can you imagine how I enjoyed their company when I could contrive to be alone with them which I did as often as possible. Ah! Jane if the partial affection of a Sister does not greatly magnify all their merits, they are charming boys, particularly the three youngest. No doubt I discern in them merits which by every body else pass unheeded. I often say to myself "I have the most affectionate brothers in the world, while I possess them, while I have you my dear Jane to whom I will ever lay open all the secrets of my heart can I ever be entirely miserable?" But no one can deprive me of the sweet consolation of pouring out my sorrows into the bosom of a brother or a friend; I young as I am flatter myself that Halifax contains several real friends to me, but it is indeed mortifying to my Brothers and me to find that amongst all those who visited at my father's house he had not one real friend. . . . I thank you my dear Jane for your inquiries about my health, I have been perfectly well since I came to Penrith excepting for a pain in my head now and then, but I think crying was the cause of it. . . . I am determined to read a great deal now, both in French and English. My Grandmr sits in the shop in the afternoons, and by working particularly hard for one hour I think I may read the next without being discovered, and I rise pretty early in a morning. . . . I am at present reading the Iliad, and like it very much. My Br Wm read a part of it. So you have got high-heeled shoes. I do not think of having them yet awhile, I am so very little, and wish to appear as girlish as possible. I wear my hair curled about my face in light curls frizzed at the bottom and turned at the ends. How have you yours? I have tied my black hat under the chin, as it looked shabby in its former state. . . . Adieu my dearest dearest girl, My very best love to all your family. Write soon. Can you read this?'[1]

Before setting out for Cambridge William returned to Penrith, and Dorothy had three blissful weeks of his company. Then a dreary winter closed in upon her. Further acquaintance with her grandparents did not increase their mutual sympathies, nor, we must add, Dorothy's respect for her elders.

'One would imagine', she writes to Jane in her next letter,[2] 'that a Grandmr would feel for her grandchild all the tenderness of a mother, particularly when that Grandchild had no other parent, but there is so little of tenderness in her manner or of anything affectionate, that while I am in her house I cannot at all consider myself as at home, I feel like a stranger. You cannot think how gravely and silently I sit with her and my Grandfr, you would scarcely know me. You are well acquainted that I was never

[1] D. W. to J. P., Aug. 5 and 6, 1787.
[2] D. W. to J. P., late autumn, 1787.

remarkable for taciturnity, but now I sit for whole hours without saying anything excepting that I have an old shirt to mend, then my Grandmr and I have to set our heads together and contrive the most notable way of doing it, which I dare say in the end we always hit upon, but really the contrivance itself takes up more time than the shirt is worth; our only conversation is about *work, work*, or what sort of a servant such a one's is, who are her parents, what places she lived in, why she left them, etc. etc. What my dear Jane can be more uninteresting than such conversation as this? Yet I am obliged to set upon the occasion as *notable* a face as if I was delighted with it, and that nothing could be more agreeable to me; notability is preached up to me every day, such an one is a very *sedate, clever, notable* girl says my grmr. My grm's taste and mine so ill agree that there is not one person who is a favourite with her that I do not dislike. You are well acquainted with the characters of those two amiable ladies the Miss Custs,[1] they are a mixture of ignorance, pride, affectation, self-conceit, and affected notability; I now see so many of those *useful* people in their own imaginations, the *notables*, that I have quite an aversion to every one that bears that character. The Miss C.s are so ill-natured too; I could bear their ignorance well enough, if they did not think so exceedingly well of themselves; for it cannot be expected that those who have not had the advantages of education can know as much as those who have. I have filled above half my paper with talking about those who are not worth my notice, and whose meanness only deserves my contempt; I will therefore, no longer vex myself with thinking of them nor you of reading about them.'

But Penrith could boast some few inhabitants neither grumpy like her grandparents nor 'notable' like the Misses Cust. Foremost among these were Mary and Peggy Hutchinson, of whom Dorothy spoke later as 'my sole companions at Penrith, who removed the tediousness of many an hour and whose company, in the absence of my brothers, was the only agreeable variety that Penrith afforded'.[2] The Hutchinsons were a family of ten. Their father, an importer and manufacturer of tobacco, had not been over-successful in business, and when he died left little provision for his family. The eldest boys, John, Henry, and

[1] On Aug. 27, 1788, D. W.'s uncle Kit married Charlotte Cust; hence, perhaps her grandmother's admiration for the Miss Custs. But when Charlotte became her aunt, D.'s opinion of her did not rise: *v.* p. 55.

[2] D. W. to J. P., Apr. 1795.

Thomas, were now with their uncle at Durham, and a younger sister Sara, afterwards an almost constant inmate of the Wordsworth household, was being brought up by a cousin of her mother's at Kendal. But Mary and Peggy, with the remainder of the family, lived at Penrith with Elizabeth Monkhouse, their mother's sister; their great-aunt, Mrs. Gamage, had settled in a house close by, in order to supervise their upbringing. Aunt Gamage, who was a disciple of Dr. Watts, Dorothy disliked almost as much as her own grandmother, but the milder aunt seems to have met with her approval, whilst there were many bonds of sympathy to draw her to Mary Hutchinson. Not only were both orphans, but their parents had been close friends. One of Mary's earliest memories was the picture of her mother 'as she sate weeping and warming herself by the kitchen fire, upon her return from the funeral' of Anne Wordsworth. And as a small boy William had been at the same dame school as Mary, perhaps had leant over her shoulder as she spelled out her letters from the copy of Addison's *Spectator*, lent her for the purpose by Aunt Gamage.[1] With Mary and Peggy Hutchinson Dorothy took many a walk in the country round Penrith, and often, on winter nights, they 'used to steal out to each others houses, and when we had had our talk over the kitchen fire, to delay the moment of parting, paced up one street and down another by moon or starlight'. And they also met at the Vicarage, where both Dorothy and the little Hutchinsons were welcome; for the Rev. Doctor Cowper's second daughter, Ann, had married Mary's uncle Monkhouse, and Dorothy's uncle William was courting the vicar's fourth and beautiful daughter Dorothy, who had already rejected the advances of his disagreeable elder brother.

William Cookson was a very different type of man from uncle Kit, whom Dorothy so cordially disliked. He had experience of a wider world than Penrith, 'that petty place', as Dorothy unkindly called it.[2] A fellow of St. John's College, Cambridge, where Wilberforce had been among his chief friends, he was a scholar and a man of taste and feeling, and he was quick to

[1] *Family Reminiscenes of M. W.* (MS.)

[2] Dorothy's contempt for Penrith society was shared by other members of her family. Thus her brother John, after visiting the town in 1800, wrote to her: 'I think P. is the most scandalous place I was ever in—everything one says and does is known to the whole town.' J. W. to D. W., Nov. 10, 1800.

detect qualities in his niece to which the rest of his family were blind. He evidently resented the way in which she was harried by her grandmother, and not only had different views of her welfare, but was able to enforce them. Mrs. Cookson thought that a girl of sixteen was more profitably occupied in plain sewing than in reading the *Iliad* or that new Scots poet whom Jane had recommended to her, whose vulgar poem on a louse seemed so amusing to the unregenerate Dorothy; but uncle William interested himself in her education, and took her off from nine to eleven every morning to do lessons in French, Arithmetic, and Geography. He sympathized, too, with her longing to pour out her heart to her distant friends, and allowed her to write letters in lesson-hours, whereas her grandmother had 'no idea one can have anything to write about, but that one is well and such stuff as that'. If she had read the letters Dorothy was writing to her dear Jane, her disapproval might have been still more strongly worded.

Dorothy responded to her uncle's kindness with all the warmth of her nature: 'I am now writing', she tells Jane, 'by that Uncle whom I so much love, he is a friend to whom (next to my Aunt) I owe the greatest obligations, every day gives me new proofs of his affection and every day I like him better than I did before.'[1] But notwithstanding her uncle's kindness she passed a dull winter, with none of the 'merry evenings and agreeable dances' that Jane was enjoying at Halifax. Her brothers were to spend their Christmas holidays with their uncle Richard at Whitehaven, but though she was invited to join them she was not allowed to go. Her dear Aunt Threlkeld paid a visit to Newcastle, and a Halifax friend who called at Penrith offered to escort her there, but this too was denied her. And the sudden death of old Mr. Cookson, three days before Christmas, did not tend to make the house more lively. No wonder that she felt more than ever her separation from her brothers ('how we are squandered abroad!' she exclaims) and longed for the cheerful society of Halifax and her heart-to-heart talks with Jane. As it is they can only exchange by the post their little gifts and words of undying devotion:

'I have sent you', she writes,[2] 'a lock of my hair, it will serve to remind you of poor Dolly whenever you see it. You cannot

[1] D. W. to J. P., late autumn, 1787.

[2] D. W. to J. P., Jan. 1788.

think how I like the idea of being called poor Dorothy or Dolly by my Halifax friends, I could cry whenever I think of it; strange as this may appear it is very natural for those who fancy they deserve pity to be affected when they know they meet with it. You will receive a thimble either by Mr. Nicholson or before, which my dear Love I hope you will accept. I wish I could send you something better or of greater value, but, trifling as it is, whenever you put it on, I hope it will serve to remind you of my affection for you. I have got the handkerchief in my pocket that you made, and marked for me, I have just this moment pulled it out to admire the letters. Oh! Jane! it is a valuable handkerchief. . . . Now do write soon my dearest, dearest girl, do not defer it longer than a fortnight. You see how punctual I have been, you wrote to me last Sunday but one. Adieu my love. Do not forget to send me a piece of hair.'

But despite these eager requests for letters it was Dorothy who proved the tardy correspondent, and the whole following summer passed without her writing a line to Jane. From this, perhaps, we may infer that life at Penrith was becoming more tolerable to her. Her intimacy with the Hutchinsons was growing, as was also her affection for her uncle William and Miss Cowper; and for part of the time at least she had her brothers' company. John, it is true, was on his first voyage to the Barbados, but Christopher must have spent his summer holidays at Penrith, and William, who passed much of his first long vacation at Hawkshead and in wandering about the Lake country, must often have come over to see her. It seems likely, indeed, that by a confusion of dates natural after so long a passage of time, it is this summer rather than the next to which he refers in the sixth book of *The Prelude*.[1] There he tells how, between his sundry wanderings, he was blest

with a joy
Above all joys, that seem'd another morn
Risen on mid noon, the presence, Friend, I mean,
Of that sole Sister, she who hath been long
Thy Treasure also, thy true friend and mine,
Now, after separation desolate
Restor'd to me, such absence that she seem'd
A gift then first bestow'd.[2]

[1] The evidence for this will be found in my edition of *The Prelude* (2nd impression, 1928), p. 608A.

[2] *Prelude* (1805), vi. 211–18.

Together they roamed the beautiful country that surrounds Penrith. They loved especially the gentle banks of the river Emont and the path through the woods from the mill below Brougham to the old quarry. On the ruins of Brougham Castle they sat for many an hour;

> when having climb'd
> In danger through some window's open space,
> We look'd abroad, or on the Turret's head
> Lay listening to the wild flowers and the grass,
> As they gave out their whispers to the wind.[1]

Their talk was often of that happy future when they would be free from the irksome control of unsympathetic guardians. William was fresh from that unforgettable experience when at sunrise, on the moors above Hawkshead, he had vowed his life to poetry, and he was already planning his first response to the poetic call, *An Evening Walk*, to be dedicated to his 'sole sister'. And Dorothy, too, was conscious of her mission, to be always at his side smoothing his path before him, and helping him with loving sympathy to be true to his chosen vocation. We can hardly doubt that their dream of a lifelong companionship now first took definite shape.

On these delightful summer rambles Mary Hutchinson often went with them, and thus Dorothy's second great friendship, which was to count for so much in her life and William's, gained a greater depth. What wonder, then, that

> o'er paths and fields
> In all that neighbourhood, through narrow lanes
> Of eglantine, and through the shady woods,
> And o'er the Border Beacon, and the Waste
> Of naked Pools and common Crags that lay
> Expos'd on the bare Fell, was scatter'd love,
> A spirit of pleasure, and youth's golden gleam;[2]

what wonder, either, if Dorothy gave to this new happiness any moment she could snatch from the tasks imposed on her by an inexorable grandmother, and put off writing to Jane from day to day, till her old friend had good reason to complain of her neglect?

[1] *Prelude* (1805), vi. 228–32. [2] Ib., 239–45.

II

FORNCETT

December 1788–February 1794 (aet. 17–22)

When summer drew to a close and her brother returned to Cambridge, Dorothy saw ahead of her another gloomy winter at Penrith; but fate had something better in store. Uncle William was appointed by his College to the living of Forncett in Norfolk, married Miss Cowper, and bore Dorothy off with him to his new home. The next letter to Jane, dated from Norwich on December 6, had many new impressions to communicate:

'I believe nearly half a year has elapsed since I last wrote to you; since that time great and unexpected changes have taken place; I have now nothing left to wish for on my own account; every day gives me fresh proofs of my Uncle and Aunt's goodness; I am sure there is not a better man in the world than my Uncle, nor a more amiable woman than my Aunt. You know how partial I always was to a country life, but I almost despaired of ever enjoying it; but to live in the country and with such kind friends! have I not every reason to be thankful? My happiness was very unexpected, for I knew nothing of it ten days before; when my Uncle told me I was almost mad with joy; I cried and laughed alternately; it was in a walk with him and Miss D. that the secret was communicated to me. You may be sure the short time I had to stay at Penrith was very busily employed in preparing my cloaths, etc. After the wedding was over we breakfasted at Mrs. Cowper's, and then set off on our journey; we got to Newcastle the next day, where we spent a fortnight very agreeably; and had not the prospect of finding a comfortable and happy home presented itself continually to my view I should have left that place with very great regret. Nothing happened worth relating on our journey between Newcastle and Cambridge, where the buildings, added to the pleasure of seeing my Brother very well and in excellent spirits, delighted me exceedingly; I could scarcely help imagining myself in a different country when I was walking in the college courts and groves; it looked so odd to see smart powdered heads with black caps like helmets, only that they have a square piece of wood at the top, and gowns something like those that clergymen wear; but, I assure you, (though a description of the dress may sound very strange) it is exceedingly becoming. We only staid a day at Cambridge, as you may be sure we were anxious to see our destined abode. At our entrance we saw Norwich to great advantage, as they were celebrating the revolution and the discovery of the gunpowder plot; the town was very well illuminated and the illuminations and ringing of bells would almost have given us spirits if we had wanted them. . . . Forncett is a little village entirely inhabited by farmers, who seem very decent kind of people; my Uncle's house is now very comfortable and may be made an excellent one; the gardens will be charming. I intend to be a great gardener and promise myself much pleasure in taking care of the poultry of which we are to have great abundance. . . . We have sketched out a plan of the manner in which we are to spend our time. . . . We are to have prayers at nine o'clock (you will observe it is winter), after breakfast is over we are to read, write, and I am to improve myself in French till twelve o'clock, when we are to walk or visit our sick and poor neighbours till three, which is our dining hour; and after tea my Uncle will sit with us and either read to us or not as he and we find ourselves inclined. . . . I enjoy the idea of spending Christmas in the country. We have had many consultations in what manner we are to keep my birthday, but we have at last agreed upon roast beef and plum pudding as the best Christmas-day dinner. It is now nearly a year since my grandfather died; you know the manner in which I spent last Christmas, how different is my present situation!. . . I dare not ask you to write soon, I will only tell you that I shall expect a letter with the greatest impatience; and I promise you I will answer it by the very next post. Adieu my very dear Friend. . . . I have not, I find, given you any account of Norwich. It is an immensely large place; but the streets in general are very ugly, and they are all so ill-paved and dirty as almost entirely to take away the pleasure of walking; we have been introduced to some of the genteelest families in the place but have visited very little on account of business. Their visiting is entirely in the rout style, and they are so ridiculous as to send invitations three weeks or a month beforehand. We had an invitation came on the 26th of November for the 18th of December for tea and cards, can any thing be more absurd? I cannot help thinking how my grandmother and the old ladies of Penrith would stare at this. They exclaim against the idleness and folly of the age; and say it is impossible to secure company unless you send two or three days before you intend to receive them. Adieu, my dear girl.'

For more than five years Dorothy's home was to be at Forncett. It is separated by three miles of narrow, winding lanes from Long Stratton, on the Norwich-Ipswich road, the nearest village of any size, so that even to-day it is sparsely populated, and remote enough from the busy hum of men and motors: its isolation a century and a half ago can easily be conceived. But the life there had all, or nearly all, that Dorothy asked for. A month after she had settled in she wrote contentedly: 'upon nearer view my prospects appear even more delightful than they did upon a more distant one. Oh! my dear friend, if you were with me how happy we should be! I often wish for you to walk with me in the garden. My room is one of the pleasantest in the house, some of the views are beautiful.'[1]

This was in the winter; and when the summer came round, the country had still more to offer her. 'I rise about six every morning, and as I have no companion, walk with a book till half-past eight if the weather permits, if not, I read in the house. Sometimes we walk in the morning, but seldom more than half an hour just before dinner. After tea we walk together till about eight, and then I walk alone as long as I can in the garden. I am particularly fond of a moonlight or twilight walk. It is at that time that I think most of my absent friends.'[2]

In those days young ladies did not venture far afield without a protector, and Dorothy records an expedition to the post at Long Stratton as an enterprise of daring. Visits to Norwich were something of an event, often entailing two or three nights away from home; and they were not an unmixed pleasure, for seats at the theatre were an inadequate compensation for painful sessions in the dentist's chair. From these excursions Dorothy returned without reluctance; and though, in days gone by, she had loved the gaieties of Halifax, she can hear of Jane's Christmas festivities without a murmur: 'sitting quietly, though very happily, at Forncett, without having been at one ball, one play, one concert. Indeed, I am sure I should make the worst rake in the world. I was at Norwich a few days in the summer and returned quite jaded and as pale as ashes.'[3] She loved her country life and entered into all its simple pleasures, for she had a genius for making the most of whatever the present had to offer.

[1] D. W. to J. P., Dec. 28, 1788.
[2] D. W. to J. P., May 23, 1791.
[3] D. W. to J. P., Dec. 7, 1791.

Thus her life pursued its even way. She had plenty of duties to occupy her time and give zest to her leisure. In the August after her arrival she started a little village school, which met on Sundays and twice in the week, when she instructed nine little scholars in reading and spelling, and taught them to repeat hymns, prayers, and the catechism. She was evidently popular with the children, and when the school was suspended owing to an outbreak of smallpox she was flattered by a question from one of them, 'Pray, miss, when shall we come to school again?' She visited the parishioners with her uncle and helped her aunt in the management of the household. And when the small family began to appear, Mary in 1790, Christopher in 1791, and William in 1792, the cares of a nurse were added to her other responsibilities. In prospect she had viewed this with some anxiety: 'I verily believe', she wrote, 'that I never took an infant in my arms that did not the moment it was there by its cries beg to be removed', but her fears proved quite groundless; her aunt's babies were as happy with her as she with them, and she never writes of them without some word of admiration or delight.

There was little society at Forncett to distract her. The Cooksons had only one near neighbour, a certain Mrs. Dix, whose idiosyncrasies gave some scope to Dorothy's satiric pen. Mrs. Dix was a widow 'with a good many of the particularities and some of the bad qualities ascribed to old maids; her appearance is rather remarkable, as she always wears long ruffles and a common stuff gown. She is rich, but lives alone and in a very plain manner. . . . Her worst fault is censoriousness; . . . on my uncle's saying what a pleasant man Dr. Enfield[1] was, she remarked that he was a *true Presbyterian*, "that he would lick the feet of his benefactors", and to prove what she said, she told us a story of which I could make out nothing at all but that her notions of religion were prejudiced and illiberal.'[2] Two miles off lived a widow, Mrs. Burroughs, with two daughters in whose company Dorothy sometimes took her walks, and three miles further still were two other families with whom the Cooksons were on visiting terms. But Dorothy, at least, got more pleasure out of the society of the robins. 'There are at present two in the room which have gone to rest; you may imagine how tame they

[1] Dr. Enfield was a Norwich clergyman of their acquaintance.

[2] D. W. to J. P., Dec. 28, 1788.

are when I tell you they hop about the room where we sit, without the least appearance of fear.'[1]

On rare occasions the Rectory welcomed visitors from the more distant world. In the summer of 1789 both her aunt Threlkeld and her brother William were at Forncett, and for a month of the following Christmas recess Wilberforce was their guest. He had already launched his great crusade for the abolition of the slave trade, and Dorothy caught some of his passion for the cause, begging Jane to solicit her father's vote for him at the next election. It is evident, too, that Dorothy made a great impression upon Wilberforce, for before he left he promised her ten guineas a year for distribution among the poor of the parish, prudently accompanying his first donation with a copy of Mrs. Trimmer's *Oeconomy of Charity*. Dorothy's enthusiasm for Mr. Wilberforce aroused in the breast of her friend Jane suspicions which recall the emotions of young ladies living some three hundred miles west of Forncett under the malicious eye of Miss Austen. Dorothy replied in the only proper vein, by reciprocating her suspicions. Jane had referred to little Mary Cookson as Dorothy's niece. 'From what', retorts Dorothy, 'could this error proceed but from absence of mind, and how shall I account for this absence so naturally as in your way? In short I see *you* want a confidante, and that all your sly raillery was designed to create a suspicion in me; that it was a picture of your own case which you applied to mine. Then to be sure, I must ask a few pretty questions and you at last modestly blushing must be obliged to confess the truth.'[2] And Jane's repeated visits to Leeds, the home of the Marshalls, from which she returns so much improved in health, suggest that Dorothy was not far wrong. For a time she plays up gallantly to her friend's mood. The Miss Burroughs, she says, have a brother, 'who is a very pleasant young man. Here I see you draw up and smile, but however you have no reason. We have a respectable and worthy man who lives in the adjoining parish who makes an excellent use of a large fortune, and a very smart good-tempered fellow his curate. Here too you look significant. . . . The seal you showed so much sagacity in your conjectures about was given me by a Penrith friend, Mary Hutchinson.'[2] Clearly the theme has an irresistible attraction for Jane, for she

[1] D. W. to J. P., Dec. 28, 1788. [2] D. W. to J. P., Mar. 30, 1790.

harps upon it till Dorothy gets heartily sick of it. 'I shall not answer your foolish raillery any more, I shall think you unkind if you say anything more to me on the subject.'[1] And so the matter drops, at least out of Dorothy's side of the correspondence.

In the latter months of 1790 she was much excited by news of the engagement and marriage of her dear Aunt Threlkeld to Samuel Rawson, a wealthy widower with cotton mills and a fine house pleasantly situated on the banks of the Calder, about three miles from Halifax. On hearing of it she told Jane, 'My joy was such as I have seldom felt on any occasion; and you are right for supposing that for a time it occupied all my thoughts. That God may grant her many years of uninterrupted happiness is my constant wish and prayer, as it must be of all her children'. Dorothy has only a vague recollection of the bridegroom, and she peppers her friend with questions: 'What sort of a man is Mr. Rawson? By this question I do not mean is he a sensible man for I know he is amiable and sensible, but I wish to know is he grave or lively, younger than my Aunt or older? little or tall? fat or thin? On looking over my letter I can scarcely help laughing at this string of womanish queries. . . . But my aunt's choice of him is a sufficient encomium.'

The Christmas of 1790 brought a visitor more welcome than Mr. Wilberforce; William spent his six weeks vacation at Forncett, before returning to Cambridge to take his degree. Though Dorothy had not seen him for eighteen months he had seldom been far from her thoughts. She had been very anxious about him during the previous summer, though her anxiety was touched with pride at his prowess, for he was on a walking tour with his friend Jones through Revolutionary France and Switzerland:

> 'I assure you,' she writes, 'when I trace his paths upon the maps I wonder that his strength and courage have not sunk under the fatigues he must have undergone; he says, however, that they have frequently performed a journey of thirteen leagues, (thirty-nine miles, you know) over the most mountainous parts of Switzerland without feeling more weariness than if they had been sauntering an hour in the groves of Cambridge, they are so inured to walking. William is a perfect enthusiast in his admiration of

[1] D. W. to J. P., Oct. 6, 1790.

nature in all her various forms, therefore he must have had the highest possible enjoyment in viewing the sublime scenes of Switzerland. I confess, however, that had he acquainted me with his scheme before its execution I should (as many of his other friends did) have looked upon it as mad and impracticable.'[1]

And she proceeds to quote from William's letter to her a catalogue of his itinerary, though, as soon as it is on paper, she realizes that it must be 'shockingly tedious' to one less interested in him than she was. But that part of her brother's letter, which we may be sure she read most often and with the deepest feeling, she does not quote—she could not share it, even with Jane. 'I have had', he had written, 'during the course of this delightful tour, a great deal of uneasiness from an apprehension of your anxiety on my account. I have thought of you perpetually; and never have my eyes burst upon a scene of particular loveliness but I have almost instantly wished that you could for a moment be transported to the place where I stood to enjoy it.'[2] And now William was at her side, sharing with her every detail of his recent experiences, discussing with her all their family affairs, their prospects of recovering from the Lonsdales their little inheritance, the future that was in store for each and all of them—above all their fixed resolve to have a home together. She is never so happy as with her brothers, and when they are absent her greatest happiness is in writing of them to the sympathetic Jane.

'I confess you are right in supposing me partial to William. Probably when I next see Kit, I shall love him as well, the difference between our ages at the time I was with him was much more perceptible than it will be at our next meeting. His disposition is of the same cast as William's, and his inclinations have taken the same turn, but he is much more likely to make his fortune; he is not so warm as William but has a most affectionate heart. His abilities though not so great perhaps as his brother's may be of more use to him, as he has not fixed his mind upon any particular species of reading or conceived an aversion to any. He is not fond of Mathematics but has resolution sufficient to study them because it will be impossible for him to obtain a fellowship without a knowledge of them. William you may have heard lost the chance, indeed the certainty, of a fellowship by not combating his inclinations; he gave way to his natural dislike of studies

[1] D. W. to J. P., Oct. 6, 1790. [2] W. W. to D. W., Sept. 6, 1790.

so dry as many parts of mathematics, consequently could not succeed at Cambridge. He reads Italian, Spanish, French, Greek, Latin, and English, but never opens a mathematical book. We promise ourselves much pleasure from reading Italian together at some time, he wishes that I was acquainted with the Italian poets, but how much have I to learn which plain English will teach me! William has a great attachment to poetry: indeed so has Kit, but William particularly, which is not the most likely thing to produce his advancement in the world; his pleasures are chiefly of the imagination, he is never so happy as in a beautiful country. Do not think from what I have said that he reads not at all for he does read a great deal, and not only poetry and those languages he is acquainted with, but history etc. etc.' [1]

With such brothers, though the Lonsdale suit seems hopeless enough, she is quite confident as to her ultimate future.

> 'While I am young,' she writes, 'I thank God I am not destitute of the means of supporting myself; . . . therefore I can bear the worst with fortitude and put myself into a situation by which I may procure a livelihood till my Brothers are able to assist me.'[1]

In the meantime she follows with an eager interest all that these wonderful brothers are doing, and duly hands it on to Jane. In the summer William is with his friend Jones in the Vale of Clwyd, enjoying the beauty of the country and also the companionship of three charming young ladies, Jones's sisters, 'and without a rival'; Kit is on a walking tour with two schoolfellows in the Lakes; John is held up at the East Indies, in consequence of the expected war with Spain; in October William is in Cambridge beginning, on his uncle's advice, a study of Oriental languages, John is back in England, grown, she hears, a tall handsome man, and she is looking forward to seeing him at Forncett before very long; in December William, who, apparently, has soon got tired of Sanskrit, is reported at Orleans whither he has gone to study French with a view to fit himself for a travelling tutorship; early in the next year John arrives at Forncett and spends four happy months with his sister.

Then came an exciting break in Dorothy's life. Her uncle was appointed Canon of Windsor, and at the end of July moved his whole household to take up a three months' residence there.

[1] D. W. to J. P., June 6, 1791.

So happy was she in her quiet village rectory, that she did not look forward to the change; but when it came she was ready enough to enjoy it. Only a year before she came to Windsor another young lady, with a pen even more lively than hers, had placed on record her impressions of the court life there: Dorothy's account is naturally less intimate than Fanny Burney's, and less piquant, for she had not the privilege of meeting Frau Swellenborg; yet, even if she does not take us behind the scenes, at least she gives us a vivid picture of the stage on which the royal party played their charming domestic comedy.

Windsor October 16th (1792)

My dear Friend,

Though I have not replied to your last affectionate letter so soon as I ought to have done, yet I am not so culpable as you may have supposed—for I did not receive it till I had been some time at Windsor. As it had no date (it was not without signature so I will only suppose you *half* in love) I know not how long it had lain at the Post-office at Long Stratton before it came to my hands. Knowing that I am at Windsor your curiosity must be sufficiently raised; it is my part therefore to gratify it as quickly as possible but how shall I set about so complicated a task? I despair of satisfying *you* as I am sure I shall not be able to satisfy *myself*. I will, however, *begin* instead of *end* with the sum total, that I am extremely happy and have enjoyed myself highly ever since my arrival at Windsor. You must set forward then, contented with this information, and, if you find my accounts so confused that you cannot guess whence I have derived my happiness be not disappointed or angry with me for the fault shall not be committed wilfully. We left Forncett on the last day of July, I travelled along with two of the maid-servants in a stage coach, and arrived at the immense city of London the following morning. My Uncle and Aunt and the children were three days upon the road, I, however, amused myself very agreeably till their arrival as my Brother was in town. I ought not perhaps to have said that I amused myself *very* agreeably as I did not like London at all, and was heartily rejoiced to quit it for Windsor exactly a week after I found myself there. I do not, however, consider myself as entitled to give my opinion of London or a London life as we did not go to any places of public amusement, and the weather was so hot that we could not even enjoy walking about. I contrived to see everything at one view and was highly gratified. I was at the top of Saint Paul's from whence on a clear day (which that fortunately was) you have a view of the whole city which is most magnificent. My Aunt was in London only three days. She left the children to my care and hastened forward to Windsor to put things in order for our reception. We followed her, namely the nurse the young ones and I, on the 9th or 10th of August. If I was disappointed with London I was charmed with Windsor. The weather was delightful; we found the kindest of friends, and in short there was nothing wanting to make me completely happy. We found the Royal Family here and they staied near a fortnight after our arrival during which time they walked upon the Terrace every night. When I first set foot upon the Terrace I could scarcely persuade myself of the reality of the scene—I fancied myself treading upon fairy-ground, and that the gay company around me was brought there by enchantment. The King and several of the Princesses were advancing, the Queen's band was playing most delightfully and all around me I saw only well-dressed, smart people. What a different scene from that I had quitted a week before! The King stopped to talk with my Uncle and Aunt, and to play with the children, who though not acquainted with the new-fangled doctrine of liberty and equality, thought a king's stick as fair game as any other man's, and that princesses were not better than mere Cousin Dollys. I think it is impossible to see the King and his family at Windsor without loving them, even if you eye them with impartiality and consider them really as *man* and women not as king and princesses, but I own I am too much of an aristocrat or what you please to call me, not to reverence him because he is a monarch more than I should were he a private gentleman, and not to see with pleasure his daughters treated with more respect than ordinary people. I say it is impossible to see them *at Windsor* without loving them, because at Windsor they are seen unattended by pomp or state, and they seem so desirous to please that nothing but ill-nature or envy can help being pleased. The King's good temper shews itself in no instance so much as in his affection for children. He was quite delighted with Christopher and Mary. Mary he considers as a great beauty and desired the Duke of York to come from one side of the Terrace to the other to look at her. The first time she appeared before him she had an unbecoming and rather a shabby hat on: We had, then, got her a new one. "Ah" says he, "Mary that's a *pretty* hat!"

You may perhaps wish to know my opinion of the persons of the Royal Family. Do not think that I am dazzled with the splendour of royalty when I say that I think I never saw so handsome a family; Princess Royal and Princess Mary are certainly the most beautiful, the former has all the dignity becoming her high rank with a great deal of grace. The latter has, perhaps equal grace, but of a different kind. Hers are the winning graces of sixteen. Perhaps at six and twenty she will not be so fine a woman as her sister. But I think I have devoted a sufficient portion of my paper to this subject but what other shall I turn to? I am bewildered in a maze of which I can neither see beginning nor end. You have undoubtedly seen views of Windsor which have given you a much better idea of the place than I possibly can by a paper description. The Castle stands upon an eminence which rises boldly from the river—I ought, indeed, rather to say from the *meadows*, for the river is at some little distance from the foot of the hill. It is an immense building, as you will suppose when I tell you that the Terrace, which extends only along one of its sides and a part of two, is the third of a mile in length. Below the Terrace is a very beautiful park, called the *Little Park* to distinguish it from one which is on the other side and much larger. In this Little Park the Queen, when we first came, used to drive a phaeton with four white ponies attended by several people on horse-back while the King and the rest of the family were walking upon the Terrace, which had a very pretty effect seen from above. She was sometimes hid entirely by the trees, sometimes we got a faint glimpse of her or some of her party, then we had a complete view of the whole. This part of the prospect aided my imagination not a little when I was half persuaded that the scene acted upon the Terrace was the work of Fairies, for her equipage and her train of horsemen looked so diminutive that it was impossible to avoid comparing them with the descriptions one has read of Fairies travelling on fairy ground. The weather has been so bad for several weeks past as is quite mortifying. We have scarcely been able to walk at all. I however made very good use of my time while it was tolerable. I thought myself very fortunate in meeting with two young ladies who were staying at Windsor when we arrived and did not leave it till the fine weather left us. They were staying at their Uncle's (Doctor Heberden's). They were country ladies, and, of course fond of the country lady's amusement, walking. We soon became attached to each other and had several very charming little excursions into the country. They, luckily, had a very agreeable young man their cousin, Mr. Heberden in the house with them and he was always at their service, therefore, we were not afraid of going far out into the country. Mrs. H. was also very kind in lending us her coach whenever they expressed a desire to go a little further than within the distance of a walk. They took me to Egham Races where we saw the Prince of Wales, Dukes of York and Clarence, and a gallant shew of company, and they took me to one of the most beautiful places near Windsor, the seat of General Harcourt, called St. Leonard's Hill. It is in the finest situation that can be conceived. It stands upon an eminence, and commands a noble view of Windsor Castle and of hills richly wooded. This view and a thousand others in the Park and Forest are a thousand times superior to that from the Terrace. We are as comfortably situated as possible, in every respect, at Windsor. We compose, as it were, one large family in the Cloisters, for we can visit each other's houses in all weathers without hat or cloak, for they are surrounded by a covered passage as, (I believe) all cloisters are. You have been at York, and you probably saw the cloisters there which may give you some idea of the sort of gloom which we inhabit. Our immediate neighbours in the cloisters are the pleasantest people in Windsor and we visit them without form which is the mode I like best. We are at present, tis true, obliged to attend a greater number of *routs* than we like, but we hope the next time we come to steer a little more clear of them. Our assemblies began a fortnight ago. They are held every Monday. I have not yet been. The nature of our assemblies is this. There is what is called a *ball* once a month; and a card assembly which generally ends with a little dance once a week. There was a ball yesterday and my aunt was so good as to give me leave to go, but I declined it, as she would not go herself. I am to go once before I leave Windsor, and I preferred going with her to going with another lady as there was no party to be there to whom I was particularly attached. I made my entrée (for I was never in a public room before) at one of the Egham Race Balls. Mrs. Heberden was my chaperon, and the Miss Wollastons, her nieces, were of the party; I had the most severe tremblings and palpitations during the first dance, that can be conceived by any trembling female. My partner was a wretched one and I had not danced for five years. The latter part of the evening, however, went off very well, and after I got to dancing with Mr. Heberden with whom I was very well acquainted I felt myself quite at ease. I am called to tea, and my letter must be sent off immediately, or I cannot get it franked, but I have told you nothing—You must think me very stupid. . . . Pray write to me soon. If you are anxious that I should make amends for this letter I am sure you will—adieu, adieu

D. WORDSWORTH.

While Dorothy, like a good aristocrat, was indulging her transports on the merits of the Royal Family, her beloved William was in France, aflame with enthusiasm for the revolutionary cause, and already planning to devote his energies to its service. She cannot have been less communicative to him than to Jane Pollard, but it is clear that he did not return her confidence. In May, indeed, he had expressed his readiness to take orders as soon as it was convenient to his uncle to give him a curacy, and though, as she read 'daily accounts of insurrections and broils', she had felt some uneasiness about him, she had comforted herself with the reflection that 'he is wise enough to get out of the way of danger'; and she looked forward without apprehension to his timely return. If she had suspected for a moment the conflict of emotions by which he was distracted she could not have been so completely happy at Windsor.

For his revolutionary ardour was not the only tie that bound him to France. Soon after his arrival at Orleans he had made the acquaintance of Marie Anne Vallon, a charming French woman, some four years older than himself. He was shy and doubtless often lonely, subject as we know to deep fits of melancholy, but with a passionate idealistic nature struggling to break through a wall of English reticence and awkward reserve; Annette was vivacious and impulsive, and if she lacked depth of intellect had a warm and generous heart. In the very contrast between them lay an irresistible attraction. Acquaintance rapidly ripened into friendship, friendship into passion, and few months had passed before 'through effect of some delirious hour', Annette,

> without the name of wife,
> Carried about her for a secret grief
> The promise of a mother.[1]

The ecstacy and the torment of this time can be read in *Vaudracour and Julia* and other poems written long afterwards; for Wordsworth drew his inspiration largely from 'hiding places ten years deep'; and when he wrote, haunted

> with familiar face,
> Returning, like a ghost unlaid,[2]

there can be little doubt whose face it was. As week succeeded

[1] *Vaudracour and Julia: Prelude* (1805), ix. 594–5, 608–10.
[2] *The Waggoner*, iv. 213–14.

week his position became more desperate. It was his urgent duty to secure an income which would enable him to marry Annette and provide for her and their expected child. But whence could he obtain it? The bulk of his patrimony had been wrested from him by Lord Lonsdale: the small remainder was eaten into by a fruitless lawsuit: from his guardians he could hope for no further advances. In September he wrote for money to his brother Richard, intending to return to England within a month: he had some poems to publish which might put him in the way of earning a livelihood. Yet he could not tear himself away from France before his child was born. In November he was in Paris, vainly seeking employment under the Girondist party; and he was still there when, on December 15, his daughter Caroline was baptized. By the end of the year he had found his way back to London.

His immediate business was to see through the press his *Evening Walk* and *Descriptive Sketches*, and they were published early in February. He was not the first young poet to come before the world with high hopes of fame and profit, nor the first to be disappointed of his hopes. At the same time the declaration of war between England and France cut him off from Annette and gave a shattering blow to his ideals; and while it did nothing to shake his revolutionary faith, lessened still further his chances of finding a lucrative employment. He might relieve his feelings by voicing his uncompromising Republicanism in a *Letter to the Bishop of Landaff*, but to publish it, even if a publisher could have been found, would have embroiled him irrevocably with those who might help him towards a livelihood. Though the idea of taking orders became more and more distasteful to him, there seemed no alternative, yet he could not honestly accept his uncle's offer of a curacy without making a clean breast of his French entanglement. Out of favour as he was already, he knew that in himself he stood no chance of success; and so he opened his heart to Dorothy, entrusting to her the advocacy of his cause.

It must have been late in February when he took this step. Since his return to England he had kept in touch with her. 'William writes regularly,' she had said in December, 'and is a most affectionate brother.' But the cheery tone of her letter to Jane on February 16 shows clearly enough that she was still ignorant of his trouble. Her chief tale is of Christopher's visit to her in the recent Christmas holidays,—but the charm of Christopher only serves to remind her of the still greater charms of William,—of the little parsonage that she is some day to share with William, above all, of William's poems:

'Your affectionate letter, my dear Friend, . . . found me happy in the society of one of my dear Brothers and one of the dearest of my Brothers. I think I have told you that Christopher and I had been separated nearly five years last Christmas; judge then of my transports at meeting him again, and judge too of my happiness during the time we spent together when I inform you that he is a most amiable young man, sensible, affectionate, and engaging. . . . He is like William; he has the same traits in his character but less highly touched, he is not so ardent in any of his pursuits but is yet more particularly attached to the same pursuits which have so irresistible an influence over William, which deprive him of the power of chaining his attention to others discordant to his feelings. Christopher is no despicable Poet, but he can become a Mathematician also, he is not insensible of the beauties of the Greek and Latin classics, or of any of the charms of elegant literature, but he can draw his mind from these fascinating studies to others less alluring; he is steady and sincere in his attachments; William has both these virtues in an eminent degree; and a sort of violence of affection, if I may so term it, which demonstrates itself every moment of the day when the objects of his affection are present with him, in a thousand almost imperceptible attentions to their wishes, in a sort of restless watchfulness which I know not how to describe, a tenderness that never sleeps, and at the same time such a delicacy of manners as I have observed in few men. I hope you will one day be much better acquainted with him than you are at present, much as I have talked to you about him. I look forward with full confidence to the happiness of receiving you in my little Parsonage. I hope you will spend at least a year with me. I have laid the particular scheme of happiness for each Season. When I think of winter I hasten to furnish our little parlour, I close the shutters, set out the Tea-table, brighten the Fire. When our refreshment is ended I produce our work, and William brings his book to our table and contributes at once to our instruction and amusement, and at intervals we lay aside the book and each hazard our observations upon what has been read without the fear of ridicule or censure. We talk over past days, we do not sigh for any pleasures beyond our humble habitation "the central point of all our joys".

Oh Jane! with such romantic dreams as these I amuse my fancy during many an hour which would otherwise pass heavily along, for kind as are my Uncle and Aunt, much as I love my sweet little Cousins, I cannot help heaving many a sigh at the reflection that I have passed one and twenty years of my life, and that the first six years only of this time was spent in the enjoyment of the same pleasures that were enjoyed by my Brothers, and that I was then too young to be sensible of the blessing. We have been endeared to each other by early misfortune—We in the same moment lost a father, a mother, a home, we have been equally deprived of our patrimony by the cruel hand of lordly tyranny. These afflictions have all contributed to unite us closer by the bonds of affection notwithstanding we have been compelled to spend our youth far asunder. "We drag at each remove a lengthening Chain"; this idea often strikes me very forcibly. Neither absence nor distance nor time can ever break the chain that links me to my Brothers. But why do I talk to you thus? Because these are the thoughts that are uppermost in my breast at the moment, and when I write to the companion of my childish days I must write the dictates of my heart. In our conversations so full of tenderness I have never constrained my sentiments; I have laid open to her the inmost recesses of my heart, then why should I impose a restraint upon myself when I am writing to her? But is it not possible that these details of my feelings and my little griefs may be insipid to her? she cannot relieve them, she perhaps may think them unreasonable.

'By this time, you have doubtless seen my Brother William's Poems, and they have already suffered the lash of your criticisms. I should be very glad if you would give me your opinion of them with the same frankness with which I am going to give you mine. The scenes which he describes have been viewed with a Poet's eye and are pourtrayed with a Poet's pencil; and the Poems contain many passages exquisitely beautiful, but they also contain many faults, the chief of which are obscurity, and a too frequent use of some particular expressions and uncommon words, for instance *moveless*, which he applies in a sense if not new, at least different from its ordinary one; by moveless when applied to the Swan he means that sort of motion which is smooth without agitation; it is a very beautiful epithet but ought to have been cautiously used, he ought, at any rate, only to have hazarded it once, instead of which it occurs three or four times. The word *viewless*, also, is introduced far too often, this, though not so uncommon a word as the former ought not to have been made use of more than once or twice—I regret exceedingly that he did not submit the works to the inspection of some Friend before their Publication, and he also joins with me in this regret. Their faults are such as a young Poet was most likely to fall into and least likely to discover, and what the suggestions of a Friend would easily have made him see and at once correct. It is however an error he will never fall into again, as he is well aware that he would have gained considerably more credit if the blemishes of which I speak had been corrected. My Brother Kitt and I, while he was at Forncett, amused ourselves by analysing every line and prepared a very bulky criticism, which he was to transmit to William as soon as he should have added to it the remarks of Cambridge Friends. At the conclusion of the Evening Walk, I think you would be pleased with those lines, "Thus hope first pouring from her blessed horn" etc., etc. You would espy the little gilded Cottage in the horizon, but perhaps your less gloomy imagination and your anxiety to see your Friend placed in that happy habitation might make you overlook the dark and broad gulph between. If you have not yet seen the Poems pray do not make known my opinion of them—let them pass the fiery ordeal. Mr. Griffith desired my Br to send him half a dozen copies as soon as they should be published which I have no doubt he has done, and by his means you most probably have seen them. I am sure I ought to ask your forgiveness for dwelling thus long on what relates merely to myself or my Brothers.

'. . . Give my kind love to my cousins when you see them and to Mrs. Rawson. Pray tell Mrs. R. that I wish to hear from her and to have her opinion of my Brother's Poems. If she *has* already read them, I wish you would tell her what I have said of them—if not wait till she has formed her own judgment. I am sure you must think that there are some very glaring faults, but I hope too, that you will discover many beauties, beauties which could only have been created by the Imagination of a *Poet*.

'Remember me very affectionately to your Father and Mother, and Sisters. Tell them that I look forward with much pleasure to seeing them again—adieu my dear girl. Believe me unalterably yours

D. Wordsworth

'Pray write immediately.'

It must have been soon after this letter had been dispatched that William unburdened his heart. There can be no doubt of the distress with which she heard his story. Her life before this had not been without its sorrows and difficulties, but now she was stricken in the deepest part of her nature. The splendid loyalty with which she stood by her brother should not lead us to imagine that she thought lightly of his offence. True enough, as critics have pointed out, it would appear less shocking than it might have done some fifty years later; for under the Georges illegitimate children were more openly referred to, and were possibly more common, than in the Victorian era; but if both by nature and by upbringing Dorothy was nothing of a prude, it is equally certain that she was still less of a cynic. Moreover one may accept the fact that such irregularities occur in society without expecting to find them in one's own family, and in the nearest and dearest part of it. But whatever she suffered, her devotion to William made her course clear to her; and she was ready to shoulder as much of his burden as he could lay upon her. At once she realized the misery and loneliness of Annette, and wrote her letters of affectionate and tender sympathy, giving a warm greeting to this unknown French woman, and assuring her of the welcome which awaits her as soon as William is able to provide a home for them all. Annette's replies, full as they are of her own sufferings, show her sensible to the difficulty of Dorothy's position, and deeply touched by the warmth of her affection.

> 'J'y répont', she wrote to William,[1] 'à (la lettre) de ta sœur. La terre n'en a pas produit deux comme elle; elle fait l'honneur de son sexe. Je désire bien que ma Caroline lui resemble. Que j'ai pleuré, mon cher Williams! quel cœur! quelle âme! comme elle partage bien les malleurs qui m'acable, mais que je suis fâchée de voir qu'elle est tourmenté raport à nous! En grâce, mon ami, tranquilise la, . . . Ta sœur me parle (de notre) petit menage avec un entousiasme qui me fait grand (plaisir). Que nous serons heureux, ô mon tendre ami; oui, (on) sera heureux. Je te le promet. . . . Je te prie, mon cher petit, de faire passer aussitôt cette lettre a ma chère sœur que j'aime de toute mon âme, de l'engagé de ne rien dire à ton oncle; ce sera un combat penible qu'elle aura à soutenire. Mais tu le juge nécessaire.'

And in a long rambling letter the poor forsaken mother pours out her sorrows to Dorothy:

'Si il est consolant pour moi, ma chère sœur, de voir l'interêt

[1] Annette Vallon to W. W., Mar. 20, 1793. For this letter in full, and Annette's letter to Dorothy, *v. W. W. and Annette Vallon*, by Émile Legouis, London, 1922.

que vous prenez à (mes trist)es chagrins, je m'afflige bien en même tems de ce qu'ils vous rendent si malheureuse. Mes sentimens sont audesus de mes expressions. Je n'en trouverois pas qui vous renderoit au naturel ma vive reconnaissance; elle égale l'attachement que j'ai pour ma chère sœur. Ces deux sentiments sont gravé dans mon âme; le tems ne fera que les augmenter, surtout quand une espasse imense ne nous séparera plus, quand je pourai dire mil fois le jour à ma sœur que je l'aime avec cette tendresse que je sens déjà bien vivement. Que vos lettres sont touchante, que j'ai de peine à en soutenire la lecture!... Votre dernière ma fait une sensation si vive; à chaque ligne je voyois le sensibilité de votre âme et cet interêt si touchant que vous prenez à mes peines.... Vous n'avez personne à qui vous puissiez librement confier l'état pénible de votre âme et que vous êtes obligée d'étouffer des larmes que votre sensibilité vous arrache... Il m'avoit bien dit, ce cher ami, qu'il avoit une sœur charmante, mais que le tableau qu'il m'a fait de votre âme est inférieur a ce que je vois dans vos écrit!'

It was easy enough to Dorothy to write words of comfort to Annette; the task of making William's peace with his uncle was a very different matter, and she must have approached it with many misgivings, if, indeed, she did not realize from the first that it was hopeless. What posterity may pardon in genius, elderly relatives find it hard to tolerate in a young man for whose genius a fond sister is the only guarantee. William had never been a satisfactory ward. As a boy he was headstrong and obstinate, as an undergraduate he had been both extravagant and idle, refusing to face the fact that he had his own way to make in the world. He wrote poetry, but when the master of his college died, and a chance of distinction was offered him in writing a funeral ode, he declined to compete for the prize; when he ought to have been reading for his final examination he made a long tour through Europe, and he threw away the chances of a fellowship by refusing to do the necessary mathematics; later, when he was advised to retrieve himself by a study of Oriental languages he had gone off to France again, and returned after imbibing the most dangerous doctrines subversive of society and religion. And now Dorothy came to her uncle with this last discreditable story. We can hardly be surprised that Canon Cookson took a serious view of the matter, and feeling that for the time at least his offer of a curacy must be withdrawn, declined to receive his refractory nephew at Forncett. We can understand, too, his opinion, even if we do not share it, that the less Dorothy saw of her brother the better.

Dorothy had failed in her mission; and her disagreement with her uncle on the subject that lay nearest to her heart could not fail to put a heavy strain upon their daily intercourse. She was deeply attached to him, and was fully sensible of his unfailing kindness to her; but her dependence on his charity had always been irksome, and now that this cloud had come between them her life at the Rectory must have been almost unbearable. Her love for William was only intensified by her uncle's disapproval; her separation from him at a time when he was in such need of her support added to her misery. Her one desire now was to get away and join him. She was already looking forward to a visit to her aunt Rawson at Halifax. The Cooksons were expecting another baby in the summer, and she would be needed at Forncett, but after that she surely might be spared; and by June she had extracted from her uncle the necessary permission. At once she dashed off a hurried note to Jane: 'Oh Jane, with what transport shall I embrace you! My dear friend, we shall live over again those days, and we shall anticipate future joys: domestic felicity, peace and retirement, when you visit me and find me united to my dear William. What thousands of things shall we have to say to each other! our midnight conversations will not then be *imaginary* ones. . . . Oh talk to me of your wish to see again your old companion, your *earliest* friend. . . . Oh how I long for a Christmas fireside, surrounded by a circle of my old friends and companions.'

Apparently it had been arranged with her uncle that as soon as their friend Mr. Griffith of Newcastle, who travelled much on business, came south and could call at Forncett, he should be her escort to Halifax: William, she knew, had already received a general invitation from the Rawsons; all she had to do was to see that their visits should coincide. But the success of her plan depended on its secrecy; for if it reached the ears of the Cooksons, it would certainly be stopped. Dorothy's letters during the summer betray the suppressed excitement in which she was living, her joy at the prospect of meeting again the friend from whom she had been parted so long, her anxiety about William, above all, her longing to be once more at his side:

'June 16. I am sure you will interest yourself in all my little schemes of felicity and assist me in painting scenes of happiness, happiness arising from the exercise of the social affections in retirement and rural quiet. Alas! my Friend, the reality may be far distant, distant do I say? Were I certain that we should ever attain it how happy should I be? but I cannot foresee the day of my felicity, the day in which I am once more to find a home under the same roof with my Brother: all is still obscure and dark, and there is much ground to fear that my scheme may prove a shadow, a mere vision of happiness; but how can we find sweeter employment than in talking of these things? It is soon enough to admit so sad a guest as Despair when Hope refuses to attend us. You know how much more readily my heart receives the suggestions of Hope than of Despair. . . . I often hear from my dear Brother William, I am very anxious about him just now as he has not got any settled employment. He is looking out and wishing for the opportunity of engaging himself as tutor to some young gentleman, an office for which even friends less partial than I am, allow him to be particularly well qualified. You have no idea how much I wish to introduce him to you, I am sure you would be pleased with him, he is certainly very agreeable in his manners, and he is so amiable, so good, so fond of his Sister! Oh Jane, the last time we were together he won my affection to a degree which I cannot describe; his attentions to me were such as the most insensible of mortals must have been touched with, there was no pleasure he would not have given up with joy for half an hour's conversation with me. It was in winter (at Christmas) that he was last at Forncett, and every day as soon as we rose from dinner we used to pace the gravel walk in the garden *till six o'clock* when we received a summons (which was always unwelcome) to tea. Nothing but rain or snow prevented our taking this walk. Often have I gone out when the keenest north wind has been whistling amongst the trees over our heads. I have paced that walk in the garden which will always be dear to me from the remembrance of these long, long conversations I have had upon it, supported by my Brother's arm. Ah Jane! I never thought of the cold when he was with me. I am as heretical as yourself in my opinions concerning Love and Friendship. I am very sure that love will never bind me closer to any human being than friendship binds me to you, my earliest female friend, and to William, my earliest and my dearest male friend. . . .

THE 'GRAVEL WALK' AT FORNCETT

'July 10th. None of this is to be read aloud, so be upon your guard. My aunt is gone to take an airing with my Uncle and Mary. The evening is a lovely one, and I have strolled into a neighbouring meadow where I am enjoying the melody of birds and the busy sounds of a fine summer's evening, while my eye is gratified by a smiling prospect of cultivated fields richly wooded, our own church and the parsonage house. But oh how imperfect is my pleasure! I am *alone*; why are you not seated with me? and my dear William why is not he here also? I could almost fancy that I see you both near me. I have chosen a bank where I have room to spare for a resting-place for each of you. I hear *you* point out a spot where, if we could erect a little cottage and call it *our own* we should be the happiest of human beings. I see my Brother fired with the desire of leading his sister to such a retreat as Fancy, ever ready at our call, hastens to assist us in painting; our parlour is furnished; our garden is adorned by magic; the roses and honeysuckles spring at our command, the wood behind the house lifts at once its head and furnishes us with a winter's shelter and a summer's noonday shade. My dear friend, I trust that ere long you will be, without imagination, the companion of my walks; perhaps in three short-*long* months we may have strolled together, and,—but here let me caution you not to read any part of what I am going to write as you will betray a secret which it is of some importance not to disclose—I was going to say and my dear William may be of our party, but this is what I charge you by our friendship not to mention for reasons which I will specify before I conclude. I cannot however resist my desire of making *you* acquainted with the scheme which we have in agitation of bringing about a meeting at Halifax. . . . It is enough for *you* that I am likely to have the happiness of introducing to you my beloved Brother. You must forgive me for talking so much of him, my affection hurries me on to the subject and makes me forget that you cannot be so much interested in it as I am. You do not know him; you do not know how amiable he is. Perhaps you reply "But I know how *you* are blinded". Well, my dearest Jane, I plead guilty at once, I must be blind, he cannot be so pleasing as my fondness makes him. I am willing to allow that half the virtues with which I fancy him endowed are the creation of my love, but surely I may be excused! he was never tired of comforting his sister, he never left her in anger, he always met her with joy, he preferred her society to every other pleasure, or rather when we were so happy as to be within each other's reach he had no pleasure when we were compelled to be divided.

Do not then expect too much of this brother of whom I have delighted so to talk to you, do not form your expectations from *my* account but from that of other people. In the first place you must be with him more than once before he will be perfectly easy in conversation; in the second place his person is not in his favour, at least I should think not; but I soon ceased to discover this, nay, I almost thought that the opinion which I first formed was erroneous. He is, however, certainly rather plain than otherwise, has an extremely thoughtful countenance, but when he speaks it is often lighted up with a smile which *I* think very pleasing—but enough, he is my Brother, why should *I* describe him? I shall be launching again into panegyric. I must for the present bid you adieu. The dew begins to fall so I think it not quite prudent to sit upon the grass. I will take a few turns at the bottom of the field where I have a sweet prospect, and I will adorn our little cottage. . . . I fear what I have written is quite illegible—a knee is not the most convenient writing desk. Adieu. . . .

'I steal a few moments before I retire into my Aunt's bedroom for the night. As I am head nurse, housekeeper, tutoress of the little ones, or rather superintendent of the nursery, I am at present a very busy woman and literally *steal* the moments which I employ in letter writing. I hope, however, very soon to have more leisure, but my aunt does not gain strength so fast as I had expected. . . . I am still obliged to sleep in her room, and she goes to bed so early as nine o'clock, which robs me of the most precious of my hours, as I go to bed at the same time, and as she sleeps very indifferently at nights I am obliged to lie very long in the mornings for fear of disturbing her. . . . *Thursday morn.* I find that I have not proceeded regularly last night and I also find that I cannot read what I have written without great difficulty; how you will decipher it I cannot tell. . . . But for my journey to Halifax and my meeting there my Brother Wm it is time I should explain myself a little more clearly. In the first place I have not heard from Mr. Griffith yet, (which has disappointed me a good deal) therefore I cannot say *when* I am to be with you. After August however, I shall only wait his convenience, but my Brother's tour will not be completed till October, at which time they will perhaps make a stand in North Wales, from whence he can very conveniently take a trip to Halifax. It is more than two years and a half since we last saw each other, and so ardent is our desire for a meeting that we are determined upon procuring to ourselves this happiness if it were even to be purchased at the price of a journey across the Kingdom, but from North Wales into Yorkshire the distance is nothing. If therefore my Brother does not meet with any employment which is likely to fix him before I go to Halifax we shall certainly meet there, but if he should be engaged we are determined to see each other at Forncett. Judge my dearest Jane of the excess of my desire to see my brother at *Halifax* when I assure you that much as I am interested that he should be established in the world and important as is his early provision to our final interests, yet I wish that he may continue at liberty so long as to allow us an interview there. In forming this wish I have a sort of conflict within my breast, but surely I am not very culpable, as in so very short a time I shall reach my dear friends at Halifax, and as he is equally desirous for our meeting, and for our meeting for a longer time than, circumstanced as we are, it would be possible for us to be together at Forncett, and besides he is impatient to be introduced into our little society at H. Here, then, the matter rests. If my Brother makes an engagement which will take him out of England or confine him to one spot for any length of time, then he is determined to come and see me at Forncett, if it be but for one day, though he has never received an invitation from my Uncle, and though he can have no possible inducement but the pleasure of seeing me. You must know that this favourite brother of mine happens to be no favourite with any of his *near* relations, except his Brothers by whom he is adored, I mean by John and Christopher, for Richard's disposition and his are totally different, and though they never have any quarrels, yet there is not that friendship between them which can only exist where there is some similarity of taste, or sentiment, or where two hearts are found to sympathize with each other in all their griefs and joys. I have not time or room to explain to you the foundation of the prejudices of my two Uncles against my dear William; the subject is an unpleasant one for a letter, it will employ us more agreeably in conversation, then, though I must confess that he has been somewhat to blame, yet I think I shall prove to you that the excuse might be found in his natural disposition,

> In truth he was a strange and wayward wight
> Fond of each gentle etc. etc.

That verse of Beattie's *Minstrel* always reminds me of him, and indeed the whole character of Edwin resembles much what William was when I first knew him after my leaving Halifax—"and oft he traced the uplands" etc., etc.

'I have been much disappointed that my Uncle has not invited Wm to Forncett, but he is no favourite with him. Alas! alas!

I shall not however at all regret it if I have the infinitely greater happiness of meeting him at Halifax which nothing forbids me to expect. I insist upon a strict silence and pray do not read aloud one word of what I have written. I do not write to you what ought to be read by everyone, but particularly when I speak of my Brothers I wish you to be silent. . . . I am particularly desirous that nothing should be said of William's intention to visit Halifax when I am there, as though after the meeting has taken place, I should by no means wish to conceal it from my uncle, yet I should be very averse to his knowing it beforehand, or even afterwards that my scheme was a *premeditated* one. For this reason I shall not say a word of it either to Mrs. Rawson or Mr. Griffith. *You* are the only person to whom it has been mentioned. I will transcribe a passage or two from my brother's letters which will give you a faint idea of his affection for me and of his desire to see me. The first which I shall transcribe is from the letter which he wrote to me in answer to mine informing him of my certainty of visiting Halifax but when he had no idea of . . . the possibility of meeting me at Halifax. He says after speaking much of the pleasure I might hope for from seeing you all again, "How, my dearest friend, could you dare to apologise for writing me a second letter particularly when its object was to inform me of an addition to your happiness? How much do I wish that each emotion of pleasure and pain that visits your heart should excite a similar pleasure or a similar pain within me, by that sympathy that will almost identify us when we have stolen to our little cottage! I am determined to see you as soon as ever I have entered into an engagement; immediately I will write to my uncle, and tell him that I cannot think of going anywhere before I have been with you. Whatever answer he gives me I certainly will make a point of once more mingling my transports with yours. Alas! my dear sister, how soon must this happiness expire, yet there are moments worth ages." In another letter, in which he informs me of his intention to accept his friend Calvert's offer he says "With reference to our meeting, this scheme will not at all affect it, as in case of my not meeting with any employment we shall probably be in North Wales about the time of your going into Yorkshire, and it will be easy for me to see you at Halifax. O my dear, dear sister, with what transport shall I again meet you, with what rapture shall I again wear out the day in your sight. I assure you so eager is my desire to see you that all obstacles vanish. I see you in a moment running or rather flying to my arms." . . . This letter is so shamefully written that much as I am accustomed to write in this illegible style I am quite ashamed of it, but I think if you knew all the circumstances under which it has been written and at how many different times, you would hold me excused. Pray tell me honestly if you are able to read it. I would have you however consider this *very* bad writing a proof of my affection for you. I would not have sent such a scrawl to any one but you or my brother William. Never I entreat you make it an excuse for not writing that you want time. Write as I have written this letter at twenty different sittings or standings whenever you find a moment to yourself. Perhaps you may have seen Mr. Griffith at Halifax. I long to know *when* he goes to London. Adieu my very dear friend. Love me always and depend on my unalterable regard. D. W.'

So Dorothy passed the summer, in anxious expectancy of her visit to Halifax; it was probably a good thing for her that she was kept so busy in attendance on her aunt. In August her worries were increased by the loss of her purse, 'a most grievous misfortune' she tells Jane, for it held 'my little store of savings for my Halifax gaieties'. At once she wrote off to her brother Richard, the only one of her family who had the means to help her:

My dear Richard,

I write to you in great distress—I have discovered this morning that I have lost my purse containing six guineas, which is more than I am worth, as I owe a guinea and a half. Never surely was anything so unlucky. It was by mere chance that I had the money at all, or that I should be so unlucky as to put so much in my purse—I had lent my Aunt six guineas last week; she had repaid it to me the night before last, and I, not finding it convenient to go upstairs immediately and put it in the box where I always keep my money, except a few shillings or a guinea, put it in my purse, and forgot to take it out again. Last night I went to Stratton, and there I suppose I lost it, as I took it out of my pocket there, and got a guinea changed. My dear Richard, it hurts me much to apply to you in this distress, but what can I do? I have not a farthing in the world. Pray be so good as to write to me by return of post, and if possible send me my allowance: at any rate write to me—I know not what I shall do—I had fancied myself so rich and I am now as poor as Job! but Riches take unto themselves wings and flee away. It is, however, no joking matter; for I know not what will become of me—My Aunt gave me five guineas the other day which was the reason of my being so rich.

I would not delay writing to you one post as I was fearful that, if I did, you might not be in London; and without some relief from you, and *immediate* relief, I must beg or be dunned. I have sent over to Stratton but can hear no tidings of the purse. . . . If you should see my Uncle, say nothing to him about it, as he would think me very careless, and there is still a chance (but alas! a very poor one, and I have no hopes) that I may find it again. I shall beg my Aunt never to tell my Uncle. Adieu, dear Richard, Believe me, very truly yours. D.W.

I shall send over to Stratton for your letter on Sunday morning, when I shall fully expect one. *Friday afternoon.* This loss is particularly unfortunate *now*, as I am so soon going from home.

In answer to this touching appeal she promptly received a £10 note, which she acknowledged with effusive gratitude. Only years afterwards, when their father's estate was finally wound up, did she discover that the prudent Richard had debited her account with the sum which she had taken as a generous and loving gift.

Her departure for Halifax was not to be so soon as she had hoped. Mr. Griffith was a good friend, but a bad correspondent, and grievously deliberate in all his movements. When she could wring a letter out of him it was only to tell her that his journey was postponed; November passed without his appearance, and the Christmas that she had imagined herself spending as of old by the happy fireside at the Pollards found her still at Forncett, amusing the Cookson babies. It was not till early in February that, with or without Mr. Griffith, she was able to effect her journey to Halifax.

III

HALIFAX AND THE NORTH

February 1794—September 1795 (aet. 22–3½)

A WARM welcome awaited Dorothy at Halifax. She rejoiced to find her dear aunt no longer immersed in the busy cares of a household overrun with nephews and nieces, but the mistress of a commodious country home, in easy circumstances, and with leisure to devote to her beloved garden; Mr. Rawson proved a kindly host, and quickly won her affection, and she entered with zest into the pleasant society that surrounded her. At Forncett she had few companions of her own age, and none who were really congenial. The Miss Burroughs might be 'sweet girls', but they lived two miles off, and her friendship with them had not gone very deep: here she was among the playmates of her girlhood, who had interests similar to her own; and the slight seniority of her cousins the Threlkelds and Fergusons, which had made them seem so old to her six years ago, counted for nothing now that she, like them, was in the twenties. Jane Pollard, whom she remembered 'in a round cap, her hair flowing about' her,

> and sweetly wild,
> Just betwixt the woman and the child.[1]

was now the charming and beautiful fiancée of Mr. Marshall of Leeds. And Dorothy, too, had changed. To Jane, indeed, who had written that she expected to find her Dolly an accomplished woman, she might protest that she 'had no acquirement to boast, and nothing to recommend her but a warm honest affectionate heart', but in truth the society of her scholarly uncle, and the study of books recommended to her by him or by William, had developed her lively intelligence as effectively as a more formal education could have done, whilst her busy life of service in separation from those she loved best had strengthened her character, and without repressing her natural buoyancy of spirit had made her wiser than her years. The letters sent by her aunt and cousins to Sam Ferguson, who had

[1] D. W. to J. P., June 16, 1793.

gone to seek his fortune in America, show clearly how deep an impression Dorothy made upon them all.

William they were ready to accept at something of his sister's valuation. He was not the best of company, for he was never at his ease among strangers; and now that trouble weighed heavy upon him it is no wonder that they often found him moody and silent; but after all he had moved in a wider world than they, a world in which they were keenly interested. The Unitarian society of a north-country town had more sympathy with revolutionary principles than could be expected from a Canon of Windsor; moreover they were quite up to date in their literary tastes, and are not likely to have underrated the poems just published by their cousin. And so, when they dubbed him an 'eccentric young man' it was more in admiration than in censure, and Dorothy had the satisfaction of feeling that her wonderful brother was properly appreciated.

Her cup of joy was indeed full. For three long years, the last of them a year of deep anxiety and distress, she had lived in anticipation of this meeting. But now he was at her side, and she could revisit with him all those scenes associated with her childhood of which she had often told him, living over again with him that part of her life from which he had been excluded; whilst in return she could hear from his own lips all those details of his experiences in France, of Beaupuis and of Annette, which no letters, however intimate, could have contained; and together they could discuss their plans for the difficult future that lay before them.

Six happy weeks at Halifax were the prelude to a time of even fuller happiness; for with the dawn of spring they set off together on what Dorothy has significantly called their 'first pilgrimage'. Taking the Whitehaven coach as far as Kendal they started on a two days' tramp to Keswick. Even to-day, straightened and widened as it is to suit an age which has sacrificed its soul to speed, this road from Kendal to Keswick is reputed the most lovely in England: it was then a narrow winding track whose every bend revealed some fresh subtle or arresting beauty. To Dorothy in that delicious spring weather, when the colours are at their brightest and most varied, it was truly enchanted ground. She was tramping for the first time a road that of all others was to be the most familiar to her, and she had the best of guides. Never afterwards could she pass through Staveley without a thrill, for it was the first mountain village she came to; and her delight grew in intensity as she caught her first glimpse of shy Winander, and of the falls of Rydal, of which William had sung in the poem dedicated to her. They reached Rydalmere at sunset, and saw, as years later she loved to recall, the rich yellow light upon the waters, and the reflection of the island there. Past Rydal they mounted White Moss Common, on which old Benjamin's horses would stop for many a breathing fit,[1] and soon after breasting the summit looked upon Grasmere, with its one green island lying peacefully at their feet. At the bottom of the hill they passed the very doors of Dove Cottage, little dreaming that it would one day be their chosen home, and in the village beyond they rested for the night. On the next day they pushed on over Dunmail Raise, along the road they were so often to traverse in quest of Coleridge or in his company, and a short mile from the little town of Keswick reached their destination, a farm house called Windy Brow. Here her brother's friends, William and Raisley Calvert, had lodgings, and they had moved into an adjacent cottage to make room for Dorothy.

From Grasmere Dorothy had written to her aunt; her impressions of Windy Brow were duly conveyed to Jane:[2]

> 'You cannot conceive anything more delightful than the situation of this house. It stands upon the top of a very steep bank, which rises in a direction nearly perpendicular from a dashing stream below. From the window of the room where I write I have a prospect of the road winding along the opposite banks of the river, of a part of the lake of Keswick, and of the town, and towering above the town a woody steep of a very considerable height whose summit is a long range of silver rocks. This is the view from the house, but a hundred yards above it is impossible to describe its grandeur. There is a natural terrace along the side of the mountain which shelters Windy Brow, whence we command a view of the whole vale of Keswick (the Vale of Elysium, as Mr. Gray calls it). This vale is terminated at one end by a huge pile of grand mountains in whose lap the lovely lake of Derwent is placed, at the other end by the lake of Bassenthwaite, on one side Skiddaw towers sublime and on the other a range of mountains not of equal size but of much grandeur, and the middle part

[1] *V. The Waggoner*, i. 30–41.

[2] D. W. to J. P., Apr. 1794.

of the vale is of beautiful cultivated grounds interspersed with cottages and watered by a winding stream which runs between the lakes of Derwent and Bassenthwaite. I have never been more delighted with the manners of any people than of the family under whose roof I am at present. They are the most honest, cleanly, sensible people I ever saw in their rank of life,—and I think I may safely affirm happier than any body I know. They are contented with a supply of the bare necessaries of life, are active and industrious, and declare with simple frankness unmixed with ostentation that they prefer their cottage at Windy Brow to any of the showy edifices in the neighbourhood, and that they believe there is not to be found in the whole vale a happier family than they are. They are fond of reading, and reason not indifferently upon what they read. We have a neat parlour to ourselves which Mr. Calvert has fitted up for his own use and the lodging-rooms are very comfortable. Till my brother gets some employment he will lodge here.'

At Windy Brow Dorothy had a brief foretaste of the life she had dreamed of for the future. Alone or with her brother she roamed the countryside, under his direction she read much in English and French, made the acquaintance of several of his old friends, and was initiated into her proud task of copying out his new or corrected verses. For William, after his long distracted wandering, had found peace in her companionship and in the quiet beauty around him, and once more gave himself to poetry, adding fresh lines to *An Evening Walk* and working hard at the *Incident on Salisbury Plain*, which he had conceived in the previous year. But this sojourn in a remote farm-house, with no protector but a revolutionary brother, was viewed askance by Dorothy's conventional relatives. When the news reached Newbiggin Hall,[1] which Uncle Christopher had inherited on the death of his mother, Aunt Crackanthorpe felt it her bounden duty to protest: such outrageously unladylike conduct could not be tolerated in a niece of hers. Dorothy's reply, discovered years afterwards in a box lying in an outhouse at Newbiggin, reveals alike the Spartan simplicity of her life, and her fine independence and dignity of character:[2]

[1] Newbiggin is situated about 2 m. E. of Temple Sowerby, and 6 m. NNW. of Appleby.

[2] D. W. to Mrs. Crackanthorpe, Apr. 21, 1794.

My dear Aunt,

I should have answered your letter immediately after the receipt of it, if I had not been upon the point of setting forward to Mrs. Spedding's of Armathwaite, where I have been spending three days. I am much obliged to you for the frankness with which you have expressed your sentiments upon my conduct and am at the same time extremely sorry that you should think it so severely to be condemned. As you have not sufficiently developed the reasons of your censure, I have endeavoured to discover them; and I confess no other possible objections against my continuing here a few weeks longer suggest themselves, except the *expense*, and that you may suppose me to be in an unprotected situation. As to the former of these objections I reply that I drink no tea, that my supper and breakfast are of bread and milk, and my dinner chiefly of potatoes from choice. In answer to the second of these suggestions, namely that I may be supposed to be in an unprotected situation, I affirm that I consider the character and virtues of my brother as a sufficient protection; and besides I am convinced that there is no place in the world in which a good and virtuous young woman would be more likely to continue good and virtuous than under the roof of these honest, worthy, uncorrupted people: so that any guardianship beyond theirs I should think altogether unnecessary. I cannot pass unnoticed that part of your letter in which you speak of my 'rambling about the country on foot'. So far from considering this as a matter of condemnation, I rather thought it would have given my friends pleasure to hear that I had courage to make use of the strength with which nature has endowed me, when it not only procured me infinitely more pleasure than I should have received from sitting in a post chaise, but was also the means of saving me at least thirty shillings.

In mentioning the inducements which I have to stay at Windy Brow a few weeks longer, it would be unnecessary to speak of the beauty of the country, or the pleasantness of the season. To these are added the society of several of my brother's friends, from whom I have received the most friendly attentions, and above all the society of my brother. I am now twenty-two years of age, and such have been the circumstances of my life that I may be said to have enjoyed his company only for a *very few* months. An opportunity now presents itself of obtaining this satisfaction, an opportunity which I could not see pass from me without unspeakable pain. Besides, I not only derive much pleasure but much improvement from my brother's society. I have regained all the knowledge I had of the French language some years ago, and have added considerably to it. I have now begun Italian, of which I expect to have soon gained a sufficient knowledge to receive much entertainment and advantage from it. I am much obliged to you and my uncle for your kind invitation, which I shall accept with great pleasure on my return from Whitehaven. I have received the kindest civilities from Mrs. Spedding of Armathwaite. She has made me promise that, if it is in my power, I will spend a little time with her. I know of nothing that would make me more happy than to cultivate the acquaintance of the Miss Speddings who are most amiable women. I beg my love to my uncle and the children, and my compliments to Miss Cust.

Believe me, my dear aunt,
Affectionately yours,
D. WORDSWORTH.

It is strange that Aunt Crackanthorpe did not destroy this crushing rejoinder; perhaps she kept it to show to her friends, when Dorothy had gone to the bad as the inevitable result of flouting good advice.

After so long an absence from the North Dorothy had naturally many dutiful visits to pay to relations whom she had not seen since she was a little girl, and first of all to her uncle and guardian Richard Wordsworth at Branthwaite, near Whitehaven. The road thither lay through Cockermouth, and she did not fail to visit with William the house of their birth. It looked forlorn and deserted, for it had not been occupied since their father's death, and the garden was sadly overgrown; but the privet hedge of the terrace was still full of roses, as it was when they had watched the sparrows nest in it nearly twenty years before. They found their uncle seriously ill, and he died on June 14, while they were still at Whitehaven. A few days later Dorothy went on to visit her cousin Mrs. Barker at Rampside, a little village on the coast near Furness Abbey. William and her cousin Robinson Wordsworth walked by her side as far as Broughton, whilst she rode upon her uncle's horse. At Broughton they parted, and her few months' holiday with William was over:[1] for more than a year they were to be separated. Early in July she was with her new friends the

[1] William's visit to Rampside, to which he alludes in *Elegiac Stanzas on Peele Castle*, did not coincide, as has been supposed, with Dorothy's, for it is now proved to have taken place in August.

Speddings at Armathwaite, and after a few weeks went on to stay with Uncle and Aunt Crackanthorpe.

Nothing but the sternest sense of duty drove her to Newbiggin Hall. Even before she received her aunt's letter of reproof she had hoped that she would not be invited, and when the invitation came she had some hesitation in accepting it; but her virtue was unexpectedly rewarded. Her aunt, indeed, was as disagreeable as she had anticipated, but her uncle surprised her by the warmth with which he received her. 'I never', she wrote, 'saw a man so agitated in my life as he was at our meeting: I am sure he felt the most affectionate sentiments towards me.' Throughout her visit, which seems to have lasted some months, he was friendliness itself, and at her departure gave her ten guineas 'which you will say was very kind; indeed it was and the manner of giving it made it doubly so'. And forgetting how much she had disliked him in his bachelor days, when he had been so cross to her and so unjust to William, she adds, 'I am convinced that his faults are chiefly owing to his wife, whom I can never think otherwise of than as a proud and selfish woman; he is a creature of impulse and when left to the workings of his own mind I am sure he would always act well'.[1] Perhaps, however, the trials of married life had softened him; perhaps, too, he found his grown-up niece more attractive than the impetuous, high-spirited, not very contented girl whom he had scolded eight years before.

Christmas and the New Year found Dorothy at Newcastle with her cousins the Griffiths, and it was the end of April before she returned to her aunt Rawson at Halifax: her route lay through Darlington and Northallerton, and between these two towns was the farm of Sockburn-on-Tees, where her friends Mary and Peggy Hutchinson now lived with their brothers, Thomas and George. She had intended merely to pass one night with them, but she stayed almost a month.

> 'You cannot think', she wrote,[1] 'what pleasure it gives me to see them so happy, situated exactly as our imaginations and wishes used to represent when there was little hope that they would be realised . . . they are quite independent and have not a wish ungratified, very different indeed is their present situation from what it was formerly, when we compared grievances and lamented

[1] D. W. to J. P., Apr. 1795.

the misfortune of losing our parents at an early age and being thrown upon the mercy of ill-natured and illiberal relations. Their brother has a farm of about £200 a year, and they keep his house. He is a very amiable young man, uncommonly fond of his sisters. The house was built by their uncle, who left them the furniture and eighteen hundred pounds which with what they had makes them very comfortable. It is an excellent house, not at all like a farm-house, and they seem to have none of the trouble which I used to think must make farmers always in a bustle, for they have very little corn and only two cows. It is a grazing estate and most delightfully pleasant, washed nearly round by the Tees, a noble river, and stocked with sheep and lambs which look very pretty, and to me give it an interesting appearance. . . . We spend our time very pleasantly in walking, reading, working and playing at ball in the meadow in which the house stands, which is scattered over with sheep and "green as an emerald".'

Upon this visit to Sockburn Dorothy first met Sara Hutchinson, now eighteen years of age, who was destined to become one of her dearest friends. In the old Penrith days, when Mary and Peggy were the companions of her daily walks, Sara was living at Kendal under the care of her cousin Margaret Patrick. She was fortunate in her upbringing. Her cousin-in-law, David Patrick, known far and wide through the north country as 'the intellectual pedlar', was a remarkable personality—to Sara's accounts of him are due many touches in the portrait of the Wanderer in *The Excursion*—he was deeply attached to her, and she always maintained 'that the best part of her education was gathered from the stores of that good man's mind'. Sara Hutchinson was not imposing in appearance. Like Dorothy only a little over five feet in height, rather plain-featured, and with a plump, dumpy figure devoid of grace and dignity, she was only redeemed from the commonplace by a delicately fair skin and a profusion of light brown hair. But those who looked closer noted in her face a peculiarly sweet expression, and she had a real distinction of mind and character. More matter of fact than Dorothy, less excitable, and without her sensitive alertness of mind, the had a keener sense of quiet fun, and was, moreover, a woman of considerable intellectual gifts, fully worthy to be the intimate friend of two great poets. 'The combination', wrote Coleridge, 'of natural shrewdness and a disposition to innocent humour joined with perfect simplicity and tenderness is what distinguishes her from her sister (Mary), whose character is of a more solemn cast.'[1]

Dorothy passed her summer at Halifax, and on August 5 saw her dear Jane married to John Marshall of Leeds: her own plans were still unsettled. The idea of returning to the Cooksons was naturally enough repugnant to her, for William was still in disfavour with them: her life with him at Windy Brow had only intensified her eager impatience to share his home. But of this there seemed no clear prospect.

Ever since his return from France William had sought in vain for an employment which would bring in a competence and yet leave him time for poetry. 'All professions are attended with great inconveniences,' he had written to his friend Mathews,[2] with a naivety common in the young aspirant to literary fame, 'I have done nothing and still continue to do nothing. What will become of me I know not. I cannot bow my mind down to take orders, and as for the law I have neither strength of mind, purse, or constitution, to engage in that pursuit.' He had tried without success to obtain a travelling tutorship: some form of journalism seemed the only resource left to him. News of this intention reached his prudent brother Richard, who somewhat naturally took fright. He knew William's revolutionary sympathies, perhaps had read in manuscript William's reply to the Bishop of Llandaff,[3] and he wrote urging him to be careful, pointing out that by the suspension of the Habeas Corpus Act the government had great powers. The chances of success in their suit with Lord Lonsdale were remote enough as it was, his Lordship had spies in every part of the country, and if the family were tarred with a revolutionary brush their chance would be remoter still. Dorothy strove to allay Richard's alarm. 'I think', she wrote, 'I can answer for William's caution about expressing his political opinions. He is very cautious, and seems well aware of the dangers of a contrary conduct.'[4]

[1] S. T. C. to Daniel Stuart, 1808.

[2] W. W. to William Mathews, Feb. 17, 1794.

[3] The full title of this pamphlet is *A Letter to the Bishop of Llandaff, on the extraordinary avowal of his Political Principles, contained in the Appendix to his late Sermon; by a Republican.* It remained in MS. till 1876.

[4] D. W. to R. W., May 28, 1794. R. W.'s letter to W. W. is dated May 23; his anxiety is emphasized by his saying 'You may read this letter to Dolly: afterwards it may be as well to burn it'.

But, in truth, it was not caution so much as opportunity that he lacked. In the depths of the country he was out of touch with the literary market; and life in London was too expensive to hazard without a certain source of income. He was in a vicious circle. As for starting a paper with Mathews, as Mathews suggested, that would require capital, and he had not a sixpence to advance. So he had wandered about the country, staying with different friends, waiting, but without Mr. Micawber's optimism, for something to turn up. In autumn he had at least the satisfaction of making himself useful. His friend Raisley Calvert had developed a rapid consumption, and William went to Windy Brow to nurse him; when Raisley thought of seeking health by a voyage to Lisbon, William offered to accompany him; and when he proved too ill to make the journey, tended him with unremitting devotion. In December he moved his friend to Penrith, probably with the object of obtaining more skilled medical attendance, and here early in January Raisley Calvert died. Before his illness he had offered to share his income with William: in his will, dated October 23, 1794 he had bequeathed 'the sum of £900 to my friend William Wordsworth'; and by a codicil of the same date he 'ordered and directed that the said sum of £900 shall be laid out by him (W. W.) in the purchase of one or more annuities for his use and benefit, granting unto him nevertheless full power to lay out such part of the said £900 as to him shall seem meet for the use and benefit of his Sister Dorothy Wordsworth'. This codicil shows clearly enough that the poet's friends were already aware of the close tie which bound him to his sister.

It was a timely benefaction. It freed William from all immediate financial anxiety, and removed the only obstacle which prevented his return to London; and forthwith he hurried there to see what prospects literature afforded. His first idea seems to have been to summon Dorothy at once to join him and share his labours, but the plan did not commend itself to Mrs. Rawson. 'Dorothy and Wm.', she wrote to Sam Ferguson (March 11), 'have now a scheme of living together in London, and maintaining themselves by their literary talents, writing and translating; not that they are altogether without other means of support, as he has had a legacy of £900, but the interest will not go far towards keeping house, and the rest they mean to procure by their pens. We think it a very bad wild scheme.' Apparently William came to think so too. Life in London, even without financial embarrassment, did not come up to his expectations. He was always subject to severe nervous headaches when exposed to heated atmosphere or loud noises, and he found that life in dreary lodgings, alternating with the excitements of revolutionary society, was unfavourable to all mental exertion, and did not help him to recover his lost peace of mind. He longed for the country, yet he saw no way of earning a living there. But he never lacked friends who had a firm belief in his genius and character, and a few of them now combined to solve his difficulty for him.

His friend Montagu, a widower living in chambers, proposed to him that he and Dorothy should take charge of his little son Basil, and their cousin Tom Myers made a similar request in favour of his little niece; at the same time young Mr. Pinney of Bristol, another friend whom he had come to know through Montagu, offered him the loan of a furnished house in Dorsetshire,[1] where he could receive the children and any other pupils who might offer themselves. Financially the scheme was sound, for the proceeds of the legacy, together with fees for the children's board, would amount to at least £180 a year, and William might add to this by the proceeds of his pen: he had already been offered ten guineas for a work that had taken him little time, and he saw no reason why that sum should not be almost indefinitely increased.

The castle which Dorothy had so often built in the air had at last some solid foundations; but the very intensity with which she had longed for it made her realize the more fully its attendant responsibilities, and she gave many a careful thought to the course she should adopt.

> 'It will', she wrote,[2] 'be a very great charge for me, I am sensible, but it is of a nature well suited to my inclinations. You know I am active, not averse to household employments, and fond of children. I have laid my plans as distinctly as I can, but many things must depend upon unforseen circumstances; I am, however, determined to adhere with the strictest attention to certain rules. In the first place economy and an attention to the

[1] The house belonged to Pinney's father, a Bristol merchant with large plantations in the West Indies, who rented it to his son at £50 a year.

[2] D. W. to Jane Marshall (*née* Pollard), Sept. 2, 1795.

over-looking every thing myself will be absolutely necessary for this purpose, not much time is necessary if it is done with regularity. I shall also have a good deal of work, (needlework) to do and I am determined to take the whole care of the children such as washing, dressing them etc., upon myself. I forgot in enumerating the comforts of Racedown (so the place is called) to tell you that we may have land to keep a cow and that there is a cow there of which we may have the use, I think it is probable that there may be a cottager near us to whose charge we may commit it for a share of the milk or some trifling recompense. I mean to keep one maidservant, she must be a strong girl and cook plain victuals tolerably well, as we shall occasionally have both Mr. Montagu and Mr. Pinney to stay with us. . . . Kitt is very much pleased with the plan, it will indeed be a great comfort to him and John to have a place to draw to and I hope we shall oftener meet than we have ever hitherto had it in our power. I confess when I think of the importance of my duties I am anxious and sometimes fearful, but resolved as I am to do all that my abilities will permit I hope I shall not fail. My Aunt says she has no doubt of me and Mr. Rawson is of the same opinion. He thinks I am quite equal to the charge. I expect to have some trouble with the children at first, but I am determined to act with resolution and steadiness —I hope I shall succeed. Basil Montagu is yet by no means a spoiled child notwithstanding the disadvantages under which he has laboured. As for the little girl I shall feel myself quite as a mother to her. I am expecting a letter from my uncle William every day with his opinion of the scheme, I think he cannot disapprove of it, there are so many arguments in its favour. One of the first and greatest is that it may put William into a way of getting a more permanent establishment, and on my account that it will greatly contribute to my happiness and place me in such a situation that I shall be *doing something*, it is a painful idea that one's existence is of very little use, which *I* really have always been obliged to feel; above all it is painful when one is living upon the bounty of one's friends, a resource of which misfortune may deprive one, and then how irksome and difficult is it to find out other means of support, the mind is then unfitted perhaps for any new exertions, and continues always in a state of dependence, perhaps attended with poverty. . . .

'I shall have to join William at Bristol and proceed thence in a chaise with Basil to Racedown, it is 50 miles. I have received a very polite invitation from the Pinneys to stay at their house on my road.'

Though the expected advent of a fifth addition to the Forncett family made Dorothy's presence there most desirable, Uncle William could hardly offer a serious opposition. His unsatisfactory nephew was at last making some effort to become self-supporting, and without Dorothy the plan would fall to the ground. Within a month of writing her letter Dorothy was installed with William at Racedown; till his death they were rarely again to be parted for more than a few weeks at a time.

IV

RACEDOWN

September 1795—July 1797 (aet. 23½–5½)

'If you want to find our situation out, look in your maps for Crewkerne, Chard, Axminster, Bridport and Lyme; we are nearly equidistant from all those places. A little brook which runs at the distance of one field divides us from Devonshire. . . . We have many very pleasant walks about us and what is a great advantage, the roads are of a sandy kind and are almost always dry. We can see the sea 150 or 200 yards from the door, and at a little distance have a very extensive view terminated by the sea seen through different openings of the unequal hills. We have not the warmth and luxuriance of Devonshire, though there is no want either of wood or cultivation, but the trees appear to suffer from sea blasts. We have hills which seen from a distance almost take the character of mountains, some cultivated nearly to their summits, others in their wild state covered with furze and broom. These delight me the most, as they remind me of our native wilds. Our common parlour is the prettiest little room that can be, with very neat furniture, a large bookcase on each side the fire, a marble chimney piece, bath stove, and an oilcloth for the floor. The other parlour is rather larger, has a good carpet, side boards in the recesses on each side the fire, and has upon the whole a smart appearance, but we do not like it half so well as our little breakfast room.'[1]

Such was Dorothy's description of her new home. Everything came up to her highest expectations. The good Pinneys had handed over the house so well equipped that she had not to lay out ten shillings upon the necessary pots and pans, and after a month's search Dorothy secured a servant. Peggy by name, whom she describes enthusiastically as one of the nicest girls she ever saw. She did not allow the cares of a household to absorb her whole time. 'I have all my domestic concerns so arranged that everything goes on with the utmost regularity. We wash once a month. I hire a woman to whom I give ninepence for one day to wash, on the next we have got the clothes dried, and on the third have finished ironing. It is the only

[1] D. W. to J. M., Nov. 30, 1795.

time in which I have anything to do in the house, but *then* I am very active, as you will suppose.'[1]

As a mother Dorothy was equally efficient. It was a disappointment to her that the little girl who was to join their family did not put in an appearance, but Basil Montagu provided material enough for that study of child psychology which was an absorbing interest to both her and her brother—not the less so, perhaps, because, as William asserted, he 'lied like a little devil'.[2] It was a satisfaction to them to see him develop under their care 'from a shivering halfstarved plant into a lusty blooming fearless boy, dreading neither cold nor rain'.[3] 'I do not think', she wrote,[4] 'there is any pleasure more delightful than that of marking the development of a child's faculties 'and observing his little occupations'; and when Jane's interest in children was kindled by the arrival of her first-born, Dorothy was able to supply her with hints which many a modern mother might do well to ponder:

'You ask to be informed of our system respecting Basil; it is a very simple one, so simple that in this age of systems you will hardly be likely to follow it. We teach him nothing at present but what he learns from the evidence of his senses. He has an insatiable curiosity which we are always careful to satisfy to the best of our ability. It is directed to every thing he sees, the sky, the fields, trees, shrubs, corn, the making of tools, carts, etc. etc. He knows his letters, but we have not attempted any further step in the path of *book learning*. Our grand study has been to make him *happy*, in which we have not been altogether disappointed, he is certainly the most contented child I ever saw; the least disposed to be fretful. At first when he came he was extremely petted from indulgence and weakness of body, and perpetually disposed to cry. Upon these occasions (perhaps this may be of use to you) we used to tell him that if he chose to cry he must go into a certain room where he cannot be heard, and *stay* till he chose to be quiet, because the noise was unpleasant to us: at first his visits were very long, and he always came out again perfectly goodhumoured. He found that this rule was never departed from, and when he felt the fretful disposition coming on he would say, "Aunt, I think I am going to cry", and retire till the fit was over. He has now entirely conquered the disposition. I dare say it is

[1] Ib.
[2] W. W. to Wrangham, Mar. 7, 1796; cf. 'Anecdote for Fathers', Oxf. W. p. 85.
[3] D. W. to J. M., Mar. 7, 1796.
[4] D. W. to J. M., Nov. 30, 1795.

three months since we have had occasion to send him into this apartment of tears. We have no punishments except such as appear to be, as far as we can determine, the immediate consequence that is to grow out of the offence. He had two mornings last week but one failed to get up when Peggy called him; he came down about an hour after. The second morning Peggy was employed, she could not wash him, we were all engaged and could not fasten his clothes for him, so he was obliged to go to bed again, where he lay till four o'clock. He has ever since risen at the first call.'[1]

At Harlescombe, the farm-house just below Racedown, lodged Joseph Gill, a cousin of the Pinneys who had come down in the world and was now acting as the general overseer of their Dorsetshire property. The Wordsworths were soon on good terms with him: he had a large store of *Gentleman's Magazines* on which William drew for light reading of an evening, and when the gardener proved refractory Gill helped to keep the place in order. In the absence of shops Dorothy obtained most of her household supplies from Gill, and from time to time he lent her little sums of money; in June 1796, when William paid a short visit to London, Gill walked three times with her to Crewkerne to fetch the letters. In December 1796 he noted in his journal 'Miss Ws Diary 10d'. Did Dorothy begin to keep a diary at Racedown, we wonder, or was this merely a journal in which to enter her accounts? With the Harlescombe farmer, John Hitchcock, Gill was always at loggerheads, but to his surprise Dorothy was able to manage even the unruly Hitchcock; for he notes in his journal: 'On Friday J. Hitchcock went to Lyme for coal for Miss Wordsworth with less difficulty than was expected as his wife has said he should not go.'[2]

By the time they had settled into their new home winter was already upon them, and about Christmas they enjoyed a five weeks' visit from the two Pinney youths. The elder, John Frederick, was fresh from Oxford and had also 'travelled a good deal by way of education, was well informed and had an uncommonly good heart and was very pleasant in conversation'. Azariah, the younger, had spent a year at Cambridge and some

[1] D. W. to J. M., Mar. 19, 1797 (wrongly dated in K. The first Marshall baby was born in May 1796).

[2] *V.* 'Racedown and the Wordsworths', by Bergen Evans and Hester Pinney, *Rev. of Engl. Studies*, Jan. 1932.

time in Germany, and was now in business with his father in Bristol; though not such a favourite with Dorothy as his brother she thought him 'a very good young man and much more pleasing in manners than the generality of young men'. Perhaps Dorothy showed her preference too plainly, for Azariah found something wanting in her. 'Miss Wordsworth', he wrote to a friend, 'has undoubted claims to good humour, but does not possess, in my opinion, that je ne sais quoi, so necessary to sweeten the sour draught of human misfortune.'

The Pinneys proved pleasant guests and entered with zest into the unconventional life of the household:

> 'We here read a good deal while they were with us (for they are fond of reading) but we have not gone on with our usual regularity. When the weather was fine they were out regularly all the morning, walking sometimes: *then* I went with them frequently[1] —riding sometimes, hunting, coursing, cleaving wood: this is a very desirable employment, and what all housekeepers would do well to recommend to the young men of their household in such a coal[2] country as this, for it produces warmth both within and without doors . . . you would be surprised to see what a small cartful we get for three or four and twenty shillings.'

The neighbours were friendly but not exciting, and William and Dorothy did not cultivate their society. But whilst the Pinneys were with them they gave what Dorothy calls 'a grand rout', and, like all such parties, 'very dull it was, except for the entertainment of talking about it before and after'.

For the rest they were thrown upon their own resources. One day was so much like another that Dorothy found little to record in her letters to Jane. But they were well content; for they both possessed those two accomplishments needful for the enjoyment of winter in the country, they could read and they

[1] D. W. to J. M., Mar. 1796. Several writers have exaggerated Dorothy's hardihood by misreading this passage to mean that she accompanied them in their hunting and coursing, but 'then I went with them frequently' is clearly a parenthesis, referring only to their walks.

[2] Printed in K. 'cold', but D. goes on to speak of it as one of the mildest winters that she can remember; and cf. also 'Goody Blake and Harry Gill'. (L. B. 1798)

> This woman dwelt in Dorsetshire,
> Her hut was on a cold hill-side,
> And in that country coals are dear,
> For they come far by wind and tide.

could walk. A two hours' tramp in the morning to the tops of the combs on Pilsdon, or Lewisdon, or Blackdown Hill, or to get a view from Lowdett's Castle, was varied at short intervals by William's expeditions, alone or with his sister, to make purchases at Crewkerne and to fetch the post. And Dorothy's needle was not idle. The amount of sewing before her—coloured frocks and shirts for Basil and the rehabilitation of William's wardrobe after six months in London lodgings—might have daunted a less intrepid heart; yet she undertook also to make shirts for her brother Richard (a task not easier for her when, with a masculine disregard of detail, he omitted to inform her of the required length, or the size of the neck-band[1]) and she still found leisure for the improvement of her mind, so that she could report quite a substantial list of books for a month's reading, including *Tristram Shandy* and a good deal of French and Italian. William, besides much other study and hard thinking, was deep in his tragedy, *The Borderers*, and when a fit of the spleen was on him, tried to work it off by composing some mediocre satire. He worked it off more effectively in hard manual labour, hewing wood, rooting up hedges, and digging in the garden with such assiduity that his London friends predicted his metamorphosis into a cabbage. But like many another he found some taste of the penalty of Adam a relief after the storm and stress of city life. Moreover Dorothy was continually at his side, and their companionship was the fulfilment of their one constant dream.

'I think Racedown is the place dearest to my recollections upon the whole surface of the island: it is the first home I had.' So she wrote some years later,[2] and her feeling is not difficult to understand. For here she entered upon the chosen vocation of her life. No easy task lay before her, and though she never alluded to it in her letters, her happiness, for the first few months at least, must have been tempered with the gravest anxieties. Would she succeed in restoring her brother to health and happiness, so as to enable him to become the great poet she knew him potentially to be? He was shattered by a double blow. The thought of Annette and her infant daughter, cut off from him by an insurmountable barrier of international hostility, filled him with remorseful longings; the thought of the French

[1] D. W. to R. W., Mar. 19, 1797.
[2] *Memoirs*, i. 94.

Revolution, on which he had built all his splendid hopes for man, now a wreck of its own ideals, had thrown him upon a barren philosophy which had dried up the springs of his emotions and made him 'yield up moral questions in despair'. Dorothy had no experience of such suffering. Part of her strength, indeed, lay in the fact that 'barren intermeddling subtleties' had never perplexed her mind. But she could sympathize with all the fervour of her passionate heart. A physician of the spirit, like a physician of the body, can prescribe the needful remedy without having suffered from the disease. Dorothy observed its symptoms clearly enough; she knew, as no other knew, what manner of man her brother had been in health; and her love told her that she had within herself the power to restore him. 'An exquisite regard for common things', a quick discernment of the one point of interest or beauty in the most ordinary sight or incident, was the secret of her spell over all who met her:

> She welcom'd what was given, and craved no more.
> Whatever scene was present to her eyes,
> That was the best, to that she was attuned
> Through her humility and lowliness,
> And through a perfect happiness of soul
> Whose variegated feelings were in this
> Sisters, that they were each some new delight:
> For she was Nature's inmate. Her the birds
> And every flower she met with, could they but
> Have known her, would have lov'd. Methought such charm
> Of sweetness did her presence breathe around
> That all the trees, and all the silent hills
> And every thing she look'd on, should have had
> An intimation how she bore herself
> Towards them and to all creatures.[1]

Loving his sister as he did, and with the experiences of his boyhood still alive, though dormant, within him, William could not long withold his response. Delight in her delight quickened his own interest in the daily life they shared: in striving to return to her something of the joy her presence gave to him his mind was gradually distracted from its twofold burden. To realize this, we have only to recall that evening, typical of

[1] *The Prelude* (1805), xi. 207–21.

many, when he led her in triumph to the orchard, to see a glow-worm which he had placed there for her delight:

Among all lovely things my Love had been;
Had noted well the stars, all flowers that grew
About her home; but she had never seen
A Glow-worm, never one, and this I knew.

While riding near her home one stormy night
A single Glow-worm did I chance to espy;
I gave a fervent welcome to the sight,
And from my Horse I leapt; great joy had I.

Upon a leaf the Glow-worm did I lay,
To bear it with me through the stormy night;
And, as before, it shone without dismay;
Albeit putting forth a fainter light.

When to the Dwelling of my Love I came,
I went into the Orchard quietly;
And left the Glow-worm, blessing it by name,
Laid safely by itself, beneath a Tree.

The whole next day, I hoped, and hoped with fear;
At night the Glow-worm shone beneath the Tree:
I led my Lucy to the spot, "Look here!"
Oh! joy it was for her, and joy for me!

In literal truth, Dorothy saved her brother's soul alive. And he fully realized it. He never forgot how, in his darkest hour of trial and perplexity,

then it was
That the beloved Woman in whose sight
Those days were pass'd, now speaking in a voice
Of sudden admonition, like a brook
That did but cross a lonely road, and now
Seen, heard and felt, and caught at every turn,
Companion never lost through many a league,
Maintained for me a saving intercourse
With my true self; for, though impair'd and chang'd
Much, as it seemed, I was no further chang'd
Than as a clouded, not a waning moon:
She, in the midst of all, preserv'd me still
A Poet, made me seek beneath that name
My office upon earth, and nowhere else.[1]

[1] *The Prelude* (1805), x. 908–21.

In an early poem Wordsworth puts into the mouth of a woman who is recalling the dawn of love for her husband the words 'And I in truth did love him like a brother'.[1] The line has sometimes been quoted as a typical example of his total ignorance of the passions; yet, to those who know the depth of feeling from which it sprang, it seems nearer to the sublime than to the ridiculous. This passionate devotion of brother and sister is among the most profoundly moving things in literary history.

But not only did Dorothy preserve the poet in him, she guided the bent of his poetic mind. As a boy his nature had lacked something of tenderness:

> but for thee, sweet Friend,
> My soul, too reckless of mild grace, had been
> Far longer what by Nature it was framed,
> Longer retain'd its countenance severe,
> A rock with torrents roaring, with the clouds
> Familiar, and a favourite of the Stars.
> But thou didst plant its crevices with flowers,
> Hang it with shrubs that twinkle in the breeze,
> And teach the little birds to build their nests
> And warble in its chambers.[2]

It was not, perhaps, her fault that the flowers she planted in the rock had at times a sickly growth, or that this genius familiar with the clouds could not always adapt himself to the homely smiles and tears of mother earth. Wordsworth, indeed, for all his theories, had not his sister's innate genius for the trivial; and not a few of his poetic failures sprang from the attempt to transmute into art such simple fugitive experiences as went to make up their daily life. Dorothy never understood this: she read his most commonplace lines in the light of their intention rather than their achievement, and became a dangerously undiscriminating critic. But that was later: at Racedown the influence of each upon the other was all to the good; Dorothy was stimulated to develop in herself that instinct for observation which was soon to flourish in her Journals: William was drawn from his broodings to realize more fully the delights that lay about him, to love what she loved, and to find joy in that.

Their second winter at Racedown brought two welcome guests. Little Basil's father, who had disappointed them a year

[1] *'Guilt and Sorrow'*, 251. [2] *The Prelude* (1805), xiii. 227–36.

before, paid them a short, unexpected visit. In his relations with John and Azariah Pinney, to whom he acted as tutor and spiritual adviser, Montagu appears as something of a self-satisfied prig, but his less agreeable qualities were not shown to William, for whom he had a deep admiration; and, like all William's friends, he quickly won Dorothy's heart. 'He is one of the pleasantest men I ever saw,' she wrote, 'and so amiable and good that every one must love him.'[1] On his departure he carried off William with him for a fortnight at Bristol, leaving Dorothy to the companionship of Mary Hutchinson, who was now spending some months at Racedown. Mary's favourite sister Peggy had died of consumption in the previous spring, and she must have rejoiced in the companionship of a friend who had long known and loved them both. To Dorothy their reunion was no less joyful. 'She is one of the best girls in the world,' she wrote to Jane, 'and we are as happy as human beings can be; that is when William is at home, for you cannot imagine how dull we feel and what a vacuum his loss has occasioned, but this is the first day: to-morrow we shall be better. William is as chearful as anybody can be; perhaps you may not think it, but he is the life of the whole house.'[1] This eager vindication of William's social gifts shows clearly enough that at Halifax three years before, when Jane had made his acquaintance, he had hardly lived up to the glowing picture that Dorothy had painted of him in her early letters; nor can we be surprised at it when we remember the mental torment from which he was then suffering. But if time and Dorothy had worked wonders on him, we can hardly be wrong in attributing some part of his present cheerfulness to the presence of Mary. They were old friends, there is good evidence that they had been lovers, and that this earlier affection,[2] which had been swept from his

[1] D. W. to J. M., Mar. 19, 1797.

[2] In the earliest surviving notebook of Wordsworth's, dating from the period spent with Dorothy at Windy Brow (1794), is a poem imitative of Horace's *Septimi Gades* and addressed to Mary, in which William invites her to share a home with him at Grasmere. This must have been written after 1790, as it holds out the Rhone valley as an alternative to Grasmere, an evident reminiscence of his journey with Jones, and it was probably written soon after his return and *before* his second visit to France, when he met Annette. If it was written *after* his second return, e.g. at Windy Brow in 1794, it would prove that his absorption in Annette was even shorter-lived and his return to Mary even more rapid.

Legouis' conclusion that W. could not have been interested in Mary on her

memory by his passion for Annette, was now beginning to revive. The present state of that passion can only be conjectured, but we can safely assume that the passage of four years had brought a change both in his feeling for Annette and in hers for him. We know that they were in correspondence, though even such of their letters as reached their destination have not survived. But it is unlikely that Annette still loved or even wished to marry him. The time when she stood most in need of a husband's protection was long over, she was known to the world as a widow, and had courageously made her own life for herself. She was an intensely patriotic Frenchwoman,[1] and an ardent Royalist who had thrown herself with zest and courage into a dangerous cause, often risking her life in its service. Hence, while she would naturally look to William for the support of their child, it is hard to believe that she would have been ready to forgo a life of so much interest and excitement, and to settle down in a strange country whose language she did not know, and with a man whose ideals and interests were diametrically opposed to her own.

However it was with Annette, one can hardly doubt that William, ready as he may have been to fulfil his obligation to her, must have realized already that a union with Annette would be fatal alike to the happiness of them both and to the achievement of his poetic ambitions. Nor can we doubt that Dorothy realized it too. As long as this interminable war went on nothing could be settled; she could only wait in hope, and, it may be, confide to Mary her dreams of what the future might have in store for all three of them.

It is natural to suppose that during his absence from Racedown Wordsworth saw something of Coleridge at Bristol, if indeed he did not actually pass a day or two with him at Nether Stowey.[2] Though two years younger than Wordsworth,

visit to Racedown because he went off with Montagu for a fortnight at Bristol is surely a little strained. Mary had already been with them for some months, and he would naturally take the chance of going away when he could leave his sister with a congenial companion.

[1] For a vivid account of her activities *v.*, Legouis, *William Wordsworth and Annette Vallon*, 1922.

[2] In a letter written to Cottle from Racedown in June Coleridge states that 'Poole's opinion of W. is that he is the greatest man he ever knew'. W. must therefore have met Poole *before* his visit to Nether Stowey in July. Of course Poole may have met W. on some unrecorded visit to Bristol, but Dykes Campbell

Coleridge was already known to a wide circle as poet, preacher, and talker; and wherever he went his brilliant genius, united as it was with an irresistible personal charm, had won him eager disciples. His old schoolfellow, Charles Lamb, worshipped the very ground he trod on, and thought his turgid *Religious Musings* the greatest poem since *Paradise Lost*; Cottle, the Bristol bookseller, published his first volume of poems, and offered him a market for any number of verses he might produce; Charles Lloyd, the gifted but hysterical son of a Birmingham banker, had come to lodge in his house, that he might sit continually at his feet; Thomas Poole, tanner and farmer of Nether Stowey, a man who combined keen intellectual interests with much practical ability and shrewd common sense, had fallen completely under his spell, and affirmed himself ready to stand by him 'in sickness or in health, in prosperity and misfortune, nay, in the worst of misfortunes, in *vice*, if vice could ever taint thee, but *it cannot*'.[1] It was to be near Poole that Coleridge had brought his wife and infant Hartley to settle at Nether Stowey, and Poole was at this time his sheet anchor. For if Coleridge was unpractical, full of schemes which he could start but never bring to fruition, he disarmed all criticism by his ready admission of his failing; he felt, he said loftily, 'the want of those inferior abilities which are necessary to the discharge of the common duties of life', and he looked with touching confidence to his friends to see him through, whilst the services they rendered him only endeared him to them the more. For their affection, at least, he always returned in ample measure. With an impulsive, hyper-sensitive nature, that had been cramped and baffled by a lonely boyhood, the one insistent craving of his nature was for love. 'Those whom I love, I love indeed', he said truly, and throughout his life he was only too ready to give his heart away. But as yet he had given it to none who could know to the full the value of the mind that went with it. In

thinks that the reference probably refers to a former visit of W.'s to Nether Stowey; and if he is right, Mar. 1797, the only recorded absence of W. from Racedown between Sept. 1795 and July 1797, except one visit to London, is the most likely time at which to place it. It is worth noting that in a letter written May 1798, S.T.C. says, 'I have now known him a year and some months'. This would point to this visit to Bristol as being the beginning of their friendship. They had first met in Sept. 1795.

[1] Thomas Poole to S. T. C., Sept. 26, 1796.

Wordsworth he found one whom, in his generous enthusiasm, he felt to be immeasurably his superior. And Wordsworth, among the friends who believed in his genius, had none like Coleridge who could meet him on equal terms. In Coleridge's power 'of throwing out in profusion grand central truths from which might be evolved the most comprehensive systems' he felt that intellectual stimulus which, together with Dorothy's loving care of him, was to complete his regeneration. The two men were made for each other.

They seem to have met first in September 1795, when Wordsworth was with the Pinneys, and there had been fitful communication between them since, but until this spring of 1797 they were no more than acquaintances. But before Wordsworth returned home he must have extracted from his new friend a promise to follow him to Racedown, and early in June Coleridge came. It was a momentous visit. Nearly half a century later Dorothy and William recalled his first arrival, how 'he did not keep to the high road, but leapt over a gate and bounded down the pathless field by which he cut off an angle'[1] to meet them. It was a symbol of the manner in which he leapt into their lives.

'You had a great loss in not seeing Coleridge' wrote Dorothy to Mary Hutchinson,[2] who had just left them. 'He is a wonderful man. His conversation teems with soul, mind and spirit. Then he is so benevolent, so good tempered and cheerful, and, like William, interests himself so much about every little trifle. At first I thought him very plain, that is, for about three minutes; he is

[1] M. W. to Sara Coleridge, Nov. 7, 1845.

[2] This letter, which we are told (*Memoirs*, i. 98) was addressed 'to a friend who had left Racedown early in 1797', can only have been written to Mary. Harper's statement (*Life*, p. 223) that Mary was still at Racedown at the time of Coleridge's visit is based on what is clearly a mispunctuation of Mary's letter to Sara Coleridge in 1845. That letter should read: 'Your father', he says, 'came afterwards to see us at R. where I was living with my sister', &c., i.e. *Wordsworth* was living there with his sister (Mary had only been on a visit). Moreover Sara had not asked for Mary's reminiscences, but for the poet's, and it is this that Mary is giving her, taking down his actual words from his dictation.

Of Dorothy's correspondents in 1797 there is none but Mary who had been staying at Racedown earlier in the year. There is evidence, too, that other letters quoted in the *Memoirs* without mention of the recipient's name were written to Mary. This interpretation of the letter is further corroborated by Mary's statement to H. C. R. (Oct. 14, 1841) that she 'passed a long winter and spring' at Racedown. If she had stayed on into June she would not thus have described the time of her visit.

pale and thin, has a wide mouth, thick lips, and not very good teeth, longish, loose-growing, half-curling, rough, black hair. But if you hear him speak for five minutes you think no more of them. His eye is large and full, not dark but grey; such an eye as would receive from a heavy soul the dullest expression; but it speaks every emotion of his animated mind; it has more of the "poet's eye in a fine frenzy rolling" than I ever witnessed. He has fine dark eyebrows, and an overhanging forehead.

'The first thing we read after he came was William's new poem, *The Ruined Cottage*, with which he was much delighted; and after tea he repeated to us two acts and a half of his tragedy *Osorio*. The next morning William read his tragedy *The Borderers*.'

Coleridge stayed at Racedown about ten days, but a long separation from his new friends was not to be thought of: before the end of the month he was back again, and he only tore himself away a second time to reappear a few days later, with a one-horse chaise in which to transport them to his cottage at Nether Stowey. His joy in their society was not unmingled with a naive elation at his management of the convoy. 'I have driven back Miss Wordsworth', he wrote to Southey,[1] 'over forty miles of execrable roads, and have always been very cautious, and am now no inexpert whip.' But when we recall that at this time Coleridge also regarded himself as an expert gardener, we are forced to view his statement with some suspicion. Neither he nor Wordsworth was ever at his best in his dealings with horses.

But fortune was kind, and somehow or other they reached their destination in safety. Dorothy spent a very happy fortnight there, adding to her circle of acquaintance Sara Coleridge and little Hartley, now a baby of nine months (later to win a place in her heart close to that of her future nieces and nephews), honest Thomas Poole and his kindly old mother. And for a week of their stay Charles Lamb was a fellow guest. He was not the cheery Lamb of later days, for he was still under the shadow of that tragedy which was the dark prelude to his life of dual loneliness; but it was now that the seeds were sown of the friendship which was to be among the precious things in Dorothy's later life.

In a letter to Cottle from Racedown[2] Coleridge had made

[1] July, 1797. [2] June, 1797.

no reference to Dorothy, so absorbed was he in the genius of his new friend: 'Wordsworth', he had written, 'admires my tragedy, which gives me great hopes. Wordsworth has written a Tragedy himself. I speak with heart-felt sincerity, and (I think) unblinded judgment, when I tell you that I feel *a little man by his side*, and yet I do not think myself a less man than I formerly thought myself. His drama is absolutely wonderful.' But when he had them both under his own roof at Nether Stowey he spoke of Dorothy as enthusiastically as of her brother, and with a subtler discrimination:

> 'W. and his exquisite sister are with me. She is a woman indeed! in mind I mean, and heart; for her person is such, that if you expected to see a pretty woman, you would think her rather ordinary; if you expected to see an ordinary woman, you would think her pretty! but her manners are simple, ardent, impressive. In every motion, her most innocent soul outbeams so brightly, that who saw would say,
>
> Guilt was a thing impossible in her.
>
> Her information various. Her eye watchful in minutest observation of nature; and her taste, a perfect electrometer. It bends, protrudes, and draws in, at subtlest beauties, and most recondite faults.'

For a week or so, however, he was denied a full enjoyment of her companionship. 'The second day after Wordsworth came to me', he writes, 'dear Sara accidentally emptied a skillet of boiling milk over my foot'; thus confined to his house and garden and to the lime-tree bower, his prison, he had to leave his guests to wander without his guidance 'on springy heath, along the hill-top edge', to wind down the dell, 'o'erwooded, narrow, deep', and then, climbing again, to view

> The many-steepled tract magnificent
> Of hilly fields and meadows, and the sea.

They were delighted with all they saw, and not the less because there was much to remind them of their native region. 'There is everything here', wrote Dorothy, 'sea, woods wild as fancy ever painted, brooks clear and pebbly as in Cumberland, villages so romantic, and William and I, in a wander by ourselves, found out a sequestered waterfall in a dell formed by steep hills covered with full-grown timber trees. The woods are as fine as those at Lowther, and the country more romantic, and it has the character of the less grand parts of the neighbourhood of the Lakes.'[1]

On the same 'wander' they lighted upon Alfoxden,[2] a large country house surrounded by a deer park. The place gave them such delight that at once, as was their wont, they pictured themselves as dwellers in a little cottage near by, if such could be found there. A few days later they heard that the house itself was to let furnished, at a merely nominal rent, and through the good offices of Thomas Poole they secured it forthwith, at £23 per annum.

[1] D. W. to M. H. (?), July 4, 1797.

[2] Alfoxden or Allfoxden is the spelling adopted by the W.s and S. T. C. But Alfoxton seems to be correct.

V

ALFOXDEN

July 1797–June 1798 (aet. $25\frac{1}{2}$–$6\frac{1}{2}$)

On July 14 they moved to their new home. Coleridge and his wife went with them to help settle them in, and four days later their first visitor appeared. This was citizen Thelwall, just released from the prison where he had been confined, without trial, during the reactionary terror of the previous year, and now in search of a quiet country retreat. Thelwall had reached Stowey at nine o'clock on the evening of July 17, whither Sara had returned 'to superintend the wash-tub', and she started back with him to Alfoxden between five and six on the next morning, arriving in good time for breakfast. 'Faith, we are a most philosophical party,' wrote Thelwall to his wife, 'the enthusiastic group consisting of Coleridge and his Sara, Wordsworth and his sister, and myself, without any servant, male or female. An old woman, who lives in an adjoining cottage, does what is requisite for our simple wants.'[1] Evidently the good Peggy, with little Basil and their other impedimenta, had not yet been fetched from Racedown. A month later[2] Dorothy sent to Mary a full description of Alfoxden and its surroundings:

'The house is a large mansion, with furniture enough for a dozen families like ours. There is a very excellent garden, well stocked with vegetables and fruit. The garden is at the end of the house, and our favourite parlour, as at Racedown, looks that way. In front is a little court, with grass plot, gravel walk, and shrubs; the moss roses were in full beauty a month ago. The front of the house is to the south, but it is screened from the sun by a high hill which rises immediately from it. This hill is beautiful, scattered irregularly and abundantly with trees, and topped with fern, which spreads a considerable way down it. The deer dwell here, and sheep, so that we have a living prospect. From the end of the house we have a view of the sea, over a woody meadow-country; and exactly opposite the window where I now sit is an immense wood, whose round top from this point has exactly the appearance of a mighty dome. In some parts of this wood there

[1] Sandford, *Thos. Poole and his friends*, i. 233; Coleridge, ed. Dykes Campbell, *Poetical Works*, p. xxxv.

[2] Aug. 14, 1797.

is an under grove of hollies which are now very beautiful. In a glen at the bottom of the wood is the waterfall of which I spoke, a quarter of a mile from the house. We are three miles from Stowey, and not two miles from the sea. Wherever we turn we have woods, smooth downs, and valleys with small brooks running down them, through green meadows, hardly ever intersected with hedgerows, but scattered over with trees. The hills that cradle these valleys are either covered with fern and bilberries, or oak woods, which are cut for charcoal. . . . Walks extend for miles over the hill-tops, the great beauty of which is their wild simplicity: they are perfectly smooth, without rocks.

'The Tor of Glastonbury is before our eyes during more than half of our walk to Stowey; and in the park wherever we go, keeping about fifteen yards above the house, it makes a part of our prospect.'

Very few of Dorothy's letters written from Alfoxden are extant, but the normal tenor of her life there can be reconstructed from her *Journal*, of which the entries of some four months (January 20–March 22, 1798) have been preserved. This *Journal* is no mere record of fact: here for the first time she reveals that delicate gift of minute observation, that exquisitely sensitive susceptibility of eye and ear which proclaim the true artist. Her earlier letters describe with a ready pen her delight in the country and country life, but show few traces of her peculiar genius. But this, two years of close companionship with her brother had quickened and brought to birth. It is at least likely that she kept her *Journal* at his suggestion and for his special pleasure. Much of what it records they had enjoyed together, something even of the language in which she records it may well have fallen from his lips rather than hers when they experienced it. But though we owe our vocabulary, and something of our experience, to the company we keep, the use we make of it depends upon ourselves: and all that Dorothy notes in her *Journal* has a freshness and a spontaneity that is hers alone. It is entirely without self-consciousness, nor is there any attempt at formal writing. The entries are often mere jottings, disjointed sentences without verbs. Yet no studied composition could convey with a surer touch the 'landscape lure of rural England'. When she visits an artificial garden laid out in the approved style of the period, with its craze for the 'Gothic', the significant cry escapes her: 'Happily we cannot shape the huge hills, or carve out the valleys according to our fancy': when she is with nature unspoilt and unadorned she sets down simply and faithfully what she sees, and drinking in the spirit of the season, distils it into telling phrase. She began her diary at that time of year when the English countryside has least attraction to common eyes, yet how she warms under the winter sunshine that has come to break up a spell of dark rainy weather!

'Alfoxden, January 20th 1798.—The green paths down the hill-sides are channels for streams. The young wheat is streaked by silver lines of water running between the ridges, the sheep are gathered together on the slopes. After the wet dark days, the country seems more populous. It peoples itself in the sunbeams. The garden, mimic of spring, is gay with flowers. The purple-starred hepatica spreads itself in the sun, and the clustering snow-drops put forth their white heads, at first upright, ribbed with green, and like a rosebud when completely opened, hanging their heads downwards, but slowly lengthening their slender stems. The slanting woods of an unvarying brown, showing the light through the thin net-work of their upper boughs. Upon the highest ridge of that round hill covered with planted oaks, the shafts of the trees show in the light like the columns of a ruin.

'Jan. 23rd.—Bright sunshine, went out at 3 o'clock. The sea perfectly calm blue, streaked with deeper colour by the clouds, and tongues or points of sand; on our return of a gloomy red. The sun gone down. The crescent moon, Jupiter, and Venus. The sound of the sea distinctly heard on the tops of the hills, which we could never hear in summer. We attribute this partly to the bareness of the trees, but chiefly to the absence of the singing of birds, the hum of insects, that noiseless noise which lives in the summer air. The villages marked out by beautiful beds of smoke. The turf fading into the mountain road. The scarlet flowers of the moss.

'Jan. 25th.—Went to Poole's after tea. The sky spread over with one continuous cloud, whitened by the light of the moon, which, though her dim shape was seen, did not throw forth so strong a light as to chequer the earth with shadows. At once the clouds seemed to cleave asunder, and left her in the centre of a black-blue vault. She sailed along, followed by multitudes of stars, small, and bright, and sharp. Their brightness seemed concentrated, (half-moon).

'Jan. 27th.—Walked from seven o'clock till half-past eight. Upon the whole an uninteresting evening. Only once while we were in the wood the moon burst through the invisible veil which enveloped her, the shadows of the oaks blackened, and their lines became more strongly marked. The withered leaves were coloured with a deeper yellow, a brighter gloss spotted the hollies; again her form became dimmer; the sky flat, unmarked by distances, a white thin cloud. The manufacturer's dog makes a strange, uncouth howl, which it continues many minutes after there is no noise near it but that of the brook. It howls at the murmur of the village stream.

'February 1st.—About two hours before dinner, set forward towards Mr. Bartholemew's. The wind blew so keen in our faces that we felt ourselves inclined to seek the covert of the wood. There we had a warm shelter, gathered a burthen of large rotten boughs blown down by the wind of the preceding night. The sun shone clear, but all at once a heavy blackness hung over the sea. The trees almost *roared*, and the ground seemed in motion with the multitudes of dancing leaves, which made a rustling sound, distinct from that of the trees. Still the asses pastured in quietness under the hollies, undisturbed by these forerunners of the storm. The wind beat furiously against us as we returned. Full moon. She rose in uncommon majesty over the sea, slowly ascending through the clouds. Sat with the window open an hour in the moonlight.

'Feb. 4th.—Walked a great part of the way to Stowey with Coleridge. The morning warm and sunny. The young lasses seen on the hill-tops, in the villages and roads, in their summer holiday clothes—pink petticoats and blue. Mothers with their children in arms, and the little ones that could just walk, tottering by their side. Midges or small flies spinning in the sunshine; the songs of the lark and redbreast; daisies upon the turf; the hazels in blossom; honeysuckles budding. I saw one solitary strawberry flower under a hedge. The furze gay with blossom. The moss rubbed from the pailings by the sheep, that leave locks of wool, and the red marks with which they are spotted, upon the wood.

'March 1st.—We rose early. A thick fog obscured the distant prospect entirely, but the shapes of the nearer trees and the dome of the wood dimly seen and dilated. It cleared away between ten and eleven. The shapes of the mist, slowly moving along, exquisitely beautiful; passing over the sheep they almost seemed to have more of life than those quiet creatures. The unseen birds singing in the mist.'

To us, as to Dorothy herself, the value of the *Journal* is enhanced by its relation with her brother's poetry. The entry already quoted under the date January 25 is verbally re-echoed in *A Night-piece*, and not everywhere do we prefer the poetic version to Dorothy's simpler prose. The asses that she notes 'pasturing in quietness under the hollies', bore their part in the inspiration of *Peter Bell*. 'In the woods of Alfoxden', said Wordsworth years later,[1] 'I used to take great delight in noticing the habits, tricks and physiognomy of asses, and I have no doubt that I was thus put upon writing the poem out of liking for the creature that is so often dreadfully abused.' On March 18 they 'sheltered under the hollies, during a hail shower. The withered leaves danced with the hailstones. William wrote a description of the storm'; and in *A Whirlblast from behind the Hill* the leaves dance as they danced in Dorothy's *Journal*. On March 19 'Wm and Basil and I walked to the hill tops, a very cold bleak day. We were met on our return by a severe hailstorm. William wrote some lines describing a stunted thorn.' He had often passed this thorn before without noticing it, but he was now inspired to make it as permanently impressive an object as it appeared to him and Dorothy in the storm.

Their walks were for the most part bounded within a radius of three or four miles, over the Quantocks, to Nether Stowey, or to 'Kilve by the green sea'; often their errand was to the baker's or blacksmith's, or to the farm for eggs, or merely to pick up sticks for firewood; yet they always returned the richer by some memorable sight or sound. At times Basil went with them; more often they could leave him behind, for near by lived a little boy who was his frequent playmate, 'a very naughty spoiled child,' says Dorothy,[2] 'but I think Basil has not suffered so much from him morally, as we expected'. Of neighbours they saw far more than when they were at Racedown—the Pooles, Chesters, and Cruikshanks, and for Thomas Poole and his mother they felt a genuine affection; but the vital change in their life sprang from the constant companionship of Coleridge. Save when he had wandered off to preach in a Unitarian chapel, or to visit a distant friend, hardly a day passed without his appearance. Their usual habit of walking in the afternoon or evening was often broken by his incursion in the early morning, and at whatever hour he left them, they would tramp

[1] I. F. *note* to *Peter Bell*.
[2] D. W. to Mrs. Rawson, June 13, 1798.

all or part of the way back with him to Stowey. Often he would stay the night, once he brought over his whole family for a ten days' visit, and whenever he had a guest of his own, his first impulse was to introduce him to Alfoxden. Twice at least he bore off William and Dorothy for a tour of several days—in November 1797 on that memorable expedition to Watchet and Linton and the Valley of Rocks, during which *The Rime of the Ancient Mariner* was plotted and begun; and in the following May to see the caves at Cheddar. For the rest they were content with their own neighbourhood, 'loitering long and pleasantly' in the combes, or beside the beloved waterfall, or striding over the Quantocks discussing the principles of poetry and reciting to each other their latest verses, whilst Dorothy followed at their heels. Not seldom Coleridge came to them in order to escape from his own pressing troubles. His buoyancy of spirit alternated with fits of the deepest dejection, for which, indeed, his circumstances gave full excuse. All through the year 1797 he was harassed by straitened means and the difficulty of providing a livelihood for his wife and child: 'every mode of life', he complained to Cottle, 'which has promised me bread and cheese, has been, one after another, torn away from me; but God remains';[1] and later, when Providence, in the shape of the Wedgwoods, partially relieved his financial stress, he suffered acutely from the defection of his disciple Lloyd, whose malicious tittle-tattle brought about a still more grievous sorrow, his alienation from Lamb. But in William and Dorothy he found a loving sympathy which never failed him. He was still on affectionate terms with his wife, but the fuller companionship of his new friends made him conscious of a difference. When Sara intervenes in his poetry it is to recall him from daring imaginative speculation to the safer ground of a sincere but conventional piety: but Dorothy was a stimulus rather than a curb, whilst 'her eye, watchful in minutest observation of nature', both guided his own and gave it a clearer vision. Echoes of *Christabel* to be found in her *Journal*—'the manufacturer's dog with his strange uncouth howl', 'the thin grey cloud', the 'night cloudy but not dark', the 'one only leaf at the top of a tree', 'the sole remaining leaf (that) danced round and round like a rag blown by the wind', 'the spring that continues to advance very

[1] Coleridge, *P.W.*, ed. Dykes Campbell, Introd. xxxvii.

slowly',—these are not mere borrowings, they testify to a common outlook and a common experience: she had the happiness of feeling that Coleridge, hardly less than William, shared in the things that made up her life, and in converse with her was finding material from which to mould his exquisite art.[1]

This joyous companionship was broken for the two months of December and January, when the Wordsworths went to London, and after a three weeks' absence returned to find Coleridge gone to Shrewsbury as prospective Unitarian minister. In London Dorothy first met Southey, dined three times at his house, and duly reported to her aunt that he was 'a young man of the most rigidly virtuous habits, but though his talents are certainly very remarkable for his years (as far as I can judge) I think them much inferior to the talents of Coleridge'.[2]

A stronger inducement than Southey's company had drawn them to the metropolis; for Coleridge had provided an introduction to the manager of Covent Garden Theatre, who promised to read *The Borderers* and to produce it without delay if he thought it likely to succeed on the stage. But the manager found the leading character in the play too 'metaphysically obscure',[3] and though, after its rejection, Dorothy persuaded herself that they had not the faintest expectation that it would be accepted, a more accurate estimate of her feelings is probably to be found in a letter written by their cousin Elizabeth Threlkeld to Sam Ferguson,[3] a letter which is additionally interesting as it reveals how keenly the circle at Halifax followed the fortunes of Dorothy and that 'eccentric young man', her brother:

> 'Dorothy and William have been in London . . . the motive of their journey was to offer a tragedy for the inspection of the Manager of Covent Garden Theatre which they were inclined to believe he would accept and that it would have a prodigious run. They had planned many schemes to follow if it succeeded, one of which was a pedestrian tour through Wales and by Yorkshire into Cumberland. This would *by many* be thought rather a *wildish* scheme, but by them it was thought very practicable and would certainly have been put into execution had not the play unfortunately been rejected. I received a very entertaining letter from Dorothy on the occasion. She says they are not disappointed with

[1] C. tells us that *Christabel* was begun in 1797; hence these phrases must have originated with him and not, as some (e.g. Harper) have thought, with D. W.

[2] D. W. to Mrs. R., July 3, 1798.

[3] E.T. to S.F., Feb. 14, 1798.

its rejection, but I cannot give *implicit* credit to her assertion. W. is not determined whether he shall publish it or no. He expects a reform to take place in the stage, and then it may be brought forward to great advantage. These are visionary plans, the distant prospect of which may be very pleasant, but which on a narrow view almost always disappoint one. However they are happy in having very fertile imaginations which are a continual source of entertainment to them, and serve to enliven many of their solitary hours.'

But attributing, as they did, the rejection of *The Borderers* to 'the debased state of the stage', they did not allow their disappointment to weigh heavily upon them, and they took up their life at Alfoxden again with even greater zest. A few months later Martha Ferguson wrote to her brother Sam: 'Dorothy, from whom we have heard lately, is deeper in plays and poetry than ever; if they publish the one they have wrote we shall certainly send it to you. It is highly spoken of by those who have read it in manuscript.' Among her relatives at Halifax Dorothy was evidently regarded as joint author with her brother. Nor in one sense were they entirely mistaken.

This spring of 1798 was probably of all Dorothy's life the time of most unclouded happiness. In the *Journal* and the few surviving letters of the period there is no trace of the restless anxiety or the wistful return upon the past that were later alike to temper and give poignancy to her deep power of joy in the present. The three friends were all in all to one another, united in a perfect bond of sympathy—in Coleridge's beautiful phrase 'three persons and one soul', and they were growing daily. Though Coleridge had already begun to indulge in opium, it had as yet no hold upon him, and rather gave a strange lustre to his imaginings than tainted his mind or clouded his perfect confidence; from time to time his genius put forth flowers which they could only regard as an earnest of a richer harvest to come; and while Dorothy watched him and William together, each spurring on the other, she was conscious too that she gave to them no less than she received. Of her brother's strenuous energy she comments to Mary, in a letter of March 5: 'William was unwell last week, oppressed with languor and weakness. He is better now, he gets up between 7 and 8 in the mornings, and I daresay he will continue it, for he is fully convinced of the relaxing tendency of lying in bed so many hours.

His faculties seem to expand every day; he composes with much more facility than he did as to the mechanism of poetry, and his ideas flow faster than he can express them.'

But their blissful life at Alfoxden was not long to continue. The neighbouring gentry viewed them askance. Their hospitality to the notorious Thelwall had made an unfortunate opening to their tenancy. Lady St. Aubyn, head of the family from whom they rented the property, addressed to Poole a sharp letter of complaint for having introduced them; and though Poole stoutly defended his friends' respectability—were they not near relations of a Canon of Windsor?—their bohemian manner of life only confirmed the suspicion that they were undesirable tenants for so august a mansion. Early in March they learnt that Alfoxden was let over their heads, and that at midsummer their lease would be determined. Faced with the problem of finding a new home they revolved many plans.

> 'It is most probable', wrote Dorothy to Mary, 'that we shall go back again to Racedown, as there is little chance of our getting a place in the neighbourhood. We have no other very strong inducement to stay but Coleridge's society, but that is so important an object that we have it much at heart. We sometimes talk of coming to see you at Sockburn this summer, as if it were not a mere dream, at other times it seems impossible. If the poems bring us in anything considerable we know not what we shall do; our wishes will turn to Sockburn, so I think it is very likely you may see us.'

Then Poole held out hopes of securing for them a pleasant house within a quarter of a mile of Alfoxden, but it came to nothing. A week later they had decided to go to Germany.

But thoughts of their coming departure did not cloud their present happiness. For the first time they witnessed together the rapid onrush of a late spring in a richly fertile country. In two or three days the larches turned from black to green, the hedges budded and blossomed, multitudes of primroses, dog violets, periwinkles, and stitchwort bordered the lanes; five days later cowslips were plentiful in the fields.[1] Their hearts responded to the gaiety of the season, and preparations for the projected volume of poems went on apace. In May Cottle was with them for a week to discuss the publication of the volume; early in

[1] *Alfoxden Journal*, Apr. 9–17.

June Hazlitt paid his memorable visit[1], and in William's absence Dorothy read him some of the manuscript poems; then, on the 25th, they said farewell to Alfoxden. After a week spent at Nether Stowey, they went on to stay with Cottle at Bristol. From his house in Wine Street Dorothy dispatched a letter[2] to Aunt Rawson, telling of their regrets at leaving Alfoxden, their plans for little Basil Montagu, and their own projected visit to Germany:

'We have long wished to go into that country for the purpose of learning the language, and for the common advantages to be acquired by seeing different people and different manners. Coleridge has had the same wish; and we have so arranged our plan that I hope we shall sail in two or three months. Our first intention was to have gone immediately to the neighborhood of one of the Universities; but as we find that the price of lodgings etc, is much greater in the towns where there are universities we have resolved to go into some small town or village, till we have acquired the language, which we imagine we shall have a good knowledge of in about twelve months, and afterwards, to draw near a university when William and Coleridge will then be better able to profit by the instructions they may have an opportunity of receiving.

'We are advised to go into Saxony. Some parts of that country are extremely beautiful and boarding is very cheap. It is our intention (William's and mine) to board in some respectable family for the benefit, or rather the obligation, of talking German constantly. The Coleridges, if they can, will take a ready-furnished house as they have two children and must of course keep a servant.

'Such are our plans for one year, at least; what we shall do afterwards it is impossible at present to say. If the state of Europe will permit we shall endeavour to get into Switzerland; at any rate we shall travel as far as the tether of a scanty income will permit. We hope to make some addition to our resources by translating from the German, the most profitable species of literary labour, and of which I can do almost as much as my Brother.

'Poor Basil! We are obliged to leave him behind, as his father, on account of having altered the course of his pursuits in the law, will not be able to pay the additional expenses which we should

[1] Hazlitt, *On my first acquaintance with Poets*. If it is true, as De Quincey affirms, that Hazlitt proposed to Dorothy, it must have been some time during this visit; but De Quincey is not a trustworthy authority.

[2] D. W. to Mrs. R., *begun* June 13, *finished* July 3, 1798.

incur on his account. This, however, might be got over as he has friends who would do it for him, but as the experiment of taking a child of his age into a foreign country is at any rate hazardous, and might be prejudicial if we were not so placed that he might see much of other children, we think upon the whole that it is better that he should not go, taking into calculation the certain expense.

'I am convinced it is not good for a child to be educated alone after a certain age. Basil has in some respects, I think, suffered from it, though no doubt in others he has gained; he has a most excellent temper, is quite free from selfishness, is extremely active, and never fretful or discontented. Much of his good temper must be owing to our regularity of temper, and the consequent equable treatment which he receives from us. If he had been more with children whose minds were upon *the same level with his own* I think he could scarcely have been without selfishness. As to his activity I believe that the solitude of Racedown tended considerably to increase it. Till a child is four years old he needs no other companions than the flowers, the grass, the cattle, the sheep that scamper away from him when he makes a vain unexpecting chase after them, the pebbles upon the road, etc etc. After the age of about four years he begins to want some other stimulus than the mere life that is in him; his efforts would be greater but he must have an object, he would run but he must run *races*, he would climb a wall but he has no motive to do it when he is alone; he must have some standard by which to compare his powers or he will have no pleasure in exercising them, and he becomes lifeless and inactive. . . .

'I have not often felt more regret than when we quitted Allfoxden; I should however have felt much more if we were not likely in so short a time to have again the pleasure of Coleridge's society, an advantage which I prize the more, the more I know him. . . .

'I am writing in a front room in one of the most busy streets of Bristol. You can scarcely conceive how the jarring contrast between the sounds which are now forever ringing in my ears and the sweet sounds of Allfoxden, makes me long for the country again. After three years residence in retirement a city in feeling, sound, and prospect is hateful. . . .

'When I am just upon the point of concluding my letter I recollect that you may perhaps think that we are going upon an expensive scheme into Germany and that our income will not suffice to maintain us. I must put you to the expense of a double letter to explain this to you. Notwithstanding Mr. Montagu, (from having changed the course of his application to the law) has not been able to fulfil his engagement respecting Basil, we have lived upon our income and are not a farthing poorer than when we began housekeeping. We can live for less money in Germany than we can in England, so that you see our regular income (independent of what we may gain by translation) will be sufficient to support us when we are there, and we shall receive before our departure much more than sufficient to defray the expenses of our journey from a bookseller to whom William has sold some poems that are now printing, for which he is to have a certain present price and is to be paid afterwards in proportion to their sale. Our expenses last year 23£ for rent, our journey to London, clothes, servant's wages etc. included, only amounted to 110£. We have parted from our servant. Poor girl! it was a hard trial for her. She would have gone to the world's end with us. I believe she was much more attached to us than to any other beings in the world. . . .'

Their business at Bristol was to see the *Lyrical Ballads* through the press; but before a week was out the noise and bustle of a city had proved hateful to both of them, and William was eager to share with his sister that lovely country where, five years before, he had thrown off the cares that weighed upon him, and recaptured for a time the glad spirits of his youth. 'We crossed the Severn ferry,' he tells us, 'and walked ten miles further to Tintern Abbey, a very beautiful ruin on the Wye. The next morning we walked along the river through Monmouth to Goodrich Castle, there slept, and returned the next day to Tintern, thence to Chepstow, and from Chepstow back again in a boat to Tintern, where we slept, and thence back in a small vessel to Bristol.'[1] No holiday that brother and sister ever took together left a deeper mark either upon their own memories, or upon English poetry. The lines composed on the last day of the tour, and finished as they re-entered Bristol, were at once William's greatest contribution to his coming volume and the fullest tribute to what Dorothy had been to him ever since she had joined him at Racedown, three years before:

For thou art with me here upon the banks
Of this fair river; thou my dearest Friend,
My dear, dear Friend; and in thy voice I catch

[1] *Memoirs*, i, p. 117.

The language of my former heart, and read
My former pleasures in the shooting lights
Of thy wild eyes. Oh! yet a little while
May I behold in thee what I was once,
My dear, dear Sister! and this prayer I make,
Knowing that Nature never did betray
The heart that loved her; 'tis her privilege,
Through all the years of this our life, to lead
From joy to joy: for she can so inform
The mind that is within us, so impress
With quietness and beauty, and so feed
With lofty thoughts, that neither evil tongues,
Rash judgements, nor the sneers of selfish men,
Nor greetings where no kindness is, nor all
The dreary intercourse of daily life,
Shall e'er prevail against us, or disturb
Our cheerful faith, that all which we behold
Is full of blessings. Therefore let the moon
Shine on thee in thy solitary walk;
And let the misty mountain-winds be free
To blow against thee: and, in after years,
When these wild ecstasies shall be matured
Into a sober pleasure; when thy mind
Shall be a mansion for all lovely forms,
Thy memory be as a dwelling-place
For all sweet sounds and harmonies; oh! then,
If solitude, or fear, or pain, or grief,
Should be thy portion, with what healing thoughts
Of tender joy wilt thou remember me,
And these my exhortations! Nor, perchance--
If I should be where I no more can hear
Thy voice, nor catch from thy wild eyes these gleams
Of past existence—wilt thou then forget
That on the banks of this delightful stream
We stood together; and that I, so long
A worshipper of Nature, hither came
Unwearied in that service: rather say
With warmer love—oh! with far deeper zeal
Of holier love. Nor wilt thou then forget
That after many wanderings, many years
Of absence, these steep woods and lofty cliffs,
And this green pastoral landscape, were to me
More dear, both for themselves and for thy sake!

Soon after their return to Bristol they moved to the village of Shirehampton, five miles off, where they could live in quiet, and yet be within reach of Cottle's printing office. Here Coleridge often joined them, and some time in August suggested to them what he has called 'a dash into Wales'. 'Our going to Wales', wrote William to a friend,[1] 'was a quite unpremeditated scheme, Mr. Coleridge proposed it to us one evening and we departed the next morning at six o'clock. We had a very pleasant tour along the banks of the Usk and Wye into Brecknockshire.' Their excuse was to pay a visit to Thelwall, who had settled down with his family at a farm-house at Llyswen near Brecon, but we can hardly doubt that its greatest delight lay in showing to Coleridge that country around Tintern which had so lately inspired his song. Before the end of the month they had started for Germany. London was reached on the 27th 'after a very pleasant journey per foot, per waggon, per coach, per postchaise, having expended for each passenger £1 18*s*. .6*d*, and been admitted into the presence chamber at Blenheim and seen the University of Oxford'.[2] Coleridge had now decided to leave his wife and family at Nether Stowey under the care of the faithful Poole, and he brought with him as a companion a young man called Chester, who, Hazlitt tells us, was attracted to his eloquent discourse 'as flies are to honey, or as bees in swarming time to the sound of a brass pan'. They all left London on September 14, and reached Yarmouth by noon of the following day.

[1] W. W. to Henry Gardiner, Oct. 3, 1798.
[2] W. W. to Amos Cottle, Aug. 28, 1798.

VI
GERMANY AND SOCKBURN
September 1798–December 1799 (aet. 26½–8)

THE party set sail for Hamburg on Sunday morning, September 16, at 11 o'clock. William referred to their crossing as 'a very pleasant voyage'[1], but Dorothy's account of it is less cheerful. 'Before we heaved anchor', she writes, 'I was consigned to the cabin, which I did not quit till we were in still water at the mouth of the Elbe on Tuesday morning at 10 o'clock.' And her comment on her feelings as she emerged from below: 'But oh! the gentle breezes and the gentle motion, I thought of returning to the cabin in the evening with a mingled sensation of shuddering and sickness', suggests clearly enough what she had undergone. Slowly they proceeded up the river with its low flat shores, here and there a farm-house, cattle feeding, haystacks, a cottage, a windmill; passed Cuxhaven 'an ugly black-looking place' and at sundown cast anchor. The next day was more interesting; they came to Blankanese, a village scattered over the side of three hills, the houses half concealed by and half obtruding themselves from the low trees. Then the houses became thicker and the banks of the Elbe more steep, and the spires of Altona came in sight. At Altona they took a boat and rowed through the narrow passages of the Elbe crowded with vessels of all nations and landed at the Boom House. William went to seek lodgings, and the rest of the party guarded the luggage.

While they awaited his return Dorothy found plenty of amusement in watching the motley crowds that thronged the busy quay-side. Like all travellers landing for the first time upon the Continent her eye was caught by novelties of dress,

> 'Dutch women with immense straw bonnets, with flat crowns and rims in the shape of oyster shells, without trimming or with only a plain riband round the crown, and literally as large as a small sized umbrella. Hamburgher girls with white caps with broad

[1] W. W. to Henry Gardiner, Oct. 3, 1798. The account of Dorothy's life at Hamburg and her journey to Goslar is based on her manuscript Journal, of which some extracts have been published by K., *Journals of D. W.*, i. 21–7.

overhanging borders crimped and stiff and long lappets of riband. Hanoverians with round borders showing all the face and standing upright, a profusion of riband. Fruitwomen with large straw hats in the shape of an inverted bowl, or white handkerchiefs tied round the head like a bishop's mitre. The ladies without hats in dresses of all fashions. Soldiers with dull-looking red coats and immense cocked hats. The men little differing from the English except that they generally have a pipe in their mouths. . . . After waiting about an hour we saw William reappear. Two porters carried our luggage upon a sort of wheelbarrow, and we were conducted through dirty, ill-paved, stinking streets to an inn where lodgings had been procured for us.'

The lodgings were not inviting in appearance.

'The first impression', says Dorothy, 'that an Englishman receives on entering a Hamburgh inn is that of filth and filthy smells. . . . On inquiry we found that we could have no dinner, as dinner was over. . . . I went upstairs to dress, a *man* servant brought up napkins, water, etc. My room was at the top of the house, the floor just washed, but I could see that the process had spread or plaistered the coating of dirt, no carpet, the floor painted brown. When I returned I found the party eating cold beef, no cloth spread, no vegetables, but some bad cucumbers pickled without vinegar, very good wine at one mark and four sous the bottle.'

Except for the wine, this was not a propitious opening to their holiday; and after a fortnight at Hamburg they had formed no high opinion of its inhabitants. 'It is a sad place;' wrote Wordsworth,[1] 'I have no doubt this city contains a world of good and honest people if one had but the skill to find them.' But as strangers, with no knowledge of the native language, they were not well equipped for the discovery. They were constantly irritated by the greed and dishonesty which they met on every hand. Their landlord, of whom Dorothy draws a vivid picture, 'while he sat with his greasy face at the head of the table, laughing with landlord-like vulgarity and complaisance at the jokes of his guests, or while he exercised the force of his mind on the best way of cutting the beef', cheated them in their bill of not less than four guineas. William's experience at the baker's, which he inserted in Dorothy's *Journal*, tells a similar story.[2]

[1] W. W. to Thomas Poole, Oct. 3, 1798.
[2] Wordsworth has been charged with appropriating to himself an experience

'I put two shillings into the baker's hands for which I was to have had four small rolls. He gave me two. I let him understand that I was to have four, and with this view I took one shilling from him, pointed to it and to two loaves and at the same time offering it to him. Again I took up two others. In a savage manner he half knocked the rolls out of my hand, and when I asked for the other shilling he refused to return it, and would neither suffer me to take bread, nor give me back my money, and on these terms I quitted the shop.' The porters were as bad as the tradesmen. 'We had two small trunks which we wished to have conveyed to the post, the distance about 300 yards. A porter had the audacity to demand 20*d.* for carrying them, and was very insolent when William refused to give it him; he offered him 8*d.* which was more than a London porter would have expected. William carried them himself through a heavy shower of rain.' And Coleridge fared no better at the hands of the coachmen.

The *Journal* which records Dorothy's first impression of a foreign country is rich in details that give a lively picture of Hamburg, its neighbourhood, and its inhabitants at the close of the eighteenth century, and she was quick to detect its points of difference from the England that she knew. The readiness of the townspeople to take advantage of their ignorance as strangers seemed to her only another expression of the inhumanity with which they treated all those who were in their power. While she was struck by the scarcity of beggars, and the absence of drunken men and noisy quarrels, she was astonished to see a man beating a well-dressed, middle-aged woman in the street, and she noted with indignation the brutal treatment to which the Jews were everywhere subjected. 'When we got nearly through the town,' she writes, 'we saw a surly-looking German driving a poor Jew forward with foul language, and making frequent use of a stick which he had in his hand. The countenance of the Jew expressed neither anger nor surprise, nor agitation; he spoke but with meekness, and unresisting pursued his way followed by his inhuman driver, whose insolence we found was supported by law; "the Jews have no right to *reign* in the city of Hamburgh", as a German told us in

which was really Dorothy's, but a glance at the MS. proves that though the incident is recorded in Dorothy's *Journal*, it is in William's handwriting.

broken English. The soldiers who are stationed at the draw-bridge looked very surly at him and the countenance of the bye-standers expressed cold unfeeling cruelty.'

Accustomed to English liberty she was irked by life in a walled town. 'While the sun was yet shining pleasantly we were obliged to think perpetually to turn our eyes to the church clock. The gates are shut at half past six o'clock, and there is no admittance into the city after that time. This idea deducts much from the pleasure of an evening walk. You are haunted by it long before the time has elapsed.' She was impressed by the dullness of the shops, arranged without order and elegance, the height and size of the houses in the city, which formed a striking contrast with the merchants' houses in the suburbs, set in their gardens imitating the English fashion—imitating it, said William rather unkindly, 'as Della-Crusca might imitate Virgil'—and the bright cleanliness of the suburban cottages, which contrasted with the filth and smells that reigned in the inns and in the streets. 'These houses are never more than two stories high, built of brick or a mixture of brick and wood, and thatched or tiled. They have all window shutters, which are painted frequently a light grey green, but always painted. We were astonished at the excessive neatness which we observed within these houses. They have all window curtains as white as snow; the floors of all that we saw were perfectly clean.' And she remarks that the inside of one of them 'would have done credit to the industry of any English dame of fifty years ago when oak chests were rubbed as bright as looking glasses'.

The dress of the people never ceased to interest her—'old ladies in the London fashions of the years '80 or '82–3, artificial flowers very common in their frizzled heads, ladies with small baskets hanging on their arms, some without handkerchiefs and their necks entirely exposed, long shawls of various colours thrown over their shoulders; the women of the lower orders dressed with great modesty'. And the men, where they differed from Englishmen, did not escape her critical eye—'officers whom we supposed to be Prussians, with long coats and leather belts round their waists, which pinch in the body and make them look like women'.

Naturally enough she has much to record of the continental Sunday. At a church into which she looked 'the audience appeared to be simply composed of singing boys dressed in large cocked hats, and a few old women, who sat in the aisles. The inferior shops open, women sitting at their doors knitting and sewing, and I saw one woman ironing. It seems there is not any imposition of either law or custom which prevents people from making Sunday as much a day of labour as any other if their avarice or it may be their industry—but alas! I fear the former motive is the moving spring of the Hamburgher's mind!—gets the better of their love of pleasure. I saw a cobbler at work and a carpenter carrying his tools. It seems however the more general practice to make Sunday a day of ease. The more wealthy citizens go out in carriages or on horseback, the rest walking—all are clean and well-dressed. Immense crowds of people walking for pleasure, and many pleasure waggons passing and repassing—were invited to view an exhibition of waxworks—the theatres open and the billiard tables attended.'

The chief event of their sojourn in Hamburg was their visit to Herr Klopstock, a prosperous merchant who treated them with unbounded kindness and invited them to meet his brother, the famous poet. Notes of William's conversation with him were published by Coleridge in *Satyrane's Letters*; Dorothy's account of the visit, if it has less value for the literary critic, is at least more entertaining:

'Dined with Mr Klopstock. Had the pleasure of meeting his brother the poet, a venerable old man, retaining the liveliness and alertness of youth, though he evidently cannot be very far from the grave. His second wife much younger than he, a fine fresh looking woman, but with an unpleasant expression of countenance, vain, and not pleasing in her manners. Mr Klopstock the merchant very polite and kind, his wife, who cannot speak a word of English or French, appears a very interesting woman. They have a little girl of 7 years old, she was dressed in a coloured frock and her neck covered up with a thick handkerchief. (N.B. Klopstock the poet's lady much exposed) The teeth of the family very bad, their complexions fair. The rest of the party consisted of a young German who spoke a little English, a niece of Mr Klopstock's, Wm and myself. We were conducted through the warehouse and counting house into a large low room, with two windows at the end and a glass door opening upon a balcony, which overlooks a part of the Elbe. The room was hung with gilt leather, a picture of Lessing and some other portraits—a bust of his brother in one corner—floor polished brown, no carpet;

mahogany tables, desks chairs etc. We had scarcely sat five minutes before we were called to dinner in the next room to which we were led by folding doors. We sate around the table without order. Mrs Klopstock on one side, her husband at the foot of the table. Mrs K. distributed all the dishes in succession. Soup 1st, 2nd stewed veal without vegetables, 3rd sausages with cabbage, 4th oysters with spinach, 5th fowls with sallad and currant jelly, desert, grapes, biscuits, pears, plumbs, walnuts, afterwards coffee. A woman servant in the Hanoverian cap waited at table. She seemed more at her ease than an English servant, she laughed and talked with the little girl. We withdrew into the next room and had tea. Mr K.'s niece brought in the candles, and washed up the tea things in a sort of passage or lobby. The party talked with much interest of the French comedy, and seemed fond of music. The poet and his lady were obliged to depart soon after six. He sustained an animated conversation with William, during the whole afternoon. Poor old man! I could not look at him, the benefactor of his country, the father of German poetry, without the most sensible emotions. We returned home at a little after 7. I had a bad headache and went to bed at 9.' [1]

After ten days Coleridge and Chester set off to Ratzeburg; two days later William and Dorothy left for Goslar. Dorothy's account of their journey throws a lurid light upon the discomforts of German travelling at the close of the eighteenth century:

'We quitted Hamburgh on Wednesday evening at 5 o'clock, reached Luneberg to breakfast on Thursday and arrived at Brunswick between 3 and 4 o'clock on friday evening. Our carriage was more than half-covered and lined with leather within—luxuries which I since found are not often to be met with in a German diligence, though when I entered it I was much more inclined to observe the wretched crazy appearance of the whole, the crevices in the basket work below and the great space all

[1] In a letter to Lady Beaumont, Apr. 11, 1805, D. recalled this visit to Klopstock: 'I was only with him two or three hours, and as I could not speak a word of German, and have only a miserable stock of French, and his French was even worse than mine, I had little of his conversation. What I was chiefly pleased with in him was his great chearfulness, even liveliness, under the burthen of old age and many diseases. His countenance disappointed me; but this might be owing to his having a full-powdered tye Wig with a high *Toupee* (I believe the word is spelt so). I mean a high hill of hair sloping back from the forehead—a head-dress which I think scarcely any dignity of expression could stand out against, when the face is puckered up with wrinkles as his was, and bearing the traces also of long sickness.'

round for the winds to blow through, than to congratulate myself upon our good luck. Before we had got four miles from Hamburgh the shaking of the carriage gave me a violent pain in my bowels which was followed by sickness. It was a very fine evening when we passed through the city gates, and the ramparts and spires looked gay and beautiful. There were fine shady walks which seemed to extend to the distance of at least two miles from the city, but I was probably not very accurate in my computation, I was in a German diligence where every mile seems doubled. We passed many gentlemen's houses with gardens, some had jet d'eaus and images. We crossed the Elbe at one o'clock. The same moon that shone when we crossed the channel, now in its wane, lighted the waters of the Elbe: and it was of great use to us during the whole of our journey. Before we reached the River we had stopped at an inn where William and the rest of the party had coffee. I took some wine and water. We were shewn into a room with a great number of people all smoking but the women, amongst the rest were the coachman and the conductor, as he is called, a man who attends to take care of the luggage. Our carriage had 7 passengers (4 [6?] within, or half in, and one on the outside) and we were attended by two waggons which contained luggage, and those passengers which ours could not admit. These waggons are entirely uncovered and only differ from our English dung cart in being longer and narrower, and not so well made or painted. All the passengers pay the same price, 12 marks from Hamburgh to Brunswick and at each station 2 schillings to the waggon master and 2 schillings to the postilion when he is changed, but the same postilion sometimes drives 2 stations.

'When we had crossed the Elbe, we stopped at least an hour at another wretched publick house. We emptied our bottle of wine and got it filled with hot water which I found a great comfort. We went on during the rest of the night without being able to sleep, and at ½ past 5 arrived at the next station. We were now in the Hanoverian dominions, and the inns were more strange and more miserable. The first we came to was a very large house without any partition. At the entrance was the kitchen, where was the fire etc., farther up the beds and still beyond stalls for the cattle and straw spread upon the ground, fowls, geese and cats in abundance. The country through which we passed to Luneberg very barren, and Luneberg a wretched miserable place. There was a fair held when we passed through, but all seemed lifeless and dead. We breakfasted here, the bread bad, but the butter very good. We paid an English shilling for our breakfast. The roads miserably bad, within a mile of Luneberg they branch out upon an immense sandy plain, into numberless courses or rather wheel-tracks. The country becomes occasionally rather interesting from its strangeness. There are woods scattered about at different distances but even they look barren, though the trees flourish; I saw very few cattle of any kind, there were a few flocks of sheep and here and there some cows, but no wild colts, and no asses, no cottages, all lifeless. After travelling till 4 o'clock we dined at a pretty little town, enquired for something to eat at the post house but were told it was no inn, that we must go to the White Horse. We could get no meat, but had eggs and butter and milk, and water soup made with flour and water, lemon skin and sugar. They charged us 4 bon gros each for our dinner. We arrived at Brunswick the next day, Friday, at between 3 and 4 in the afternoon. This city stands upon a sandy plain, at a little distance from the town seemingly incapable of cultivation, but the numerous gardens and potatoes, cabbages, and turnip fields which are near the city shew strongly the good effects of human industry. The road on the Hamburgh side of Brunswick is so sandy that it is only marked by the irregular tracks of cart wheels, and it is at the mercy of the winds to carry it where they please. After waiting a considerable time to arrange our baggage we sallied forth in search of an inn. The English arms, or the King of England was not far distant and there we were taken in. As in all German houses that I have seen the best part of it was lost in the entrance, a huge place fit for a senate or a council chamber. We were shewn into a parlour, not so neat as the parlour of an English inn, though much more in the English style than at Hamburgh. After waiting a considerable time hungry and faint we sate down to dinner. We had mutton chops, potatoes after the English fashion, fowls, veal and salad, and some excellent pears. Our party was of six, we had two bottles of wine and a bottle of beer. The beds were excellent. Our share of the expense amounted to half a Louis. We had taken places in the Goslar diligence, and were to set off at 8 o'clock in the morning, so we rose at a little after seven. I ought to have mentioned that we walked about the city of Brunswick after we had dined. It is an old silent dull looking place, but has some good houses in it. We saw none of the bustle or gaiety of Hamburgh, there were few ladies to be seen, and they looked dismal from their manner of dressing. The ramparts are like those of Hamburgh only much less considerable. The Duke's Palace is a large white building. There is nothing of elegance in its external appearance, but the gardens seemed as if they would be very pleasant. We peeped through a gate-way but were told it was too late to enter. When we left our inn Wm carried the portmanteau and I the small parcel. He left them under my charge, and went in search of a baker's shop. He brought me his pockets full of apples, for which he paid two bon gros, and some excellent bread. Upon these I breakfasted, & carried Kubla[1] to a fountain in the neighbouring market-place, where I drank some excellent water. On Saturday 6th October we entered the Goslar [diligence].' (Here the manuscript breaks off.)

They found lodgings with a Frau Dippermaer, a widow with five children, who kept a small draper's shop. Why they had chosen to settle at Goslar, except in the belief that living was cheap there, it is difficult to understand.

'It is not', said Dorothy[2] after some experience of it, 'a place where it is possible to see anything of the manners of the more cultivated Germans, or of the higher classes. Its inhabitants are all petty tradespeople, in general a low and selfish race; intent upon gain, and perpetually of course disappointed. They cannot find it in their hearts to ask of a stranger a fair price for their goods. The woman of this house, who is a civil and good kind of a respectable woman *in her way* could not refrain from cheating us of halfpence and farthings when we first came.'

And they were debarred even from such poor society as Goslar had to offer; for they found that a man accompanied by his wife or sister was expected to give entertainments, and this they could not afford to do. So that while Coleridge was disporting himself at Ratzeburg 'in high life among barons, counts and countesses', they had to be content with the company of a French émigré priest, and a young apprentice to the drapery business who spent his evenings in their room. What wonder that they made little progress with the language, so that William complained that he acquired more French in two months than he would acquire German in five years, living as he did. But then at Goslar there was no Annette to talk to. Before November was out they were anxious to try their luck elsewhere, but the severity of the weather kept them prisoners; for the heaviest winter had set in that had been known for a century.

[1] A manuscript copy of '*Kubla Khan*'?
[2] D. W. to C. W., Feb. 3, 1799.

At Christmas 'the cold', wrote Dorothy,[1] 'was so excessive that when we left the room where we sit we were obliged to wrap ourselves up in great coats etc. in order not to suffer much pain from the transition, though we only went into the next room or downstairs for a few minutes', and the contrast between their stove-heated room and the external air 'set the flesh creeping', whilst William's attic bedroom was so arctic that he was often congratulated on emerging from it alive. They took their walk 'for an hour each day, often much more', clad in the thickest furs they could procure; but as there were no closed coaches plying from Goslar, and any journey they made would have to be taken at night and in an open cart, we cannot wonder that they shrank from the perilous attempt.

But though they were thus cut off from the outer world in a frozen dead-alive city, Coleridge, despite his counts and countesses, could yet envy them their lot.

William my head and my heart! dear William and dear Dorothea!
You have all in each other; but I am lonely, and want you!

he wrote to them, and touched by the truth and poignancy of the sentiment they forgave the lameness of his hexameters. For nothing in their life was more real or more precious than their love for Coleridge: 'I hear as often from Wordsworth', wrote Coleridge to his wife, 'as letters can go backward and forward in a country where fifty miles a day and night is expeditious travelling'; and the arrival of a letter from Coleridge was an event eagerly awaited by both brother and sister and passionately enjoyed. 'First let me speak', wrote Dorothy[2] in one of their joint replies, 'of the joy we felt at seeing your handwriting again; I burst open the seals and could almost have kissed them in the presence of the postmaster, but we did not read a word till we got to the inn when we devoured them separately, for at least two hours.' As far as distance and an erratic postal service would allow, they strove to keep up the united life of the happy Alfoxden days. William asked his friend's opinions on German poetry, discoursed to him of Theocritus and Burns, and English comedy, and spoke of his own work's progress: Dorothy copied out poems which, had

[1] D. W. to C. W., Feb. 3, 1799.
[2] W. W. and D. W. to S. T. C., Feb. 27, 1799.

Coleridge been with them, would have been read aloud to him, and interspersed her own comments:[1]

'You speak in raptures of the pleasure of skating—it must be a delightful exercise, and, in the North of England amongst the mountains whither we wish to decoy you, you might enjoy it with every possible advantage. A race with William upon his native lakes would leave to the heart and the imagination something more dear and valuable than the gay sight of ladies and countesses whirling along the lake of Ratzeburg. I will transcribe some lines which are connected with this subject and of course will be interesting to you now. It is from a description of William's boyish pleasures. [And she copies the famous account of skating on Esthwaite: *Prelude* (1805), i. 452–89.] I will give you a lake scene of another kind. I select from the mass of what William has written, because it may easily be detached from the rest, and because you have now a lake daily before your eyes. [And she copies the episode of the stolen boat on Ullswater: ib. i. 372–427.] I will now transcribe a nutting scene (I think I shall not tire you) It is like the rest, laid in the North of England, whither wherever we finally settle you must come to us at the latter end of next summer, and we will explore together every nook of that romantic country. You might walk through Wales and Yorkshire and join us in the county of Durham and I would follow at your heels and hear your dear voices again. William's foot is on the stairs. He has been walking by moonlight in his fur gown and a black fur cap, in which he looks like any grand Signior. William begs that you will preserve any verses which we have sent you, in the fear that in travelling we may lose the copy. farewell! God bless you, dear Coleridge, our very dear friend. D. Wordsworth.'

To Coleridge in his loneliness these letters were a veritable godsend. In Dorothy's tender frank affection the constant hunger of his life was for the time satisfied: as he read the lines she copied for him he felt the presence of that genius which he had been the first to proclaim. 'That "uncertain heaven received Into the bosom of the steady lake"', he wrote, 'I should have recognised anywhere: and had I met these lines running wild in the deserts of Arabia, I should instantly have screamed out "Wordsworth"'. At no time, indeed, was his friend's genius more vigorous. 'As I have no books', wrote William,[1] 'I have been obliged to write in self-defence. I should have written

[1] W. W. and D. W. to S. T. C., n.d., but Dec. 1798 or Jan. 1799.

five times as much but that I am prevented by an uneasiness at my stomach and side with a dull pain about my heart. I have used the word pain, but uneasiness and heat are words which more accurately express my feeling. At all events it renders writing unpleasant. Reading is now become a kind of luxury to me. When I do not read I am absolutely consumed by thinking and feeling, and bodily exertions of voice or of limbs, the consequences of those feelings.' And the ever-anxious Dorothy notes that 'he is always active, indeed too much so. He over-wearies himself.' But if she felt the anxiety she had a rich compensation. No verse of William's appealed to her more strongly than that which told of the early days when she was separated from him, days of which she loved to hear him talk. But William's poetic activity was not confined to those reminiscences of his boyhood which are the glory of *The Prelude*: it was now that he wrote his unique ballad *Lucy Gray*, founded on a story which Dorothy had told him: now, too, he wrote his most precious lyrics. Whether the lovely little poems to Lucy had their original inspiration in an early unrecorded episode in his life or are the pure creatures of his imagination we shall never know; but this at least is certain, and Dorothy could not fail to recognize it, that much of their feeling sprang from his present passionate devotion to her. Coleridge's intuition cannot be astray when he says that he always felt that the sublime epitaph *A slumber did my spirit seal* had been prompted by the thought of Dorothy's death: the exquisite lines on the education of the child framed by Nature to be a lady of her own, which precede the epitaph, are clearly connected with it both in thought and feeling; and just as we know that the poem to Lucy on the glow-worm recalls an evening of their life at Racedown, so it is at least probable that the incident recorded in *Strange fits of passion I have known*, where the poet riding home at night is suddenly overwhelmed by an irrational fear that Lucy is dead, had a similar inspiration. It is 'a favourite of mine' wrote Dorothy, significantly. She knew within herself how much she had given and was giving to her beloved brother.

Thus fruitfully for William, and happily for Dorothy, passed their five months' seclusion at Goslar: about the middle of February, on the first signs of the breaking up of winter, they decided to take their courage in both hands, and, entrusting their luggage to the dreaded open diligence, to walk across the Hartz Forest to Nordhausen. It was a bold step for the time of year, and from day to day they were forced to put off starting; but before the end of the month Dorothy was able to send to Coleridge a lively account of their adventures on the way:

Nordhausen Wednesday evening
27th February (1799)

My dear Coleridge,

We have at last received your long desired letters. Our patience was rewarded, or our cowardice flattered, by a most delightful morning which made its appearance last Saturday. Our baggage had been long ready, packed and repacked. We had gone to bed, the friday night being very stormy, without any hope—I called William in the morning; he saw the sun shining upon the garden, up he got, we put together our last parcel, conveyed it to the post-house, and set off on foot in the afternoon at one o'clock. Goslar lies on the edge of some high hills; mountains they cannot be called, at the skirts of the Hartz Forest. After walking about a mile we began to ascend through a pine forest which with the accompaniments of tiny waterfalls alias "Mittenrachs" might, as Wm says, remind a traveller of the Alps in the same way as a little kitten may suggest recollections of a full-grown tiger. Some of the pine-trees are extremely beautiful. We observed that when they seemed to be past maturity, and perhaps sooner in a close situation, their boughs which had before ascended, making an acute angle with the trunk, descend till they shoot out horizontally or make an obtuse angle with the upper part of the tree. This is effected by the twigs, which from the weight of their foliage drag down the boughs and hang like long threads of ivy in festoons of different lengths, the upper part of the branch being always bare. Some of these threads appear to be two or three yards long. In the very old trees the festoons are interwoven with grey or green moss, giving to the whole tree a very venerable and impressive appearance. We observed that the brilliant green of the earth-moss under the trees made our eyes ache after being so long accustomed to the snow. The peasants in the *plains* adjoining to Goslar are extremely well clothed and decent in their appearance. We had often seen in Goslar women inhabitants of the hills, but we did not imagine them to be so rude and barbarous a race as we found them. They carry enormous burthens in square baskets hung over their shoulders, their petticoats reach very little below their knees, and their stockings are dangling about their ankles without garters. Swellings in the throat are very common amongst them which may perhaps be attributed to the straining of the neck in dragging those monstrous loads. They rarely travel without a bottle of German brandy, Schnapps as they call it. Many of them go weekly from Clousthall to Brunswick, they perform this journey, a distance of thirty five miles in two days, carrying ass-loads, parcels, etc., and letters clandestinely. These people are chiefly inhabitants of Clousthall, a large Hanoverian town cursed with the plague of a vicious population. We arrived there in the dusk of the evening, found an excellent inn, with beautiful bed-linen, good coffee, and a decent supper. The charge was about the same rate as in England; perhaps a little cheaper. The town lies in the centre of the Hartz Forest. We left it on sunday, a mild morning, saw little that was remarkable till we came to the decaying posts of an old gibbet—We had scarcely passed it when we were saluted with the song of a pair of larks, a sweet, liquid and heavenly melody heard for the first time, after so long and severe a winter. I ought to have said that before this we had a view of the Brocken, the Mont Blanc of the Hartz Forest, and the glory of all this part of Germany. I cannot speak of its height as compared with any of our British mountains, but from the point from which we saw it, it had nothing impressive in its appearance. The day continued chearing and delightful, and we walked through a country presenting forest views of hill and valley, one of which a deep valley with a village built of wood scattered in the bottom was very interesting. We lingered under the shades of the trees and did not arrive at Osterode till four o'clock in the afternoon. It is also a Hanoverian possession, a small city lying at the edge of the Hartz Forest, in a kind of low wide valley. The appearance of the people as we passed through the streets was very little favorable—they looked dirty impudent and vulgar, and absolutely the whole town being at the windows or in the streets as we unluckily met them coming from church, we were stared completely out of countenance, at least I was; William stoutly denies that he was at all uncomfortable; however this was we had not courage to stop at an inn till we had walked through the whole town, and just on the other side of the city gates, we called at one where they told us they could give us nothing to eat. While we stood pondering what we should do, inquiring for another Wirts-haus, and half resolved to go a league further where we were told we could be accomodated, one of the Under-officers of the town, who was drinking with a sort of rabble, in the Wirts-haus where we had been refused admittance, accosted us, and civilly assured us that we should be admitted into the house, but he brought out one of his comrades a little step above him in place and about equal in self-importance and insolence, who questioned us respecting our business etc etc and would not let us pass without a passport. He conducted William to the Burgomaster who promised to grant him the said passport in the morning after he had seen our letters which were to come by the post-waggon with our trunk in the evening. In the meantime I was left in one of those towers which you always see at the entrance of cities; amongst a set of soldiers who were furbishing their dress, a woman who was engaged in some kind of Taylor's business, and a man who had an iron ring and chain hanging to his hand, I suppose as a punishment for some felony. You may be sure I was not a little impatient for William's return. He brought back his friend the officer in great good humour both with himself and him, for he took care to flatter his vanity, and we were admitted into the Wirts-haus; where we had some cold veal to supper, *decentish* beds, and a large quantity of excellent coffee in the morning for the value of one shilling and elevenpence English money. Though we rose at seven o'clock, owing to the delays of office we did not leave our inn till after ten. It was a mild morning the sun shone occasionally through the patches of broken clouds and the larks regaled us with a never ceasing song. We had still the Hartz forest on our left, and crossed a very delightful valley through which our road ought to have taken us but the floods had swept away the bridge. The country through which we passed was in general pleasant and tolerably peopled, but the ways dreadful; we were often obliged to walk as in the mines at Stowey, above the ankles in water, and sometimes as high in clay. We left the town of Hartzburg on our left; it has a huge decaying castle built upon the edge of a steep hill richly wooded and commanding a very fine prospect of hills clothed with Beech wood and a wide meadow valley through which runs a respectable river. After we left this place the roads grew worse and worse, the darkness came on, and we were near being stopped by a water [?] when a waggon overtook us which conducted us safely to an Inn at Schazefeld, where we got a good supper, that is cold beef, indifferent soup, and cabbage, straw beds and coffee and bread and butter for 1 shilling and tenpence. In the night we had a hard frost and the first part of our yesterday's journey was very delightful; the country charming, something like the widest of the Welsh valleys, the widest and tamest, but afterwards the roads grew worse, still however we had a pleasant walk, and reached our inn at 4 in the afternoon. We had sausages and boiled milk to supper, coffee etc for 1 shilling and ninepence, we slept in company with our host and hostess, and four children, a facetious shoe-maker, a Prussian tax-gatherer and a journeyman hat-maker, who had travelled all over Germany working a month here and a few days there, to see the world—William advised him to go to England as he was so fond of travelling. 'England? was ist das für ein land gehört? ist an dem Konig von Danemark? wo liegt es? nein, nein, man ist nicht ruhig darin.' If my report does not exactly accord with the strict rules of German Grammar I hope you will be so good as to attribute it to the hat-maker. Our landlord had been in the Prussian service, a fine looking man, extremely fond of his children and seeming to be very happy with a very good tempered wife. We were struck with the extreme folly of people who draw conclusions respecting national character from the narrow limits of common observation. We have been much with German hosts and hostesses and notwithstanding the supposed identifying tendency first of national manners, and then of particular occupations, these persons appeared in every respect as if made in contrast to each other, but this will be a more proper subject for conversation. This morning was very rainy, so we got into the post-waggon, in which conveyance we travelled ten miles, and arrived at the post-haus in the afternoon. We are now at a tolerable inn but we don't know what we have to pay.'

For another two months they rambled about Germany; though no record of their journeyings has survived, it seems likely that, among other places, they visited Weimar, Eisenach, and Erfurt; but we know that towards the end of April they passed a day or two with Coleridge, who had moved on from Ratzeburg to Göttingen, and that early in May they were back in their own country. 'We have spent our time pleasantly enough in Germany', wrote William to Cottle, on his arrival, 'but we are right glad to find ourselves in England, for we have learned to know its value.'

William's more prudent relatives had hoped that on his return from abroad he would at last grapple with the problem of earning a decent livelihood; but again he disappointed them. His one desire, as it was Dorothy's, was to see Mary, and on landing they made straight for Tom Hutchinson's farm at Sockburn-on-Tees, and here they settled down to enjoy the summer. 'How they propose to add to their incomes I cannot tell,' wrote Aunt Rawson with some asperity to Sam Ferguson, 'if by their pens they will be at a great distance from the capital';[1] and a reference of Sam's to the *Lyrical Ballads* she met with a 'lament that he is spending his youth in so unprofitable a manner'. But if, as is likely, she wrote to Dorothy in a similar vein, neither sister nor brother were seriously disturbed by it. More disturbing to them was the fact that their letters to Coleridge elicited no answer. He had returned from Germany at the end of June, and they were longing for him to join them. That he and Mary, so dear to them both, should remain strangers to one another was not to be thought of. But at length the news that Wordsworth was dangerously ill roused him from his silence, and on October 26 he appeared, and, as was his wont, made a rapid conquest of all hearts. At once he realized, what he had not known before, the love of William and Mary, and Mary became, like Dorothy, his 'sister'; almost at once his insatiable craving for undivided love and sympathy drew him irresistibly to Sara Hutchinson;[2] and now began that fervid passion that of all his many loves went the deepest and lasted the longest.

Whether the ever-anxious Dorothy had exaggerated the gravity of William's illness, or the arrival of Coleridge had effected a rapid cure, we cannot tell; but anyhow, they both were ready, after a few days, to start off upon a walking tour in the Lake country. The two friends were joined by John Wordsworth, now returned from one of his distant cruises, and together, by way of Haweswater, Bowness, and Hawkshead, they reached Grasmere and put up at Robert Newton's inn there. It was Coleridge's first visit to his friends' native country, and he was enchanted with every part he saw, though, as he said, Rydal and Grasmere gave him the deepest delight. 'It was to me the vision of a fair country', he wrote. 'Why were you not with us, Dorothy, why were you not with us, Mary?'[3] It was no new spell that Grasmere exerted upon William. Years before he had pictured to himself a home there with Mary, and now once more it laid a hold upon him. 'You will think my plan a mad one', he wrote to Dorothy,[3] 'but I have thought of building a

[1] June 28, 1799.

[2] The evidence for this is to be found in S. T. C.'s private notebooks, *v.* T. H. Rayson, *Coleridge and Asra* (*Studies in Philology*, July 1929).

[3] S. T. C. and W. W. to D. W., Oct. 1799.

house there by the Lake side. John would give me £40 to buy the ground and for £250 I am sure I could build one as good as we can wish. . . . There is a small house at Grasmere empty which we might take, but of this we will speak. But I shall write again when I know more of this subject.' The plan of building was given up and the small house was taken. In this same letter William was able to tell Dorothy that her Uncle Crackanthorpe, who had just died, had left her a legacy of £100; with this sum they could purchase all the necessary furniture. Before the end of the year William and Dorothy were at Dove Cottage.

WILLIAM WORDSWORTH (1805)

From a tinted pencil drawing by

HENRY EDRIDGE, A.R.A.

VII
DOVE COTTAGE
(December 1799–1802 (aet. 28–31)

EARLY on Tuesday morning, December 17, while the moon still shone upon the river Tees, Dorothy and William left Sockburn, William on one horse, and Dorothy mounted behind George Hutchinson upon another. After fourteen miles' riding they reached Richmond; eight miles farther on, at the little village of Wensley, George returned with the horses and they proceeded up the dale on foot, reaching Askrigg, twelve miles distant, about six o'clock in the evening. At Sedbergh, twenty-one miles on, they spent the following night. It was wild wintry weather, keen frost and snow showers interspersed with bright sunshine. Eager though they were to reach their destination, they found time to turn out of their course to visit the three waterfalls that are the pride of Wensleydale. They were in high spirits; and with a strong wind behind them walked the ten miles from Hardraw to Garsdale, over a high mountain road, in two hours and a quarter by the watch, and then, after a short rest, the next seven miles in an hour and thirty-five minutes, 'a marvellous feat', said William, 'of which D. will long tell!'[1] The third morning they went on to Kendal, and spent the rest of the day in laying out a part of Uncle Crackanthorpe's legacy in furniture and other household needments. On Friday, the 20th, they hired a postchaise which deposited them at Dove Cottage at half-past four.

Throughout their journey they had felt that peculiar thrill known only to the traveller who returns after long absence to the land of his childhood. In Dorset and Somerset those features of the country had most rejoiced them which recalled to their minds their native hills and valleys: Grasmere was the very centre of their beloved Lake country. It was the spot where William, years ago, had in imagination placed his first home; which, only two months before, had given most delight to Coleridge. Here they would be among their own people, with the habits and traditions in which they had been bred, and listen

[1] W. W. to S. T. C., Dec. 24, 1799.

daily to the dialect and accent which was endeared to them from childhood. As they drew near to Grasmere the very sky seemed to give them a passionate welcoming:

> Embrace me then, ye hills, and close me in.
> Now in the clear and open day I feel
> Your guardianship: I take it to my heart;
> 'Tis like the solemn shelter of the night.
> But I would call thee beautiful; for mild,
> And soft, and gay, and beautiful thou art,
> Dear valley, having in thy face a smile,
> Though peaceful, full of gladness. Thou art pleased,
> Pleased with thy crags, and woody steeps, thy Lake,
> Its one green island, and its winding shores,
> The multitude of little rocky hills,
> Thy Church, and cottages of mountain stone
> Clustered like stars some few, but single most,
> And lurking dimly in their shy retreats,
> Or glancing at each other cheerful looks,
> Like separated stars with clouds between.

So wrote William,[1] and his words spoke for Dorothy as fully as for himself. One of these cottages was to be her home. To have such a dwelling had been the dream of her girlhood: it would be their own with a completeness unattainable at either Racedown or Alfoxden.

Dove Cottage,[2] formerly an inn known as the Dove and Olive Bough, was one of a group of some half-dozen small houses which stood on the old road from Rydal to Grasmere, about six hundred yards short of the church. Its outlook in those days was not blocked by a congested mass of ugly buildings; from the front windows was an uninterrupted view over meadows to the lake. It stood alone on the east side of the road, its little garden and orchard rising steep up the fell behind; across the road, some few yards on each side of it, were two other cottages. This group of buildings, together with two cottages a little way up the hill towards Rydal, was known as Town End; another group of about the same size lying two miles to the North, on the road to Keswick, constituted Town Head; there was a third, rather larger, close to the church.

[1] *On Nature's invitation do I come*, 28–43, *Oxf. W.*, 622.

[2] It is uncertain when the cottage first became known as 'Dove Cottage'. The W.s only speak of living at 'Town-end', and head their letters 'Grasmere'.

Other cottages or small farmsteads were dotted about the lane that led to the church, on the Keswick road, at the foot of the Easedale valley, and on the western bank of the lake. There cannot have been more than forty or fifty of them in all, for the population of the whole valley was but two hundred and seventy. Of this number some twenty-six were statesmen, or freeholders with small plots of land which they farmed themselves; the rest comprised their families and those who worked for them or plied the homely trades of a normal village community. Grasmere, indeed, was 'a perfect republic of shepherds and agriculturists'; and the whole valley bore that unpretentious aspect which, thirty years before, had charmed the poet Gray. 'Not a single red tile,' he had said, 'no flaring gentleman's house or garden wall breaks in upon this little unsuspected paradise; but all is peace, rusticity, and happy poverty, in its neatest and most becoming attire.'

Dove Cottage itself, as Dorothy wrote, was 'truly and literally a cottage, not an advertisement cottage with coach house and even stable, but a little low-roofed building with the entrance through the kitchen'. This kitchen hall, a low room, sixteen feet by twelve, wainscoted with dark oak, and with its little diamond-paned windows overlooking the road and lake, was the main room on the ground floor; leading out of it in front was a smaller room which the Wordsworths made into a bedroom; behind, a small kitchen or laundry. On the first floor were two rooms facing the front, the one above the hall to be their main living room, the other another bedroom; above the back kitchen was a lumber room and a tiny annex hardly bigger than a cupboard, which could be used as an extra bedroom.

When they reached the cottage on that memorable evening they found their neighbour, old Molly Fisher, waiting to receive them. She had kept a small fire burning in the parlour for the previous fortnight that it might be dry and comfortable, and she loved in after years to recall Dorothy's appearance as she stood on the hearth, warming herself after her long winter drive. 'Aye,' Molly would say, 'I mun never forget t'laal striped gown and t'laal straw bonnet as ye stood here.' Two welcome letters from Coleridge greeted their arrival, and though four days slipped by before leisure could be found to send an answer, Coleridge was never long from their thoughts. 'My dear friend,' wrote William, 'we talk of you perpetually, and for me I see you everywhere'; and he went on to tell how they had fared since they left Sockburn, and to give a first impression of their new quarters. Despite Molly's forethought they had 'both caught troublesome colds in the new and almost empty house'; one of the chimneys had smoked like a furnace, everything was 'in confusion, painting the rooms, mending the doors, and heaven knows what, and Dorothy has so much work for her needle among the bed curtains, etc., that she is absolutely buried in it. She has scarcely been out since our arrival; one evening I tempted her forth; the planet Jupiter was on the top of the hugest of the Rydale mountains, but I had reason to repent that I had seduced her from her work, as she returned with a raging toothache.' But neither colds nor toothache could dull their happiness. 'Dorothy', he reports, 'is much pleased with the house and appurtenances, the orchard especially; in imagination she has already built a seat with a summer shed on the highest platform in this our little domestic slip of mountain. The spot commands a view over the roof of our house, of the lake, the church, Helm crag, and two thirds of the vale. We mean to enclose two or three yards of ground between us and the road, this for the sake of a few flowers, and because it will make it more our own.'[1]

Without the small addition to their slender income derived from the care of little Basil, they had to practise an economy even more rigid than at Racedown. So they decided to keep no servant, but 'partly out of charity, partly for convenience' engaged Molly Fisher for two hours a day, with a little extra time on Saturdays and when they had visitors. For this service they arranged to give her two shillings a week and her dinner. 'We could', says William, 'have had this attendance for eighteen pence, but we added the sixpence for the sake of the poor woman, who is made happy by it.'[1] And without a maid living in the house they could save the kitchen fire for the greater part of the day, only lighting it for dressing the dinner and the subsequent washing up. Breakfast and supper Dorothy could cook herself on 'the half-kitchen half-parlour fire' upstairs. Molly was not an ideal servant. She was sixty years of age, 'very

[1] W W. to S. T. C., Dec. 24, 1799.

ignorant, very foolish, and very difficult to teach',[1] says Dorothy, 'so that I once almost despaired of her'; and only after much perseverance was she taught to do mechanically the housework and the rougher parts of the cooking. But what she lacked in efficiency she made up in zeal and devotion, and proved herself 'as good and honest as ever was human being'. She took an immense pride in her work, exulting in her own importance, and in her good luck at having secured a position so far above her most sanguine dreams. 'Aye, mistress,' said she,[2] 'them 'at's low laid would have been proud creatures could they but have seen where I is now, fra what they thought mud be my doom!' Molly remained in their service for more than four years, and was a constant source of entertainment to Dorothy and her guests. To Coleridge she was 'that drollery belonging to the cottage', and he had a story of how, when he called there in his friends' absence, Molly would not let him go beyond the kitchen because his boots were dirty. Hazlitt immortalized her as 'the woman who had never heard of the French Revolution ten years after it had happened', whilst the Lambs long remembered with pleasure her old friendly face, and when they wrote to the cottage sent her loving greetings. With only Molly to help her, Dorothy found plenty to occupy her in the house; but such duties did not weigh heavily upon her. 'It is natural for me', she said,[3] 'to do everything as quick as I can, and at the same time', and she was always at her brother's call, ready to talk or walk with him, to help him in the garden, to write his letters or to copy out his poems.

Before many weeks had passed they had settled down at Grasmere as though they had lived there all their lives. From the first they established friendly relations with their neighbours. The Fishers, Molly's brother and his wife, lived just across the way, and John Fisher would often lend a hand in the garden; on the other side of them was John Ashburner, a statesman in reduced circumstances; he brought their coal from Keswick, and his wife and five children would pop in and out of the cottage, eager to run their errands for them; in the peat house adjoining the Ashburners, Fletcher, the carrier, kept his horses and carts, and he was always ready to take letters and

[1] D. W. to J. M., Sept. 10, 1800. [2] *Journal*, Mar. 5, 1802.
[3] D. W. to Lady B., Dec. 25, 1804.

parcels for them to and from Keswick; only a little farther off were the Dawsons and the Lewthwaites, families upon whom they were to draw for faithful servants in years to come.

> 'They are excellent people,' wrote Dorothy,[1] 'friendly in performing all offices of kindness and humanity, and attentive to us without servility, if we were sick they would wait upon us night and day. We are also', she adds, 'on very intimate terms with one family in the middle rank of life, a clergyman with a very small income, his wife, son and daughter. The old man is upwards of eighty, yet he goes fishing to the tarns on the hilltops with my Brothers, and he is as active as many men of fifty. His wife is a delightful old woman, mild and gentle, yet chearful in her manners, and much of the gentlewoman, so made by long exercise of the duties of a wife and a mother, and the charities of a neighbour, for she has lived 40 years in this vale and seldom left her home. The daughter, though much inferior to her mother, is a pleasant kind of woman, and the son is an interesting man; he is about 40, manages his father's glebe-land, reads a little, and spends much time in fishing.'

These were the Sympsons, who lived at Broadrain, Town Head, and few days passed without some intercourse between the two families. With an official clerical call they were not troubled, for the rector of Grasmere had been for more than fifty years a hopeless imbecile, and the curate in charge did not take his pastoral duties too seriously; no social claims forced their life into a prescribed routine, and they could keep their own hours. 'Our employments', Dorothy wrote to Jane,[2] 'are not very various, yet they are irregular. We walk every day and at all times of the day, we row upon the water, and in the summer sit a great part of our time under the apple trees of the orchard, or in a wood close by the lake-side. Wm. writes verses and we read the books we have and such as we can procure. I read German partly as preparatory to translating, but I am unfit for that task alone, and Wm. is better employed so I do not know when it will turn to much account.'

In putting the final touches to the cottage they had the help of their sailor brother John: he was spending a long furlough in England between two of his voyages to the East, and from late January to the end of September made his home with them.

[1] D. W. to J. M., Sept. 10, 1800.

[2] Ib.

Dorothy had seen nothing of him for more than seven years; but he had accompanied William and Coleridge on their walking tour some three months earlier, and Coleridge with a poet's intuition at once discerned his intrinsic character. 'John is one of you,' he had written, 'a man who hath solitary musings of his own intellect, with a subtle tact, a swift instinct of Truth and Beauty.' Dorothy soon found that Coleridge was right. Like them, John

> 'loved solitude and he rejoiced in society; he would wander alone among these hills with his fishing rod, or led on merely by the pleasure of walking—or he would walk with William or me or both of us, . . . he had so fine an eye that no distinction was unnoticed by him, and so tender a feeling that he never noticed anything in vain. Many a time has he called me out in an evening to look at the moon or stars, or a cloudy sky, or this vale in the quiet moonlight; but the stars and moon were his chief delight. . . . Then he was so happy by the fireside—any little business of the house interested him, he loved our cottage, he helped us to furnish it, and to make the garden.'[1]

Without the nervous excitability of his brother or sister, or their gift for expression, John had been slow to develop, and he had been set down as the dunce of the family; but now they recognized in him 'a silent poet', and the bond of kinship, always strong in them, was made stronger by a real intimacy of heart and mind. And he was devoted to them with all the depth of his modest, reserved, self-effacing nature. William he wellnigh worshipped, and had unshakable faith in his genius; it was his life's ambition to re-establish the family fortunes, so that Dorothy might live in comfort and William pursue his poetic calling, free from all care for the morrow: for them, he said, he would work, William was to do something for the world. There was, in fact, every prospect that he would achieve his purpose; for it was the recognized custom of officers in the employ of the East India Company to do a little trading on their own account, so that with reasonable luck he could look forward at no distant date to the acquisition of a comfortable income. But now he was on holiday, living the simple life that he loved, that he hoped in a few years to be able to share with them; and when in the early spring Mary Hutchinson joined

[1] D. W. to J. M., Mar. 16, 1805.

them on a six weeks' visit, his happiness was increased, and he came to love her only less than he loved William and Dorothy.

Before Mary left the cottage Coleridge came to them for a month, Joanna Hutchinson, too, the 'wild-hearted maid', was probably their guest during the spring,[1] and then, in mid-May, the two brothers went off for three weeks to pay a return visit to Mary at Gallow Hill, near Scarborough in Yorkshire, whither the Hutchinsons had lately moved from Sockburn. Dorothy was left entirely to herself. 'During their absence', she wrote to Jane,[2] 'I felt myself very lonely; while I was within doors I wanted my little companion Basil, and poor old Molly did but ill supply the place of our good and dear Peggy, who was quite as a friend to us.' It was her first experience of complete solitude, and with that capacity for suffering which is the price all must pay for real happiness, she felt with a peculiar poignancy her dependence upon William. The very intensity with which for the last four years she had entered into every detail of his life left her with a sense of emptiness when he was not at her side. Love for her brother, she said,[3] was 'the building up of my being, the light of my path': in his absence her lively imagination saw life falling into ruins, and her bright path darkened. By temperament over-anxious, she often suffered torments of fear for his health when he was with her: how could she keep back her fears when he was out of her sight? And now that he was gone to Mary she could not fail to think of that time, soon to come, when she would no longer be mistress of his home.

It is clear that she had played no small part in bringing the lovers together. She realized that, though he was everything to her, his life was still incomplete. He must have a wife, and a family, for she knew no less than he, that 'wisdom doth live with children round her knees'. His marriage, indeed, would not entail separation from him—that was unthinkable—but though in love 'to divide is not to take away', the thought was not the less bitter that at no distant future she would have to share with another a companionship which had been all her own. Yet there was no trace of selfishness in her; and in her

[1] Otherwise how could the poem *To Joanna* (*Oxf. W.* 147) have been composed in Aug. and published before the end of the year?

[2] D. W. to J. M., Sept. 10, 1800.

[3] D. W. to Lady B., Mar. 17, 1805.

inevitable sadness there was the exaltation of sacrifice. It was in something of this mood that she resumed, at Grasmere, the *Journal* that she had kept at Alfoxden and in Germany.

> 'May 14 1800. Wm and John set off into Yorkshire after dinner at half-past two o'clock, cold pork in their pockets. I left them at the turning of the Low-wood bay under the trees. My heart was so full that I could hardly speak to Wm. when I gave him a farewell kiss. I sate a long time upon a stone at the margin of the lake, and after a flood of tears my heart was easier. The lake looked to me, I knew not why, dull and melancholy, and the weltering on the shores seemed a heavy sound. I walked as long as I could amongst the stones of the shore. The wood is rich in flowers; a beautiful yellow (palish yellow) flower that looked thick, round, and double, and smelt very sweet (I supposed it was a ranunculus), crowfoot, the grassy-leaved rabbit-toothed white flower, strawberries, geranium, scentless violets, anemones two kinds, orchises, primroses, the heckberry very beautiful, the crab coming out as a low shrub. Met a blind man, driving a very large beautiful bull and a cow. He walked with two sticks. Came home by Clappersgate. The valley very green; many sweet views up to Rydalehead, when I could juggle away the fine houses; but they disturbed me, even more than when I have been happier; one beautiful view of the bridge, without Sir Michael's. Sate down very often, though it was cold. I resolved to write a journal of the time till Wm and J. return, because I will not quarrel with myself, and because I shall give William pleasure by it when he comes home again. At Rydale, a woman of the village, stout and well-dressed, begged a half-penny. She had never, she said, done it before, but these hard times! Arrived at home with a bad headache, set some slips of privet, the evening cold, had a fire, my face now flame-coloured. It is nine o'clock. I shall go to bed soon. Oh that I had a letter from William!'

So she jots down, day by day, her occupation in house and garden, and her minutest observations in her walks, for nothing that concerns her is too trivial to interest William. Her usual walk is to Ambleside to get the post, and though William writes every few days there is often the despairing interjection, 'no letters', or 'only a letter from Coleridge, I expected a letter from William'. One day, such is her eagerness, she starts off after breakfast, forgetting that the post is not due till evening, and she has to go again. The time of his return is uncertain; two days before his arrival she will not go far from home lest she should not be there to welcome him: the next day, as she comes in from a short stroll she slackens her pace as she approaches the cottage, fearing to find that he is not come, and at night she lies awake, listening to every barking dog. At last, 'sitting at work till after 11 o'clock I heard', she says, 'a foot go to the front of the house, turn round, and open the gate. It was William! After our first joy was over, we got some tea. We did not go to bed till 4 o'clock in the morning, so that he had an opportunity of seeing our improvements. The birds were singing; and all looked fresh, though not gay. There was a greyness on earth and sky. We did not rise till near 10 in the morning.'

Dorothy's Grasmere *Journal*, begun in May 1800, runs on to the January of 1803. In the extant manuscript books there is a gap of nine months in 1801, but it is more likely that the record for this period has been lost than that it was not written. These three years were the richest in her life, and of no others have we so intimate a revelation. The *Journal* tells a tale of plain living and high thinking, but it does not ignore those trivialities that make up a significant part in all existence. Many a prosaic detail is set down—bare entries are frequent enough, such as 'Mrs Coleridge came with Derwent. Sweeping chimneys', or 'I was not very well, mended stockings', or 'Mr Sympson drank tea with us', or 'A cold evening. Molly stuck the peas. I weeded a little. Did not walk.' At times her entire lack of self-consciousness becomes a lack of humour,[1] and she reveals

[1] In a letter to Miss Anne Scott, written in 1833, Coleridge tells an amusing story of Dorothy's deficiency in a sense of humour—'a certain degree of obtuseness in this respect', he says, 'I have ever considered among the characteristic traits, nay, *charms* of Womanhood: & have a hundred times noticed it, not only in amiable females, but in the most intelligent, & of the finest talents. . . . Once, she being present, I told (a story) of a surgeon, who, having restored to life two or three persons who had attempted to hang or drown themselves; & having afterwards been importuned by them for help & maintenance on the plea, that having forced life upon them against their own will & wish, he was bound to support it: had ventured, that he would never interfere in any such accidents without having first ascertained whether the individual wished it or no. On a summer day while on a water-party, one of the Rowers in some unaccountable way fell overboard & disappeared. But on his re-emersion the Surgeon caught hold of his hair, & lifting his head & chest above the water said—"Now, my good Fellow! did you really mean to drown yourself? What is your own wish?" "O—O—O!" (sobbed out the man)—"a sickly Wife—& seven small children!" "Ha! poor Fellow! No wonder then!" exclaimed the surgeon, & instantly popped him under again. The party were all on the brink of a loud laugh, when Dorothy Wordsworth, with tears sparkling in her eyes, cried out—"Bless me! but was not that very *inhuman!*"

the naivety of a child, as in this sentence which occurs in the account of a day passed on the hills. 'William and Coleridge repeated and read verses; I drank a little brandy and water, and was in heaven.' But the stark fidelity with which she sets down whatever might pass through her mind gives to the whole journal the stamp of a living human document, and throws into stronger relief her power as an artist to recreate the world about her in pictures of a beauty proportionate to the intensity of her feeling. Since the days when she wrote her Alfoxden journal she had grown both in depth and breadth of character; her feelings had become even more acute and sensitive, her range of sympathies far wider. Her eager response to the sights and sounds about her is charged with a deeper personal emotion; the eye of a poet was hers before: now she reveals more of the poet's heart and mind. Thus, for example, she describes 'our favourite birch-tree': 'It was yielding to the gusty wind with all its tender twigs. The sun shone upon it, and it glanced in the wind like a flying sunshiny shower. It was a tree in shape, with stem and branches, but it was like a spirit of water. The sun went in and out and it resumed its purplish appearance, the twigs still yielding to the wind, but not so visibly to us. The other birch trees that were near it looked bright and cheerful, but it was a creature by its own self among them.' Her favourite walk, particularly when she was alone, was that which led her through Rydal to Ambleside; and intimacy never dulled for her its beauty or its wonder. Here are three separate impressions of it:

'May 16. 1800. I went round by the stepping stones. Rydale was very beautiful, with spear-shaped streaks of polished steel. Grasmere was very solemn in the last glimpse of twilight. It calls home the heart to quietness.

'June 2. 1800. crossed the stepping stones at the foot of Grasmere, and pursued my way on the other side of Rydale and by Clappersgate. I sate a long while to watch the hurrying waves, and to hear the regularly irregular sound of the dashing waters. The waves round about the little Island seemed like a dance of spirits that rose out of the water, round its small circumference of shore.'

This stroke of exquisite simplicity & true singleness of heart, made us almost roll off our chairs; but was there one of the party, that did not love Dorothy the more for it? I trust, not one.' Coleridge, *Letters*, ed. Griggs, vol. ii, pp. 449–50.

Returning, she is accompanied part of the way by the Ambleside post-mistress, who thinks she must be lonely. 'This was very kind, but God be thanked, I want not society by a moonlight lake.'

And here is a third impression of the same walk:

> 'March 18. 1802. Rydale vale was full of life and motion. The wind blew briskly, and the lake was covered all over with bright silver waves, that were there each the twinkling of an eye, then others rose up and took their place as fast as they went away. The rocks glittered in the sunshine. The crows and the ravens were busy, and the thrushes and little birds sang. I went through the fields and sate half an hour afraid to pass a cow. The cow looked at me, and I looked at the cow, and whenever I stirred the cow gave over eating . . . came along Ambleside vale in the twilight. It was a grave evening. There was something in the air that compelled me to serious thought.—the hills were large, closed in by the sky.. . . Night was come on, and the moon was overcast. But, as I climbed the moss, the moon came out from behind a mountain mass of black clouds. O, the unutterable darkness of the sky, and the earth below the moon, and the glorious brightness of the moon itself! There was a vivid sparkling streak of light at this end of Rydale water, but the rest was very dark, and Loughrigg Fell and Silver How were white and bright, as if they were covered with hoar frost. The moon retired again, and appeared and disappeared several times before I reached home. Once there was no moonlight to be seen but upon the island-house and the promontory of the island where it stands. "That needs must be a holy place," etc., etc. I had many very exquisite feelings, and when I saw this lowly Building in the waters, among the dark and lofty hills, with that bright, soft light upon it, it made me more than half a poet.'

When she reaches home after this walk she cannot settle down to reading, and tries to write verses; but 'alas!', she says, 'I gave up, and went soon to bed'. She had, indeed, no metrical gift, and those technical difficulties which stimulate the imagination of the true poetic artist, only benumbed hers. She was, as she confessed, 'only half a poet'; yet 'exquisite feelings' she had in plenty, and when she voices them in the simple prose that came natural to her, her language often takes on a music with which she might well have rested content.

Dorothy had not merely grown in sensitiveness to natural

beauty: her extended sympathies now responded to all that was going on about her. There is no sign that at Racedown or Alfoxden the doings of her neighbours concerned her nearly: at Grasmere she threw herself with an intense and loving interest into the life of the whole village. In this she was at one with her brother. In *The Prelude* he has told how, on his return from France,

> the lonely roads
> Were schools to me in which I daily read
> With most delight the passions of mankind,

and how converse with humble men and women helped him to regain his lost faith in human nature. 'Strip my neighbourhood of human beings', he wrote to Sir George Beaumont,[1] 'and I should think it one of the greatest privations that I could undergo.' But Dorothy had a genius, denied to him, for getting into close touch with all who crossed her path. De Quincey justly noticed that on their walks she was the 'one who took upon herself the whole expenses of the flying colloquies exchanged with stragglers on the road'; no wonder, then, that her *Journal* gives a lively impression of the daily life of a Lakeland village, the character and habits of its people, their dress and manner of speech. Here William found much raw material for his poetry; and once at least, in his lines on *The Beggars*, Dorothy's language was so inevitable as to hinder him in his attempt to reshape it in verse. 'After tea', she writes,[2] 'I read to William that account of the little boy belonging to the tall woman, and an unlucky thing it was, for he could not escape from those very words, and so he could not write the poem.' And where her words have not directly inspired a poem, they often supply a valuable commentary upon it. Thus the following two entries have a special interest in their bearing upon the theme of *Michael*:

> 'John Fisher talked much of the alteration of the times, and observed that in a short time there would be only two ranks of people, the very rich and the very poor, "for those who have small estates", says he, "are forced to sell, and all the land goes into one hand".
>
> 'Sent Peggy Ashburner some goose. She sent me some honey, with a thousand thanks. "Alas! the gratitude of men has" etc.

[1] W. W. to Sir G. B., Oct. 17, 1805. [2] Mar. 13, 1802.

She talked about Thomas's having sold his land. "Ay," says she, "I said many a time he 's not come fra London to buy our land, however." Then she told me with what pains and industry they had made up their taxes, interest, etc. etc., how they all got up at 5 o'clock in the morning to spin and Thomas carded, and that they had paid off a hundred pounds of the interest. She said she used to take such pleasure in the cattle and sheep. "O how pleased I used to be when they fetched them down, and when I had been a bit poorly I would gang out upon a hill and look over t'fields and see them, and it used to do me so much good you cannot think." Molly said to me when I came in, "Poor body! she 's very ill, but one does not know how long she may last. Many a fair face may gang before her." '

Thus simply Dorothy entered into the joys and sorrows of her neighbours, and made them her own. The very triviality of some of her entries, at times even their inconsequence, stamps them as a transcript from real life; in her more detailed sketches, such as this picture of a pauper's burial, she reveals clearly enough that vital sympathy which was the true secret of her power:

'went to a funeral at John Dawson's. About 10 men & 4 women. Bread, cheese, and ale. They talked sensibly and cheerfully about common things. The dead person, 56 years of age, buried by the parish. The coffin was neatly lettered and painted black, and covered with a decent cloth. They set the corpse down at the door; and, while we stood within the threshold, the men with their hats off sang with decent and solemn countenances a verse of a funeral psalm. The corpse was then borne down the hill, and they sang till they had passed the Town-End. I was affected to tears while we stood in the house, the coffin lying before me. There were no near kindred, no children. When we got out of the dark house the sun was shining, and the prospect looked as divinely beautiful as I ever saw it. It seemed more sacred than I had ever seen it, and yet more allied to human life. The green fields, neighbours of the churchyard, were as green as possible; and, with the brightness of the sunshine, looked quite gay. I thought she was going to a quiet spot, and I could not help weeping very much. When we came to the bridge, they began to sing again, and stopped during four lines before they entered the churchyard. The priest met us. He did not look as a man ought to do on such an occasion. I had seen him half-drunk the day before in a pot-house. Before we came with the corpse one of the company observed he wondered what sort of cue our Parson would be in! N.B. It was the day after the Fair.'[1]

Reading entries like these we feel that Coleridge was not exaggerating when he said that at Grasmere Dorothy was 'exceedingly beloved, enthusiastically'.

But the *Journal* is most precious when it reveals the life of those with whom she was in closest intimacy. In their first summer at Grasmere, passing beside Thirlmere, a happy company of friends had cut upon a rock, known afterwards as the Rock of Names, their initials—W.W., M.H., D.W., S.T.C., J.W., S.H., and two years later, as a writer pausing in his composition for words that fit his idea may scribble half unconsciously the names which recur most often in his thoughts, so Dorothy wrote on the blotting-paper that interleaved her diary:

S. T. Coleridge.
Dorothy Wordsworth. William Wordsworth.
Mary Hutchinson. Sara Hutchinson.
William. Coleridge. Mary.
Dorothy. Sara.
16th May
1802.
John Wordsworth.

Here was the world of which she was the vital centre. Other friends, who came and went, they had in plenty. William's college friend, Robert Jones, who had walked with him through the Alps, was with them in the September of their first year at Grasmere, and Mr. Marshall, Jane's husband, came from Leeds, bringing news of Jane and stirring Dorothy to a recollection that she had long owed her old friend a letter; the Clarksons,[2] too, would come over from Eusemere, their house at the foot of Ullswater. In the next year they welcomed Sam Ferguson, now home on a visit from America, and some others of the old Halifax circle; the Hutchinson brothers came too, and more than once Mrs. Coleridge and her children. And other names than the Sympsons are noted in the *Journal* as neighbours with

[1] Sept. 3, 1800.

[2] 'Mr Clarkson is the man who took so much pains about the slave trade. . . . Mrs C. is a pleasant woman.' So wrote D. W. to J. M., Sept. 10, 1800. Mrs C. was soon to become her most intimate friend.

whom they exchanged an occasional visit—the Olliffs, the Luffs, the Lloyds. Charles Lloyd, whom they had known at Alfoxden, now lived at Brathay, four miles from Grasmere, and as his sister Priscilla was engaged to Christopher Wordsworth, they felt obliged to be civil; but they had not forgotten his treatment of Coleridge some three years earlier, and they did not relish his incursion into their midst. 'He is perpetually forming new friendships,' wrote Dorothy to Jane, on his arrival, 'quarrelling with the old ones, and upon the whole a dangerous acquaintance'; and later she had no reason to alter her opinion. 'The Lloyds called in a chaise,' she wrote to Mary,[1] 'luckily we did not see them, we are determined to cut them entirely as far as *will* goes; there is one chain about us, Priscilla, but she shall only drag us to Brathay about once a year.' But though, apart from Lloyd, such gentry of the district as they knew were congenial enough, they counted for little in their lives. In the visits of their brother John and of Coleridge, of Sara and Mary Hutchinson, they had all the society they wanted.

Coleridge, as we have seen, had joined them for a month in the spring of 1800, and at the end of June he had returned, bringing his wife and little Hartley to stay till July 23; then he moved on to Greta Hall, Keswick, where the Wordsworths had found a house for him: doubtless he would have settled nearer, at Grasmere or Ambleside, if an empty dwelling had been available. Thus the old intimate life was resumed. Daily intercourse, as at Alfoxden, was not possible, for Dove Cottage and Greta Hall were separated by thirteen miles of mountain road; but if their meetings were not so frequent they were more prolonged, lasting as a rule for several days at a time. Within a week of Coleridge's departure for Keswick he was at the cottage again for three days, and took William back with him till the 1st of August; on the 8th William and Dorothy set off for Keswick, and stayed there a week or ten days. On the 31st Coleridge appeared again at Grasmere; and so, whilst Coleridge was in the North, their life proceeded. When they were parted letters passed almost daily between them, but at any hour Coleridge might burst in upon them, and he was always welcome. Never was there more delightful comrade for lighter or more serious hours. Often they had discovered some new nook,

[1] D. W. to M. H., June 14, 1802.

or rillet in the hills to which their friend must be taken, so that he might share their pleasure in it; additions to the forthcoming *Lyrical Ballads*, or other verse written since his last visit, must be read to him, and the new *Preface*, now in process of composition, had to be discussed. It arose, Coleridge tells us, 'out of conversations so frequent that with few exceptions we could scarcely either of us positively say who first started a particular thought'. And if too seldom he brought with him a fresh poem of his own, his talk, at least, was alive with poetic suggestion. The following entries in the *Journal* are typical:

'Aug. 31 (1800). At 11 o'clock Coleridge came, when I was walking in the still clear moonshine in the garden. He came over Helvellyn. Wm. was gone to bed, and John also. . . . We sate and chatted till half-past three, Wm. in his dressing gown. C. read us a part of *Christabel*. Talked much about the mountains etc etc.

'Sept. 1. We walked in the wood by the lake. W. read *Joanna* and the *Firgrove* to Coleridge. They bathed. The morning was delightful, with something of an autumnal freshness. After dinner Coleridge discovered a rock-seat in the orchard. Cleared away the brambles. Coleridge obliged to go to bed after tea. . . . The evening somewhat frosty and grey, but very pleasant. I broiled Coleridge a mutton chop, which he ate in bed. Wm was gone to bed. I chatted with John and C. till near 12.

'Oct. 4. Coleridge came in while we were at dinner, very wet. We talked till twelve o'clock. He had sate up all the night before, writing essays for the newspaper... Exceedingly delighted with the second part of *Christabel*.

'Oct. 5. Coleridge read *Christabel* a second time; we had increasing pleasure. A delicious morning. Wm. and I were employed all the morning in writing an addition to the *Preface*. Wm. went to bed, very ill after working after dinner. Coleridge and I walked to Ambleside after dark with the letter. Returned to tea at 9 o'clock. Wm still in bed and very ill. Silver How in both lakes.

'Oct. 6. A rainy day. Coleridge intending to go, did not get off. We walked after dinner to Rydale. After tea read *The Pedlar*. Determined not to print *Christabel* with the L.B.'

But the joy which Coleridge brought to both brother and sister was soon to be tempered with the keenest sorrow. On December 20 (1800) is the significant entry: 'Coleridge came. Very ill, rheumatic, feverish. Rain incessantly.' With all his immense vitality, and his capacity for spasmodic bursts of physical energy, Coleridge's health had never been robust. An acute attack of rheumatic fever, from which he suffered in his last year at school, the result of neglecting to change his clothes after he had swum across a river, left him with a constitutional tendency to all those ills which are aggravated by a damp climate; and his youthful imprudence had not taught him the most obvious precautions against them. He could hardly have chosen a worse district in which to settle than the Lake country; and this illness at the close of 1800 was only the prelude to a long series of ailments—pains in the stomach, lumbago, swelling of the joints, gout or rheumatism in every conceivable part of the body. 'Never', said Southey, 'was poor fellow tormented with such pantomimic complaints; his disorders are perpetually shifting, and he is never a week together without some one or other.' But worse than all was his addiction to opium. He had taken the drug in his Nether Stowey days, but without harmful results; but now, reading in a medical journal that laudanum was an infallible remedy for swellings of the knee, he had regular recourse to it, and rapidly became its slave. This disastrous habit destroyed a will already weak by nature, and engendered deceit and suspicion of others, which gradually undermined his relations even with his dearest friends.

Coincident with this wreckage of his physical health came the growing discord of his home life. His marriage, for which Southey and pantisocracy were largely responsible, had been contracted whilst he was still smarting under his rejection by Mary Evans, his early love; and it had, indeed, brought him a brief happiness. To Hartley, his baby child, he was devoted, and at Alfoxden the society of William and Dorothy seemed rather to complete his family circle than to clash with it. But on his return from Germany he realized how empty his home was when they were beyond its reach; and when he rejoined them at Sockburn, and to their love was added that of Mary and Sara Hutchinson, he found the sympathy and complete understanding that he missed at his own hearth. Drawn irresistibly to their society he brought his wife to Keswick; but even if Mrs. Coleridge was ignorant of the depth of his passion for the other Sara, she could not long be blind to the fact that however much she, as his wife, might have proprietary rights over him, he belonged in spirit to Sara and Mary Hutchinson, to William, and to Dorothy. His constant visits to his friends and their almost as frequent appearance at Greta Hall could hardly fail to gall her. Her bearing to the Wordsworths and the Hutchinsons seems always to have been friendly, but she would have been more than human had she given her husband no signs of her resentment; and his nervous and sensitive nature, made doubly sensitive by illness, was constantly exasperated by what he called her 'inveterate habits of puny thwarting and unintermittent *dys*pathy'. In health, but still more in sickness, when he could not escape from it, his home became a place of torment to him; and with growing distress his four friends observed his misery. Dorothy's letter to Mary, written after a visit to Greta Hall in April 1801, reveals clearly enough at once the depth of their sympathy and Coleridge's need for it:

Grasmere. Wednesday, April 27th 1801.

My dearest Mary,

We left poor Coleridge on Monday evening: we had been with him a week and a day. You know that I wrote to Sara on the Friday evening before we went to Keswick giving her the joyful tidings that C. was better, but alas! on Saturday we had a sad account of him. I was determined not to give you unnecessary uneasiness, therefore I did not write. We left home at one o'clock on Sunday, and reached Keswick, at about six. We both trembled, and till we entered the door we hardly durst speak. He was sitting in the parlour, and looked dreadfully pale and weak. He was very, very unwell in the way that Sara can describe to you: ill all over, back, and stomach, and limbs, and so weak that he changed colour whenever he exerted himself at all. Our company did him good, and the next day he was much better. Since that time he has been upon the whole greatly improved in his looks and strength, but he was never quite well for more than an hour together during the whole time we were there, though he began to form plans and schemes for working, but he was unable to do anything. The weather was very fine when we were there, such as one would have thought might have set him up at once, but these frequent attacks make him more weak in recovering from them. I do think he will never be quite well till he has tried a warm climate. If he were to live for six months at Lisbon, in the South of France, or at one of the Western Isles, he would probably be restored to perfect health and might keep himself well with tolerable care. He and Hartley are to come over in the first returned Chaise after tomorrow, Hartley is to stay some time with us and to go to Grasmere school. Dear little fellow! he will be as happy as a young lamb playing upon the green turf in the Church-yard with our bonny little lasses. We hope that C. will grow well in a short time after he comes to us, but there is no security for his continuing so. We should have stayed longer at Keswick but our company not being so new did not do him so much good as at first, and then we are never comfortable there after the first two or three days. This of course we do not mind while we are of any essential service to him, but the same cause which makes us uncomfortable at Keswick prevents him from having all the good from us that he otherwise would have. Mrs C. is in excellent health. She is indeed a bad nurse for C., but she has several great merits. She is much, very much to be pitied, for when one party is ill-matched the other necessarily must be so too. She would have made a very good wife to many another man, but for Coleridge!! Her radical fault is want of sensibility, and what can such a woman be to Coleridge? She is an excellent nurse to her sucking children (I mean to the best of her skill, for she employs her time often foolishly about them). Derwent is a sweet lovely Fatty—she suckles him entirely—he has no other food. She is to be sure a sad fiddle faddler. From about ½ past 10 on Sunday morning till two she did nothing but wash and dress her 2 children and herself, and was just ready for dinner. No doubt she suckled Derwent pretty often during that time.

When I say I would not give you any unnecessary uneasiness about Coleridge, do not fear that I shall not inform you at all times when he is very ill, but as his relapse was only a common one I did not like to give you pain. I will write to you immediately after he arrives, and I hope and trust I shall be able to tell you he is better.

So passed summer and autumn;[1] in November Coleridge went to London to work for *The Morning Post.* All the year he had done little to add to his slender income; his health could hardly be worse; away from Greta Hall, with its atmosphere no less damping to the spirit than to the body, he might well hope it would be better. But his friends could not bear to think of what might befall him when he was beyond the reach of that

[1] Some time during this period William paid his first visit to Scotland, in order to be present at the second marriage of his friend Montagu. Whether Dorothy stayed at the Cottage in his absence, or went on a visit, is unknown.

sympathy on which he was so pathetically dependent; and at no time did Dorothy's heart go out to him with a more delicate, tender affection: 'Coleridge has a sweet day for his ride', she wrote on November 10th, 'Every sight and every sound reminded me of him—dear, dear fellow, of his many walks to us by day and night, of all dear things. I was melancholy and could not talk, but at last eased my heart by weeping—nervous blubbering, says Wm. It is not so. O! how many many reasons have I to be anxious for him.' But Dorothy knew well enough that the brusqueness with which her brother tried to rouse her from her distress of mind was only a cover for the same anxious thoughts as her own; and to the diary, which she wrote for his eyes no less than for herself, she went on confiding in her own tender way her constant thoughts of their absent friend. 'Dec. 12. The birches on the crags beautiful, red brown and glittering. The ashes glittering spears with their upright stems. The hips very beautiful and so good!! and, dear Coleridge! I ate twenty for thee, when I was by myself.'

During this winter many letters came from Coleridge, and they were for the most part gloomy reading, for he chose those moments to write them when he was sick and lonely, and felt most need of their support.

'Dec. 13. The boy brought letters from C. and from Sara. Sara in bad spirits about C.

'Dec. 21. 4 letters, 2 from Coleridge. . . . C.'s were melancholy letters. He had been very ill. We were made very unhappy. Wm. wrote to him.

'Dec. 25. a letter from C. His letter made us uneasy about him. I was glad I was not by myself when I received it.

'Jan. 29. a heart-rending letter from C. We were sad as we could be. Wm wrote to him. We talked about Wm's going to London.

'Feb. 6. Two very affecting letters from C.; resolved to try another climate. I was stopped in my writing and made ill by the letters. W. a bad headache. He made up a bed on the floor, but could not sleep.

'Feb. 8. We broke the seal of C's letter and I had light enough to see that he was not ill. I put it in my pocket, but at the top of White Moss I took it to my bosom, a safer place for it.'

As one reads these touching entries it is hard to keep back feelings of resentment at the way in which Coleridge exploited his friends' devotion; he would have been more worthy of it had he made some effort to bear his own burdens. Accounts of the time he was spending in London and at Stowey, where he went for a month at Christmas, suggest that, though he was often ailing, his health was in no desperate condition. He knew well enough the suffering that he caused them, and that in so writing his 'better mind was fled'. He was, indeed, like the child who shows his love for his mother by running to her whenever he is hurt; despite his intellectual brilliance the affection he inspired had always in it something of the protective and half maternal; and such was his charm that he seldom lacked the sympathy for which he craved. 'God bless you, dear Coleridge. We are sadly grieved for your poor eyes, and the rest of your complaints, but we sorrow not without hope. Oh, for one letter of perfect uncomplainingness!' So Dorothy had written to him in the previous May, when he was still accessible to them; but now that they could not reach him, and the complaints became more piercing and more constant, their sorrow was deeper than their hope. But their love at least never failed.

In the following March Coleridge reappeared in Grasmere. 'His eyes', says Dorothy, 'were a little swollen with the wind. I was much affected by the sight of him, he seemed half-stupified . . . Coleridge went to bed late, and William and I sate up till four o'clock. . . . My spirits were agitated very much.' What they talked of in the early hours of the morning we can only surmise, but it seems likely that in that conversation William broke to his sister the cause of their friend's stupefaction, and now for the first time she learnt of his slavery to opium. Coleridge returned to Keswick, whither they followed him a few days later; a month afterwards he came to Grasmere and 'repeated the verses he wrote to Sara. I was affected with them,' says Dorothy, 'and was on the whole, not being well, in miserable spirits. The sunshine, the green fields, and the fair sky made me sadder; even the little happy, sporting lambs seemed but sorrowful to me. . . . I went to bed after dinner, could not sleep.' Can we wonder at her distress? For these 'verses to Sara' were the first version of the 'Ode to Dejection', pathetic enough as Coleridge published it some six months later, but in its first, more personal, form truly heartbreaking as a revelation of his weakness and his mental suffering. He reproaches himself for the pain which his outpourings of misery have brought upon Sara, and all those whom he most dearly loves:

> For O! was this an absent friend's employ
> To send from far both pain and sorrow thither
> Where still his blessings should have called down joy?

yet, at the same time, he contrasts his fate with theirs in a manner that can only intensify their pain:

> My own peculiar lot, my household life
> It is and will remain, indifference or strife.
> While *ye* are *well* and *happy*, 'twould but wrong you
> If I should fondly yearn to be among you—
> Wherefore, O wherefore! should I wish to be
> A wither'd branch upon a blossoming tree?[1]

So Coleridge has written in his solitary dejection: but in the company of William and Dorothy he could still forget his troubles, and they had many happy meetings during the summer. At Keswick, also, for a time, things went better with him. In July he wrote to Estlin 'I am at present in better health, though by no means strong and well, and at home all is peace and love'. He even went so far as to press William and Dorothy to come as lodgers to Greta Hall—perhaps to that part of the house later occupied by Southey. But this Dorothy wisely declined. A letter she had written to Mrs. Coleridge, though Mrs. Coleridge affected to ignore it, seems to have been in part responsible for the improvement, but she was not hopeful as to the future. 'Mrs C.', she writes to Mary, 'is a most extraordinary character, she is the lightest, weakest, silliest woman! She sent some clean clothes on Thursday to meet C. (the first time she ever did such a thing in her life) from which I guess that she is determined to be attentive to him. She wrote a note, saying not a word about my letter, and all in her very lightest style. Is not it a hopeless case? So insensible and irritable, she can never come to good, and poor C!'

The tender affection with which Dorothy writes of Coleridge has led some readers to conclude that he held the first place in her heart, and that a frustrated passion for him was the secret tragedy of her life. Such a view appeals alike to the

[1] From the first (unpublished) version of 'To Dejection'.

sentimentalist and the psycho-analyst, but to hold it is to misread her. That Dorothy loved Coleridge with a depth of devotion of which few human beings are capable, and that his later deterioration under the influence of opium was the most harrowing sorrow of her life, cannot be questioned; but if her life had its tragedy, it was not that she loved Coleridge, but rather that her passion for her brother was so intense as to preclude her from feeling for any man an emotion which would have satisfied the physical as well as the spiritual side of her nature. Coleridge himself must have realized this absorption in William: frank and open as she was, she could not have concealed from him the character of her feeling for either of them.

Every page of the *Journal* reflects the intensity with which she lived in and for her brother: whether present or absent he is the pivot of her life. After saying good-bye to him one winter's morning when he was off on a short visit to Mary she takes an anxious look at the moutains to make sure if he will 'have a safe passage over Kirkstone', and at night, to ease her loneliness, she sleeps in William's bed. 'But I slept badly,' she writes, 'for my thoughts were full of William.'[1] Two days later is the entry: 'A fine morning, but I had persuaded myself not to expect Wm., I believe because I was afraid of being disappointed . . . he came in just at tea time . . . he had had a difficult journey over Kirkstone . . . his mouth and breath were very cold when he kissed me. We spent a sweet evening.' And this is her tale of another of his short absences:[2] 'since he left me at half-past 11, (it is now 2) I have been putting the drawers into order, laid by his clothes which we had thrown here and there and everywhere, filed two months' newspapers and got my dinner, 2 boiled eggs and 2 apple tarts. I have set Molly on to clean the garden a little, and I myself have helped. I transplanted some snowdrops—the Bees are busy. Wm. has a nice bright day. It was hard frost in the night. The Robins are singing sweetly. Now for my walk. I *will* be busy. I *will* look well, and be well when he comes back to me. O, the Darling! Here is one of his bitten apples. I can hardly find in my heart to throw it into the fire. I must wash myself, then off! (*Later*) I walked round the two Lakes, crossed the stepping stones at Rydale foot. Sate down where we always sit. I was full of thoughts about my

[1] Feb. 14, 1802. [2] Mar. 4, 1802.

darling. Blessings on him. . . . I worked and read the L.B., enchanted with the *Idiot Boy*. Wrote to Wm. then went to bed.' The next day she writes to him again, and the day after that 'in came William, I did not expect him till to-morrow. How glad I was. After we had talked about an hour, I gave him his dinner, a beefsteak. We sate talking, and happy . . . He brought two new stanzas of *Ruth*.' Another day when he is away she goes out into the lane to collect a few mosses to make the chimney gay against 'my darling's return'. And here is the close of a typical day when William was at home:[1]

> 'I went and sate with W. and walked backward and forwards in the orchard till dinner time. He read me his poem. After dinner we made a pillow of my shoulder. I read to him, and my Beloved slept . . . A sweet evening, as it had been a sweet day, a grey evening, and I walked quietly along the side of Rydale lake with quiet thoughts—the hills and the lake were still—the owls had not begun to hoot, and the little birds had given over singing. I looked before me and I saw a red light upon Silver How as if coming from out of the vale below,
>
> There was a light of most strange birth,
> A light that came out of the earth,
> And spread along the dark hill-side.
>
> Thus I was going on when I saw the shape of my Beloved in the road at a little distance. We turned back to see the light but it was fading—almost gone. The owls hooted when we sate on the wall at the foot of White Moss; the sky broke more and more, and we saw the moon now and then. John Green passed us with his cart; we sate on. When we came in sight of our own dear Grasmere, the vale looked fair and quiet in the moonshine, the Church was there and all the cottages. There were huge slow-travelling clouds in the sky, that threw large masses of shade upon some of the mountains. We walked backward and forwards, till I was tired. William kindled and began to write the poem. We carried cloaks into the orchard, and sate a while there. I left him, and he nearly finished the poem. I was tired to death, and went to bed before him. He came down to me, and read the poem to me in bed.'

And in the following passage[2] it is hard to say whether one is more moved by the artistic sensibility or the tenderness of feeling: 'He is now reading Ben Jonson. It is about 10 o'clock,

[1] Mar. 17, 1802. [2] Mar. 23, 1802.

a quiet night. The fire flutters, and the watch ticks. I hear nothing else save the breathing of my Beloved, and he now and then pushes his book forward, and turns over a leaf.'

Absorbed as she was in her love for William she felt no detail of their life together too trivial or too intimate for record. On one day she makes the entry[1] 'William's head was bad after Mr Simpson was gone, I petted him on the carpet'; on another,[2] she sets down this vivid picture of the poet at work, oblivious of all but his muse:

> 'William had slept badly; he got up at nine o'clock, but before he rose he had finished *The Beggar Boys* and while we were at breakfast, that is (for I had breakfasted) he, with his basin of broth beside him untouched, and a little plate of bread and butter, he wrote the Poem to a Butterfly. He ate not a morsel, nor put on his stockings, but sate with his shirt neck unbuttoned, and his waistcoat open while he did it. The thought first came upon him as we were talking about the pleasure we both always feel at the sight of a butterfly. I told him that I used to chase them a little, but that I was afraid of brushing the dust off their wings, and did not catch them. He told me how they used to kill all the white ones when he went to school because they were Frenchmen. I wrote it down and the other poems, and I read them all over to him.'

As the life he shared with Dorothy was the inspiration of many poems, so Dorothy was their first critic and helped him to give them their final form. Thus on April 18, 1802, she enters in her Journal, 'William met me at Rydale with the conclusion of the poem of the Robin. I read it to him in bed. We left out some lines'; on the 28th, 'when we came in we corrected the Chaucers'; on June 17, 'when I came home I found William at work attempting to alter a stanza in the poem on our going for Mary, which I convinced him did not need altering'. And when a volume was being prepared for press, these eager discussions were carried on to the latest possible moment. Years afterwards Mrs. Nicholson, the old Ambleside postmistress, loved to tell how brother and sister would appear at her house late at night, in order to make some alteration in a manuscript that had already been posted.

> ' "At that time," said Mrs. N., "the mail used to pass through at one in the morning, so my husband & me used to go early to

[1] Jan. 31, 1802. [2] Mar. 14, 1802.

bed; but when Mr & Miss W. came, let it be as late as it would, my husband would get up & let them in & give them their letter out of the box, & then they would sit up in our parlour or in the kitchen, discussing over it & reading & changing till they had made it quite to their minds, & then they would seal up the packet again, & knock at our bed-room door, & say, "Now, Mr Nicholson, please will you bolt the door after us? Here is our letter for the post. We'll not trouble you any more this night." And, oh, they were always so friendly to us & so loving to one another." '[1]

Dorothy's deepest joy sprang, perhaps, from her knowledge of the part she played in her brother's poetic life, and she accepted its fruits with an unquestioning delight. Though she might point out, here and there, a slight flaw in detail, and suggest how to amend it, that detachment with which she had criticized *The Evening Walk* was now impossible to her. If it was true, as he said, that she had given him eyes, it was no less true that she accepted with an eager assent his poetic rendering of the vision; and she was as sensitive as he to any undervaluation or misreading of it. When William wrote to admonish Sara for her failure to appreciate his *Leechgatherer*, Dorothy added the significant postscript:

Dear Sara,

When you happen to be displeased with what you suppose to be the tendency or moral of any poem which Wm writes, ask yourself whether you have hit upon the real tendency and true moral, and above all never think that he writes for no reason but merely because a thing happened—and when you feel any poem to be tedious, ask yourself in what spirit it was written—whether merely to tell the tale and be through with it, or to illustrate a particular character or truth.

In so far as this reproof applies to Sara's strictures on *Resolution and Independence* good critics would probably side with Dorothy: but she would have been as ready to take up the cudgels for verses more justly assailable. It is idle to suggest that if she had not loved so blindly, but had tempered her enthusiasm with judgement, she would have done him a greater service. She could only be herself. After all he did not lack critics, and despite the stubborn front with which he faced them, he was

[1] From Mrs. Davy's manuscript 'Memories of W. W.', 1850, quoted Harper, p. 315–16.

beset with doubts and fears. The anguish with which he revised and corrected his verses is proof enough how hard he found it to satisfy himself. 'We read the Pedlar', writes Dorothy, 'thinking it done, but lo! though Wm could find fault with no one part of it, it was uninteresting and must be altered. Poor Wm!' To have continually at his side one who accepted his achievement in the light of his intention gave him the strength of which he often stood in need. And she had at least the rich reward of knowing that her passionate devotion was returned. No tribute more beautiful was ever paid by poet-lover to the source of his inspiration than is uttered in those lines written in the early days at Grasmere:

> Mine eyes did ne'er
> Fix on a lovely object, nor my mind
> Take pleasure in the midst of happy thoughts,
> But either she, whom now I have, who now
> Divides with me this loved abode, was there,
> Or not far off. Where'er my footsteps turned,
> Her voice was like a hidden Bird that sang;
> The thought of her was like a flash of light
> Or an unseen companionship, a breath
> Or fragrance independent of the wind.
> In all my goings, in the new and old
> Of all my meditations, and in this
> Favourite of all, in this the most of all.[1]

But the days were numbered in which Dorothy would be sole mistress of Dove Cottage. All through February and March 1802, letters were passing between William and Annette. Their import can only be conjectured, but it is hardly fanciful to suppose that neither William nor Mary could contemplate their union with happiness until Annette had expressed her acquiescence in it. On March 20 William and Dorothy have a little talk about going abroad, on the 21st 'a sweet and tender conversation', and on the 22nd a letter comes 'from poor Annette. We resolved to see Annette and that William should go to Mary'.

At a time of such tense emotional stress Dorothy could not be left alone in the cottage; so on the 24th they started together for Keswick, and after a week spent there with Coleridge went

[1] 'On Nature's invitation do I come', *Oxf. W.*, p. 622.

on to Eusemere, where Dorothy could stay with the Clarksons till William returned from his visit to Mary. On April 7, his birthday, William set off for Middleham where Mary was staying, and Dorothy walked six miles with him on his way; on the 12th Dorothy received a joint letter from the two lovers, telling her, doubtless, of their decision to be married in the autumn. Her conflict of emotions can be felt in the manner in which she records her receipt of the letter. Before she had time to read it an inquisitive neighbour questioned her on its contents 'like a catechiser'. 'Every question', she says, 'was like the snapping of a little thread about my heart. I was so full of thought of my half-read letter and other things. I was glad when he left me. Then I had time to look at the moon while I was thinking over my own thoughts. The moon travelled through the clouds, tinging them yellow as she passed along, with two stars near her, one larger than the other. These stars grew and diminished as they passed from, or went into, the clouds. At this time William, as I found the next day, was riding by himself between Middleham and Barnard Castle, having parted from Mary.'

Beneath that last sentence is a depth of meaning that might easily escape the careless reader: for it was when William was riding between Middleham and Barnard Castle that he wrote for her his poem on the Glow-worm, recalling an incident in their life together at Racedown.[1] After 'having parted from Mary' there would have been no wonder if Dorothy had been forgotten, yet it was just then that his heart had gone out to her with the tenderest passion. No livelier proof could have been given her of his unalterable love, and the thought brought her an ecstasy of joy.

The next day, on her return from a quiet evening walk by the lakeside, 'William was come. The surprise shot through me'; and after another day at Eusemere they turned their steps homewards. It was an unforgettable walk. One incident, at least, in it, which William records in verse,[2] is more lovely in Dorothy's unstudied prose.

'When we were in the woods beyond Gowbarrow Park we saw a few daffodils close to the water-side. We fancied that the lake

[1] *V. Journal*, Apr. 20.

[2] 'I wandered lonely as a cloud', *Oxf. W.*, p. 187.

had floated the seeds ashore, and that the little colony had so sprung up. But as we went along there were more and yet more; and at last, under the boughs of the trees, we saw that there was a long belt of them along the shore, about the breadth of a country turnpike road. I never saw daffodils so beautiful. They grew among the mossy stones about and about them; some rested their heads upon these stones as on a pillow for weariness; and the rest tossed and reeled and danced, and seemed as if they verily laughed with the wind, that blew upon them over the lake: they looked so gay, ever glancing, ever changing. This wind blew directly over the lake to them. There was here and there a little knot, and a few stragglers a few yards higher up, but they were so few as not to disturb the simplicity, unity and life of that one busy highway.'

The rest of their walk is fully described in the *Journal*; even more beautiful in its expression of tender feeling is the letter which Dorothy wrote to Mary on their arrival at Grasmere.

> Friday evening—¼ past 11 by the watch, but you know it is a little wrong headed—it is only ¼ past 10. April 16th (1802)

My dearest Mary

We are sitting by our own fireside and we have been here since the first beginnings of twilight. We are both well—that is comfort for you before I begin to tell you about our journey—and indeed I can say nothing on that subject till I have spoken about yourself. My dear, dear Mary! I am deeply concerned to hear that you are so thin. Till I had seen William I had no idea how thin you were. I cannot doubt but that you *will endeavour* to take [care] of yourself, yet I am very fearful that your ardour of mind may lead you to do imprudent things. For God's sake do not measure your exertions by your own self supposed ability, but put restrictions upon yourself, and do not overpass them on any account. Take no more exercise than would be proper for the regaining of your strength supposing that you were nearly as *weak* as you are *thin*—above all, my dearest Mary, seek quiet or rather amusing thoughts. Study the flowers, the birds and all the common things that are about you. O Mary, my dear Sister! be quiet and happy. Take care of yourself,—keep yourself employed without fatigue, and do not make loving us your business, but let your love of us make up the spirit of all the business you have. We are very anxious to know how you got home after you had parted with William, since he told me that you had owned that you felt

black and green, the birches
here & there greenish bu
there is yet more of pur
to be seen on the Twigs.
We got over into a field to
avoid some cows – people
working, a few primroses
by the roadside, woodsorr
flowers, the anemone, scentless violets, strawb
starry yellow flower which
C calls pile wort. When we
were in the woods beyond
Gowbarrow park we saw a
few daffodils close to the wa
side, we fancied that th
lake had floated the seeds
ashore & that the
little colony had so sprung
up – But as we went along
there were more & yet mo

FROM DOROTHY WOR

⟨&⟩ at last under the boughs
⟨of⟩ the trees we saw that there
was a long belt of them ~~along~~
~~[illegible]~~ along the
shore about the breadth
⟨of⟩ a country turnpike road.
⟨I⟩ never saw daffodils so
⟨be⟩autiful they grew among
the mossy stones about & about
⟨the⟩m, some rested their heads
⟨u⟩pon these stones as on a
⟨p⟩illow for weariness & the
⟨r⟩est tossed & reeled & danced
⟨&⟩ seemed as if they verily
⟨la⟩ughed with ~~the wind~~ ~~[illegible]~~ ~~that blew upon them~~
⟨lo⟩oked so gay ever glancing
⟨Th⟩is wind blew directly over the lake to them
⟨ev⟩er changing. There was
⟨h⟩ere & there a little knot
⟨an⟩d a few stragglers a few
⟨ya⟩rds higher up but they
⟨w⟩ere so few as not to disturb

JOURNAL, 15 APRIL 1802

weak, and have been very uneasy about you. We shall surely have a letter on Monday.

Now for Grasmere, Eusemere, and William and myself. I was walking out alone when he arrived—I had gone by the lake side towards Martindale. Jane met me and told me he was come,—I believe I screamed, when she said so, and ran on. I then recollected myself, and told her to run on before and tell him that I was coming, in order that he might meet me; but she was stupid, and so I met him in the parlour—he looked delightfully, but it was a sort of flushing in his face, for he was fatigued with his long ride—he got tea and very soon went to bed.

We left Eusemere yesterday afternoon at about ½ past 2—Mrs Clarkson, being very well, set off with us intending to go to Watermillock, but she got no further than into the lane at the foot of Dunmallet, for she durst not face the furious wind that blew against us—Indeed we could hardly stand it—If we had been going *from* home we certainly should have turned back, but we pushed on boldly—It sometimes almost took our breath away, we rested wherever we found a shelter, and reached Stybarrow Crag about sunset. A heavy rain came on, and when we passed Luff's house we were very wet; we turned in however to see the lower rooms, and as there was no hope that the storm would abate we pushed forward. I had Joanna's beautiful shawl on over my Spenser—Alas the *Gloss* is gone from it! but indeed I do not see that it is the worse. When we reached the Inn we were very wet. The Landlady looked sour enough upon us—I believe because she could not help it, for she was very civil; but there was a young woman, I suppose a visitor, very smart in a Bonnet with an artificial flower, who was kindness itself. She did more for me than Mrs Coleridge would do for her own Sister under the like circumstances. She made a smart Lady of me at once, and I came down to William, who was sitting by a bright fire that had sprung up as if by magic in my absence,—he had got dry clothes and was comfortable. We wished for you. We had a good supper: ham, veal cutlets, preserved plums, ale, rum and water, dry beds and decent breakfast. We paid 7/ —one shilling too much. The morning was delightful—you have been at that Inn, Mary! What a beautiful prospect there is from the chamber windows! I was exceedingly impressed by it when I opened my curtains in the morning, and saw the mountains, lake and fields all chearful and quiet, and the sun shining upon them so bright that one would almost wonder how it could be after such a night.

We set forward at about ½ past 10. William had shaved himself,—he looked bonny and well. You ought to have been with us, we saw so many sweet things. Every foot of the road was new to me, and all that we saw was interesting, yet for ever changing. We sauntered and rested, loved all that we saw, each other, and thee, our dear Mary—sauntered and rested, lounged and were lazy. I left William sitting upon the Bridge near the foot of Brothers water and walked up the Lake. When I returned I found him writing the poem which I send you[1]—We dined at the foot of Kirkstone upon some pies which Ellen made us. We came to Ambleside before sunset; the vale looked green and very beautiful. Poor Luff is in the Gout. We called, but we did not see them for the Boddingtons were there. We sauntered on towards home, and while we were sitting on the wall just beyond Rydale Jane Ashburner overtook us with an empty cart. We got in and rode nicely. She looked fresh and pretty, and amused us with an account of Mr Olliff's sale—most things sold beyond their worth, so we have nothing to regret in not having been here. The day was going away when we saw Grasmere. It looked, as it always does at that time of night, peaceful and homelike. We found all well except Aggy Ashburner who has lamed herself, and is at home. Jane was driving John Green's cart. She is there instead of her sister. Molly is well; she looked clean and handsome, and the house is a perfect model of neatness; there is nothing like it anywhere—I went into the garden and I think things here have come on nicely, but there was not much daylight to see by, and the moon had not reached it. William is now writing to Coleridge. We found a letter from him—he says he has been ailing for two or 3 days. This is sad news—poor fellow! I fear he has his own torments. He says if we wish to see him he will walk over next week, so perhaps he will be here before the week is over. Dear Mary, we are glad to be at home. No fireside is like this. Be chearful in the thought of coming to it. I long for a letter. Best love to Miss Weir—also to Joanna, and a thousand thanks for the shawl.

Farewell—my dear Mary—write often—I wish you were at Gallow Hill—I heard from Sara last Saturday—Farewell again dear Mary—

The next three months passed in the same close companionship. Their happiness was not unclouded. Coleridge's deep spiritual dejection, which he had revealed to them on his first visit after they returned, preyed upon them even more grievously

[1] 'The cock is crowing', *Oxf. W.*, p. 190.

than his bodily ailments, so that they often passed sleepless nights thinking of their friend. And Dorothy suffered more acutely than ever from fears for her brother's health. Entries such as 'Wm. nervous and jaded in the extreme', 'I was oppressed and sick at heart, for he wearied himself to death', 'He will be tired out, my heart fails me', reveal the constant anxiety in which she lived. No wonder that she was often ill herself, though, as she wrote to Mary, 'it is almost a pleasure to be ill, he is so good and loving to me': but how infinitely worth while she felt it all to be! The following entry[1] may raise a smile at its naive simplicity, yet it is eloquent of her triumphant heart: 'My tooth broke to-day. They will soon be gone. Let that pass. I shall be beloved. I want no more.' And the troubles of her daily life, with her own searchings of spirit, are but the background that throw into stronger relief those calm moments of spiritual attainment in which her life seemed to have reached its goal: 'We went to John's Grove, sate awhile at first;[2] afterwards William lay and I lay under the fence—he with his eyes shut listening to the waterfalls and the birds. There was no *one* waterfall above another—it was a sound of waters in the air—the voice of the air. W. heard me breathing, and rustling now and then, but we both lay still, and unseen by one another. He thought that it would be as sweet thus to lie so in the grave, to hear the peaceful sounds of the earth, and just to know that our dear friends were near.'[3]

During all this summer Dorothy was preparing for the reception into their home of her future sister. The garden was tended with an extra care that it might be the more lovely when Mary came; many affecting letters were received from her and duly answered, and Mary was not far from her thoughts even when she was barely conscious of it. Thus she had always found one of her chief delights in the varied bird-life that went on about her, hardly a page of her *Journal* is without some reference to it. In one place she notes 'a pair of stone-chats, with their restless voices as they skimmed along the water, following each other, their shadows under them'; in another 'the bullfinches in their particoloured raiment, poising themselves like wire-dancers on the twigs and shaking off the blossoms', at

[1] May 31, 1802. [2] Apr. 29, 1802.
[3] Cf. *Ode. Intimations of Immortality*, ll. 121–4, *Oxf. W.*, p. 589.

another she notes 'the owl with his human shout', and 'the raven with his hoarse voice echoed back by the mountains in a musical bell-like tone'. It is hardly fanciful to connect with her thoughts of William and Mary, who were soon to mate together, this exquisite bird idyll, which runs like a streak of silver through the journal of the period. June 16, 'the swallows come to the sitting room window as if wishing to build, but I am afraid they will not have courage for it; but I believe they will build in my room window. They twitter, and make a bustle and a little cheerful song, hanging against the panes of glass with their soft white bellies close to the glass and their forked fish-like tails. They swim round and round, and again they come.' Three days later we read: 'The swallows were very busy under my window this morning', and on June 25

> 'I went, just before tea, into the garden. I looked up at my swallow's nest, and it was gone. It had fallen down. Poor little creatures, they could not themselves be more distressed than I was. I went upstairs to look at the ruins. They lay in a large heap upon the window-ledge; these swallows had been ten days employed in building this nest, and it seemed to be almost finished. I had watched them early in the morning, and in the day many and many a time, and in the evenings when it was almost dark. I had seen them sitting together side by side in their unfinished nest, both morning and night. When they first came about the window they used to hang against the panes, with their white bellies and their forked tails, looking like fish; but then they fluttered and sang their own little twittering song. As soon as the nest was broad enough, a sort of ledge for them, they sate both mornings and evenings, but they did not pass the night there. I watched them one morning for more than an hour. Every now and then there was a feeling motion in their wings, a sort of tremulousness, and they sang a low song to one another.'

A page of the *Journal* is here torn out; somewhere on it Dorothy must have told how the birds made good their disaster; for on June 29 is the entry: 'It is now eight o'clock. I will go and see if my swallows are in their nest. Yes! there they are, side by side, both looking into the garden. I have been out on purpose to see their faces. I knew by looking at the window that they were there.'

Ten days later comes the time when Dorothy and William

must start on the journey from which they are to return with Mary.

'In the afternoon after we had talked a little, W. fell asleep. I read the *Winter's Tale*, then I went to bed, but did not sleep. The swallows stole in and out of their nest, and sate there, *whiles*[1] quite still, *whiles* they sung low for two minutes or more at a time, just like a muffled robin. . . . (*In the evening*) We walked first to the top of the hill to see Rydale. It was dark and dull, but our own vale was very solemn. . . . We walked backwards and forwards on the White Moss path; there was a sky-like white brightness on the lake. Glowworms out, but not so numerous as last night. O, beautiful place! Dear Mary, William. The hour is come. *Friday morning*—so I must give over. William is eating his broth —I must prepare to go. The swallows, I must leave them, the well, the garden, the roses, all. Dear creatures! they sang last night after I was in bed; seemed to be singing to one another just before they settled to rest for the night. Well, I must go. Farewell.'

[1] *Whiles* is a Cumberland dialect word, but it is also Spenserian; and we know that D. and W. were reading Spenser much at this time.

VIII
CALAIS. WILLIAM'S MARRIAGE. RETURN TO GRASMERE AND BIRTH OF JOHNNY

1802–1803 (*aet.* $30\frac{1}{2}$–$31\frac{1}{2}$)

WILLIAM's forthcoming marriage naturally raised the question of Dorothy's future maintenance. Since childhood she had relied for money upon casual gifts from her brothers and other relatives and friends, but dependence, even on those she loved, had always irked her. It now occurred to Richard, as the business head of the family, that some effort should be made to give her a definite allowance, and he wrote to ask her wishes in the matter. Her reply reveals the modesty of her financial ambition no less than her practical good sense.

(June 10th 1802)

'As you express a desire to know what are my wishes or expectations respecting a settlement upon me, I will explain to you frankly how I feel, though relying as I do, and have ever had reason to rely, upon the affection of my Brothers and their regard for my happiness, I do not doubt that, according to their power, they would meet the full extent of my wishes, without my making them known myself.

'I shall continue to live with my Brother William, but he having nothing to spare, nor being likely to have, at least for many years, I am obliged (I need not say how much he regrets the necessity) to set him aside, and I will consider myself as boarding through my whole life with an indifferent person. Sixty pounds a year is the sum which would entirely gratify all my desires. With sixty pounds a year I should not fear any accidents or changes which might befal me. I cannot look forward to the time when, with my habits of frugality, I could not live comfortably on that sum. (Observe I am speaking now of a provision or settlement for life, and it would be absurd at my age (30 years) to talk of anything else.) At present with 60 pounds per ann. I should have something to spare to exercise my better feelings in relieving the necessities of others, I might buy a few books, take a journey now and then—all which things, though they do not come under the article of absolute necessaries, you will easily perceive that it is highly desirable that a person of my age and with my education should occasionally have in her power. As to the *mode* of doing this for me I will say no more than that it seems to be absolutely necessary, to give it any effect, that it should, as much as possible, be independent of accidents of death or any other sort that may befal you or any of my Brothers, its principal object being to make me tranquil in my mind with respect to my future life. Having dealt thus openly with you, my dear Brother, I must add that I should be very loth to be oppressive to you, or any of my Brothers, or to draw upon you for more than you could spare without straitening yourselves. I am sure that John will meet your utmost wishes in the business, and Christopher will do all that he can afford. But when he marries he will be in a different situation from what he is in now, and though he may, and probably will, be as rich or richer even as a married man, yet this is uncertain; therefore he may not be able to make a permanent and unconditional engagement. I received 10£ from him this year before last, and 20£ last year, and he promised me the same sum annually as long as he should continue a Fellow of Trinity.'

Only a week after writing this letter she heard that at last the difficulty was solved. Lord Lonsdale had died on May 24, and on June 18 news reached them that his heir had resolved to pay all just debts upon the Lowther estates;[1] henceforward Dorothy would be her own mistress, and if not rich, at least would have a competence equal to her frugal desires. She did not receive her father's legacy at once. Not only has the law its delays, but Richard was fitted for his profession by a nature more than commonly dilatory; it was fully three years before the Wordsworth estate was finally parcelled out, and even then the deeds were so carelessly drawn up that on Richard's death in 1816 Dorothy was in serious danger of losing her inheritance. But from this time on she could ask with an easy conscience for whatever money she needed, and when the £1800 which proved to be her share had been invested, she had an income which must well have passed her modest expectations.

On Friday, July 9, she set out with William for Gallow Hill. Their obvious route was through Kendal; but travel to them was

[1] It has generally been supposed that William's marriage was consequent on this increase of his income. But dates prove that before he had any expectations of this he had fixed his marriage for the autumn. His visit to Mary (recounted in the last chapter, p. 137) took place early in April; Lord Lonsdale died on May 24; on May 29 W. had already 'finished his poem on going for Mary'. News of the new Lord Lonsdale's resolve to pay the family debts was only received on June 18.

not merely a means of getting from one place to another, it was a joyous adventure; and even though they were going to Mary they were not over-eager to reach their destination. Besides, so fateful a journey as this could not be taken without another sight of Coleridge; so they bent their steps towards Keswick, and passed the week-end there; and on the Monday Coleridge went with them for six or seven miles on the road to Eusemere, where they had arranged to pass the next two nights. 'We had', says Dorothy, 'a melancholy parting, after having sate together in silence by the road-side.'[1] The thought of their own happy errand could not fail to throw into dark relief the troubled home to which their friend was returning. But their spirits soon revived: though they had still some ten miles in front of them, they turned aside to explore a new and delightful piece of country, and when they reached the river at the foot of Ullswater paused awhile to watch 'the swallows flying about and under the bridge'.[1] They reached the Clarksons' at eight o'clock 'having lingered and loitered and sate down together that we might be alone'.[1] Two days later they walked to Emont Bridge and took the coach to Leeming Lane, a distance of some sixty miles. 'We had', says Dorothy, 'a chearful ride, though cold, till we got to Stainmoor, and then a heavy shower came on, but we buttoned ourselves up both together in the Guard's coat, and we liked the hills and the rain the better, for bringing us so close to one another. I never rode more snugly. At Greta Bridge the sun shone chearfully, and a glorious ride we had over Gaterly Moor. Every building was bathed in golden light. The trees were more bright than earthly trees, and we saw round us miles beyond miles. We reached Leeming Lane at about nine o'clock: supped comfortably, and enjoyed our fire.'[2]

The next morning they were up before seven and off in a post-chaise to Thirsk, where the hostess of the inn set a good breakfast before them; but when she learnt that they intended to walk on, her opinion of them fell rapidly and she 'threw out some saucy words in their hearing'.[3] And Dorothy herself wished for once that they were carriage folk; the day was intensely hot, and the tramp over Hambledon Hills left her footsore and exhausted, so that when they reached the ruins of Rievaulx

[1] *Grasmere Journal*, July 12, 1802.
[2] Ib. July 14.
[3] Ib. July 15.

Abbey she longed to rest till evening in their solemn quiet; but William was anxious to press on to the comfortable inn at Helmsley. On the Friday morning they passed through Kirby and Pickering, and met Mary and Sara seven miles from Gallow Hill, which they reached about seven o'clock. They had spent just a week upon their journey.

At Gallow Hill they rested till Monday, and Dorothy took the opportunity to replenish her wardrobe with some of Sara's gowns: it was not the only time she profited by being of the same diminutive size as her friend. By Thursday they were in London, and then, 'after various troubles and disasters',[1] of which Dorothy gives no details, they started for Calais. The crossing of Westminster Bridge at dawn was the memorable event in this last stage of their journey. 'The city,' says Dorothy, 'St. Paul's, with the river and a multitude of little boats, made a most beautiful sight. The houses were not overhung by their cloud of smoke, and they were spread out endlessly, yet the sun shone so brightly, with such a fierce light, that there was even something like the purity of one of nature's own grand spectacles.'[1] How the spectacle moved William no lover of English poetry can forget.

At Calais Annette and Caroline were awaiting them, and they settled down in lodgings for four weeks. The weather was very hot, but almost every evening they walked by the seashore, alone, or with Annette and Caroline. Dorothy was deeply stirred by the beauty of these summer evenings,

> 'seeing far off in the west the coast of England like a cloud crested with Dover Castle, which was but like the summit of the cloud—the evening star and the glory of the sky. The reflections in the water were more beautiful than the sky itself, purple waves brighter than precious stones, for ever melting away upon the sands. The fort, a wooden building, at the entrance of the harbour at Calais, when the evening twilight was coming on, and we could not see anything of the building but its shape, which was far more distinct than in perfect daylight, seemed to be reared upon pillars of ebony, between which pillars the sea was seen in the most beautiful colours that can be conceived. Nothing in romance was ever half so beautiful. Now came in view, as the evening star sunk down, and the colours of the west faded away, the two lights of England, lighted up by Englishmen in our country to warn

[1] Ib. July 29.

vessels off rocks or sands. These we used to see from the pier, when we could see no other distant objects but the clouds, the sky, and the sea itself—All was dark behind. The town of Calais seemed deserted of the light of heaven, but there was always light, and life, and joy upon the sea. One night, though, I shall never forget—the day had been very hot, and William and I walked alone together upon the pier. The sea was gloomy, for there was a blackness over all the sky, except when it was overspread with lightning, which often revealed to us a distant vessel. Near us, the waves roared and broke against the pier, and they were interfused with greenish fiery light. The more distant sea always black and gloomy. It was also beautiful, on the calm hot night, to see the little boats row out of harbour with wings of fire, and the sail boats with the fiery track which they cut as they went along, and which closed up after them with a hundred thousand sparkles, balls, shooting and streams of glow-worm light. Caroline was delighted.' [1]

'Caroline was delighted.' This is all Dorothy records of William's child; and of Annette there is nothing. But they had not come to Calais merely to observe the effects of light upon the water; lovely as this passage is, we would rather that she had set down in her *Journal* something of the impression which Annette had made upon her. Her silence is not reassuring. Did she see nothing of the charm which, ten years before, had proved so irresistible to William? Did she appreciate, as fully as she ought, the courage with which Annette had rebuilt her ruined life, the splendid daring with which she had thrown herself into the Royalist cause? The two women belonged, indeed, to wholly different worlds; and Dorothy, with her imperfect knowledge of spoken French, must have found it difficult to get into close touch with her. But however slight their intercourse, we may be sure that Dorothy did not regret the journey. To make it had shown, at least, some moral courage on William's part, to desire it a fine generosity on the part of Annette; and whilst Annette and Caroline, belonging as they did to William's past life, could not but be dear to her, we know that she kindled in them a more than passing affection. After four weeks at Calais, they crossed again to Dover, and sitting upon the cliffs 'looked upon France with many a melancholy and tender thought'. On the 30th of August they were in London.

[1] *Grasmere Journal*, Aug. 1802.

For the next three weeks they were the guests of William's friend Montagu, but two days were given to a visit to uncle Cookson at Windsor. Dorothy had not seen him since the time, eight years before, when William was in disgrace and she had slipped off to Halifax without venturing to disclose the chief object of her journey; but apparently William's delinquencies were now forgiven, for, she says, 'we passed our time very pleasantly at Windsor'. At Montagu's the Lambs were their near neighbours, and Charles tells how one evening, after they had dined with him, he was 'their guide to Barthelmy Fair':[1] they had much to talk about, for Charles and Mary were just back from a visit to Coleridge at Keswick, and on their return they had spent a night or two in company with the Clarksons at Dove Cottage. Now, too, they had their first family reunion since the days, fifteen years before, when they had foregathered at their grandfather's house at Penrith; for Richard was in chambers at Staple Inn, Christopher, now a Fellow of Trinity, Cambridge, had come to town to see them, and, best of all, their beloved John had just returned from his Indian voyage. John's arrival was the chief news which Dorothy had to communicate in her letter to Mary. 'He was grown fat', she reports, 'and looked very handsome.'[2] Their departure for Gallow Hill would now be delayed, 'for we cannot find it in our hearts to leave him till we have been a few days together'.[2] This was a feeling, as Dorothy knew, with which Mary could sympathize. She, too, loved John as a brother, and had already sent a letter of welcome to await him. And John's brief reply, added at the bottom of the sheet on which Dorothy had written, reveals that tender sincerity which made him so dear to them all:

> I have been reading your Letter over and over again, my dearest Mary, till tears have come into my eyes and I know not how to express myself—Thou art a kind and dear Creature. But whatever fate befall me I shall love thee to the last, and bear thy memory with me to the grave.
>
> Thine afft
>
> JOHN WORDSWORTH.

On September 24 William and Dorothy were once more at Gallow Hill. 'Mary first met us in the avenue. She looked so

[1] Charles Lamb to S. T. C., Sept. 8, 1802.

[2] D. W. to Mary Hutchinson, Sept. 12, 1802.

fat and well that we were made very happy by the sight of her; then came Sara, and last of all Joanna. Tom was forking corn, standing upon the corn cart.'[1] Dorothy was dismayed to learn that she had just missed seeing her old friend Jane Marshall, who was staying at Scarborough and had come over a few days before, on purpose to see her. Writing to Jane[2] to tell of her mortification, she confides to her something of the tensity of emotion with which she viewed William's approaching marriage:

> 'My dear Jane, if this letter reaches you before next Monday you will think of me, travelling towards our own dear Grasmere with my most beloved Brother and his wife. I have long loved Mary Hutchinson as a sister, and she is equally attached to me; this being so, you will guess that I look forward with perfect happiness to this connection between us; but, happy as I am, I half dread that concentration of tender feelings, past, present, and future, which will come upon me on the wedding morning. There never lived on earth a better woman than Mary H., and I have not a doubt but that she is in every respect formed to make an excellent wife to my Brother, and I seem to myself to have scarcely anything left to wish for but that the wedding was over, and we had reached our home once again.'

Her account of the day itself is thus set down in the *Journal*:

> 'On Monday, 4th October 1802, my brother William was married to Mary Hutchinson. I slept a good deal of the night, and rose fresh and well in the morning. At a little after eight o'clock I saw them go down the avenue towards the church. William had parted from me upstairs. When they were absent, my dear little Sara prepared the breakfast. I kept myself as quiet as I could, but when I saw the two men running up the walk, coming to tell us it was over, I could stand it no longer, and threw myself on the bed, where I lay in stillness, neither hearing or seeing anything till Sara came upstairs to me and said, "They are coming". This forced me from the bed where I lay, and I moved, I knew not how, straight forward, faster than my strength could carry me, till I met my beloved William, and fell upon his bosom. He and John Hutchinson led me to the house, and there I stayed to welcome my dear Mary. As soon as we had breakfasted, we departed.'

It was a strange wedding. Three of Mary's brothers were

[1] *Grasmere Journal*, Sept. 24, 1802.
[2] D. W. to J. M., Sept. 29, 1802.

present, but no relative of William's. The sisters who were dearest to both bride and bridegroom did not attend the service. And when the party returned to the house William had Dorothy, not Mary, upon his arm.

Dorothy's tale of their journey home together is touched by that beauty which illumines all her writing when her feelings are deeply stirred, and is a signal example of her gift for drawing into the present all the wealth of past memories: 'We had sunshine and showers, pleasant talk, love and chearfulness. . . . Every foot of the road was of itself interesting to us, for we had travelled along it on foot, William and I, when we went to fetch our dear Mary, and had sate upon the turf by the roadside more than once. Before we reached Helmsley, our driver told us that he could not take us any further, so we stopped at the same inn where we had slept before. My heart danced at the sight of its cleanly outside, bright yellow walls, casements overshadowed with jasmine, and its low, double gavel-ended front. Mary and I warmed ourselves at the kitchen fire. We then walked into the garden and . . . I prevailed on William to go up with me to the ruins.' The next day they passed Rievaulx. 'We stopped upon the bridge to look at the Abbey, and again when we had crossed it. Dear Mary had never seen a ruined Abbey before except Whitby. We recognised the cottages, houses and the little valleys as we went along.' The day after they joined the route which she had taken with William three years before on their way from Sockburn to Grasmere. 'When we passed through the village of Wensley my heart melted away with dear recollections—the bridge, the little waterspout, the steep hill, the church. They are among the most vivid of my own inner visions, for they were the first objects that I saw after we were left to ourselves, and had turned our whole hearts to Grasmere as a home in which we were to rest.' At Aysgarth they 'alighted and walked down to see the waterfalls. . . . We saw the pathway which William and I took at the close of evening, the path leading to the rabbit-warren where we lost ourselves.' After spending the night at Hawes they reached Sedbergh by midday and 'dined in the same room where we had spent the evening together in our road to Grasmere'. At Kendal 'Mary and I went to see the house where dear Sara had lived. . . . We arrived at Grasmere about six o'clock on Wednesday evening the 6th of October 1802. Molly was overjoyed to see us; for my part I cannot describe what I felt and our dear Mary's feelings would, I dare say, not be easy to speak of. We went by candle light into the garden, and were astonished at the growth of the brooms, Portugal laurels, etc. etc. The next day, Thursday, we unpacked the boxes. On Friday 8th, Mary and I walked first upon the hillside, and then in John's Grove, then in view of Rydale, the first walk that I had taken with my sister.'

In this spirit of tranquil happiness Dorothy opened a new chapter of her life. To attain it was a triumph of spirit which those only can realize who have entered with imaginative sympathy into her emotions of the last five years. But she had her reward in a love only less wonderful than that which she had inspired in William. For half a century she was to live with Mary under the same roof, and in the same devoted service, and there was never a trace of jealousy or disagreement between them. In Mary she had a friend who knew what William was to her, and, with an unselfishness no less than her own, was ready to share husband, children, all that was most precious.

The rest of the year slipped quickly by. Autumn is always the most lovely season in the Lake country; the *Journal* shows how deeply its beauty harmonized with Dorothy's mood:

> 'Oct. 30. William is gone to Keswick. Mary went with him to the top of the Raise. She is returned and is now sitting near me by the fire. It is a breathless, grey day, that leaves the golden woods of autumn quiet in their own tranquillity, stately and beautiful in their decaying. The lake is a perfect mirror.
>
> 'Oct. 31. Mary and I walked to the top of the hill and looked at Rydale. I was much affected when I stood upon the second bar of Sara's gate.[1] The lake was perfectly still, and the sun shone on hill and vale, the distant birch trees looked like large golden flowers. Nothing else in colour was distinct and separate, but all the beautiful colours seemed to be melted into one another, and joined together in one mass, so that there were no differences, though an endless variety, when one tried to find it out. The fields were of one sober yellow brown.'

But now that she had the constant companionship of Mary, and the tense nervous strain of the last six months was over, she

[1] The name which the Wordsworth family had given to the Wishing Gate.

'SARA'S GATE', FROM 'JOHN'S GROVE'

felt less inclination to spend time upon her journal. In November the jottings are brief and cover no more than the first week; of December only three days are recorded. Early in the New Year, however, like so many of us, she vowed to turn over a new leaf. 'I will take a nice Calais[1] Book and *will* for the future write regularly and, if I can, legibly; so much for this my resolution on Tuesday night, January 11th 1803.' But on the 12th all she has to say is 'very cold, and cold all the week', and then, after three blank days, she breaks off with an entry which, despite its triviality, combines those elements which give to the journal its peculiar quality, her infallible sense of the details that make a picture, her lively sympathy with the life of all about her, and her watchful love for William:

> 'Sunday the 16th. intensely cold—Wm. had a fancy for some gingerbread—I put on Molly's cloak and my Spenser, and we walked towards Matthew Newton's. I went into the house. The blind man and his wife and sister were sitting by the fire, all dressed very clean in their Sunday clothes, the sister reading. They took their little stock of gingerbread out of the cupboard, and I bought six pennyworth. They were so grateful when I paid them for it that I could not find it in my heart to tell them that we were going to make gingerbread ourselves. I had asked them if they had no thick. "No" answered Matthew "there was none on Friday, but we'll endeavour to get some." The next day the woman came just when we were baking—We bought two pennyworth.'

With the cessation of Dorothy's *Journal* her correspondence becomes once more the chief source of our information about her. To Jane she wrote less often; her fullest and most intimate letters were now to Mrs. Clarkson, to whom, as the friend also of William and of Coleridge, and, moreover, one who knew and loved her own dear Lakeland, she could pour out more readily all that concerned her outer and inner life.

They had first met soon after she had settled into Dove Cottage; their friendship may be dated from about a year later. On February 12, 1801, Mrs. Clarkson had written to a friend at Cambridge:[2]

> 'I think I told you in my last that I expected Wordsworth and his Sister to visit us, well—they have been here and staid more than three weeks and have left us with a very favourable opinion

[1] Presumably a notebook bought in Calais.

[2] C. C. to the Rev. R. E. Garnham, Feb. 12, 1801.

of them. You must buy W's two volumes of Lyrical Ballads and tell me what you think of them. . . . I am fully convinced that Wordsworth's genius is equal to the Production of something very great, and I have no doubt that he will produce *something that Posterity will not willingly let die*, if he lives ten or twenty years longer. I was very much affected by "the Brothers". . . . Lucy Gray is I think inimitable.'

Mrs. Clarkson's enthusiasm was not viewed too seriously in all quarters; among the friends of her youth she had a reputation 'for taking up opinions in a very hasty manner before she had digested them'. 'Her intimacy with the Poet Wordsworth', Thomas Robinson informed his brother,[1] 'has, I am told, made her a very pretty enthusiast. She is become a religionist and a believer. Her faith receives little or no aid from written revelation—but God has spoken to her heart in a most sublime and mystical manner. In short she is a species of Quaker—a great admirer of the conduct and sentiments of Madame Guyon . . . it is highly probable that it is a state of things which will remain but a short time in her mind.' But this callow cynicism belies her true character, for however variable she may have been in the past, the poetry of Wordsworth became from this time forward a permanent influence upon her life. There could have been no surer road to Dorothy's affection; and the tribute paid her years later by Crabb Robinson, her life-long friend, is evidence that she had qualities of mind and temper which made her worthy of it. 'She was', he wrote, 'the most eloquent woman I have ever known with the exception of Madame de Stael. She had a quick apprehension of every kind of beauty, and made her own whatever she learned.'

With so much in common, her intimacy with Dorothy had been of rapid growth. It will be remembered that when William had gone to arrange his marriage with Mary, Dorothy had stayed with the Clarksons, and that she and William had spent two days with them on their way to visit Annette at Calais. But early in the summer of 1803 Mrs. Clarkson's health broke down, and she was forced to leave the district in search of skilled medical advice. It was on returning from a farewell visit to her at Eusemere that Dorothy wrote her the first of that large bundle of letters which Mrs. Clarkson so carefully preserved:

[1] T. R. to H. C. R., Sept. 8, 1803.

My dear Friend

. . . I reached home before five o'clock on Sunday afternoon without being in the least heated or fatigued. I daresay Mr Clarkson was anxious about me, for he would see the clouds upon the tops of the mountains. There they were, but they never touched me, they only made my walk more interesting. They connected the whole vale of Brother's Water, with the sky enclosing it, so that there seemed no place beyond; and indeed, it seemed as beautiful a place as there need be in a beautiful world. I met William at the top of the hill above our own house. He was on the look-out for me. Mary was at home—Dear creature! she was overjoyed to see me, after this short absence. She looked much better than she did when I left her. . . . Our garden is in great beauty. The brooms are covered with blossom, and we have a fine stock of flowers. I wish you could see it at this moment. Then I should wish the rain to stop, so that you might sit on the orchard seat by the bower. . . . Oh! my dear friend, what a beautiful spot this is! the greenest in all the earth, the softest green covers the mountains even to the very top. Silver How is before my eyes, and I forget that I have ever seen it so beautiful. Every bit of grass among the purple rocks (which are of all shades of purple) is green. Every now and then I hear the chirping of a little family of swallows that have their abode against the glass of my windows. The nest was built last year, and it has been taken possession of again about six weeks ago, needing no repairs whatever. William calls me again. God bless you, my very dear friend.

This letter is undated, but from the reference to the swallows, who had been in possession of the nest for six weeks, it can hardly have been written before the second week in June; on the 18th William's first son was born. The child's advent was as vital to Dorothy as to either of its parents. Ever since her attendance on her uncle's babies at Forncett she had loved children; to the little Coleridges, Hartley, Derwent, and the infant Sara, she was devoted; now she had one whom she could regard as her very own. It brought to her another joy which she could share with William, and she felt for it all a mother's ecstasy. On June 29 she dashed off a hurried scrawl to Mrs. Clarkson:

'My dear Friend, I was exceedingly hurt that I did not see Mr L.[1] and your Br. and that they did not see our little Babe—

[1] Probably Luff, a friend of the Clarksons and W.s who lived a mile or two from Patterdale.

I have only one moment to say that Mary and the Child are quite well. She has never ailed anything since his Birth. I hope we shall hear from you in a day or two—we are anxious about you, as you may well believe. Oh my dear friend how happy we are in this blessed Infant! He sleeps sweetly all night through, loves the open air—he has been out two hours to-day at one time, and by snatches at different times all the day through. He is a noble looking Child, has a very fine head, and a beautiful nose, and thrives rarely. He takes no food but his mother's milk. Our Nurse left us last Tuesday morning, and we have had no want of her, Mother and Child have gone on so nicely. I have been their sole attendant. The only thing that has let us down is that poor old Molly is very far from well—indeed has been *ill.*—No more—Coleridge is going off to Keswick—not a moment more. God bless you for ever. D. WORDSWORTH.'

A fortnight later she found leisure to write a fuller account of this wonderful baby:

Grasmere. 15th July. (1803)

My dear Friend

Mary and I have never ceased to regret that you did not see our own darling Child before your departure from this country—It would have been very sweet to us to think that you had carried away an image of what we so dearly love. When you see him he will be a different creature and we should have liked that you had known perfectly what he is now; or rather what he was then, for he is much grown since that time, though indeed he does not appear to us to be much altered. He has blue eyes, a fair complexion, (which is already very much sunburnt) a body as fat as a little pig, arms that are thickening and dimpling and bracelets at his wrists, a very prominent nose which *will be* like his Father's and a head shaped upon the very same model. I send you a lock of his hair sewed to this letter. To-day we have all been at Church—Mary was *churched* and the Babe christened—Coleridge my Brother Richard and I were Godfathers and Godmother, old Mr Sympson answered for my brother Richard and had a hearty enjoyment of the christening cake, tea and coffee, this afternoon.—The child sleeps all night, and is a very good sleeper in the day.—I wish you could see him in his Basket, which is neither more nor less than a meat Basket which costs half a crown. In this basket he has [Not like Moses in his cradle of rushes, but in a boat, mind that. *Note added by William in the margin*] floated over Grasmere water asleep and made one of a dinner party at the Island, and we often carry it to the orchard-seat where he drops asleep beside us. My dear Friend, we are very anxious to hear how you have borne the journey. . . .

God bless you my ever dear Friend—May God restore you to health and may you come back to us with a Body as fit for enjoyment among these noble and quiet Mountains and Vales as your heart is. . . .

yours ever and ever DOROTHY WORDSWORTH.

For many years to come Johnny, and the sisters and brothers that followed him into the world, were a theme upon which Dorothy was right voluble; and if ever her letters become tedious it is when she is dilating upon their charms and recording the minutiae of their size and growth—matters in which, a cynic might be tempted to observe, the little Wordsworths were, after all, not wholly unlike other children. But no baby-worshipper will blame her, and she herself was quite impenitent. 'William was frightened', she interjects into one of these effusions,[1] 'when he saw me with this long sheet of paper, and called out that I was not to say a great deal about John, for it would be quite tiresome—indeed my dear Friend, I have no such fears (nor do I believe that *he* had in his heart). I feel deeply every hour of my life the riches of the Blessings which God has given us, and you who have nursed your own Babe by a cottage fireside know what peace and pleasure, wakefulness and hope there is in attending on a healthy infant, and that one's thoughts are never tired when so employed.'

And in truth, to Dorothy, as to so many others of nervous, anxious temper, a baby brought that calm which is of all things the most healing; as she watched over the tiny Johnny she could gain something of his serene detachment from the troubles that harass an older world, forgetting for the time her fears for William and for Coleridge.

It had been arranged that as soon as it was safe to leave Mary in the less experienced hands of Sara or Joanna Hutchinson, Dorothy should go off for a rambling holiday in Scotland with William and Coleridge. 'Our dear Mary', she writes,[2] 'does not look forward to being left alone with one gloomy thought, and indeed, how could she with so sweet a Babe at her Breast? . . . William and C. talk of our tour with thorough enjoyment and I have no doubt I shall be as happy as they when I am fairly

[1] D. W. to C. C., Nov. 13, 1803. [2] D. W. to C. C., July 15, 1803.

off, but I do not love to think of leaving home and parting with the dear Babe, who will be no more the same Babe when we return.'

While they were still at Grasmere, absorbed in little Johnny, Sir George and Lady Beaumont had come to Keswick and taken rooms in the unoccupied part of Greta Hall. The Beaumonts were prominent figures among the London intelligentsia: it is difficult to-day to share the enthusiasm which was felt for Sir George's work as a painter, and modern critics might feel some sympathy with old Molly's judgement on one of his landscapes—'To be sure, the frame's varra bonny, but, for my part, I can mak nowt on't': he has greater claim to distinction as a liberal patron of all the arts, and as probably the finest connoisseur of painting in his generation. He had been the intimate friend of Sir Joshua Reynolds, had unbounded admiration for the work of Claude, had the discernment to recognize in Wilson the founder of a new school of English landscape painters, and was the first to hail the genius of Wilkie and Landseer. Later he crowned a life devoted to the service of art and artists by presenting to the nation his own valuable collection of pictures, and by inducing the government, by the purchase of the Angerstein Collection, to found our National Gallery. He was a man of upright character and generous impulse, and whilst his chief pleasure in life lay in the discovery and assistance of struggling artists, the courtesy and delicacy with which he helped them made of him their friend rather than their patron. Poetry he loved hardly less than pictures. Before this visit to Keswick in 1803 he does not seem to have heard of Wordsworth, but Coleridge he admired already, and the hope of meeting him was probably one of his inducements in making the journey.

For a few days he disliked Coleridge cordially, and then fell another victim to his eloquence, whilst Coleridge's susceptible heart was captivated at once by Sir George, and still more by his gracious and charming wife. And no one could be long in Coleridge's company without hearing of his wonderful friend, and realizing how much each of them owed to the other. 'Sir George and Lady B.', he wrote enthusiastically to William,[1]

[1] S. T. C. to W. W., *prob.* Aug. 6, 1803. It is interesting to notice that both these new friends of Dorothy's, Mrs. Clarkson and Lady Beaumont, are compared by those who knew them to Madame Guion.

'are half mad to see you. Lady B. told me that the night before last, as she was reading your poem on *Cape Rash Judgment*, had you entered the room she believes she would have fallen at your feet. . . . I can describe her to you in few words. She is a miniature of Madame Guion—a deep enthusiast, sensitive, trembles, and cannot keep the tears in her eye. Such ones do love the marvellous too well not to believe it. You may wind her up with *any* music, but *music* it must be, of some sort or other'; and when he had known her a little longer he asserted that she 'has verily a soul in point of quick enthusiastic feeling so much like Dorothy's, only not Dorothy's powers'.[1]

Before he left Keswick, Sir George had bought a small property at Applethwaite, at the foot of Skiddaw, to present to Wordsworth: 'I had the most ardent desire',[2] he wrote, 'to bring you and Coleridge together. I thought with pleasure on the increase of enjoyment you would receive from the beauties of Nature, by being able to communicate more frequently your sensations to each other; and that this would be the means of contributing to the pleasure and improvement of the world, by stimulating you both to poetical exertions.'

This plan for the future of the two poets was not destined to be fulfilled, but Dorothy was not the less deeply affected by the generous impulse that had prompted it; while the glowing enthusiasm with which Coleridge spoke of her to Lady Beaumont, and of Lady Beaumont to her, made each of them eager to know the other. Three years were to elapse before they met; but during the last two of them they were exchanging letters of a steadily growing intimacy. Indeed the warmth with which Lady Beaumont wrote gave Dorothy some qualms. Modest as she was, she could not suppress the fear that her impulsive friend had formed an image of her wholly unlike her real and, as she thought, very ordinary self:

> 'I was', she replied to one of these effusions,[3] 'so deeply affected with the tender kindness of your last letter—If I could have done anything I should have written immediately for my own heart's comfort to tell you how happy, how proud I am of your friendship, or rather I ought to be proud in them to whom I chiefly

[1] S. T. C. to W. W., Feb. 16, 1804.
[2] Sir George B. to W. W., Oct. 24, 1803.
[3] D. W. to Lady Beaumont, Jan. 5, 1805.

owe the gift, for to my Brother, surely, if I am in myself worthy of your esteem I owe it; or if I am in any degree worthy of the great affection which Coleridge feels for me: but when I think how great his regard for me is, knowing that all you know of me is from him, I really, (it is no false modesty, as my Brother, who knows well all my thoughts, could tell you) I really, (much as I desire to see you) am almost afraid of it, you will find me so different from what you have imagined, and (believe me) so much inferior. I have not those powers which Coleridge thinks I have—I know it—my only merits are my devotedness to those I love, and I hope a charity towards all mankind. Perhaps it may seem to you that I have said too much about myself, that it is but one of the shapes which vanity puts on, and this thought would have kept me silent but for the high value which I set on your esteem, and for that cause my strong desire that you should judge and expect of me as I am.'

This letter, so characteristic of Dorothy, can only have corroborated what Lady Beaumont had already heard of her, and made her new friend look forward with an even greater impatience to the day of their meeting.

IX

THE SCOTCH TOUR. COLERIDGE'S DEPARTURE FOR MALTA

August 1803–April 1804 (aet. 32)

ON August 11 or 12, 1803, the Beaumonts left Greta Hall; on the evening of the 12th Wordsworth arrived with his wife, sister, and baby. They lost no time in visiting Applethwaite; then on the 14th Mary and Johnny returned to Dove Cottage, and a day later William, Dorothy, and Coleridge started upon their tour. Up to the last moment Coleridge was uncertain whether he would go. The chance of rainy weather and damp beds daunted him. The rough Irish dog-cart which they had bought to convey them had given him some misgivings before they set out. 'I begin to find', he had written, 'that a Horse and Jaunting Car is *an anxiety*,—and almost to wish that we had adopted our first thought and *walked*; with one pony and side saddle for our Sister Gift-of-God'.[1] After a few days he found that the noise of the wheels grated on his nerves, that sitting in an open carriage in the rain was death to him, that Wordsworth was too silent and hypochrondriacal a companion. Of Dorothy he says nothing. 'Somehow or other', he explained, 'I had not been quite comfortable.'[2] Evidently he was in a state neither of body nor of mind to enjoy the adventure; he bore up for a fortnight, and then decided to leave them. It was the first time on record that the society of his friends had failed to satisfy him.

Dorothy and William made a full use of the six weeks they were away from home. In the first they got as far as Lanark, travelling by way of Dumfries, where they viewed the home and grave of Burns; two days later they had seen the Falls of Clyde and were at Glasgow. From Glasgow they made for the Highlands going by Dumbarton and the vale of Leven to Luss on Loch Lomond, and thence to Tarbet, Loch Katrine, and the Trossachs. They had now been a fortnight on the road. Retracing their steps to Tarbet they crossed the hill to Arrochar on Loch Long; here Coleridge parted from them, and they pursued a westward

[1] S. T. C. to W. W., Aug. 6 (?), 1803. [2] S. T. C. to Mrs. C., Sept. 1, 1803.

course to Inveraray, then northwards to Dalmally, westward again by the side of Loch Awe and the lower end of Loch Etive to the Ferry, and then north along the coast by the Strath of Appin to Ballachulish. Turning eastwards along the vale of Glencoe they reached the King's House at the end of their third week. In the fourth they proceeded by way of Inveroran, Tyndrum, Loch Tay, Aberfeldy, Blair Atholl, and the Pass of Killicrankie to Callander. Then, after a few days spent in revisiting the Trossachs and Loch Lomond, they returned to Callander and made for Edinburgh, and thence by Hawthornden and Lasswade to Peebles. In their last week they turned their steps homewards through the vales of the Tweed, Teviot, and Esk.

A detailed account of their journey can be read in Dorothy's *Recollections of a Tour made in Scotland.*[1] Two-thirds of it she set down during the following winter and, after laying it aside for more than a year, completed it in the spring of 1805. She wrote it, she tells us, 'for the sake of my friends who, it seemed, ought to have been with us', and though it was not published till long after her death, it was handed round among a wide circle. Of all her writings it is the most carefully composed; while it has not the intimacy of some of her Letters, or of the Journals which she wrote only for her own eye and for William's, it is yet perfectly free from all pose or affectation. With no attempts at fine writing she sets down, faithfully and with a sensitive beauty of language, her impressions of the country and its people. 'On going into a new country', she says, 'I seem to myself to waken up, and afterwards it surprises me to remember how alive I have been to the distinctions of dress, household arrangements etc. and what a spirit these things give to the wild, barren or ordinary places.' So vivid and minute is her story that it is often spoken of as a diary of the tour; even Professor Harper states[2] that it was written from copious notes taken day by day, but this is contrary to her own express assertion. 'I am writing', she says,[3] 'not a Journal, *for we took no notes*, but *recollections* of our Tour in the form of a journal.'

[1] Ed. Shairp, 1874; D. W.'s *Journals*, ed. Knight, 1897. On its composition and later revision, *v.* Appendix, pp. 405–15. [2] *Life of W. W.*, ed. 1929, p. 391.

[3] D. W. to C. C., Nov. 13, 1803. Dorothy always insisted on this point: cf. her letter to J. M., July 26, 1812, 'By the bye, its title is not properly a Journal or Tour, but "*Recollections* of a Tour etc.". So, too, in a letter to Lady B., Jan. 19, 1806, she speaks of 'my journal, or rather *recollections*'.

Here lies, in part at least, the secret of her success. Where the mere diarist sets down, day by day, a laborious record of passing events, simply because they happened and irrespective of their relative importance, Dorothy, trusting to her memory, reinforced, doubtless, by talks with William, only records that which after a passage of time is still a vital experience; and thus her work gains something of the perspective of a work of pure imagination. The result is one of the most readable, because it is one of the most living, of all books of travel. Dorothy did not share her brother's passion for this kind of literature, and she viewed her own contribution to it with her usual modesty. 'You will be amused at it', she wrote to Mrs. Clarkson, 'for our sakes, but I think Journals of Tours, except as one is interested in the Travellers, are very uninteresting things.' But we may claim an interest in the travellers as genuine, in its own way, as Mrs. Clarkson's; and even were it not so, an impression of Scotland as it struck an alert and sensitive observer at the opening of the last century would hardly come amiss.

Except in its weather, it was a very different country from the Scotland that is now so woefully betouristed. Even the main thoroughfares were unfrequented: the travellers met only one stage-coach and very few private carriages: off the highroads, save for a stray wayfarer on horseback or on foot, they rarely saw any but natives, to whom a visitor from the outer world was an event. 'A laugh was on every face', says Dorothy, 'when William said we were come to see the Trossachs: no doubt they thought that we had better have stayed at our own homes.' Their journey, indeed, was not without its spice of perilous adventure. 'The outlandish Hibernian vehicle', which they had bought to convey them, was the source not only of wonder and innocent merriment to others, but of constant anxiety to themselves. None of them was really competent to manage it. Coleridge had entirely lost the youthful confidence with which he had driven Dorothy from Racedown to Nether Stowey; when it was his turn to take charge he thought it more prudent to lead the horse. If William was not quite so inefficient as in the Alfoxden days, when after several vain attempts to remove a horse collar, he pronounced the feat to be 'wholly impracticable', he was still very awkward and clumsy with the harness, and he drove somewhat as Chaucer's shipman rode upon his rouncy, 'as he couthe'. The poor animal, by nature nervous and obstinate, was not slow to detect their inexperience. On the very first day he nearly involved them in two serious accidents: later on, when they were ferrying over Loch Etive, his wild vagaries almost cost them their lives. 'Driven over rough stones, which were as slippery as ice with slimy sea weed, he was in terror before he reached the boat', and when he was embarked

> 'the poor creature fretted, and stamped with his feet against the bare boards, frightening himself more and more with every stroke. . . . the motion of the boat and the noise and foam of the waves terrified him still more, and we thought it would be impossible to keep him in the boat, and when we were just far enough from the shore to have been all drowned he became furious, and, plunging desperately, his hind-legs were in the water, then, recovering himself, he beat with such force against the boat-side that we were afraid he should send his feet through.'

On the next day he had another access of nerves.

> 'We travelled close to the water's edge, and were rolling along a smooth road, when the horse suddenly backed, frightened by the upright shafts of a roller rising from behind the wall of a field adjoining the road. William pulled, whipped, and struggled in vain; we both leapt upon the ground, and the horse dragged the car after him, he going backwards down the bank of the loch, and it was turned over half in the water, the horse lying on his back, struggling in the harness, a frightful sight! I gave up everything; thought that the horse would be lamed, and the car broken in pieces. Luckily a man came up in the same moment and assisted William in extricating the horse, and, after an hour's delay, and with the help of strings and pocket-handkerchiefs, we mended the harness and set forward again, William leading the poor animal all the way, for the regular beating of the waves frightened him, and any little gushing streams that crossed the road would have sent him off.'

To their anxieties about their horse were added others which sprang from the primitive character of the country they were exploring. The inns were for the most part as rough and unaccommodating as any they had come across in Germany. Sometimes they would arrive at the end of a long day's journey and find no room, or if the house was empty they would meet with a 'demur respecting beds', and though they were cold and wet they would be told that 'the mistress was not varra willing to gie fire'. Dorothy was continually disgusted with the slovenliness and dirt near the doors of the Highland huts, 'so different from the cottages of Somersetshire covered with roses and myrtle and their small gardens of herbs and flowers', and even more with the filth and disorder of their interiors as compared with the scrupulous neatness of the poorest Westmorland homes. 'How light the labour in such a house as this,' she reflected in one of them, as she recalled her own strenuous domestic labours, 'little sweeping, no washing of floors, and as to scouring the table, I believe it was a thing never thought of.' Their food was often as primitive as their lodging. Though eggs and fowls were usually to be had, they seldom saw wheaten bread, and the oatcake defied the efforts of Dorothy's feeble teeth. Arriving at the King's House in Glencoe after sunset, tired and hungry, they sat shivering for three-quarters of an hour in one of the large rooms before they could get a fire, and another hour before supper was served them—'a shoulder of mutton so hard that it was impossible to chew the little flesh that might be scraped off the bones, and some sorry soup made of barley and water, for it had no other taste', and the sheets for their beds were so wet that they spent hours in trying to dry them before a wretched peat fire that refused to do more than smoulder. But such hardships they bore with cheerfulness. 'As long as people were civil we were contented', says Dorothy, and civility is too tame a word to describe the reception they often met. At the inns which catered for more ostentatious patrons, they might perhaps receive off-hand treatment, and have to endure the lazy impertinence of a waiter 'who is too great a man to speak three words more than he can help'; at Luss their landlady was 'a cruel and hateful looking woman. (She was overgrown with fat and sitting with her feet and legs in a tub of water for the dropsy—probably brought on by whisky drinking)'; but their usual experience, at least at the less frequented places, was to be welcomed with a beautiful courtesy and a real if somewhat dilatory hospitality. At the first Highland hut they had occasion to visit they had a sample of true Highland manners.

> 'We entered by the cow-house, the house-door being within, at right angles to the outer door. The woman was distressed that she had a bad fire, but she heaped up some dry peats and heather, and, blowing it with her breath in a short time raised a blaze

that scorched us into comfortable feelings. A small part of the smoke found its way out of the hole of the chimney, the rest through the open window-places, one of which was within the recess of the fire-place, and made a frame to a little picture of the restless lake and the opposite shore, seen when the outer door was open. The woman of the house was very kind; whenever we asked her for anything it seemed a fresh pleasure to her that she had it for us: she always answered with a sort of softening down of the Scotch exclamation, "Hoot!" "Ho, yes, ye'll get that," and hied to her cupboard in the spence. . . . We got oatmeal, butter, bread and milk, made some porridge and then departed—It was rainy and cold, with a strong wind.'

When they returned there in the evening, wet to the skin and sick with cold,

'the good woman had provided, according to her promise, a better fire than we had found in the morning; and indeed when I sate down in the chimney corner of her smoky biggin' I thought I had never been more comfortable in my life. . . . We could not prevail upon the man of the house to draw near the fire, though he was cold and wet, or to suffer his wife to get him dry clothes till she had served us, which she did, though most willingly, not very expeditiously. . . . We asked for sugar, butter, barley, bread and milk, and with a smile and a stare more of kindness than wonder she replied "Ye'll get that", bringing each article separately.

'We caroused our cups of coffee, laughing like children at the strange atmosphere in which we were: the smoke came in gusts, and spread along the walls and above our heads in the chimney, where the hens were roosting like light clouds in the sky. We laughed and laughed again, in spite of the smarting of our eyes, yet had a quieter pleasure in observing the beauty of the beams and rafters gleaming between the clouds of smoke. They had been crusted over and varnished by many winters, till, where the firelight fell upon them, they were as glossy as black rocks on a sunny day cased in ice. When we had eaten our supper we sate about half an hour, and I think I had never felt so deeply the blessings of a hospitable welcome and a warm fire. The man of the house repeated from time to time that we should often tell of this night when we got to our homes, and interposed praises of this, his own lake, which he had more than once, when we were returning in the boat, ventured to say was "bonnier than Loch Lomond".'

William and Coleridge spent the night on the hay in the barn, for there was no room for them in the hut:

'I went to bed some time before the family. The door was shut between us, and they had a bright fire, which I could not see; but the light it sent up among the varnished rafters and beams, which crossed each other in almost as intricate and fantastic a manner as I have seen the under-boughs of a large beech-tree withered by the depth of the shade above, produced the most beautiful effect that can be conceived. It was like what I should suppose an underground cave or temple to be, with a dripping or moist roof, and the moonlight entering in upon it by some means or other, and yet the colours were more like melted gems. I lay looking up till the light of the fire faded away, and the man and his wife and child had crept into their bed at the other end of the room. I did not sleep much, but passed a comfortable night, for my bed, though hard, was warm and clean: the unusualness of my situation prevented me from sleeping. I could hear the waves beat against the shore of the lake; a little "syke" close to the door made a much louder noise; and when I sate up in my bed I could see the lake through an open window-place at the bed's head. Add to this, it rained all night. I was less occupied by remembrance of the Trossachs, beautiful as they were, than the vision of the Highland hut, which I could not get out of my head. I thought of the Fairyland of Spenser, and what I had read in romance at other times, and then, what a feast would it be for a London pantomime-maker, could he but transplant it to Drury Lane, with all its beautiful colours!'

The night spent at this Highland hut was perhaps Dorothy's richest experience in the whole tour. At inns with large rooms and bustling waiters she never felt wholly at her ease, and at the pretentious hostelry of Arrochar, where they had an excellent dinner, 'would gladly have exchanged our roasted lamb and pickles, and the gentleman waiter with a napkin in his pocket, for the more homely fare of the smoky hut at Loch Kettrine, and the good woman's busy attentions'.

The scenery through which they passed could not fail to enchant her. 'Scotland', she writes, 'is the country above all others that I have seen, in which a man of imagination can carve out his own pleasures . . . I can always walk over a moor with a light foot. I seem to be drawn more closely to nature in such places than anywhere else, or rather I feel more strongly the power of nature over me.' Her quickness to catch the essential features of the ever-varying landscape, and her fidelity in recording them bear witness to that power. But she was always happiest when she saw the beauty and the grandeur about her as the setting to human life and emotion. Her one regret, on their return, was that they had had so few chances of intimate contact with the people, 'especially the peasantry in lonely places': such chances as they had were not lost upon her. Taking an evening stroll along Loch Katrine they met two women; 'one of them said to us in a friendly, soft tone of voice, "What, you are stepping westward?"[1] I cannot describe', she adds, 'how affecting this simple expression was in that remote place, with the western sky in front, yet glowing with the departed sun.' Deeply impressed on her mind was the gay friendliness of two girls at Inversneyde, who placed at her disposal all the resources of their wardrobes, repeating at least half a dozen times, as they helped her into a blue linsey petticoat and a light-coloured sprigged cotton gown, 'you never had on the like o' that before'. They had overtaken the girls as they descended the hill to Loch Lomond:

> 'One of them was exceedingly beautiful, and the figures of both of them, in grey plaids falling to their feet, their faces only being uncovered, excited our attention before we spoke to them; but they answered us so sweetly, that we were quite delighted at the same time that they stared at us with an innocent look of wonder. I think I never heard the English language sound more sweetly than from the mouth of the elder of these girls, while she stood at the gate answering our inquiries, her pronunciation was clear and distinct, without difficulty, yet slow, like that of a foreign speech. . . . She made me think of Peter Bell's Highland girl
>
> As light and beauteous as a squirrel,
> As beauteous and as wild.[2]
>
> She moved with unusual activity, which was chastened very delicately by a certain hesitation in her looks when she spoke, being able to understand us but imperfectly.'

Dorothy, indeed, treasured every scrap of conversation which seemed to her characteristic of the people in their manners or their outlook upon life, such as the comment of a woman when she was told that William was married and had a baby—'And the man's a decent man too', or the 'pious seriousness and perfect simplicity' of another who, learning that Dorothy was single,

[1] Cf. *Oxf. W.*, p. 289.
[2] Cf. *Oxf. W.*, p. 246.

comforted her with the assurance that 'there is great promise for virgins in heaven', and hastened to retail to her the sorrows of her own married life. And often when no words were exchanged, a human figure had merely to cross their line of vision to invest the landscape with an added beauty and significance. Just as that 'sweet Highland girl' was to William the very spirit of 'the lake, the bay, the waterfall',[1] so many a lonely figure touched with human emotion the scene of which he was the foreground.

> 'An old man, the first we had seen in a Highland bonnet, walking with a staff at a very slow pace by the edge of one of the moorland cornfields: he wore a grey plaid, and a dog was at his side. There was a scriptural solemnity in the man's figure, and a sober simplicity, which was most impressive.'

Another time,

> 'we stopped suddenly at the sound of a half articulate Gaelic hooting from the field close to us. It came from a little boy whom we could see on the hill between us and the lake, wrapped up in a grey plaid. He was probably calling home the cattle for the night. His appearance was in the highest degree moving to the imagination; mists were on the hillsides, darkness shutting in upon the huge avenues of mountains, torrents roaring, no house in sight to which the child might belong; his dress, cry and appearance all different from anything we had been accustomed to. It was a text, as William has since observed to me, containing in itself the whole history of the Highlander's life—his melancholy, his simplicity, his poverty, his superstition, and above all, that visionariness which results from a communion with the unworldliness of nature.'

Thus they had, as she puts it, 'many most interesting feelings connected with man in dreary solitariness'; if Byron, in his famous controversy with Bowles, had wanted further support of his contention that 'a ship confers its own poetry on the waters and heightens theirs', he could have found no more eloquent illustration of his meaning than in Dorothy's account of how, as they rounded a point of Loch Awe, a vessel hove in sight:

> 'She floated steadily through the middle of the water, with one large sail spread out, fully swollen by the breeze, that blew her right towards us. I cannot express what romantic images this vessel brought along with her—how much more beautiful the

[1] *Oxf. W.*, p. 288.

mountains appeared, the lake how much more graceful. There was one man on board, who sate at the helm, and he, having no companion, made the boat look more silent than if we could not have seen him.'

During their tour Dorothy added both Rogers and Scott to her literary acquaintance. With Rogers they had only a chance meeting on the road, but years later in his *Table Talk* he recalled[1] how when travelling with his sister 'we fell in with Wordsworth, Miss Wordsworth, and Coleridge, who were at the same time making a tour in a vehicle that looked very like a cart. Wordsworth and Coleridge were entirely occupied in talking about poetry; and the whole care of looking out for cottages where they might get refreshment and pass the night, as well as of seeing their poor horse fed and littered, devolved upon Miss Wordsworth. She was a most delightful person, so full of talent, so simple-minded, and so modest!' If his statement as to the poor horse is an error, and his account of Wordsworth and Coleridge's conversation a mere conjecture, we can at least accept his vivid impression of Dorothy. It does not seem to have been reciprocated, for she makes no mention of Rogers in her *Journal*.[2] But of Scott she has much to say. Both she and William were delighted with 'the frank cordiality which marked his manner, his lively entertaining conversation, his unaffected modesty about himself, and his cheerful and benevolent views of man and the world'. 'They met', says Lockhart, 'as if they had not been strangers, and they parted friends.' With a fine disregard of the conventions they had called at his home at Lasswade before he or Mrs. Scott had risen; they breakfasted with him and stayed till two o'clock; and when they left, Scott accompanied them back to Roslin. Two days later he joined them at Melrose, and in his absence they found his friendship the best of passports. 'Mr Scott', wrote Dorothy, 'is respected everywhere, I believe that by favour of his name one might be hospitably entertained throughout the borders of Scotland.' When they were at Jedburgh he came to the assizes in his capacity of Sheriff and spent all his spare time in their company: dined at their lodgings, where they had a bottle of wine in his honour, and stayed late into the evening reciting to them, in an

[1] *Table Talk of S. R.*, ed. Dyce, 1887, pp. 208–9.
[2] i.e., in the first version: in the second she adds a short reference to the meeting.

enthusiastic kind of chant, his new poem, *The Lay of the Last Minstrel.* The next day, when the business of the courts was over, he sent off his own gig with the groom, and taking a seat in their Irish car was their guide through much of the Border country. At Hawick he left them. 'We wished', adds Dorothy, 'we could have gone with Mr Scott into some of the remote dales of this country, where in almost every house he can find a home and a hearty welcome. But after breakfast we were obliged to part with him, which we did with great regret; he would gladly have gone with us to Langholm, eighteen miles further.'[1] Two days later we 'arrived at home between eight and nine o'clock, where we found Mary in perfect health, Joanna Hutchinson with her, and little John asleep in the clothes-basket by the fire'.

When she was at home every one asked her ' "do you like the Scotch or the English Lakes better?" A question I do not like to answer. There is no comparison to be made where everything is so different except a part of Loch Lomond which is like Ullswater, but there is certainly nothing so *beautiful* in Scotland as parts of this country. Notwithstanding this if any body should make the same journey that we did, having had fine weather, and not having received a very high pleasure, I should say it was their fault.'[2]

While on her tour Dorothy had not written to Mrs. Clarkson. 'I was always tired', she says, 'when I reached the Inn at night and glad to put my body in the state to receive all possible enjoyment of the few comforts that a Scotch Inn affords. I was glad to lay my legs up and loll in indolence before the fire'; and when she was home again she had no wish to forestall her *Journal*—she had enough to tell of the joys and the anxieties of the present. Johnny, of course, was more wonderful than ever.

[1] 'When we were in Scotland we spent several days in company with Mr Scott—we were at his house, he limped by our side through the groves of Roslin, went with us along the shores of Teviot and the Tweed, led us to Melrose Abbey, and pointed out every famous hill, and told some tale of every old Hall we passed by. His local attachments are more strong than those of any person I ever saw—his whole heart and soul seem to be devoted to the Scottish streams, Yarrow and Tweed, Teviot and the rest of them, of which we hear in the Border Ballads, and I am sure that there is not a story ever told by the firesides in that neighbourhood that he cannot repeat, and many more that are not so familiar. He is a man of very sweet manners, mild, cordial, and chearful.' D. W. to Lady B., May 4, 1805.

[2] D. W. to C. C., Oct. 9, 1803.

'If I were not afraid of making even you laugh at me,' she writes,[1] 'I should say that he looks as if he was not the child of ordinary parents. . . . It is very affecting to us to see how much he is beloved in the neighbourhood. Peggy Ashburner dotes on him as if she were his grandmother, and Molly Ashburner and Sally are never more happy than when John smiles at them. . . . By the bye, his eyes are not fine ones, they are small; but that, you know, makes him seem more like his father, and they have frequently the very same expression as his father's—that same mild light when he smiles . . . if it were possible to tire you with a long story of him you will be tired now. But oh that you could see him! I am sure you would not soon be tired with quietly watching him, and it would do you good, soul and body. . . . Old Molly is well; she has put on her gown this afternoon to nurse John—it is her Sunday afternoon's treat to sit in the parlour belowstairs and nurse him. Poor creature! she told him (for she always talks to him whenever we will let her) several times in the week that she would dress herself for him on Sunday.'

So Dorothy rambles on, with more to the same effect.

The joys of being at home again, and of witnessing the vale and mountains of Grasmere in the fullest pride of their beauty, with an autumn colouring more gorgeous even than usual, were tempered by agitation about the French wars, and by increased anxieties for Coleridge. The short-lived peace signed at Amiens had only lasted fourteen months, and since May the growing fear of invasion had roused the country to a pitch of excited patriotism. Years before this the rise of Napoleon had cured William of his republican sympathies with France, and a fortnight after their return from Scotland Dorothy reports that he has 'gone to Ambleside to volunteer his services with the greatest part of the men of Grasmere'.

'Alas, alas, Mary and I have no other hope than that they will not be called upon out of these quiet far off places except in the case of the French being *successful* in their landing, and in that case what matter? We may all go together. But we wanted him to wait till the body of *the people* should be called. For my part I thought much of the inconvenience and fatigue of going to be exercised twice or thrice a week; however, if he really enters into it heart and soul and likes it, that will do him good, and surely there was never a more determined hater of the French, nor one

[1] D. W. to C. C., Nov. 13, 1803.

more willing to do his utmost to destroy them if they really do come. . . . We have not seen Coleridge since our return. He is taking a violent medicine in the hope of bringing his disease to a fit of the gout . . . he is often dreadfully ill.'[1]

Coleridge had long come to the conclusion that nothing but a warmer and drier climate could restore his health. Two years back he had planned a trip to the Azores, and William had written to Poole to try and raise the necessary funds for the voyage; earlier in this year, he had applied to John Wordsworth to take him to China; he then decided on Sicily, whither, he affirmed, Wordsworth and his family would accompany him. He now determined to try Malta or Madeira. On December 20 he appeared at Grasmere bringing little Derwent with him, for a few days' stay before he proceeded to London. But he was again taken seriously ill, and for more than three weeks, as he said, 'Mary and Dorothy were my kind nurses who tended me with a sister's and mother's love, and often, I well know, wept for me in their sleep and watched for me even in their dreams' Dorothy's account of this melancholy farewell visit was dispatched to Mrs. Clarkson on January 15:

My dear Friend.

I received your last letter the day before Coleridge came to us with Derwent intending to spend a few days only here, and proceed to Devonshire either by Bristol or London. Day after day he was detained by sickness, or bad weather, or both, (for when the weather was damp or wet he never failed to be very ill) and yesterday he left us in indifferent health, though on a fine sunny morning. . . . Derwent is still with us and very sorry we shall be to part with him, but we must send him by the first opportunity as he has now been nearly a month absent from his Mother. . . . But I must tell you about Coleridge—he walked to Kendal yesterday. William accompanied him almost to Troutbeck and C was not tired when he parted from him, but two or three days before he was lame with Gout, stomach-sick, haunted by ugly dreams, screamed out in the night, durst not sleep etc, etc.—he still thinks nothing but a warmer climate *can* restore him to health. I have told you that he was the cause of my not writing—the uncertainty in which we were respecting him, that alone perhaps would not have prevented me, but I had so much uneasiness about him and *so much to do* that I seemed to have scarcely the quiet and leisure

[1] D. W. to C. C., Oct. 9, 1803.

necessary to make me feel fit to write a letter that would give you any comfort. Mary had a very bad cold most of the time, which weakened her and made her unable to take an equal share with me in the business of the house—Molly was poorly, Coleridge continually wanting coffee, broth or something or other—the bed was moved into the sitting room night and morning, and with Derwent and the liveliest of Johnnys you may think we were busy enough in our small house.'

In about three weeks they were cheered by good news. Coleridge, after a gay, convivial time with his London friends, was enjoying the hospitality of the good Beaumonts at Dunmow in Essex.

'I was not received here', he wrote,[1] 'with mere kindness. I was welcomed *almost* as you welcomed me when I first visited you at Racedown. . . . My health is greatly improved, and rich and precious wines (of several of which I had never before heard the names) agree admirably with me, and I fully believe, most dear William! they would with you. . . . We talk by the long hours about you and Hartley, Derwent, Sara, and Johnnie; and few things I am persuaded would delight them more than to live near you. I wish you would write out a sheet of verses for them, and I almost promised for you that you should send that delicious poem on the Highland Girl at Inversneyde. But of more importance, incomparably, is it that Mary and Dorothy should begin to transcribe *all* William's MS poems *for me*. Think what they will be to me in Sicily!'

The request did not fall on deaf ears, for their one desire was that, even in absence, Coleridge should still share with them the best part of their life. Ever since he left them William had been hard at work on that poem in which, 'as if to thee alone in private talk',[2] he related the history of his mind, to that friend 'who in my thoughts art ever at my side'.[3] 'He walks out every morning', says Dorothy,[4] 'generally alone, and brings us in a large treat every time he goes. The weather with all its pleasant mildness has been very wet in general—he takes out the umbrella, and I daresay stands stock-still under it, during many a rainy half-hour, in the middle of a road or field'; she and Mary were

[1] S. T. C. to the Wordsworths, Feb. 8, 1804.
[2] *Prelude* (1805), x. 373.
[3] Ib., iii. 200.
[4] D. W. to C. C., Feb. 13, 1804.

eager to make their own humbler contribution to their friend's happiness. For the next few weeks every spare moment was given to copying. The task proved more exacting than they had anticipated. 'I have been literally at work from morning till night', she says,[1] '... the manuscripts were in such a wretched condition, and so tedious to copy from—besides requiring William's almost constant superintendence—that we considered it as almost necessary to save them alive that we should recopy them; for I think William would never have had the resolution to set us to work again. Judge then how fully we have been employed, what with nursing and the ordinary business of the house, which is really not a little.' But by March 6 she is able to report to Coleridge that 'we have transcribed all William's smaller poems for you, and begun the poem on his life and *The Pedlar*', and after setting his mind at rest upon that score, she runs on to tell him something of their doings at the cottage—'a short and meagre letter' she calls it, but it is full of just those intimate details he most longed to hear, such as would bring him in imagination into their midst again.

My dear Friend,

We have waited post after post in expectation of another letter from you—in so doing I feel that we have done wrong for I begin to write now as a duty, rather than a work of pleasure and sympathy. But why have you not written to us again? . . . I am sorry you have left Dunmow, because the Beaumonts are so good and kind-hearted that I think you must there have had home feelings about you, something like being amongst us, and, surely you might, at their house in the country, have more time to yourself, and more quiet for going on with your work (independent of the chance of better health) than in London. I wish you would stay there till you go to Sicily, if you can. . . . It will, I am sure give William great pleasure to send some of his poems to Lady Beaumont, and we shall be most glad to copy them when the necessary business is over, indeed I do not know what I should *not* like to do for so amiable a woman, one who has been so tender and kind to you. . . .

In the morning William and I had so much enjoyment that regrets forced themselves on us continually that you were not with us, at least had not seen the place where we were. Mary is to go

[1] D. W. to C. C., Mar. 24, 1804.

to-morrow. William found it out by himself—it is a little slip of the river above Rydale, that makes the *famous* waterfalls, about two hundred yards in length, it is high up towards the mountains, where one would not have expected any trees to be, and down it tumbles among rocks and trees, trees of all shapes, elegant birches and ancient oaks, that have grown as tall as the storms would let them and are now decaying away, their naked branches like shattered lances, or the whole tree like a thing hacked away and dismantled, as William says, to impale malefactors upon. On one of them was an old glead's nest. With these are green hollies and junipers, a little waterfall, endless, endless waterbreaks, now a rock starting forward, now an old tree, enough to look at for hours, and then the whole seen in a long prospect. It is a miniature of all that can be conceived of savage and grand about a river, with a great deal of the beautiful. William says that whatever Salvator might desire could there be found. . . .

Mary, though very thin, and not *very* strong, is on the whole well . . . the babe is flourishing and healthy. He is indeed as noble a creature as ever was beheld, the joy and comfort of us all, and wherever he goes he is looked on with delight. 'What a stout fellow!' 'I never saw so large a child' we hear from all quarters. You will be delighted to hear, that he does not, as W. in his tenderness to us was pleased to say 'take a weary deal of nursing'—he is far less trouble, (if trouble I *must* call it) than he was. He sleeps generally in the evenings and is far more happy in the day when we leave him to himself upon the carpet with good store of playthings than when he is upon our knees. Give him but a work-basket full of tape and thread and other *oddments*, and he riots among them like a little pussy-cat. He can sit upright on the carpet, and so we leave him—sometimes he gets a good bump on his head and lustily he roars, but no matter, he cannot hurt himself seriously, so we are not afraid of him and he will soon learn to take care of himself. His countenance is very intelligent. Could you but see him look up at you when he is sitting upon the ground, it would fill your heart top-full of pleasure, then he *does* look *beautiful*, though I am far from being so blind as to think him a beautiful child.

Then after telling her latest news of Mrs. Clarkson, and of a four days' illness from which she had suffered herself, she goes on:

'Poor dear Sara has had another sore throat—happily but a slight one and she is well. Farewell, my beloved friend. William, who is sitting beside me reading *Hamlet*—(we are both at the little green round table by the fireside, the watch ticking above our heads. Mary is with the sleeping baby below stairs, writing to Sara)—William exhorts me to give over writing; so farewell, my dearest Coleridge. May God bless you! and your faithful and affectionate Dorothy Wordsworth.

'Kind love to the Lambs. I hope you have talked to Mary Lamb about my regard for her, and my *seeming* neglect in not writing to her.

'William gets on rapidly with his poem. It is truly delightful, and makes us all happy. I am about to read Shakespeare through, and have read many of the plays; so you see I do not absolutely do nothing. This I tell you, because I know it will give you pleasure. The Journal is at a stand at present on account of the copying.'

For another fortnight the fevered work of copying went on; and as the date of Coleridge's departure drew nearer, Dorothy's fears increased, lest the precious volumes should not be ready for him in time; her mind was not at ease till she had heard of their safe arrival in London. 'Thinking of his banishment,' she wrote to Mrs. Clarkson,[1] 'his loneliness, the long distance he will be from all the human beings that he loves, it is one of my greatest consolations that he has those poems with him.' Then came the distressing news that whilst staying with the Beaumonts in Grosvenor Square he had had another violent attack of illness, and had only been nursed to convalescence by the devoted care of his hostess. In the hope of getting into touch with him once more before he sailed they wrote off at once:

March 29, 1804.

My dearest Coleridge,

There is little chance that this letter will reach you: therefore I shall write but a few words. Our hearts are full of you. May God preserve you, and restore you to us, in health of Body and peace of mind! I cannot express to you how deeply we were shocked at your late terrible attack nor how very thankful we are to the Beaumonts for their kindness to you. Indeed I love them most affectionately for it. We have had the severest gales of wind that we remember this winter in the beginning of the week; at first we did not know but you might be out at sea in them, and we were happy indeed to hear that you were not. Your letter

[1] D. W. to C. C., Mar. 24, 1804.

informing us of the arrival of all the poems did not reach us so soon as it ought to have done by several days. It had been missent to Keswick.

William has begun another part of the Poem addressed to you. He has written some very affecting lines, which I wish you could have taken with you. He is perfectly well at present, works in the garden, and walks daily. To-day Mary, John, William, and I had a walk together in Bainriggs, and after we left W. he wrote twenty lines in the three quarters of an hour before dinner. John is a rosy-cheeked fellow, very strong, happy as a bird in the open air, and delights in every sound he hears,—the crows high up in the sky, the wind in the trees, the little sykes by the roadsides. He is of an impatient temper. We expect him very soon to get up from the ground in a passion, for when we do not go to him the moment he wants us the efforts he makes are astonishing. . . . Before your Return I hope we shall be blessed with another little baby. I shall be thankful if it be a girl, but not disappointed if it is not. . . . Mrs Coleridge in her last letter said she would come over with the children. We hope in her next she will fix a time. They must all come, for we can have Thomas Ashburner's bed. Could you but see them playing with our Grasmere darling! . . . I am very well at present. I am going on with my *Journal*. I wish I could send you a copy of it when it is done. It is a tiresome thing to read long descriptions of places, but in Italy it would not seem tiresome, so far, far from us. If you get this letter, write to us yet once again; and never, dearest friend! never miss an opportunity of writing when you are abroad. . . .

. . . Farewell, my beloved Coleridge, dear friend, farewell. Believe me evermore your faithful friend,

DOROTHY WORDSWORTH.

On the same sheet William added:

My dearest Coleridge,

Your last letter but one informing us of your late attack was the severest shock to me I think I have ever received. I walked over for the letter myself to Rydale and had a most affecting return home, in thinking of you and your narrow escape. I will not speak of other thoughts that passed through me, but I cannot help saying that I would gladly have given three fourths of my possessions for your letter on *The Recluse* at that time. I cannot say what a load it would be to me, should I survive you and you die without this memorial left behind. Do, for heaven's sake, put this out of the reach of accident immediately. We are most happy that you have gotten the poems, and that they have already given you so much pleasure. Heaven bless you for ever and ever. No words can express what I feel at this moment. Farewell, farewell, farewell.

W. W.

On April 9 Coleridge left Portsmouth in the *Speedwell*, bound for Malta; on the 14th Dorothy opened a correspondence with Lady Beaumont. Her ostensible purpose was to acknowledge the receipt of a cask of brown stout which the kindly Sir George had sent them, but her real theme was their dear absent friend:

'I have many things to thank you for—I have been indebted to you and Sir George for many pleasures; but chiefly let me speak of the comfort we have had in the thought that our Friend was under your roof after his last illness. Believe me, my dear Madam, we feel no common gratitude for the consolation and happiness you bestowed on him by your affectionate care and tendance. But for you I know not how he would have got over the melancholy days of weakness and sickness previous to his departure from London. We have had only one letter from him since his arrival at Portsmouth, but three days ago Mrs Coleridge informed us that she had heard from him, and that he was on the point of going on board the vessel. I fear we shall not hear again, for when he is in bad spirits he has not heart to write, and I dare not hope that he could be otherwise till he had lost sight of his native land, and found himself alone with his own thoughts.'

But before she could put down her pen the post arrived with a farewell letter from Coleridge, 'concluded in the moment when the ship was going to sail'. 'It was like another parting to us', she adds, 'when we were assured that the last step was taken, that he is now really gone.'

And it would have been well for them all had this parting been the last; for that same Coleridge, with whom, for the last eight years, they had lived in rarest intimacy, 'three persons but one soul', was never to return.

X

BIRTH OF LITTLE DOROTHY (DORA). JOHN WORDSWORTH DROWNED. EXCURSION TO ULLSWATER

May 1804–December 1805 (aet. 32–34)

'YOU will be inclined to smile at me for talking of business and want of leisure in this solitude', wrote Dorothy to Lady Beaumont on May 24, but the tale of her doings suggests that she was probably as fully occupied as her friend, who was 'in the throng of her London engagements'. Earlier in the month she had spent a fortnight at the foot of Ullswater, whither she had gone to welcome Tom and Sara Hutchinson into the district, and help them to settle into their new farm. They had been forced to quit Gallow Hill, where they were comfortable and happy; for they had so improved the house and garden that their landlord's wife took a fancy to it as an extra residence for herself; and they had now moved into Park house,[1] a farm which stands on a hill between Dacre and Stainton, about two miles from Ullswater and three from Penrith. The surrounding country was already dear to Dorothy from its associations with her girlhood and from her visits with William to the Clarksons, and naturally enough her first walk after her arrival was to Eusemere; she was anxious to show it to Sara, and she knew too that Mrs. Clarkson would be hungry for news of it.

> 'The walk from here', she wrote,[2] 'is very pleasant over Dacre Beck (they are miserable stepping stones to be sure: we got wet-shod, but that may easily be remedied) through the fields and through your own Dunmallett. Could you but have heard the thrushes and seen the thousand thousand primroses under the trees! . . . We strolled about in the garden for about half an hour. The afternoon was warm and we sat down upon the grass, the Lake was beautiful and all about the house neat and flourishing—need I say how full our hearts were? Ellen gave us a kind welcome. We drank tea by the kitchen fire and had nice bread and everything comfortable. We went upstairs and when we entered the drawing room the view from the window struck upon us both

[1] Park house: so Dorothy always writes it.

[2] D. W. to C. C., May 9, 1804 (misdated by D. W. 'April').

in the same moment in the same way, as if it were an unearthly sight, a scene of *heavenly* splendour.'

Dorothy returned home to labours even more strenuous than those which had occupied her at Park house. 'Our old servant has left us', she wrote,[1] 'and we have been engaged in a Whitsuntide cleaning, colouring and painting etc. . . . it is an affair of great consequence to us that we should be well served, and that all things in our little establishment should be regularly arranged, which has not been the case for the last six weeks, while we have had no servant but a little girl—therefore my sister not being very strong, I was glad to take upon myself the charge of putting things in order.'

Old Molly Fisher had been with them ever since they came to the cottage; but her sister-in-law had just died, and she was now 'promoted to the high office of her brother's housekeeper and attendant upon his single cow. It is a great comfort to us', adds Dorothy,[2] 'that Molly has been taken from us in so quiet and natural a way, for we were afraid of breaking her heart by telling her that she was not fit for her place.' The Wordsworths had the true North country standard of household management, which Molly had long failed to reach; but still Molly was better than no one, and we are not surprised to hear that in her single-handed spring cleaning, Dorothy was 'overwrought with positive labour', so that a month's solitude at the cottage, while the others paid a visit to Park house, did not come amiss.

On their return Mrs. Coleridge arrived with her three lively children, filling the cottage and overflowing into the Ashburners' across the road. While Coleridge was abroad the Wordsworths made a point of seeing as much as possible of his family, and if Mrs. Coleridge was not particularly congenial, the Coleridge children were only less dear to them than Johnny—Hartley, who has 'so much thought and feeling in his face that it is scarcely possible to look at him with indifference', and fat, sweet-tempered little Derwent, said by Coleridge to be Dorothy's favourite, and Sara 'a slender, delicate creature, fair as a snowdrop and almost as pale[3] . . . such a little Fairy, a spirit, a thing that hardly seems to touch the earth as she skims along, though

[1] D. W. to Lady B., May 25, 1804.
[2] D. W. to C. C., May 3, 1804.
[3] D. W. to Lady B., June 20, 1804.

occasionally a little Vixen too, in action and voice; and look, if it were not for her soft blue eyes. Johnny and she were bitter enemies at first, but now they can agree very well together, for a few minutes, can run about in a friendly way till something takes their fancies which both cannot have, and *she* squalls and *he* roars, and we are obliged to part them by force.'[1] A happy but hardly a peaceful household; it was perhaps fortunate that William had acquired a habit of composing his poetry out of doors.

Then, on August 6, a month before she was expected, Johnny's little sister arrived. They had already decided that the new baby would be a girl, and had eagerly discussed the name that was to be given her. But William insisted that she must be called after her aunt, and though Mrs. Coleridge, a little tactlessly, 'exclaimed against it', and Dorothy herself did 'not like that the child should be saddled with such a name for my sake',[1] Mary took William's side, and Dorothy had to submit. From the first she undertook all the duties of nurse.

> 'Your goddaughter', she wrote to Lady Beaumont[2] (Lady Beaumont had asked to be allowed to stand godmother), 'grows a very pretty baby—she is her Father's darling. I think he is more tender over her than he ever was over her Brother. She wins her way into all our hearts, though at first we were often hurt to think that she did not seem so much prized among us as John was in the first fortnight of his life. Now, however, we make all up—but Johnny is very jealous and often gives her a blow that makes her cry—indeed he is so boisterous that we are obliged to keep constant watch over him when he is near her. . . . These are nursery tales—I will ask you to excuse them—I only prattle in this way to those whom I love and who, I believe, love me and those I love.'

To Mrs. Clarkson, who asked her to compare her feelings for the new baby and for Johnny, she replied:[3]

> 'I am sure I do not love her less—sometimes I fancy that I love her more, but there is certainly a difference which may possibly be sufficiently accounted for by the novelty of a first child. Everything that it does is curious and keeps one perpetually wakeful

[1] D. W. to Lady B., July 25, 1804.

[2] Sept. 23 (misdated by D. W. Aug. 23) 1804. In all the earlier letters D. W. calls her niece 'Dorothy', then, occasionally, 'Sissy', the name by which her brothers and sister seem to have called her. She only became first 'Doro', and then 'Dora', when she was grown up.

[3] D. W. to C. C., Feb. 10, 1805.

and alive; besides, the care which the first child continues to demand interferes with the *extra* attentions which otherwise would be paid to the second. On the other hand I think bringing more knowledge with the love makes us more tender, not so proud, not so much elated with the joy of possessing such a gift, but inwardly as happy in thinking of it. There is some difference in the sex of the children—something of delicacy about Dorothy as a girl that makes one love her as if one's love fortified her, independent of any consideration of future helplessness, while the courage and strength of the boy keeps alive the pride we have always had in him.'

As Mary and the baby throve apace, Dorothy was rewarded for her devoted care of them by a little holiday with her brother.

'We seized the first fine autumnal days and took our car to Keswick.[1] . . . The next day William and I set off on our Tour. We passed over the mountains of Whinlatter along the Cockermouth Road, and through the Vale of Lorton, and by Loweswater to Ennerdale. You must have crossed Whinlatter and will recollect what a lonely and wild road it is among the high mountains—one scene impressed me very much—there was neither stone-fence nor hedge, nor any work of men but the Road for a considerable way before us between the hills, a mile-stone, and a wall upon the sloping ground at the foot of the mountain built by the shepherds in the form of a cross[2] as a shelter for their sheep—it is strange that so simple a thing should be of so much importance, but the mountains and the very sky above them, the solitary mountain vale, all seemed to have a reference to that rude shelter—it was the very soul of the place. We dropped down soon after into the fertile vale of Lorton, and went to visit a Yewtree which is the Patriarch of yewtrees, green and flourishing in very old age—the largest tree I ever saw. We have many large ones in this country, but I have never seen one that would not be but as a Branch of this. When you come we must take you to it. I had never been at Ennerdale and I was very anxious to see every mountain top for the sake of old Walter Ewbank[3] and his Grandsons, but the mists had obstinately taken possession of them, and it rained all the time we were there. At Wasdale we did

[1] D. W. to Lady B., Oct. 7, 1804.

[2] Cf. *An Evening Walk* (1793), ll. 117–18.

> Beside their sheltering cross of wall, the flock
> Feeds on in light, nor thinks of winter's shock.

To which W. added the note: These rude structures, to protect the flocks, are frequent in this country; the traveller may recollect one in Withburne, another upon Whinlatter.

[3] *V. The Brothers*, *Oxf. W.*, 95–102.

better. . . . Wasdale is exceedingly wild, but in entire simplicity; the mountains are large and steep—in great masses—the borders of the lake on one side without any wood, on the other nearly so. We were very hospitably entertained at the house of a *statesman* at Wasdale Head, for there is no inn here, and the next day we went to his Cousin's who keeps an alehouse at Seathwaite in the vale of Duddon, one of the most romantic of all our vales, and one of the wildest, but in perfect contrast to Wasdale. In Duddon vale hills, rocks, bushes, and trees are striving together for mastery, green fields and patches of green are to be spied wherever the eye turns, with their snug cottages half-hidden by the rocks, or so like them in colour that you hardly know rock from cottage. We were received by the good people of the publick house with the same hospitality as by their kinsfolk in Wasdale. We said to each other that we here saw what the natives used to be in this country before it was so much visited. In the morning we asked for our Bill, which I will copy for you, as it is a curiosity. Observe that we had Tea, Supper and Breakfast, excellent cream and delicious bread and butter, broiled Char fresh out of the Tarn to supper. Tea 1s—Supper 1s—Breakfasts 1s—Horse 1s—ale 6d—Total 4s 6d!'

When they reached home, Montagu and Lamb's friend, George Dyer, were with them for a few days, and brother Richard followed; then they settled down to a quiet winter at the cottage, broken only by a short visit to Park house at the New Year.

'The day before New Year's Day', wrote Dorothy,[1] 'was one of the most delightful days that ever was felt; we were all taking our pleasure upon the ice, William and George Hutchinson pushed us along in their skates (Grasmere Water is entirely frozen over) and we carried the children on our knees, John and even little Dorothy. In our good spirits we resolved with true courage, and perhaps a little rashness it might seem, to come to see Sara the next day if the weather was not changed. It proved a fine morning, and we had a delightful journey; the children were no worse, but owing to our being overheated in climbing Kirkstone, both Mary and I suffered for it. She has been ill in the tooth ache unable to stir out ever since we came and I caught a very bad cold. All this would have been spared if William would have allowed us a little more time, but he was so much afraid of our being too late at night and hurried us up the hill—I carried

[1] To C. C., Jan. 6, 1805.

Dorothy in my arms, Mary had enough to do to carry herself and her clothes, William bore Johnny, and G. Hutchinson took care of the horse.'

But though, curiously enough, Dorothy does not mention it, William was the worst sufferer from the effects of his anxious hurry, for he dated the disease of his eyes, by which he was troubled intermittently for the rest of his life, from an inflammation caught on this occasion on the top of Kirkstone.[1]

Returning home, they took the less exposed route by Threlkeld and Dunmail Raise. William now busied himself over *The Prelude*; Mary and Dorothy had their hands full with the house and children. Since the birth of the little girl the arrival of any visitor had made them feel sadly cramped for space, and they began to look about for a more roomy dwelling. 'We cannot, however, hear of a house,' wrote Dorothy,[2] 'and though we are very industrious inquirers, yet I think we are half glad of it, for though when we have any single person staying with us we are forced to wish ourselves in another place, when we are alone we gather ourselves together, and looking round our lowly sitting room we feel as if we could never find another home.' It was partly to ease the situation that they now set about the building of a little shed or hut at the top of the orchard, 'a sort of larger Bird's nest (for it is lined with moss) a place for my Brother to retire to for quietness on warm days in winter, and for a pleasure-house, a little parlour, for all of us in summer—it is large enough for a large party to drink tea in'.[3] 'It is coated with heather and seated all round and thatched with straw. It will be circular but for the doorplace which is wide, but not near so wide as the diameter of the hut.'[4] They delighted in imagining how, when

[1] In the I.F. note (1843) to *A little onward lend thy guiding hand* (1816), after attributing the complaint in his eyes to this journey, he goes on: 'Frequently has the disease recurred since, leaving my eyes in a state which has often prevented my reading for months, and makes me at this day incapable of bearing without injury any strong light by day or night.' The only allusion to W.'s eye trouble before this expedition over Kirkstone, is, I believe, one made by D. W. in a letter to Lady B., May 25, 1804, when she speaks of him as 'troubled with a weakness in one of his eyes'. The trouble must have been seriously increased by the smoky chimneys at Allan Bank and the Rectory (1808–13), but there are few allusions to it in the correspondence till after the return from the Continent in 1820, when they become frequent.

[2] To Lady B., Oct. 7, 1804.

[3] D. W. to Lady B., Dec. 25, 1804.

[4] D. W. to C. C. Feb. 10, 1805.

summer came round again, they would entertain their friends there, the Beaumonts and Mrs. Clarkson, above all, Brother John and Coleridge.

Coleridge was never out of their minds. Not a letter was written without some wistful reference to him. 'Our enjoyments', she says,[1] 'are always damped by an inner sense of uncertainty respecting our beloved friend.' They had little news of him. His first letter had not reached them till September, and others followed only at rare intervals. In these days of secure postal service, speeded up with air mails, it is hard to realize how slow and uncertain, at the beginning of the last century, was all communication with a friend wandering on a war-distracted continent. They were ignorant of the state of his health, of his whereabouts, of the time of his return, of any plans that he might have formed for the future. On one point, however, they were quite clear, 'His returning to live in the North of England is quite out of the question, therefore we intend to keep ourselves unfettered, ready to move to any place where he may chuse to settle with his family.' At one time they think of Kent, where Mr. Clarkson tells them that land is cheap. 'But oh, my dear Friend,' Dorothy exclaims,[2] 'it will be a hard thing to leave these dear mountains without having some home here to draw us back again from time to time!' Perhaps two humble cottages might be found for them somewhere in Switzerland, and Dorothy suggests that the Beaumonts might take a third. 'But alas', she adds,[3] 'these things are to be guided by agents greater than we are. What is to become of Buonaparte? or when shall we be suffered again to pass quietly from place to place?' And the excitement with which they followed in the newspapers the fortunes of the war was stimulated by their knowledge of the danger it meant to those they loved.

Coleridge was not their only anxiety. During the summer and autumn John was on the high seas, and at any time his ship might be captured by the French. In December, however, they were relieved to hear that he was safely back in England, and they eagerly pressed him to visit them. 'Come if only for a fortnight', wrote William. 'We long to see you.' But urgent

[1] D. W. to Lady B., Jan. 5, 1805.
[2] D. W. to C. C., Oct. 14, 1804.
[3] D. W. to Lady B., Oct., 7, 1804.

business kept John in London. Through the influence of Wilberforce he had obtained the command of the ship *Earl of Abergavenny*, and was busy with preparations for his next voyage, from which he hoped to return a rich man; and for the pleasures of the present he would not risk any postponement of that happy day for which he worked, when he would be able to settle down for good, close beside his beloved brother and sister. On January 24 he wrote to William that his investment was well laid in and that he had no doubt but that he would 'make a very good voyage of it, if not a *very great* one'; the *Earl of Abergavenny* had reached Portsmouth, and he expected to sail on the following day. On February 10 Dorothy passed on this news to Mrs. Clarkson. 'John', she says, 'is in great spirits.' On the 11th came a short letter from Richard, informing them that the *Earl of Abergavenny* had struck a rock off Weymouth and gone to the bottom. Of the four hundred souls on board the great majority had perished, and among them their brother John.

It was the most terrible blow that either William or Dorothy had ever suffered; and their grief was uncontrollable. That same evening William wrote to Richard:

My dear Brother,

The lamentable news which your Letter has brought has now been known to us seven hours, during which time I have done all in my power to alleviate the distress of poor Dorothy and my Wife.—Mary and I were walking out when the Letter came; it was brought by Sara Hutchinson who had come from Kendal where she was staying, to be of use in the house and to comfort us; so that I had no power of breaking the force of the shock to Dorothy or to Mary. They are both very ill, Dorothy especially, on whom the loss of her beloved Brother will long take deep hold. I shall do my best to console her. But John was very dear to me, and my heart will never forget him. God rest his soul! When you can bear to write do inform us, not generally but as minutely as possible, of the manner of this catastrophe. It would comfort us in this lonely place, though at present nobody in the house but myself could bear a word on the subject. It is indeed a great affliction to us!

God bless you my dear Brother: Dorothy's and Mary's best love. We wish you were with us, God keep the rest of us together! the set is now broken. Farewell, dear brother

WM WORDSWORTH.

To Sir George Beaumont he wrote:

'I can say nothing higher of my ever dear brother than that he was worthy of his sister who is now weeping beside me and of the friendship of Coleridge,—meek, affectionate, silently enthusiastic, loving all quiet things, and a poet in everything but words. . . . I shall do all in my power to sustain my sister under her sorrow, which is, and long will be, bitter and poignant. We did not love him as a brother merely, but as a man of original views and an honour to all about him. Oh! dear friend, forgive me for talking thus. We have no tidings of Coleridge. I tremble for the moment when he is to hear of my brother's death; it will distress him to the heart—and his poor body cannot bear sorrow. He loved my brother, and he knows how we at Grasmere loved him.'

For the time they gave themselves up completely to their grief. To a letter of sympathy received the next morning from Southey William replied: 'We weep much to-day, and that relieves us. As for fortitude I hope I shall show that, and that all of us will show it, in a proper time, in keeping down many a violent pang hereafter. But grief will (as you say) and must have its course: there is no wisdom in attempting to check it under the circumstances which we are all of us in here.' For the present they found their only comfort in helping one another to bear the burden; and naturally enough their thoughts turned with anxious love to their absent brothers, Richard and Christopher, whose sorrow they longed to share. Eagerly they looked for letters, and when a fortnight had passed and nothing further had come from Richard, they became alarmed. On the 27th Dorothy wrote urging him to send a line, if only to say that he was well, and five days later, as Richard was still silent, she repeated her entreaty:

My dear Brother,

Being exceedingly anxious and uneasy about you I wrote to you, (the first letter I had been able to write since our dear Brother's death) to beg that you would write and let us know how you were. As we have had no letter from you I am afraid that mine has never been received, for it was entrusted to a carrier who has most likely lost it or neglected to put it in the post-office. I cannot be easy till we hear from you—Mary is very anxious about you also, indeed so are we all—we know how deeply you must have suffered from the first agony of the shock, and your mind must now be harassed and perplexed by many dismal affairs in connection with it. You will be continually seeing people who have had concern with poor John and his ship and probably have many painful inquiries to answer. We are indeed afraid that your health should sink under it, and cannot get it out of our minds that you are ill. Pray, my dear Richard, write to us, if only to tell us how your health is. I need not add that if you have leisure and have anything to communicate respecting our Brother John that may give us comfort, we shall thankfully receive it—we go about our house and garden with dismal hearts—John knew this place and loved it well—everything I see reminds me of him.—Mary is a sincere mourner with us—but she has been a great comfort and consolation to us—we are all pretty well. God bless you, my dear Brother.

Believe me ever your affectionate Sister

D. WORDSWORTH.

One thing let me say.—If there is anything saved from the wreck that belonged to my dear Brother, I should wish that some trifle may be preserved for me and Wm, or if he left any Book or anything in your Rooms that you can part with.

And William adds:

'I cannot say that the burthen of our affliction in this house is yet much lighter; to time we must look for ease. Dorothy though not ill is very thin and weak. Do write to us—we are very anxious about you, and if you would tell us anything about John and his behaviour in his dreadful trial, do: for we are almost heart-broken.'

But Richard's reply to their pathetic inquiries makes it clear that they need not have felt alarm on his account:

'I received your kind letter for which you will accept my warmest thanks. I hope you are by this time completely composed and that William, and Mary and yourself are in tolerable health. I have been as well as could be expected, and am getting up my spirits. It is impossible for me to enter into the particulars of the melancholy catastrophe. It will be enough to say that our dear Brother did everything that man could do on so trying and arduous an occasion. This must be a great consolation to us all. I have no reason to think that any of us shall suffer in our Property. I have taken out administration. The Insurance was considerable. . . . You will excuse me for not writing sooner, for the Truth is, I have no relish for writing. Let me hear from you soon, how you all are—Remember me affect.ly to William and Mary and believe me most sincerely and affectionately (Give John a shake by the hand) R. WORDSWORTH.'

William's acknowledgement of this epistle suggests that he realized, as indeed, in normal conditions, they knew well enough, that the phlegmatic Richard moved on a different plane of feeling from theirs.

'God defend any body from suffering what we have suffered, and still do suffer. No words can express the love we had of poor John, and the daily and perpetual pleasure we had in looking forward to the time when he would be at liberty to settle among us. He loved everything which we did, and every thing about us here incessantly reminds us of him and our irreparable loss. But I will not distress you, for you can give us no relief.'

Richard was in truth, as Dorothy delicately put it some years later, a 'curious' brother.

More than a month elapsed before she could command enough self control to respond to the loving sympathy which reached her from many quarters. Then in turn she wrote to her aunt Rawson, to Jane, Lady Beaumont, and Mrs. Clarkson.

To Lady Beaumont (March 17th). 'I know it will give you pleasure to see my handwriting again. God be praised, I am quiet and composed and able to write! But I must not give myself up to past things. Blessings be upon you, my dear and good Friend! for ever blessed will you be by me while my heart can beat! If my poor lost brother could have known you I should have even greater comfort in thinking of your goodness—but it could not be. It was the will of God that he should be taken away from all care and sorrow, and he has left behind with us what we shall never part from; the memory of his retired virtues, his modesty, his tenderness, his deep affections. Wherever we go we shall know what would have been John's sentiments and feelings, if he had been at our side—for he was true and constant as the light of heaven—he seemed to have been made for the best sort of happiness which is to be found in this world, for his whole delight was in peace and Love and the beautiful works of this fair Creation.—I cannot speak of him as he was—I must have done.

'I take the pen again and resolve not to trust myself into the depths of our affliction. I must only say that I hope I shall in a little time profit as I ought from the many consolations which remain to us, above all from the solemn recollections which we have of our departed Brother; and I have a task of my own to perform, and therein I must not be remiss, that of aiding my Sister to raise up the spirits of my dear Brother William, and contribute to make him fit to accomplish the work he meditates. This is an awful thought, and trust me I will do my utmost. I have begun again to attend to the children; the quietness of the little Girl is very soothing to me, and I have great delight in her, but John is too boisterous. We walk out whenever the weather is tolerable—these walks feed our melancholy, but in the end they are tranquillizing, and we are the better for them—but this Vale is changed to us, it can never be what it *has been*, and as we cannot spend our days here the sooner we remove the better, for if we stay long we shall be attached to it by our painful feelings even more strongly than we have been heretofore by those of hope and gladness or fearless peace—and the parting will be a fresh sorrow, which if it were to happen within a few months would scarcely be felt as such.

'Since I wrote the above I have been walking with my Brother. We were two hours in the open air, and the day was uncommonly delicious. We have had many fine days since we heard the dismal tidings; but sunshine and darkness, starlight and moonlight, calm weather and fierce winds were all doleful to us. As your tender sympathy suggested to you it would be, the placid weather which followed the lamentable sixth of February was beyond description melancholy. I had even a feeling of *joy* the first time I heard the wind in my bed after we heard the tidings—but why dwell upon these things? I am distressing you—and this morning we have had some chearful sensations, while we sate down together talking of you and Coleridge, and all the time we thought of our beloved Brother. . . .'

The letter to Mrs. Clarkson, written on the next day, is blotted with tears:

'. . . My dear Friend what a struggle we have gone through! and how much sorrow have we not yet to endure! but I trust that the example of our dear Brother, who though taken from our earthly sight is for ever with us and will be so to our dying day, that his example will teach us to submit to the divine Will—and that the memory of his happy and innocent life, his joy in all good and lovely things will help us again to take pleasure in the same objects as before and with a more holy feeling, though it can never be so gladsome. Blessings be with him for evermore, his lovely happy ways. Oh my friend! I must have done—I could have had no pleasure greater than that of pouring out my heart to you because you are one of those who knew something of John's greatest merits which were never known but to a very few, and you can sympathize with us to the full contentment of our dejected hearts, but I have forborne to do it for fear of distressing you, and now, weak creature that I am! I have been unable to write with calmness—but I have much comfort for you: we are all in tolerable health.'

A little later they were helped to bear their loss by news of the calm heroism with which John had met his fate. From a Mr. Evans, a survivor from the wreck, they received a letter which touched them deeply, and Charles Lamb, with a ready sympathy, spared no pains in collecting all such information of the disaster as he felt would bring them comfort. 'I have great pleasure', wrote Dorothy to Mrs. Clarkson on April 19, 'in thinking that you may see Miss Lamb. Do not miss it, if you can possibly go without injury to yourself. They are the best good creatures, blessings be with them! They have sympathized in our sorrow as tenderly as if they had grown up in the same town with us, and known our beloved John from his childhood. Charles has written to us the most consolatory letters, the result of diligent and painful enquiry of the survivors of the wreck—For this we must love him as long as we have breath. I think of him and his sister every day of my life, and many times in the day, with thankfulness and blessings.'

Only gradually was Dorothy able to take up the threads of her old life.

'When I do not seem to know it,' she writes on May 4th,[1] 'I am sensible of my loss. I can never again have a *perfect*—that is an unchastized—joy in this world. You understand me—I did not know what sorrow was till now, which made me oversecure in what I loved and rejoiced in, and think it too good and too perfect. . . . Oh! my dear Friend, you have been good in listening. I know not what I am doing to give you pain now—I cannot see my paper for my tears. . . . I take my pen again—it does not look like composure and tranquillity thus to be led away—but believe me I have done a good deal. I keep myself constantly employed and seek after chearful thoughts for the sake both of the living and the dead. I am never, I am sure, two minutes without some image of my brother John; how could it be otherwise, for he loved every thing that is dear to me, but I think that this constant presence of him, which I have never striven against, has done more to calm me than anything else.'

[1] To Lady B.

On June 11th she is able to write[1] in a calmer frame of mind:

My dear Friend,

It will give you pleasure to hear that I have delayed writing to you in consequence of full employment—I do not mean employment that made it impossible or inconvenient; but I had determined within myself not to write till our work was ended. In the first place we turned to the melancholy garden, and put it into order; the orchard hut, which had remained unfinished since last autumn, we have completed;[2] and our own dwelling house, which had fallen into disorder like other things, we have had set to rights. While these labours were going on I took a small share in them, but nursing was my chief business. Since that time I have been engaged in finishing a copy of a journal of our tour in Scotland[3]—this was at the first beginning a very painful office. I had written it for the sake of Friends who could not be with us at the time, and my Brother John had been always in my thoughts, for we wished him to know everything that befell us. The task of re-copying this journal, which at first when it was proposed to me after his death, I thought I could never do, I performed at last, and found it a tranquillizing employment. I write to you from the Hut, where we pass all our time except when we are walking—it has been a rainy morning, but we are here sheltered and warm, and in truth I think it is the sweetest place on earth—the little wrens often alight upon the thatch and sing their low song, but this morning *all* the Birds are rejoicing after the rain. Before my eyes is the Church, and a few houses among trees, and, still beyond, the hollow of Easedale which I imagine but cannot see, and the quiet mountains shutting all up. Where I sit I have no view of the Lake, but if I chuse to move half a yard further along the seat, I can see it; and so on, going all round, we have a different view. My Brother is at Patterdale, he took his fishing rod over the mountains, there being a pass from Grasmere thither. My Sister and I accompanied him to the top of it, and parted from him near a Tarn under a part of Helvellyn—he had gone up on Saturday with a neighbour of ours to fish there, but he quitted his companion and poured out his heart in some beautiful

[1] To Lady B.

[2] 'William Mary and I finished the Moss Hut on the afternoon of June the sixth 1805—After the work was ended we all sate down in the middle of the seat, looking at the clouds of the west—a very beautiful Evening—as it had been a very fine sunny day.' *Mem.* written at the end of D. W.'s *Recollections of a Tour in Scotland.*

[3] Another note states 'Finished copying this Journal May 31st 1805 in the Moss Hut at the end of the Orchard. D.W.'

verses to the memory of our lost Brother,[1] who used to go there sometimes alone, for the pleasure of angling in part, but still more for his love of solitude and of the mountains. Near that very Tarn William and I bade him farewell the last time he was at Grasmere, when he went from us to take command of the ship. We were in view of the head of Ullswater, and stood till we could see him no longer, watching him as he *hurried* down the stony mountain—Oh! my dear Friend, you will not wonder that we love that place. I have been twice to it since his death—the first time was agony, but it is now a different feeling—poor William was overcome on Saturday—and with floods of tears wrote those verses—he parted from us yesterday very chearfully, and indeed his spirits are far better than I could have thought possible at this time. He will return to us we hope in three days—he went for the sake of relaxation having finished his long poem,[2] and intending to pause a short time before he begins the other. You will judge that a happy change has been wrought in his mind when he chuses John's employments, and one of John's haunts (for he delighted in the neighbourhood of Patterdale) for such a purpose.

The summer season brought them even more visitors than usual, in July Mrs. Coleridge and little Sara, later Humphrey Davy and Richard Sharp,[3] Walter Scott and his wife. 'I have often', writes Lockhart[4], 'heard Scott speak with enthusiastic delight of the reception he met with in the humble cottage which his brother poet then inhabited on the banks of Grasmere', and twenty years later when Scott visited the Lakes, and found Wordsworth living in a state of comparative splendour, he recalled 'the little cottage, and his sister and wife dressing the mutton leg in the same room where it was to be eat'. Then Mrs. Threlkeld and her daughter Elizabeth came from Halifax: they had not seen Dorothy for some years and were deeply shocked at her worn and aged appearance. 'Elizabeth', wrote Edward Ferguson[5] to his brother Sam in America, 'gives a sad

[1] *Elegiac Verses, in Memory of my Brother.* 'The Sheepboy whistled', *Oxf. W.*, p. 580.

[2] *The Prelude.*

[3] Richard Sharp, 1759–1835, M.P. on the Whig side 1806–12 and 1816–19; all his life keenly interested in politics and literature, and so brilliant a talker that he was known as 'Conversation Sharp'. In his youth he knew Johnson and Burke, and later was the 'close and intimate friend' of Rogers. He knew both W. W. and S. T. C. well, and often visited the Lake country.

[4] *Life of Scott*, chap. xiv.

[5] E. F. to S. F., July 22, 1805.

account of poor Dorothy, who is grown so thin and old that they should not have known her, lost many of her teeth, and her cheeks quite sunk that it has entirely altered her profile.' Brother Richard came also, and fearing that Dorothy was overtaxing her strength by too much walking, presented her with a pony and side-saddle. It was a timely gift, for William could often borrow for himself a neighbour's horse, or walk by her side; and for their longer expeditions this was a pleasanter means of travel than in the old Irish car, especially in a country which can only be enjoyed to the full when the roads are left behind.

But of all their visitors none was so welcome as Mrs. Clarkson, for whom they took lodgings at Robert Newton's in the village. Mrs. Clarkson was still a great invalid, often suffering from acute attacks of pain, but that did not prevent her from being 'cheerful, and often lively, and even merry and the cause of mirth by our fire-side'.[1]

An unusually wet summer was followed by a glorious autumn, and Mrs. Clarkson stayed on into the middle of October; early in November William and Dorothy started off on a week's tour to explore the region of Ullswater. 'William on foot, and I upon the pony, with William's greatcoat slung over the saddle-crutch, and a wallet containing our bundle of "needments".'[2] They had left it too late, and the weather had already broken; but this did not damp their spirits, for they never felt closer to one another than when they were on the tramp. 'As the mist

[1] D. W. to Lady B., Aug. 7, 1805. Mrs. Clarkson's devotion to Dorothy, and admiration for her genius, is attested by the fact that during this visit she made a complete copy of her friend's *Recollections of a Tour in Scotland*. Her manuscript is beautifully written in a small clear hand, with hardly an erasure: it is divided into three parts numbered separately, 1–70, 1–98, 1–70. Appended is the following note: 'This copy of my beloved friend's Journal was begun at Grasmere the beginning of September and finished at Patterdale this day (the 1st of November 1805). When I began the work I scarcely indulged the hope of finishing it myself, my health being so indifferent that every little exertion of mind or body fatigued me exceedingly; but instead of a difficult task I have found it the easiest and pleasantest employment that ever I engaged in; and now though the possession of such a treasure makes me very happy, yet I am sincerely sorry that my work is ended. The whole (except a very few pages, the writing of which was the only toilsome part of the undertaking) was written in bed, and the whole by myself, except the title pages and the divisions of the work wh. were written by Mr. George Hutchinson brother of my two dear friends Mrs. Wordsworth and Sara Hutchinson, and the title on the first page of the work, which my Husband had the kindness to interrupt himself, when he was exceedingly busy in his own work, to write for me. C. C.'

[2] *Journals of D. W.*, ed. Knight, ii. 153.

thickened', writes Dorothy, 'our enjoyments increased, and my hopes grew bolder: and when we were at the top of Kirkstone (though we could not see fifty yards before us) we were as happy travellers as ever paced side by side on a holiday ramble. At such a time and in such a place every scattered stone the size of one's head becomes a companion.'[1] The next day she wrote to Lady Beaumont[2] from the cottage of their friend Luff, in the valley at the head of Ullswater: 'I look over the level bed of the valley, intersected with hedgerows (it seems as level as a bowling-green); horses and cows are feeding in the fields which are of a soft yellow hue, through which you hardly perceive the tinge of the fading green, a colour that harmonizes exquisitely with that of the trees upon the mountain opposite, where a thick cloud is resting; and through that veil rocks and craggy points now appear, and then are hidden again. This is a wonderful country; the more wonderful the more we know of it. . . . Yesterday we had visions of things, imperfectly seen as we passed along, that might have employed our fancy happily for hours, if they had not been replaced by others as beautiful.'

Dorothy wrote a journal of this tour which her brother afterwards recast and appended to his *Guide to the Lakes*: few readers will prefer his more formal, 'literary' version to Dorothy's, which has the same vivid beauty of feeling and expression that characterizes her *Recollections of a Tour in Scotland*. Thus she tells how one day William 'pitched upon the spot where he should like to build a house better than in any other he had ever yet seen', and they went out by moonlight to view it. 'The vale looked as if it were filled with white light when the moon had climbed up to the middle of the sky; but long before we could see her face, while all the eastern hills were in black shade, those on the opposite side were almost as bright as snow. Mrs. Luff's large dog lay in the moonshine upon the round knoll under the old yewtree, a beautiful and romantic image—the dark tree with its dark shadow, and the elegant creature as fair as a spirit.' Another day they explored Boar Dale, a deep bare valley behind Place Fell, and saw at its head the ruins of a chapel where the villagers of Martindale and Patterdale used to meet

[1] *Journals of D. W.*, ed. Knight, ii. 153.

[2] D. W. to Lady B., Nov. 7, 1805. (D. W.'s dating of her *Journal* is throughout one day wrong.)

for worship. The place was associated with an incident later to be recorded in one of the finest passages in *The Excursion*.[1] 'Whether it was ever consecrated ground or not I know not; but the place may be kept holy in the memory of some now living in Patterdale; for it was the means of preserving the life of a poor old man last summer, who, having gone up the mountain to gather peats had been overtaken by a storm, and could not find his way down again. He happened to be near the remains of the old chapel, and, in a corner of it, he contrived, by laying turf and ling and stones from one wall to the other, to make a shelter from the wind, and there he lay all night'; the next morning he was found 'huddled up in the sheltered nook. He was at first stupified and unable to move; but after he had eaten and drunk, and recollected himself a little, he walked down the mountain and did not afterwards seem to have suffered.' But perhaps the most delightful excursion to Dorothy was one which brought back to her the days of her youth. From Yanwath, the home of their good Quaker friend Thomas Wilkinson, they walked by way of Brougham Castle through the woods to Lowther, passing the quarry which had been the boundary of those evening walks taken years ago, at times with William, more often with Mary and Peggy Hutchinson, when she escaped from the stern eye of her grandmother. 'The sun did not shine when we were there, and it was mid-day; therefore if it had shone, the light could not have been the same; yet so vividly did I call to mind those walks, that, when I was in the wood, I almost seemed to see the same rich light of evening upon the trees which I had seen in those happy hours.'

When they reached home it was Mary's turn for a release from household duties, and she went off on a visit to Park house; and as William divided his time between her and Grasmere, Dorothy was left much to herself. There was a maid to help her with the children, and she was now sole mistress of her leisure; it was at such times, and especially in the quiet evenings, when she felt most keenly the need of companionship, that she wrote her best, and most revealing letters:

Friday evening—Grasmere—November 29th.

I received the first of your short letters on Monday, the second not till today: judge of the mismanagement of our Post-office!—

[1] *Excursion*, ii. 725, *ad fin.*

regular office indeed we have none, but the Post now comes four times a week; yet (so do they arrange it) on the Sunday evenings he brings as many letters as all the rest of the week put together. I do not know why I have troubled you with this my lamentation at this time except that in future it may serve to explain to you if there should be any extraordinary delay when you may have written what may demand an immediate answer. My Brother and Sister are at Park house—She left home last Monday, and William yesterday morning; and I do not expect them at home before the end of next week. Perhaps my Sister may stay longer, as she is still not in *strong* health, and we think that change of air may be of service to her. She will bring Miss Hutchinson to spend the winter with us.

My dear Lady Beaumont, you are so affectionate and kind to me that I often feel a restless desire that you should know me better, which impels me to write to you; for while I write I seem to draw nearer to you and to bring you more near to me. I have many dear and chearful thoughts, and many melancholy ones in my solitude—these L sometimes seek, but at others they master me, and I turn my cowardly heart to some other employment—I read—I copy some of my Brother's Poems (a work which he has left me to do) or I write a letter. The Children are now in bed. The evening is very still, and there are no indoor sounds but the ticking of our Family watch which hangs over the chimney piece under the drawing of the Applethwaite Cottage,[1] and a breathing or a beating of one single irregular Flame in my fire. No one who has not been an Inmate with Children in a *Cottage* can have a notion of the quietness that takes possession of it when they are gone to sleep. The hour before is generally a noisy one, often given up to boisterous efforts to amuse them, and the noise is heard in every corner of the house—then comes the washing and undressing, a work of misery, and in ten minutes after, all is stillness and perfect rest. It is at all times a sweet hour to us, but I can fancy that I have never enjoyed it so much as now that I am quite alone. Yet it is a strange kind of pleasure, for the Image of our departed Brother haunts me with many a pang in the midst of happy recollections of him and glorious hopes—he loved this fireside—he paced over this floor in pride before we had been six weeks in the house, exulting within his noble heart that his Father's Children had once again a home together. We did not know on what day he would come, though we were expecting him every hour, therefore he had no reason to fear that he should

[1] A picture given to them by Sir George Beaumont.

surprize us suddenly; yet twice did he approach the door and lay his hand upon the latch, and stop, and turn away without the courage to enter (we had not met for several years)[1]—he then went to the Inn and sent us word that he was come. This will give you a notion of the depth of his affections, and the delicacy of his feelings. While he stayed with us he busied himself continually with little schemes for our comfort. At this moment when I cast my eyes about I scarcely see anything that does not remind me of some circumstance of this kind, and my tears *will* flow by fits in spite of my inner and habitual sense of the many consolations which he has left for us (chiefly in his innocent life and noble death) and that all our regrets are selfish. *His* Hope, and mine, our Brother William, is yet spared to me—and I have many blessings which poor John did not share; he knew and affectionately loved my Sister, but he never saw her after her marriage, and he had only heard the names of their dear Children—Oh! what a beautiful spectacle are they, as I have just left them this evening upon their pillows! how divine an image of peace! But I was seeking consolation, and I find I am further from it, for then came a bitter pang—I was weak enough to grieve for *his* Loss, thinking what happiness would have been his, could he have beheld their blessed countenances——

——I begin again after a pause—Poor Coleridge! we must not talk of him—I hope we shall not see him this winter; yet I cannot in my mind depend upon it, for I *know* that his earnest desire to return is the cause of his silence—he has nothing decisive to communicate and therefore has not heart to write—Heaven preserve him from captivity in France!

The very morning after I wrote to you the tidings of Lord Nelson's Fate reached us at Patterdale. We were at Breakfast when Mr Luff's maidservant opened the door, and shewing only her head, with an uncouth stare and a grin of pleasure told us that there had been a great victory, and Lord Nelson was shot. It was a blow—*I* was not collected enough to doubt, and burst into tears; but William would not believe all at once, and forced me to suspend my grief till he had made further inquiries. At the Inn we were told that there were "great rejoicings at Penrith—all the Bells ringing"—"Then", I exclaimed, "he cannot be dead!" but we soon heard enough to leave us without a doubt, and bitterly did we lament for him and our Country. Your account of what you have heard of him interests me very much—I believe

[1] In 'we' she only refers to herself and John. W. and J. had taken a short tour together in the previous October (*v.* p. 107).

that every truly *brave* Man, in the highest sense of the word, is, as you describe Lord Nelson to have been, tender and humane in all the daily acts of life. I was sure that you would be pleased with the stanzas on the Solitary Reaper. There is something inexpressibly soothing to me in the sound of those two Lines

> Oh listen! for the Vale profound
> Is overflowing with the sound—

I often catch myself repeating them in disconnection with any thought, or even I may say recollection of the Poem.

My Brother has not yet begun fairly with his great work, but I hope he will after his return from Park house. We shall then in right earnest enjoy winter quiet and loneliness; besides, starlight walks and winter winds are his delight—his mind I think is often more fertile in this season than any other. I am now engaged in making a fair and final transcript of the Poem on his own Life—I mean *final*, till it is prepared for the press, which will not be for many years. No doubt before that time he will, either from the suggestions of his Friends, or his own, or both, have some alterations to make, but it appears at present to be finished. . . .

We spent a delightful day at Lowther—indeed the whole week was delightful—we ranged from one beautiful scene to another—I came home in perfect health, and we boasted of my wonderful strength; but last week I was confined to my bed four days by a violent pain in my left side—I was bled, blistered, etc. and am now perfectly well, and the apothecary tells me I have no reason to apprehend a return of the disease in consequence of having once had it. It being a new disease, I believe I was unduly alarmed, else, now that it is over, I think I should not have thought it worth while to mention it to you.

At another time I should have told you *by way of consolation* on coming to the end of this letter, that it may probably be a long time before you receive another of equal length, for when our household is gathered together again I shall have less leisure; but you so kindly encourage me to believe that all that happens to us is interesting to you, that I am not afraid that even *this* letter will tire you. Believe me I consider your delight in hearing from me as a sure proof of your affection; for what have I to communicate but our daily goings-on (which hardly vary from day to day) and my own peculiar feelings; and to make these interesting love must be in your heart.

Adieu, my good and dear Friend,

your ever affectionate

DOROTHY WORDSWORTH.

When Christmas came Mary was still at Park house, and William with her: Dorothy spent the day with the children, and in communion with absent friends and with her own thoughts:

'John', she wrote[1] to Mrs. Clarkson, 'is all alive at the thought of two plumb-puddings which are now rumbling in the pot, and a sirloin of beef that is smoking at the fire. Old Molly and John Fisher are in the kitchen, but when dinner is ready they are to come up stairs and partake with us, and "Johnny and all". . . . Perhaps you may remember that this is my birthday. . . . Six Christmases have we spent at Grasmere, and though the freshness of life was passed away even when we came hither, I think these years have been the very happiest of my life,—at least, they seem as if they would bear looking back upon better than any other,—though my heart flutters and aches, striving to call to my mind more perfectly the remembrance of some of the more thoughtless pleasures of former years, and though till within this late time I never experienced a real affliction.

'Poor John was in London last Christmas, all his heart set upon the accomplishment of that fatal voyage as the termination of his Labours, and so it proved, and to him a happy and glorious termination of them,—to us only the sorrow and pain. Dear and blessed creature, he in those last moments of trial bequeathed us a large share of consolation and enobling thoughts, and confident trust in the goodness of divine providence. But my heart (fills?) fast and I shall betray myself into tears and grief, and give you pain also. In numbering over the Blessings of the last six years first and foremost are present with me the pleasures and consolations of Friendship. How many excellent and kind friends have been tried and proved to me, within that time! When we came here, you were but a *name* to me!'

To Lady Beaumont she wrote:

Your kind and interesting letters gave me true pleasure; indeed, my dear Lady Beaumont, the proofs which I so frequently receive from you of your sympathy in my daily feelings and common concerns are very affecting to me. You yourself are far removed from many of the cares, anxieties and even pleasures that occupy my mind, which makes your sympathy doubly touching; and for that cause I am the more grateful for it. I began this letter yesterday, on Christmas day, but was interrupted. It is a day of dear

[1] Dec. 25, 1805.

and interesting remembrances, and to me peculiarly, therefore I was unwilling to take another sheet of paper for the Date's sake. I yesterday completed my thirty fourth year—a birthday is to everybody a time of serious thought, but more so, I should think, when it happens to be upon a day of general festivity, and especially on Christmas day, when all persons, however widely scattered, are in their thoughts gathered together at home. I can almost tell where every Birthday of my life was spent, many of them even *how* from a very early time. The day was always kept by my Brothers with rejoicing in my Father's house, but for six years (the interval between my Mother's death and his) I was never once at home, never was for a single moment under my Father's roof after her death, which I cannot think of without regret for many causes, and particularly that I have thereby been put out of the way of many recollections in common with my Brothers of that period of life, which, whatever it may be actually as it goes along, generally appears more delightful than any other when it is over.—Poor Coleridge was with us two years ago at this time—he came over with Derwent on his way to London, and was detained week after week by sickness. We hear no further tidings of him, and I cannot help being very uneasy and anxious: though without any evil, many causes might delay him; yet it is a long time since he left Malta. The weather is dreadful for a sea voyage. Oh my dear Friend, what a fearful thing a windy night is now at our house! I am too often haunted with dreadful images of Shipwrecks and the Sea, when I am in bed and hear a stormy wind, and now that we are thinking so much about Coleridge it is worse than ever. My Sister is not yet returned, we expect her at home tomorrow, if the day be tolerable, but wind, rain and snow are driving down the Vale, and the chimney every now and then roars as if it were going to come down upon us. I am very anxious that this boisterous day should be followed by a gentle one (as often happens)—I should be exceedingly disappointed if my Sister should not come home—she has stayed much longer than she intended, and is anxious to be with us again and to see the children—John is grown very much during her absence, and Dorothy, till within these three days, has been advancing rapidly, but she is now very poorly having caught cold, and will be quite thrown back again when her Mother sees her, which is mortifying to me. You are very good in taking so much thought about us. It is true that Miss Hutchinson will be of great use in assisting us in the care of the children; not that when we are both well we are over-fatigued with them but even at (all?) times it would be better if we had more time for the cultivation of our minds by reading. I do not read much—very little, indeed; but in this house it would be exceedingly unpleasant to have two servants, not to speak of an *insurmountable* objection, the want of room for another person; but as soon as we can meet with a suitable house in a situation that we like, we are resolved to remove, and by keeping a couple of cows (even if my Sister should have no more children) we shall have sufficient employment for two servants, and she and I might have much more leisure. I have been summoned into the kitchen to dance with Johnny, and have danced till I am out of breath. According to annual custom our Grasmere Fiddler is going his rounds, and all the children of the neighbouring houses are assembled in the kitchen to dance. Johnny has long talked of the time when the Fiddler was to come; but he was too shy to dance with anybody but me, and, though he exhibited very boldly when I was downstairs, I find they cannot persuade him to stir again. It is a pleasant sound they make with their little pattering feet upon the stone floor, half a dozen of them, Boys and Girls; Dorothy is in ecstasy, and John looks as grave as an old man.

I am very glad you hear so frequently from your Sister. If the Lyrical Ballads do but give her half the pleasure which you have received from them it will be very gratifying to me. I have no thoughts more soothing than those connected with the hope that my dear Brother and Coleridge may be the means of ministering consolation to the unhappy, or elevating and worthy thoughts to many who live in solitude or retirement, or have too much of the bustle of the world without unhappiness.

. . . The day grows worse and worse—I fear we shall have sad tidings from the sea-coast. Heaven grant that Coleridge may be somewhere or other safe on Land! Adieu, my dear Friend. May you enjoy many years of life with health and tranquillity! Coleridge, I believe, was at Dunmow about five weeks after this time two years ago—Oh! that he were with you there now!

Yours ever

Dorothy Wordsworth.

XI

BIRTH OF THOMAS. RETURN OF COLERIDGE. COLEORTON. LAST DAYS AT DOVE COTTAGE

1806–1808 (*aet.* 34–36)

SHORTLY after Mary's return to Grasmere Sara Hutchinson joined her there; for the rest of her life she was to make her home with the Wordsworths. Mary was her favourite sister, Dorothy her closest friend, and her chief interests and sympathies were bound up with theirs. She felt, too, that she was not really needed at Park house, for her brother Tom had Joanna to keep house for him: at Grasmere, if she helped to look after the children, Mary and Dorothy might have a little more leisure. But with one more permanent inmate at the cottage they were 'crammed in their little nest edge-full',[1] and the problem of finding another house became still more acute. Yet nothing could be decided in Coleridge's absence, and the strain of their uncertainty about his movements became more and more harassing. Ever since the previous May they had been expecting him; in the summer they had postponed a projected holiday tour because they could not bear the thought of his possible arrival in their absence; again, early in December, they heard that he was on his way home, and might be with them at any moment; then for another three months they had no news. They did not know whether he was travelling by land or sea, and in either case were apprehensive of the dangers that would threaten him. 'The tidings from the Continent', says Dorothy,[2] 'are so dismal that I dread to hear anything fresh when the newspapers arrive . . .' 'and oh what dreadful winds we have had lately, I never remember such a winter of storms.[1] . . . We were wearied out with conjectures, and expectations worn out, [*sic*] for though every post-day we trembled when the news was coming upstairs "no letters", yet we had scarcely anything like expectation left . . . when I was alone in bed at night I could not banish the most dreadful images, and Mary and Sara have suffered in the same way.'

William was in a like state of restless excitement; and they

[1] D. W. to C. C., Mar. 2, 1806. [2] D. W. to Lady B., Jan. 19, 1806.

all felt that a change of scene would do him good. He had not been south since his marriage, and so at the end of March they packed him off for a five or six weeks' visit to London, to stay with his brother Christopher, now rector of Lambeth, and with Sir George Beaumont in Grosvenor Square; and as they now heard once more that Coleridge was on his way home there was another incentive to his journey. 'We have great delight', wrote Dorothy[1] to Lady Beaumont, 'in thinking of the possibility of Coleridge's reaching London before his return, and all meeting under your roof.'

While in London William sends a history of every day that he passes. None of these letters survive, for the Wordsworths kept very little of their family correspondence, but the tender passion of Dorothy's replies can be conjectured from a scrap which she wrote upon a letter she was forwarding to him;—it reads more like the missive of a young wife to her husband than of a middle-aged woman to her brother:

> 'By this same post we shall send a letter to you directed to *Mr Lambe*;[2] you will probably receive this first. I have just finished my part of the letter. It is 10 o'clock. Mary is much better, and Dorothy is very calm and happy. We get nothing done. I have read one play *The Bashful Lover* and one or two of Plutarch's *Lives* since we wrote last. I need not advise you to go to Lamb's for your letter—this however may keep down your anxiety, for we are all going on well. God bless thee my dearest William. Thy letter arrived to-day along with thy letter of last Saturday. It is a pity that this bit should go away without a word. While Mary is undressing to go to bed I take the pen. The wind is howling and the rain beats. Oh my dear William that thou wast humming thy own songs to it and untying thy many strings or resting thy hands upon thy knees as thou art used in musing while work pauses. But thou art happy and it is better perhaps that we should sometimes be separated even if thou didst not take such pleasure in things (as thou dost). God bless thee. This scrap will keep down thy impatience till the long letter arrives. Mary is just ready to slip into bed. Farewell. Good night.

[1] Mar. 2, 1806.

[2] On Feb. 19, 1804, S. T. C. wrote to his wife 'Direct "Mr. Lambe, East India House, London".' 'The misspelling', says Ernest Hartley C., 'which was intentional, was an intimation to Lamb that the letter was not to be opened.' *Letters of S. T. C.* (ed. E. H. C.), p. 460. Apparently the W.'s had the same arrangement with Lamb.

I wish I could give a better account of the disposal of our time. It is a sad pity that we can do nothing. Farewell, I am going to bed to my little darling; I always kiss her for thee.'

On May 23 William was back at Grasmere; his second son, Thomas, was born on June 15.

'There was something peculiarly affecting to us', writes Dorothy,[1] 'in the time and manner of this child's coming into the world. It was like the very same thing over again which happened three years ago; for on the 18th of June, on such another morning, after such a clear and starlight night, the birds singing in the orchard in full assembly as on this 15th, the young swallows chirping in the self-same nest at the chamber window, the rose-trees rich with roses in the garden, the sun shining on the mountains, the air still and balmy,—on such a morning was Johnny born, and all our first feelings were revived at the birth of his brother two hours later in the day, and three days earlier in the month; and I fancied that I felt a double rushing in of love for it, when I saw the child, as if I had both what had been the first-born infant John's share of love to give it, and its own.'

Of Coleridge they had no further news; the Beaumonts had offered them the loan of the house-farm on their estate at Coleorton, in Leicestershire, and they were anxious to accept it, for they could not face the thought of another winter in the crowded cottage; yet without knowing of Coleridge's plans they could decide nothing. Then on August 15 came the 'blessed news' that he was in quarantine off Portsmouth, at last 'in sight of his own dear country',[2] and by the 21st a short letter from him told them that he was uncommonly well, staying in Lamb's chambers in London. Were they unreasonable in expecting that he would at once hurry northwards to them and to his family at Keswick? But days passed and he did not appear. He would make no plans for himself, and totally ignored their repeated statements that all their movements depended upon his. At last his delay was explained. 'He dare not go home', William writes[3] to Sir George Beaumont. 'He recoils so much from the thought of domesticating with Mrs Coleridge, with whom, though on many accounts he much respects her, he is so

[1] D. W. to Lady B., June 17, 1806.
[2] D. W. to C. C. and to Lady B., Aug. 15, 1806.
[3] n.d., but probably Sept.

miserable that he dare not encounter it. I have written to him to say that if he does not come immediately I must insist on seeing him somewhere. If he appoints London I shall go. I believe if anything good is to be done for him it must be done by me.' But to William's urgent appeal he sent no answer; and at last they learned from Mrs. Coleridge that he was expected at Keswick on September 29.

> 'My dear friend,' wrote Dorothy[1] to Lady Beaumont, 'you will judge how much we have suffered from anxiety and distress within the last few weeks. We have long known how unfit Coleridge and his wife were for one another; but we had hoped that his ill-health, and the present need his children have of his care and fatherly instructions, and the reflections of his own mind during this long absence would have so wrought upon him that he might have returned home with comfort, ready to partake of the blessings of friendship, which he surely has in abundant degree, and to devote himself to his studies and his children. I now trust he has brought himself into this state of mind, but as we have had no letters from him since that miserable one which we received a short time before my brother mentioned the subject to Sir George, I do not know what his views are. Poor soul! he had a struggle of many years, striving to bring Mrs Coleridge to a change of temper, and something like communion with him in his enjoyments. He is now, I trust, effectually convinced that he has no power of this sort, and he has had so long a time to know and feel this, that I would gladly hope things will not be so bad as he imagines when he finds himself once again with his children under his own roof. . . . While he imagined he had anything to hope for, no wonder that his perpetual disappointments made him [miserable]. But suppose him reconciled to that great want, an utter want of sympathy, I believe he may live in peace and quiet. . . . When we meet you at Coleorton I trust we shall have been with Coleridge long enough to know what comfort he is likely to have. . . . I hope everything from the effect of my brother's conversation upon Coleridge's mind.'

All through October they were kept in the same miserable suspense. They could put off their journey to Coleorton no longer. Whooping cough had been rampant in Grasmere during the summer, and the children, despite a tardy removal to Park house, had all succumbed to it: it would not be safe

[1] n.d., but late Sept.

for them to travel later in the year; moreover the Beaumonts were on the point of leaving Coleorton, and they felt bound to see them before their departure. On Sunday, October 26, they all left Grasmere for Kendal, and two days later Mary, Dorothy, the three children and the servant took a private conveyance, William and Sara following in the public coach. It was a troublesome journey. 'John and Dorothy were weary with three days confinement in a post chaise, and towards night whined after Grasmere and old friends, and poor Thomas's cough was and is very bad.' They reached Coleorton on the 30th. What they had suffered during the past weeks, with its climax in their pathetic meeting with Coleridge at Kendal, is recounted in Dorothy's letter of November 6 to Mrs. Clarkson:

Coleorton, Ashby de la Zouche, Leicestershire,
November 6th, 1806, begun the 5th.

My dear Friend,

I hope you have hit upon the true reason of my long silence, or you may have felt as if I were either negligent or positively unkind. In fact from Coleridge's arrival till the time when we saw him at Kendal we were so unhappy on his account, and so distracted with doubt and painful conjectures, that I could not bear to write. You could do us no good, and to set about explaining so perplexing a distress would have been a miserable task. William would have gone up to London before we received your letter, but he was afraid of missing him on the road; and when C. wrote in answer to Wm.'s proposal, he replied in three lines that he was coming, and wrote to Mrs. C. to the same effect time after time. Meanwhile Wm. knew not what to do. . . .

During the last week of our stay at Grasmere we had reason (from his having told Mrs. C. that he should be at Keswick by the end of the preceding week) to expect him every day, and judge of our distress at being obliged to set off without having seen him; but when we got to Kendal we heard from Sara Hutchinson that she had just received a letter from him from Penrith, written immediately on his arrival there, i.e. little more than half an hour after her departure from P. to meet us at K[endal]. He said he *could* not come to Kendal, just to see us, and then to part. Notwithstanding this, however we resolved to see him and wait one day at Kendal for that purpose: accordingly we sent off a special messenger to Keswick to desire him to come over to us; but before seven o'clock that evening he himself arrived at an inn, and sent for William. We all went thither to him, and never never did I feel such a shock as at first sight of him. We all felt exactly in the same way—as if he were different from what we have expected to see; almost as much as a person of whom we have thought much, and of whom we had formed an image in our own minds, without having any personal knowledge of him. . . .

Mary and I stayed with him from Sunday evening till Tuesday morning at nine o'clock; but Sara H. and Wm did not part from him till the following morning. Alas! what can I say? I know not what to hope for, or what to expect; my wishes are plain and fair, that he may have strength of mind to abide by his resolution of separating from Mrs. C., and hereafter may continue unshaken; but his misery has made him so weak, and he has been so dismally irresolute in all things since his return to England, that I have more of fear than hope. He is utterly changed; and yet sometimes, when he was animated in conversation concerning things removed from him, I saw something of his former self. But never when we were alone with him. He then scarcely ever spoke of anything that concerned him, or us, or our common friends nearly, except we forced him to it; and immediately he changed the conversation to Malta, Sir Alexander Ball, the corruptions of government, anything but what we were yearning after. All we could gather from him was that he must part from her or die and leave his children destitute, and that to part he was resolved.

We would have gone back to Grasmere, or taken a house near Hawkshead (Belmont), but this he was against, and indeed it would have been worse than useless, for he gave us a promise to come to us here in a month; and, if he do part, the further the better. So matters stood when we left him, and we are now in anxious expectation of a letter from him. He did not complain of his health, and his appetite appeared to be not bad; but that he is ill I am well assured, and must sink if he does not grow more happy. His fatness has quite changed him—it is more like the flesh of a person in a dropsy than one in health; his eyes are lost in it—but why talk of this? you must have seen and felt all. I often thought of Patty Smith's[1] remark. It showed true feeling of the divine expression of his countenance. Alas! I never saw it, as it used to be—a shadow, a gleam there was at times, but how faint and transitory! I think however that, if he have courage to go through the work before him, William's conversation and our kind offices may soothe him, and bring on tranquillity; and then, the only hope that remains will be in his applying himself to some grand object connected with permanent effects.

[1] A daughter of W. Smith, M.P. for Norwich. She was a friend of the Clarksons

The Beaumonts received their guests like old friends, and Dorothy, as she had expected, found them 'delightful affectionate good people'. After a few days she felt quite at home in her new quarters, and though she missed her beloved mountains admitted that the flat midland country had its compensations:

'We like the place more and more every day,' she wrote on November 14,[1] 'for every day we find fresh comfort in having a roomy house. The sitting room, where by the fireside we have seen some glorious sunsets, we far more than like—we already *love* it. These sunsets are a gift of our new residence, for shut up as we are among the mountains in our small deep valley, we have but a glimpse of the glory of the evening through one gap called the Dunmail Gap, the inverted arch which you pass through in going to Keswick. On Wednesday evening my brother and I walked backwards and forwards under the trees near the hall just after the sun was gone down, and we felt as if we were admitted to a new delight. From the horizon's edge to a great height the sky was covered with rosy clouds, and I cannot conceive anything more beautiful and glorious and solemn than this light seen through the trees, and the majestic trees themselves.'

Two days later she is able to report[1] the receipt of four letters from Coleridge:

'in all he speaks with the same steadiness of his resolution to separate from Mrs Coleridge, and she has fully agreed to it, and consented that he should take Hartley and Derwent, and superintend their education, she being allowed to have them at the holidays. I say she has agreed to the separation, but he tells us that she breaks out into outrageous passions, and urges continually that one argument (in fact the only one which has the least effect upon her mind), that this person, and that person, and every body will talk. . . . My Brother has written to advise him to bring the boys to us.'

A few days before Christmas he arrived with little Hartley, and he stayed with them for nearly two months. 'I think', wrote Dorothy,[2] 'that I was never more happy in my life than when we had had him for an hour by the fireside: for his looks were much more like his old self, and though we only talked of common

[1] To Lady B.
[2] D. W. to Lady B., Dec. 23, 1806.

things, and of our friends, we perceived that he was contented in his mind, and had settled things at home to his satisfaction.' And when, in the evenings that followed, William read aloud the poem written to him during his absence, and 'round them both' was

> That happy vision of beloved faces,[1]

Mary and Dorothy and Sara, it seemed as if they were taking up again the old blissful life of open-hearted comradeship. But this was not to be. A change had come over Coleridge.

> Sense of past youth, and manhood come in vain,
> And genius given, and knowledge won in vain[1]

weighed heavily upon him, and to remorse at his own tragic failure were added less worthy feelings. Over-indulgence in alcohol and narcotics not only had weakened a will already weak by nature, but had begun to undermine his affections and to play havoc with his moral sense. At times, indeed, he still felt the old self-effacing admiration for his friend,

> my comforter and guide,
> Strong in thyself, and powerful to give strength;[1]

but he was subject to moods in which love and gratitude were crossed with resentment, even with jealousy. He could not rejoice in the thought of William's happy home life without bitter reflection upon his own homelessness. 'The blessings of friendship', which, as Dorothy had said, 'he surely has in abundant degree' did not satisfy the cravings of his heart: much as he received, it did not seem a full exchange for what he gave. He had long been tortured with the conviction that he was incapable of inspiring a single-hearted passion. He realized that the blend in William of the brusque with the tender was more attractive to women than his own softer and more querulous nature; that the love he awakened sprang less from hero-worship than from pity, that it had in it more of the protective, maternal instinct than a lover's adoration; and he now feared that William not only came first with Mary and Dorothy, but was supplanting him in the affections of Sara. The private notebooks to which he committed these fears and suspicions make pathetic reading. He knew them to be unworthy alike of his friends and of himself, and bitterly reproached himself even

[1] *V.* Coleridge's poem *To a Gentleman* [W.W.] composed Jan. 1807.

as he wrote them down; but by committing them to paper and brooding over them he gave them a stronger hold upon him; he 'plucked the poisons of self-harm', and instead of casting them from him, pressed them to his bosom. In his friends' company he became silent and moody and reticent. They had, as yet, no idea of what was passing through his mind; they only saw that he was no longer the happy confiding companion of earlier days. William voiced his sense of the change in 'A Complaint'.[1] The 'consecrated fount of murmuring, sparkling, living love' was now, he lamented, 'a comfortless and hidden well'.

> A well of love—it may be deep—
> I trust it is,—and never dry;
> What matter? if the waters sleep
> In silence and obscurity.
> —Such change, and at the very door
> Of my fond heart, hath made me poor.

Dorothy felt the change no less deeply. For a time she tried to persuade herself that renewed difficulties with his wife were the cause of their friend's dejection. 'Coleridge', she writes,[2] 'called me upstairs to read a letter from Mrs C., who, poor woman, is almost frantic, being now convinced that C. is determined not to live with her again, which she never believed before, though she herself, as far as words would go, had fully assented to it.' But whereas in the old days the greater Coleridge's distress the more whole-heartedly he sought their sympathy, he now shrank more and more into himself, and a few months later Dorothy had to make the bitter confession that 'we had long experience at Coleorton that it was not in our power to make him happy'.[3]

At the end of February Coleridge went off with Hartley to stay with Montagu in London, and here William and Mary joined him for the month of April: when William returned to Coleorton he brought Scott with him for a few days' visit, and on Scott's departure brother and sister accompanied him for a stage or two on his way homewards:[4] in June the whole Wordsworth family set out for Grasmere. They broke the

[1] *Oxf. W.*, p. 111.
[2] D. W. to C. C., Feb. 17, 1807.
[3] D. W. to C. C., Dec. 28, 1807.
[4] Cf. chap. xviii, p. 366.

journey for a fortnight at Halifax, among Dorothy's old friends the Pollards, Rawsons, and Threlkelds. 'I had', she said, 'great pleasure in the revival of many old recollections, and in finding every favourite valley more beautiful than I had ever imagined.' From Halifax they moved on to spend a week-end with Jane Marshall at Leeds; then Mary, Sara, and the children were dispatched in a post chaise to Kendal, whilst Dorothy and William joined the Marshalls and Aunt Rawson in a carriage expedition to Otley, and up the Wharfe as far as Bolton Abbey. Here they parted, but the few days' companionship with Jane had been enough to bring back to its old warmth the friendship which a busy life and new ties had allowed to fall into the background: henceforward they kept once more in close touch with one another; and when a few years later the Marshalls took a house on Ullswater, first at Watermillock and then, in 1815, at Hallsteads, there was constant intercourse between the two families.

From Bolton William and Dorothy set off on a few days' ramble into the heart of the Yorkshire moors, over the bare hills to Gordale, on to Malham Cove, to Settle, Ingleton, and Giggleswick. At Kendal they picked up the rest of the family, spent a day at Levens, and reached Grasmere on July 3.

They had been away less than nine months, but they found changes in the village which saddened their home coming. 'On our arrival here', wrote Dorothy,[1] 'our spirits sank, and our first walk in the evening was very melancholy. All the trees at Bainriggs are cut down; and even worse, the giant sycamore near the parsonage house, and all the finest firtrees that overtopped the steeple tower.' And several once familiar faces had vanished—among them old Mr. Sympson and his son, the friends they had made on their first arrival at Grasmere seven years before, and 'young George Dawson, the finest young man in the Vale'.

Once more they packed into their tiny cottage. It was a tight fit, William and Mary in one room, Johnny and little Dora in another, Dorothy with the baby in a third. If a visitor appeared he had to sleep with Johnny, whilst Dora and the servant went across the road to the Ashburners. And in the daytime there was not much peace. They had hired Sally

[1] D. W. to C. C., July 19, 1807.

Green, the fourteen-year-old daughter of a poor statesman in Easedale, to help mind the children, but every sound could be heard from one end of the cottage to another, and in bad weather, when all were confined to the house, the strain upon the nerves was almost unbearable. Dorothy, as usual, saw the situation chiefly as it affected William. 'I cannot', she wrote,[1] 'but admire the fortitude, and wonder at the success, with which he has laboured in that one room, common to all the family, to all visitors, and where the children frequently play beside him!' Judge, therefore, of their delight when they learned that a large house was to let which for the last two years had been slowly rising on a hill at the north end of the Lake. They had viewed its erection with little favour. Up to this time Grasmere had been immune from all pretentious gentlemanly residences, and the Wordsworths, like all dwellers in a quiet and primitive countryside, deeply resented such an innovation.

> 'Woe to Grasmere for ever and ever!' William had written,[2] 'A wretched creature, wretched in name and nature, of the name of *Crump*, goaded on by his still more wretched wife, has at last begun to put his long impending threats in execution; and when you next enter the sweet paradise of Grasmere you will see staring you in the face, upon that beautiful ridge that elbows out into the vale, (behind the church, and towering far above its steeple) a temple of abomination, in which are to be enshrined Mr. and Mrs. Crump. Seriously, this is a great vexation to us, as this house will stare you in the face from every part of the vale, and entirely destroy its character of simplicity and seclusion.'

Dorothy shared William's feeling; 'the first object', she had written,[3] 'which now presents itself after you have clomb the hill from Rydale is Mr Crump's newly-erected large mansion, staring over the Church Steeple', and she had contemplated its erection as a 'public sorrow'; as she sat in the moss hut at the orchard top 'Mr Crump's ruinous mansion' seemed 'the only object that is not chearful and in harmony with the sheltering mountains and the quiet vale', and she recorded, with no expression of regret, that a part of it had fallen down.[4] But if an ugly house

[1] D. W. to Lady B., Feb. (?), 1808. [2] W. W. to Richard Sharp, Feb. 1805.

[3] D. W. to Lady B., Nov. 7, 1805.

[4] 'Has my brother told you', she asks Lady Beaumont, 'that one third of it is fallen down?' (Apr. 20, 1806). An amusing account of this incident will be found in De Quincey's *Lake Reminiscences* (*Works*, ed. Masson, ii. 359). But on July 23, 1806, she writes to C. C. 'Mr Crump's monster of a house is built up again'.

is built in a beautiful and commanding situation it is at least better to be inside than outside it, and in this 'temple of abomination' they found the solution of their acute housing problem. It was not to be ready for at least six months, but they could bear the present overcrowding if they knew it to be only for a time. And they could ease it by paying visits. Sara arranged to stay with friends at Kendal, Appleby, and Penrith till after Christmas; in early August Dorothy spent twelve days with the Beaumonts at Keswick; and when she returned William and Mary went off for a time to Eusemere, and then for a week's tour to Wastdale and Whitehaven; later in the year Mary was away for six weeks and William for three, visiting Henry Hutchinson at Stockton-on-Tees. 'I am very happy amongst my little ones', wrote Dorothy,[1] 'but oh! how glad shall I be when William and Mary come back again.' They returned only just in time for Christmas, when they had hoped, vainly as it turned out, to move into the new house.

Before their last absence a new friend had been welcomed into their circle. To a letter written on November 4 to Mrs. Clarkson Dorothy adds:

> 'Half an hour after I had closed this letter I heard a tumult in the house and Mary shouted; I was alarmed, and guess my surprise and joy at seeing Hartley skipping about the room; his Mother and Derwent and Sara were at the door in a chaise and a Mr. De Quincey, a young Oxonian who long ago addressed a letter to William expressive of his gratitude and veneration, and since that time they have corresponded occasionally. He found out Coleridge and is come for a week purposely to see William. Mrs C. is just as usual only more friendly than ever with us, looks well and is in great spirits. . . . The Coleridges stayed with us all night, and left us after dinner to-day. By lodging two at Peggy Ashburner's we contrived to harbour the whole party, not excepting Mr. De Quincey.'

De Quincey's own account of this visit, from which his description of Dorothy has already been quoted, is among the most vivid as it is among the most trustworthy of his reminiscences.[2]

Dorothy took to him at once, for he had the best passport to her favour—'He is a remarkable and very interesting young

[1] D. W. to C. C., Dec. 7, 1807.

[2] *V.* De Quincey, *Works*, ed. Masson, ii. 235–41, 306–13; quoted, pp. 1, 2.

man,' she told Lady Beaumont, 'very diminutive in person, which, to strangers, makes him appear insignificant; and so modest, and so very shy, that even now I wonder how he ever had the courage to address my brother by letter. I think of this young man with extraordinary pleasure, as he is a remarkable instance of the power of my brother's poems over a lively and contemplative mind, unwarped by any established laws of taste.'[1] For some days after Mrs. Coleridge had left he stayed on with them, and before his visit was over Dorothy was already on affectionate terms with him; for the next few years he was to count almost as one of the family.

The news which Mrs. Coleridge brought of the state of affairs between her and Coleridge was not calculated to ease their minds. Her 'great spirits' were due, not to any reconcilement between them, but rather to the success with which she was still keeping up appearances.

> 'When we were alone together she entreated us to say nothing to Mr. De Q. that should make him suspect anything amiss between her and C., spoke of the disgrace of a separation, that she had never mentioned it, nor would mention it, to any living soul, and a great deal more. To this Mary and I answered that their present or rather past way of going on *was* disgraceful, but that if each declared openly that they were separated we could see no disgrace whatever that was likely to follow, that there would be a buzz, and all would be over, whereas now every body was ready to sneer. "Well," she replied, "he may stay away if he likes, I care nothing about it, if he will not talk about it", and then she began again about disgrace, and the children. As to the children, we replied, that the evil was mighty indeed; but, however they went on, she saw plainly that *they* were not likely to be much with both parents at once.'[2]

But much as Dorothy resented the callous conventionality of Mrs. Coleridge's point of view, she had to admit that the fault was not all on one side; for, as she said,[2] he was continually putting her 'into disagreeable situations, by his delays in coming to her at the time promised, and the like'. She had been 'kept several weeks at Bristol in hourly expectation of him. These things are very wrong, and it is a sad pity that he should have done anything at such a time, which his best friends cannot help

[1] Dec. 6, 1807.

[2] D. W. to C. C., Dec. 2, 1807.

condemning. If after he came home he had acted with dignity and firmness, how easy it would have been, compared with what it is!'

Coleridge was treating them no better than he was treating his wife. One of their chief reasons for embarking on the expense of so large a new house had been that they might have room for him and his two boys. They realized that they would incur odium in this, and that gossips would charge them with abetting him in the desertion of his wife; but this they were prepared to face if it was for his health and happiness. But now they were uncertain whether he would come after all. For months they had received no direct news of him. 'He has never written to us', says Dorothy,[1] 'and we have given over writing to him. For what is the use of it? we believe that he has not opened one of our letters. Poor soul! he is sadly to be pitied. I fear all resolution and strength of mind have utterly deserted him.' When at last, on November 17, he wrote that he would 'certainly be with them in March', they doubted whether he would have the strength of mind to carry out his resolve, nor, she admits,[2] 'do we now even think it would be prudent for us to consent to it, C. having been so unsteady in all things since his return to England. . . . I do not say that we *should not consent*, but it would be with little hope'. From tales which reached them of the irregularities of the life he was now leading they feared, with good reason, that his presence in their house would disturb their domestic peace without any compensating advantage to him. But when, in the following February, they heard from Mrs. Coleridge and from Southey that he was again alarmingly ill, their love, and the hope which love engenders, prevailed over these fears. 'My brother has determined', writes Dorothy,[3] 'to go up to London and see him, and if he be strong enough, to endeavour to persuade him to return with him to this country.'

On the next day she wrote again: 'William left me yesterday. . . . The day was delightful, warm and sunny; the lake glittered, the birds sang in full concert, and we could not but be cheered at parting. It seemed as if the Heavens looked favorably upon our hopes.'

[1] D. W. to C. C., Nov. 4, 1807.
[2] D. W. to C. C., Dec. 28, 1807.
[3] D. W. to J. M., Feb. 23, 1808.

For more than a month William was in devoted attendance upon him, seeing little of his other friends. Though Coleridge had 'solemnly assured Southey that he could not live three months', his illness was rather of the mind than of the body. William had often to wait till four o'clock in the afternoon to gain admittance to him, and then saw no appearance of disease which could not have been cured, or at least prevented, by himself. But that did not make the task lighter. 'When I was in town', he wrote afterwards to Coleridge, 'I had only one object which interested me, viz. the state of your health and what could be done to save you.' His efforts were not unavailing. 'We have had frequent letters from Coleridge,' wrote Dorothy on March 28, 'and his health seems to be much amended. He has been too much employed in thinking of his friends to have time to brood over his own misfortunes.' William's company took him out of himself and gave to both his intellectual and his emotional natures the stimulus they needed. But a month or two after William had left him, though he suffered no physical relapse, he sank to depths as low as he ever plumbed. His irregular manner of life had inevitably laid him open to a criticism to which his diseased mind was abnormally sensitive; and he now persuaded himself that he was the object of a most cruel, and wellnigh universal, persecution. The Insurance Company had declined to allow him to increase his insurance, at which, indeed, we can hardly be surprised, his brother had treated him shamefully, Wedgwood, his benefactor, was unjustly accusing him of the basest ingratitude; he felt that the whole world was in conspiracy against him, and he retaliated by attacking those friends whose loyalty and devotion none of his shortcomings had been able to shake. To Grasmere he sent a letter of passionate recrimination. The letter is not extant, but a surviving draft of Wordsworth's reply, in which he met it point by point, leaves no doubt as to its character and contents. After accusing him of petty jealousy, and of lukewarm friendship even when he was not actually siding with his enemies against him, Coleridge went on to make 'many most reprehensible and ungrateful accusations against those whom I best love.' 'There is', says Wordsworth in his reply, 'more than one sentence in your letter which I blushed to read, and which you yourself would have been unable to write, could never have thought of writing, nay, the matter of which could never have passed through your mind, had you not acquired a habit which I think a very pernicious one, of giving pen and voice to your most lawless thoughts, and to your wildest fancies an external existence, and thus furnishing the bad Soul, as well as the Good, with an ever ready Companion and Encourager, finding by insensible reconcilement fair and attractive bosom-inmates in productions from which you ought to have recoiled as monsters.' Among these 'lawless thoughts' and 'fancies' was the charge against Dorothy and Mary that they read all the letters which passed between him and Sara Hutchinson and 'infused into Sara's mind the notion that your attachment to her has been the curse of all your happiness'. 'So far', replies Wordsworth, 'from our having done this the very reverse is the truth. They (i.e. Mary and Dorothy) did not venture to deny (for my part I have meddled little with the affair) that your passion was the source to you of much misery; but they always told her that it was a gross error to appropriate this to herself; that your mind must have had such a determination to some object or other, and that as far as *you* were concerned she might congratulate herself'; if his passion had settled on an unworthy object his sufferings would have been incalculably greater.

A letter such as Coleridge's would have been the death-blow to any common friendship, but the Wordsworths realized that it had not been written by the Coleridge whom they knew and loved, but by a man in 'a lamentably insane state of mind', and they trusted that the fit would pass. Before the end of the following September Coleridge was with them at Grasmere.

XII

THE *POEMS* OF 1807. *THE WHITE DOE OF RYLSTONE.* THE TRAGEDY OF THE GREENS

OF the many letters that Dorothy wrote to William during his absence from Grasmere in the spring of 1808 only two are extant, and neither of them reached him before his return, if, indeed he ever saw them; but they have a more than common interest, for they deal with matters that were vital to both brother and sister,—his poetry and the life of the village community.

The *Poems in Two Volumes*, published in the previous May, contained much that not only is characteristic of Wordsworth's genius in its happiest and most exalted moods, but is bound up with the dearest intimacies of his daily intercourse with his sister. The lines on the Butterfly and the Sparrow's Nest had been inspired by talks of their happy childhood,[1] those on the Glow-worm by an incident in their life at Racedown; the poem on the Daffodils and 'The cock is crowing' recalled their memorable walk from Eusemere; there were lovely reminiscences, too, of their tour in Scotland; their visit to France lived again in the sonnet on Westminster Bridge, and in others dated from either Calais or Dover, and written, as he recorded in one of them, 'with such a dear companion at my side'. 'Beggars' was a poetic transcription from her private diary: together they had met the Leech Gatherer; the lines in the great Ode:

> to whom the grave
> Is but a lonely bed without the sense or sight
> Of day or the warm light,
> A place of thought where we in waiting lie,[1]

though condemned as 'a frightful notion' by Coleridge, enshrined what was to both of them a cherished fancy. In these two slender volumes Dorothy found transmuted into song much that was most precious in her life. They brought to her heart, she knew, a deeper meaning than they could ever bear to the world at large, yet she fully expected that the audience fit to receive them would be larger than it actually proved to be. She felt, moreover, that the labourer was worthy of his hire; but as

[1] *V.* the passage from the *Grasmere Journal*, quoted on p. 141.

yet William's reward lay solely in the praise of a few friends and in his own conviction of immortality; and this, however gratifying, did not help him to meet the growing demands upon his purse. Writing to congratulate Mrs. Clarkson on the success of her husband's book, *The Portraiture of Quakerism*, which was published in 1806 and reached its third edition in the following year, she had added:[1] 'I wish I could give you like histories of the flowing in of wealth from our literary concerns, but alas! poetry is a bad trade, and William's works sell slowly; yet we do hope that in the course of a twelve month the present Editions will be sold off, and then there will be two hundred pounds more, which we shall greatly need to meet the expenses of fitting up our new house and the high rent.'

But the reception accorded to the new volumes by the Reviews, in particular by the *Edinburgh*, and by the *Critical Review*, which William not unjustly described as 'a miserable heap of spiteful nonsense', was worse than Dorothy had thought possible, and it effectively stopped their sale. She was bitterly disappointed; yet when, in the following January, he had finished *The White Doe of Rylstone*, she was confident that now at last he would come into his own. 'I can never', she admitted,[2] 'expect that poem, or any which he may write, to be immediately popular, like *The Lay of the Last Minstrel*, but I think the story will help out those parts which are above the common level of taste and knowledge, and that it will have a better sale than his former works, and perhaps help them off.' William thought otherwise; all confidence in his power to attract readers had now left him; but he allowed himself to be over-persuaded, and before he left Grasmere was 'fully determined to publish the poem in quarto and ask 100 guineas for an edition of 1000'. No sooner, however, had he reached London than he repented of his decision. He found that Lamb did not like the poem, whilst Coleridge, though he thought it 'beyond any other in rhyme, illustrative of your peculiar excellences', and regarded that quarter of it which dealt with Emily as 'most exquisite', put his finger unerringly on its weakness of construction, and gave his opinion that it was unlikely to please the general public.

Dorothy heard with dismay of William's change of mind:

[1] July 19, 1807.
[2] D. W. to C. C., Mar. 28, 1808.

'We are exceedingly concerned', she wrote,[1] 'to hear that you, William! have given up all thoughts of publishing your Poem. As to the outcry against you, I would defy it. What matter, if you get your 100 guineas into your pocket? Besides it is like as if they had run you down, when it is known you have a poem ready for publishing, and keep it back. It is our belief, and that of all who have heard it read, that the *Tale* would bear it up—and without money what can we do? New House! new furniture! such a large family! two servants and little Sally; we *cannot* go on so another half-year; and as Sally will not be fit for another place, we must take her back again into the old one, and dismiss one of the servants, and work the *flesh off our poor bones*. Do dearest William; do pluck up your courage, and overcome your disgust to publishing. It is but a *little trouble*, and all will be over, and we shall be wealthy, and at our ease for one year, at least.'

On William's return to Grasmere she resumed her attack. She had now additional motives. As usual, he was wearing himself out in attempts to improve the poem, and only, she felt, after its publication would he be able 'to get it out of his head';[2] besides, Coleridge in his lectures had just been dealing with Wordsworth's system of composition and, as she wrote to him, if the poem appeared 'before the buzz of your lectures is settled',[2] its sale must inevitably profit. But though William hesitated again, she did not gain her point, and *The White Doe* remained for another eight years in manuscript. However much he leant on Dorothy for sympathy and understanding he knew that Coleridge was right both as to the prospects of his poem and Dorothy's inability to guage them.

'God forbid', Coleridge had written,[3] 'your sister should ever cease to use her own eyes and heart, and only her own, in order to know how a Poem *ought* to affect mankind; but we must learn to see with the eyes of others in order to guess luckily how it *will* affect them. Neither do I wish her to learn this: but then I would have her learn to entertain neither warm hopes nor confident expectations concerning events dependent upon minds and hearts *below* the distinct ken of her sympathies. Let her only reflect that even excluding the effect of Routs and continued personal gossip etc., yet the great majority of modern buyers of new Poems

[1] D. W. to W. W., Mar. 31, 1808, enclosed in a letter to S. T. C.; William had left London before the letter arrived.

[2] D. W. to S. T. C., May 1, 1808.

[3] S. T. C. to W. W., May 1808.

read at least 20 whole Novels of 2, 3, 4, 5 volumes each for *one* poem.'

It was a just criticism of Dorothy;[1] but if she had not 'entertained warm hopes and confident expectations' she would not have been herself. Of contemporary literature she knew little, of contemporary taste still less. The flaws which Coleridge detected in *The White Doe* did not exist for her; her estimate of it was upheld by Mary and Sara, by Mrs. Clarkson and the Beaumonts, and she could not conceive that its effect would be different upon 'any feeling mind'.

But if she had long lost the power of judging impartially her brother's poetry, not even his approval could convince her that there was any merit in her own. Two years before this William had read some of her verses to Lady Beaumont, but to Lady Beaumont's entreaties that she should take herself seriously as a poet she had replied:[2]

> 'And you would persude *me* that I am capable of writing poems that might give pleasure to others besides my own particular friends!! indeed, indeed, you do not know me thoroughly; you think far better of me than I deserve. I must tell you the history of those two little things[3] which William in his fondness read to you. I happened to be writing a letter one evening when he and my Sister were last at Park house; I laid down the pen and thinking of little Johnny (then in bed in the next room) I muttered a few lines of that address to him about the Wind, and having paper before me wrote them down, and went on till I had finished. The other lines I wrote in the same way, and as William knows everything that I do, I shewed them to him when he came home, and he was very much pleased; but this I attributed to his partiality; yet because they gave him pleasure and for the sake of the children I ventured to hope that I might do something more at some time or other. Do not think that I was ever bold enough to hope to compose verses for the pleasure of grown persons—Descriptions, Sentiments, or little stories for children

[1] Less just was his suggestion, in the same letter, that her judgement was 'in danger of warping from money motives in affairs which concern, if not your fame, yet your thereto introductory reputation'. And there is a pathetic irony in Coleridge expressing himself 'grieved by your sister's exceeding anxiety about pecuniary matters' as indicating 'a decaying of genial hope and former light-heartedness'. For if W. and D. had less hope and light-heartedness than formerly, the chief cause lay in Coleridge himself.

[2] Apr. 20, 1806.

[3] Probably 'Address to a child', *Oxf. W.*, p. 80, and 'The Cottager to her infant', *Oxf. W.*, p. 117.

was all I could be ambitious of doing, and I did try one story, but failed so sadly that I was completely discouraged.[1] Believe me, since I received your letter I have made several attempts (could I do less, as you requested that I would *for your sake*?) and have been obliged to give it up in despair; and looking into my mind I find nothing there, even if I had the gift of language and numbers, that I could have the vanity to suppose could be of any use beyond our own fireside, or to please, as in your case, a few partial friends; but I have no command of language, no power of expressing my ideas, and no one was ever more inapt at moulding words into regular metre. I have often tried when I have been walking alone (muttering to myself as is my Brother's custom) to express my feelings in verse; and *ideas* such as they were, I have never wanted at those times; but prose and rhyme and blank verse were jumbled together and nothing ever came of it.'

Her modest judgement upon her rhymes was just enough; it was an old trouble to her that she was but 'half a poet'; but when prose was her medium, and she wrote of what stirred her heart and mind, her power of expression never failed her; and before William had returned from his attendance on Coleridge she had a tale to tell him that moved her to the depths of her nature:

I trust my dearest Love, that this is the last letter we shall have to send to you further than Kendal, for at Kendal we will meet you with one—God be thanked we are all well. . . . But we have been, and the whole vale—since Monday after noon in the greatest consternation. . . . George Green and his wife, our Sally's Father and Mother, went to Langdale on Saturday to a Sale, the morning was very cold and about noon it began to snow, though not heavily but enough to cover the ground. They left Langdale between 5 and 6 o'clock in the evening and made their way right up the Fells, intending to drop down just above their own cottage, in Easedale—(Blenkrigg Gill under Miles Holmes's Intack).[2] They came to the highest nose of the hill that can be seen from Langdale in good time, for they were seen there by some people in Langdale; but alas! they never reached home. They were probably bewildered by a mist before daylight was gone, and may have either fallen down a precipice or perished with cold—six children had been left in the house, all younger than Sally, and the youngest an infant at the breast. Poor things they sate up till 11 o'clock

[1] The story is extant: her criticism of it is not too severe.

[2] *Intack*, an enclosed piece of fell-side pasture.

on Saturday night, expecting their parents, and then went to bed, satisfied that they had stopped all night in Langdale on account of the bad weather; the next day they felt no alarm; but stayed in the house quietly and saw none of the neighbours, therefore it was not known that their Father and Mother had not come back till Monday noon, when that pretty little Girl, the eldest of the household (whom you will remember, having admired the exquisite simplicity and beauty of her Figure one day when you were walking with Mary in Easedale)—this Girl went to George Rowlandson's to borrow a cloak. They asked why, and she told them she was going to *lait*[1] their folk who were not come home. George Rowlandson immediately concluded that they were lost and many men went out to search upon the Fells. Yesterday between 50 and 60 were out, and to-day almost as many, but all in vain. It is very unfortunate that there should be so much snow on the Fells. Mary and I have been up at the house this morning, two of the elder daughters are come home, and all wait with trembling and fear, yet with most earnest wishes, the time when the poor creatures may be brought home and carried to their graves. It is a heart-rending sight—so many little, *little* creatures. The Infant was sleeping in the cradle, a delicate creature the image of Sara Coleridge. Poor Sally is in great distress. We have told her that we will keep her till we can find a nice place for her, and in the mean time instruct her in reading, sewing etc. We hope she will continue to be a good girl. . . . This very moment three, nay four of the poor orphans (for Sally was with them) have left the room. The three had been at Mrs North's who has sent them home with a basket of provisions—and will visit them herself with clothes for all the younger, being very ragged. That sweet Girl looks so interesting, has such an intelligent, yet so innocent a countenance that she would win any heart. She is a far nicer Girl than Sally and one that we could not but have more pleasure from; but poor Sally has fallen to us, and we cannot cast her off for her Sister; but we hope that Mrs North will take *her*, or at least send her to school. . . . I really think I have nothing more to say for I have not heart to talk of our own little concerns, all being well with us. We have been strangely unsettled for these three days. Pray bring Sally a new Testament—you can buy it at Kendal. . . .

God bless thee my dearest William and grant that we may see thee again in good health and soon—thine evermore

DOROTHY WORDSWORTH.

Grasmere Wednesday November [*sic for* March] 23rd.

[1] *lait*, seek.

I open my letter to tell you that we are at ease—the poor lost creatures are found. John Fisher has called at the window to tell us; he says they had rolled a great way, and were found just above Benson's. Where that is I cannot tell; but it must have been low down. She was near a wall, and he lying a little above her.[1]

The whole neighbourhood was profoundly stirred by the tragedy. A fund was opened for the relief of the destitute orphans, and in less than six weeks £300 had been raised, in sums ranging from ten guineas down to the threepences willingly given by the poorest labourers in the vale. William and Dorothy wrote round to many of their friends, and the success of the appeal was largely due to their exertions: in the meantime Mary joined a committee of six ladies who undertook to place the children in suitable homes, and when a sudden illness to Johnny tied Mary to the house, Dorothy acted as her deputy. The committee was not entirely harmonious; for among its members was a Mrs. North of Liverpool, whose husband had recently bought Rydal Mount. Wholly ignorant of village life and character, she was already unpopular from her tactlessness in forcing her charity on those whose pride of independence was greater than their need; and now Dorothy found her 'a busy meddling woman who takes much upon her and would fain have everything of her own management'. Without consulting her colleagues she arranged that all the children should board with an old woman 'who was totally unfit to look after them', and when Dorothy protested, 'she was very rude and impertinent to me and in my person to the whole committee'.

Mrs. North's high-handed ways provoked much resentment in the village, but this was the only note of discord. Dorothy was deeply impressed by the sympathy that the tragedy had awakened in every inhabitant of the vale, and even more by what they now learnt of the life and character of the Greens before the disaster—of their cheerful independence, their heroic poverty, their passionate attachment to their small inheritance.

[1] This letter was addressed Thomas De Quincey Esqre, Worcester College, Oxford. *For Mr Wordsworth.* (Wordsworth had intended to return to Grasmere *via* Oxford, and was only prevented by anxiety to reach home earlier on account of Sara's illness.) Both Japp and Knight, however, print it as though it were written to De Q., omitting the opening lines, and altering its conclusion to 'Your affectionate friend'. It is not uncharacteristic of Dorothy that she dates her letter *November* instead of *March*.

William saw in it an eloquent testimony to those virtues in the plain people which he loved to celebrate in verse, and he urged his sister to write a full account of it, and 'give a minute detail of all the particulars which had come within her notice . . . leaving behind a record of human sympathies, and moral sentiments, either as they were called forth or brought to remembrance by (this) distressful event'. Dorothy's 'simple and fervid memoir', as De Quincey has called it, 'addressed to a friend', (probably Mrs. Clarkson) is a masterpiece of narrative; but it is wholly characteristic of her that when the Clarksons begged her to publish it she could not be persuaded.

'My dear friend,' she wrote,[1] 'I cannot express what pain I feel in refusing any request of yours, above all one in which dear Mr Clarkson joins so earnestly, but indeed I cannot have that narrative published. My reasons are entirely disconnected with myself, much as I should detest the idea of setting myself up as an Author. I should not object on that score as, if it had been an invention of my own, it might have been published without a name, and nobody would have thought of me. But on account of the family of the Greens I cannot consent . . . by publishing this narrative, I should bring the children forward to notice as individuals, and we know not what injurious effect this might have upon them. Besides it appears to me that the events are too recent to be published in delicacy to others as well as to the children. . . . Thirty or forty years hence, when the characters of the children are formed and they can be no longer objects of curiosity, if it should be thought that any service would be done, it is my present wish that it should then be published, whether I am alive or dead.'

From the extracts which follow the reader will perceive that the judgement of De Quincey and the Clarksons was not at fault. After an account of the tragedy, similar to that which she had given in the letter already quoted, her narrative continues:

'Soon after the alarm had been spread on Monday afternoon (and from that moment all were convinced of the truth; for it was well known that if the Mother had been *alive* she would have returned to her sucking babe) two or three women friends of the family (*Neighbours* they call themselves, but they live at the opposite side of the dale) went to take care of the poor children, and they found them in a wretched state—"all crying together". They

[1] D. W. to C. C., Dec. 1810.

had passed two whole days (fróm Saturday noon till Monday noon) without seeing anybody, waiting patiently and without fear; and when the word came that their father and mother must have died upon the hills it was like a thunder-stroke. In a little time however they were somewhat pacified; and food was brought into the house, for their stock was almost exhausted, their parents being the poorest people in the Vale, though they had a small estate of their own and a cow. This morsel of land, now deeply mortgaged, had been in the possession of the family for many generations, and they were loth to part with it; consequently they had never had any assistance from the parish. George Green had been twice married. By his former wife he had left one son and three daughters, and by her who died with him four sons and four daughters, all under sixteen years of age. They must very soon have parted with their land if they had lived, for their means were reduced by little and little till scarcely anything *but* the *land* was left. The cow was grown old, and they had not money to buy another; they had sold their horse and were in the habit of carrying any trifles they could spare out of house or stable to barter for potatoes or meal. Luxuries they had none. They never made tea, and when the neighbours went to look after the children they found nothing in the house but two boilings of potatoes, a very little meal, little bread, and three or four legs of lean dried mutton. The cow at that time did not give a quart of milk in the day. You will wonder how they lived at all; and indeed I can scarcely tell you. They used to sell a few peats in the summer, which they dug out of their own heart's heart, their Land; and the old man (he was sixty-five years of age) might earn a little money by doing jobs for his neighbours; but it was not known till now (at least by *us*) how much distressed they must have been; for they were never heard to murmur or complain. See them when you would, both were cheerful; and when they went to visit a friend or to a sale they were decently dressed. . . .

'It would not be easy to give you an idea of the suspense and trouble in every face before the bodies were found; it seemed as if nothing could be done, nothing else thought of, till the unfortunate pair were brought again to their own house. The first question was, "Have you heard any thing from the Fells?" On the second evening I asked a young man, a next-door neighbour of ours, what he should do to-morrow? "Why, to be sure, go out again", he replied, and I believe that though he left a profitable employment (he is by trade a shoemaker) he would have persevered daily if the search had continued many days longer—even weeks.

'My Sister Mary and I went to visit the orphans on the Wednesday morning,—we found all calm and quiet. Two little boys were playing on the floor; the infant was asleep; and two of the old man's upgrown daughters wept silently while they pursued the business of the house; but several times one of them went out to listen at the door. "Oh!" said they, "the worst for us is yet to come! we shall never be at rest till they are brought home; and that will be a dreadful moment." Their grief then broke out afresh, and they spoke of a miserable time, above twenty years ago, when their own mother and brother died of a malignant fever—nobody would come near them, and their father was forced himself to lay his wife in her coffin. "Surely", they often repeated, "this is an afflicted house!" and indeed in like manner have I since frequently heard it spoken of by persons less nearly concerned, but who still retain a vivid remembrance of the former affliction. It is, when any unusual event happens, affecting to listen to the fireside talk in our cottages; you then find how faithfully the inner histories of families, their lesser and greater cares, their peculiar habits and ways of life are recorded in the breasts of their fellow-inhabitants of the Vale; much more faithfully than it is possible that the lives of those, who have moved in higher stations and had numerous friends in the busy world, can be preserved in remembrance, even when their doings and sufferings have been watched for the express purpose of recording them in written narratives. I heard a woman a week ago describe in as lively a manner the sufferings of George Green's family, when the former two funerals went out of the house, as if *that* trouble had been the *present* trouble. Among other things she related how friends and acquaintances, as is the custom here when any one is sick, used to carry presents; but instead of going to comfort the family with their company and conversation, laid their gifts upon a wall near the house, and watched till they were taken away.

'It was, as I have said, upon the Wednesday that we went to visit the orphans. A few hours after we had left them John Fisher came to tell us that the men were come home with the bodies. A great shout had been uttered when they were found, but we could not hear it, as it was on the Langdale side of the mountains. The pair were buried in one grave on the Friday afternoon. My Sister and I attended the funeral. A great number of people of decent and respectable appearance were assembled at the house. I went into the parlour where the two coffins were placed with the elder of the mourners sitting beside them; the younger girls gathered about the kitchen fire, partly amused perhaps by the unusual sight of so many persons in *their* house; the baby and its sister Jane (she who had been left by the mother with the care of the family) sate on a little stool by the chimney-corner, and, as our Molly said after having seen them on the Tuesday, "they looked such an innocent pair!" The young Nurse appeared to have touches of pride in her important office; for everyone praised her for her notable management of the infant, while they cast tender looks of sorrow on them both. The child would go to none but her, and while on her knee its countenance was perfectly calm—more than that—I could have fancied it to express even thoughtful resignation.

'We went out of doors and were much moved by the rude and simple objects before us—the noisy stream, the craggy mountain down which the old man and his wife had hoped to make their way on that unhappy night—the little garden, untilled—with its box-tree and a few peeping flowers! The furniture of the house was decayed and scanty, but there was one oaken cupboard that was so bright with rubbing that it was plain it had been prized as an ornament and a treasure by the poor woman then lying in her coffin.

'Before the bodies were taken up a threepenny loaf of bread was dealt out to each of the guests. Mary was unwilling to take hers, thinking that the orphans were in no condition to give away anything; she immediately however perceived that she ought to accept it; and a woman who was near us observed it was an ancient custom now much disused; but probably, as the family had lived long in the Vale and had done the like at funerals formerly, they thought it proper not to drop the custom on this occasion. The funeral procession was very solemn passing through the solitary valley of Easedale, and altogether I never witnessed a more moving scene. As is customary here, there was a pause before the bodies were borne through the Church-yard gate, while part of a psalm was sung, the men standing with their heads uncovered. In the Church the two coffins were placed near the Altar, and the whole family knelt on the floor on each side of the father's coffin, leaning over it. The eldest daughter had been unable to follow with the rest of the mourners, and we had led her back to the house before she got through the first field. The second fainted by the grave-side; and their brother stood like a Statue of Despair silent and motionless; the younger girls sobbed aloud. Many tears were shed by persons who had known little of the deceased; and all the people who were gathered together appeared to be united in one general feeling of sympathy for the helpless condition of the orphans. After the funeral the family returned to their melancholy home. There was a sale of the furniture on the Thursday following, and the next day the house was left empty and silent. . . .

It was a village custom to board out orphan children, at the parish expense, with any poor families that were willing to receive them, and such children were often seriously neglected. But the subscription that had been raised for the Greens to supplement the parish bounty made it possible to secure comfortable homes for them, and Dorothy goes on to tell how she 'had the satisfaction of seeing all the five children hospitably welcomed':

'It had been declared with one voice by the people of the parish, men and women, that the infant and her Sister Jane should not be parted. The woman, who was to have the care of these two, was from home, and had requested a neighbour to be in the way to receive them when they should come. She has engaged to instruct Jane in sewing and reading, being according to the phrase in this country "a fine Scholar". Her husband is living but she has never had any children of her own. They are in good circumstances having a small estate of their own, and her husband is a remarkably ingenious and clever man, a blacksmith by trade; she appears to be a kind-hearted woman, which is shown by her motives for taking these poor children. She said to my sister with great simplicity and earnestness: "I should not have done it if we had not been such near relations, for my Uncle George's (namely the late George Green's) first wife and my husband's mother were own sisters", from which odd instance of relationship you may judge how closely the bonds of family connexion are held together in these retired vallies. Jane and her Sister took possession of their new abode with the most perfect composure; Jane went directly to the fireside and seated herself with the babe on her knee; it continues to call out "Dad!" and "Mam!" but seems not to fret for the loss of either; she has already transferred all her affections to her Sister, and will not leave her for a moment to go to anyone else. This same little girl, Jane, had been noticed by my brother and sister some months ago when they chanced to meet her in Easedale, at first not knowing who she was. They were struck at a distance with her beautiful figure and her dress, as she was tripping over the wooden bridge at the entrance of the valley; and when she drew nearer, the sweetness of her countenance, her blooming cheeks, her modest, wild and artless appearance quite enchanted them. My brother could talk of nothing else when he came home and he minutely described her dress—a pink petticoat peeping under a long dark blue cloak, which was on one side gracefully elbowed out, or distended as with a blast of wind by her carrying a basket on her arm—and a pink bonnet tied with a blue ribband—the lively colours harmonizing most happily with her blooming complexion. Part of this dress had probably been made up of her elder sister's cast-off clothes, for they were accustomed to give to their father's family whatever they could spare; often I believe more than they could well afford. Little did my brother at that time think that she was so soon to be called to such important duties; and as little that such a creature was capable of so much; for this was the child who was left by her parents at the head of the helpless family, and was as a mother to her brothers and sisters when they were fatherless and motherless, not knowing of their loss. Her conduct at that time had been the admiration of everybody. She had nursed the baby, and without confusion or trouble provided for the other children who could run about. All were kept quiet—even the infant that was robbed of its mother's breast. She had conducted other matters with perfect regularity, had milked the cow at night and morning, wound up the clock and taken care that the fire should not go out—a matter of importance in that house so far from any other—a tinder-box being a convenience which they did not possess. This little girl I saw, as I have told you, take her place in her new home with entire composure—I know not indeed how to find a word sufficiently strong to express what I mean. It was a calmness amounting to dignity, which gave to every motion a perfect grace.

'We next went with the two boys in petticoats to a neat farm house; the man and his wife came down the lane a hundred yards to meet us, and would have taken the children by the hand with almost parental kindness; but they clung to Miss Knott, the lady who had fetched them from their father's house on the day of the funeral and had treated them tenderly ever since. The younger sate upon her lap while we remained in the house, and his brother leaned against me; they continued silent, but I felt some minutes before our departure by the workings of his breast that the elder boy was struggling with grief at the thought of parting with his old friend. I looked at him and perceived that his eyes were full of tears. The younger child with less foresight continued calm till the last moment, when both burst into an agony of grief. We have since heard that a slice of bread and butter quieted their distress; no doubt the good woman's kind looks, though she gave to the bread and butter the merit of consoling them, had far more effect. She is by nature loving to children, mild and tender—inclining to melancholy which has grown upon her since the sudden death of a son, twenty years of age, who was not only the pride of his father's house but of the whole Vale. She has other children, but they are scattered abroad except one daughter who is only occasionally with her, so that she has of late spent many hours of the day in solitude, and the husband yielded to her desire of taking these poor orphans, thinking they might divert her brooding thoughts. She has begun to teach them to read, and they have already won the hearts of the rest of the family by their docility and quiet affectionate dispositions. My sister thought when she was at the house a few days ago that she perceived more cheerfulness in the kind woman's manners than she had observed in her for a long time. They, poor Things! are perfectly contented; one of them was overheard saying to the other while they were at play together, "My Daddy and Mammy's dead, but we will never go away frae this house!"

'We next went with the last remaining one of our charge, a boy seven years old. His sorrow gathered while we were in the chaise at the apprehension of parting from his friend; he repeated more than once however that he was glad to go to the house whither we were taking him; and Miss Knott turning to me said he told her he should like to live with John Fleming (that was the man's name), for he had been kind to his father and mother and had given them two sheep last year. She also related what seemed to me a remarkable proof of the child's sensibility. There had been some intention of fixing him at another place, and he was uneasy at the thought of going thither because, as he said, the master of the house had had a quarrel with his father. It appears that George Green and John Fleming had had a particular regard for each other; he was the Godfather of his friend's daughter Jane, to whom he says he will give a fleece of wool every year to spin for her own stockings, and from the day that the death of their parents was known he expressed a wish to have the care of little John. The manner in which he greeted the boy, who could not utter a word for weeping, corresponded with this. He took hold of him and patted his head as lovingly as if he had been his Grandfather, saying, "Never fear mun! thou shalt go upon the hills after the sheep; thou *kens my* sheep!" then addressing himself to us he went on, "This little lad and his brothers and sisters used always to come to our *clippings*, and they were the quietest bairns that ever I saw; we never had any disturbance among them". Meanwhile poor John did not cease crying, and continued to weep as long as we remained in the house, but we have since seen him as happy and contented as plenty of food and kindness could make any child. His master is feeble and paralytic, but he spends most of his time out of doors, looking about his own fields or following the sheep. In these walks he had formerly no companion but his dog and his staff; now at night and morning—before and after school hours—the boy goes with him. I saw them last night on their return homewards, little John was running here and there as sportive as a mountain lamb; for the child may wander at will after his own fancies and yet be a faithful attendant upon his master's course; for *he* creeps at a slow pace with tottering steps. Much as the old man delights in his new charge his housekeeper appears to have little less pleasure in him. I found her last night knitting stockings for him out of yarn spun from the master's fleeces, which is a gratuitous kindness, their allowance being half a crown weekly for board and lodging. I said to her that I hoped the boy was dutiful to her; and she replied that there was no need to give him correction, for he did nothing amiss, and was always peaceable—and happy too; and she mentioned some little circumstances which proved that she had watched him feelingly. Among the rest, that on Saturday, his weekly holiday, he had gone with her and her master to a mountain enclosure near Blintarn Gill, where they had some sheep. They passed by his father's door, and the child said to her (looking about, I suppose, in one of the fields which had belonged to his parents) "My Mother's ewe has got a fine lamb!" The woman watched his countenance, as she told us, and could not perceive that he had any painful thoughts, but was pleased to see the new-dropped lamb and his mother's ewe. . .

'I am almost afraid that you may have thought my account of the characters of the children but a Romance, a dream of fanciful feeling proceeding in great measure from pity—pity producing love; yet I hope that the few facts which I have mentioned concerning them will partly illustrate what I have said. You will conclude with me that if the parents had not shown an example of honesty, good temper and good manners these happy effects could not have followed; but I believe that the operation of their example was greatly aided by the peculiar situation of themselves and their children. They lived in a lonely house where they seldom saw anybody. These children had no playfellows but their own brothers and sisters; and wayward inclinations or uneasy longings, where there was no choice of food or toys, no luxuries to contend for, could scarcely exist,—they seeing nothing of such feelings in their parents. There was no irregular variety in the earlier part of their infancy and childhood, and when they were old enough to be trusted from home they rarely went further than their own fields, except to go on errands; so that even then they would be governed by the sense of having a duty to perform. No doubt many families are brought up in equal solitude and under the same privations, and we see no such consequences, and I am well aware that these causes have often a baneful effect if the parents themselves be vicious; but such very poor people as in their situation most resemble these are generally in a state of dependence, and the chain which holds them back from dishonesty or any disgraceful conduct is by no means so strong; while George and Sarah Green held possession of the little estate inherited from their forefathers they were in a superior station; and thus elevated in their own esteem they were kept secure from any temptation to unworthiness. The love of their few fields and their ancient home was a salutary passion, and no doubt something of this must have spread itself to the children. The parents' cares and their chief employments were centred there, and as soon as the children could run about even the youngest could take part in them, while the elder would do this with a depth of interest which cannot be felt, even in rural life, where people are only transitory occupants of the soil on which they live.

'I need not remind you how much more such a situation as I have described is favourable to innocent and virtuous feelings and habits than that of those cottagers who live in solitude and poverty without any out-of-doors employment. It is pleasant to me here to recollect how I have seen these very children (with no overlooker except when it was necessary for the elder to overlook the younger) busied in turning the peats which their father had dug out of the field near their own house, and bearing away those which were dry in burthens of three or four upon their shoulders. In this way the family were bound together by the same cares and exertions; and already one of them has proved that she maintained this spirit after she had quitted her father's roof. The eldest, Mary, when only fourteen years of age, spared a portion of her year's wages to assist them in paying for the funeral of her Grandfather. She is a girl of strong sense, and there is a thoughtfulness and propriety in her manners which I have seldom seen in one so young—this with great appearance of sensibility which showed itself at the time of her parent's death, and since in her anxiety for her brothers and sisters. . .

'The neighbours say that George and Sarah Green had but one fault; they were rather "too stiff", unwilling to receive favours, but the "*keenest payers*", always in a hurry to pay when they *had* money, and for this reason those who knew them best were willing to lend them a little money to help them out of a difficulty—yet very lately they had sent to the shop for a loaf of bread, and because the child went without ready money the shopkeeper refused to let them have the bread. We in our connexion with them have had one opportunity of remarking (Alas! we gained our knowledge since their death) how cheerfully they submitted to a harsh necessity, and how faithful they were to their word. Our little Sally wanted two shifts; we sent to desire her mother to procure them; the father went the very next day to Ambleside to buy the cloth and promised to pay for it in three weeks. The shifts were sent to Sally without a word of the difficulty of procuring them, or anything like a complaint. After her parent's death we were very sorry (knowing now so much of their extreme poverty) that we had required this of them, and on asking whether the cloth was paid for, intending to discharge that debt, we were told by one of the daughters that she had been to the shop purposely to make the inquiry, and found that two or three days before the time promised her father had himself gone to pay the money. Probably if they had lived a week longer they must have carried some article of furniture out to barter for that week's provisions. I have mentioned how very little food there was in the house at that time—there was no money—not even a single half-penny! The pair had each threepence in their pockets when they were found upon the mountains. With this eagerness to discharge their debts their unwillingness to receive favours was so great that the neighbours called it *pride* or as I have said "*stiffness*". Without this pride what could have supported them? Their cheerful hearts would probably have sunk, and even their honesty might have slipped from them.'

At the close of her narrative Dorothy expresses the fear that she has spun it out to a tedious length. 'I cannot give *you*', she says, 'the same feelings that *I* have of them as neighbours and fellow inhabitants of this vale; therefore what is in my mind a full and living picture will be to you but a feeble sketch.'

But this 'feeble sketch' is a beautiful piece of writing, precious not only as a faithful, living picture of life in a lowly village a hundred years ago, but as a revelation of her rare power of entering into that life with imaginative sympathy, and making it an integral part of her own.

XIII

LIFE AT ALLAN BANK. BIRTH OF CATHARINE AND OF WILLY. ESTRANGEMENT FROM COLERIDGE

1808–1813 (*aet.* 36–41)

On April 6, William returned from his attendance on Coleridge to an afflicted household. Alarming news of Sara Hutchinson's health had brought him back sooner than he had intended, and for more than a year afterwards they were haunted with the fear that, like her sister Peggy, she was consumptive: on the very night of his arrival Johnny was taken dangerously ill, with all the symptoms of water on the brain. 'We resigned ourselves to his loss,' writes Dorothy, 'and contemplated the poor Innocent's sufferings with awful dread.' But the crisis passed, and on the 21st she was able to report: 'The little darling is now sleeping quietly, beautiful as an angel though different from himself, his features enlarged, for he is grown so thin: but his countenance is quite divine; he more resembles his father than ever. Nothing of the disease seems now to remain but the weakness, and we hope that will quickly pass away—but we are very anxious to be in the new house both on his account and on dearest Sara's.'

Towards the end of May they moved into Allan Bank. As usual, the bulk of the work fell upon Dorothy's shoulders. Sara was still too weak to do more than a little sewing, Mary had sprained her arm and could not use it even to write a letter, and '*William*, you know, is not expected to do anything'.[1] Dorothy had hoped, indeed, to get William out of the way altogether; 'for as to his *company* we could have no enjoyment of it, and he would not by his help pay for the trouble of cooking, which we women can do very well without.'[2] But she had taken the precaution of securing an efficient substitute for him in Henry Hutchinson, Mary's sailor brother, whose calling had fitted him better than William's for the practical business in hand. 'Harry', she writes,[2] 'is the handiest creature in the world—can sew, cook, wash dishes, put up beds,—anything you can name. Poor fellow!

[1] D. W. to C. C., June 6, 1808 (misdated by D. W. April).
[2] D. W. to C. C., May 10, 1808.

I love him better because once or twice he reminded me of my dear brother John—it was something in his *manner* but for a single moment, and he is like him in taking interest in all little domestic goings-on'.... 'Being very poor we are determined to make the carpets and do everything ourselves; for [Henry] is as good as a tailor, and at the same time a very pleasant companion and fellow-labourer. Judge how busy I must have been for this fortnight past—papers, linen, books, everything to look over in the old house and put by in the new—besides curtains to make etc. etc. etc. In another fortnight all will be over, we hope, for Henry and I work body and soul, and with less we should never be done.'[1] But even in the desolate chaos of a removal she could look on the brighter side of things, and despite her fond regrets for the cottage which was no longer to be her home, she admitted that the situation of the new house was as lovely, and was far better for the children, who could now wander up and down the green fields that surrounded them without fear of carriages and horses; above all, their elders would have some chance of a little privacy.

> 'Sara and I', she writes,[1] 'have a delicious view from our several windows—both look to the East—the mighty mountains of Fairfield and Seat Sandal, now green to their very summits. Oh! that you could see that mass of clouds now resting on the pass which we used to traverse in our visits to you, that pass where William and I were near being lost for ever.[2] Oh that you could see the bonny cottages and their tufts of trees and the sweet green fields. It is a soothing scene, and I trust you will one day behold it, and sit with me in this my little castle, where I now write. We already feel the comfort of having each a room of our own, and begin to love them—but the dear cottage! I will not talk of it.'

It was during this summer that they became intimate with John Wilson, afterwards known as Christopher North, a young Scottish Oxonian who was building himself a house at Elleray above Windermere, and living in a cottage there with his mother and sister. Dorothy describes him as 'a man of fortune, of good understanding and most affectionate heart and very pleasing manners. The origin of our first acquaintance was his enthusiastic admiration of my Brother's poems, and he is now

[1] D. W. to C. C., June 6, 1808.
[2] *V. Grasmere Journal*, for Jan. 23, 1802 (*Journals of D. W.*, i. 81).

scarcely less enthusiastic in his admiration of my Brother. It seems as if he and his whole family thought they could hardly do enough to express their liking to us all—no doubt in consequence of their reverence for him.'[1] It does not seem to have occurred to her that her own society had anything to do with the attraction. Wilson often had parties of college friends to stay with him, and they were a cheerful, even boisterous company. 'Wilson and his merry men', William used to call them, and they would often take him off with them to fish, or organize for the Wordsworth family a picnic party. 'By the bye what is the origin of the word picnic?', asks Dorothy. 'Our Windermere gentlemen have a picnic almost every day.'[1] And as Mary's cousin, Mary Monkhouse,[2] a charming girl of twenty-one, was at Grasmere during part of the summer, her visit was made the occasion of many pleasant expeditions on the lake or over the hills. Wilson, indeed, paid her such marked attention that Sara mockingly dubbed him her 'lover'. 'You must have him, Mary, if you can get him,' she wrote after Mary's departure, 'he is a nice creature and would fain be better than he is. I am sure if he were near William he would never seek those wild companions of his any more . . . he says that it is only "a sense of his own unworthiness" that makes him come so seldom to Grasmere, and not his preference for other society. He wrote Wm a nice letter on the subject.'[3] For the next few years the Wilsons

[1] D. W. to C. C., Aug. 3, 1808.

[2] Mary M. and her two brothers, John and Thomas, from this time on played a large part in the intimate life of the Wordsworth family. Mary (1787–1858), first cousin of M. W. and S. H., became their sister-in-law on her marriage, in 1812, with Mary's favourite brother Thomas. With him she lived at Hindwell, near Radnor, till 1824, and then at Brinsop Court, near Hereford, till 1846, when they moved to their son George's Rectory, near W. Malvern. Her last three years were passed at Grasmere. John M. (1782–1866), went into partnership in farming with his cousin Thomas H. and settled with him at Hindwell in March 1809, but on his sister's marriage moved to Stow, near Whitney, on the banks of the Wye. He won a wide renown for his skill and success as a farmer, despite total blindness for the last 35 years of his life. He was a man of wide culture and a great reader, and is reputed to have known the whole of *Paradise Lost* by heart. Thomas M. (1785–1825) was in business at Budge Row, London; he was a man of considerable wealth and famous for his generous hospitality. He was keenly interested in literature and numbered among his friends and acquaintances Lamb, Coleridge, Kenyon, Moore, Keats, Haydon, and Crabb Robinson. With D. W. and S. H. he was on terms of great affection. W. W. spoke of him as one of his dearest friends, and Lamb referred to him as 'Wordsworth's noble-hearted kinsman'.

[3] Letters of Sara H. to Mary M., Nov. 1808 and Mar. 1809.

added much to the happiness of the Wordsworth household, joining them not only on summer outings, but by the fireside at Christmas, which they enlivened 'by their pleasant mixture of merriment and thoughtful discourse'.

On September 6 Mary gave birth to a second daughter, named Catharine, after her godmother Mrs. Clarkson; before the end of the month both Coleridge and De Quincey were members of the Wordsworth household. De Quincey stayed with them till February, and returned for a month in the following November, after which he settled into Dove Cottage, where he was to make his home for the next six years. In his absence Dorothy kept him in touch with all that was going on at Grasmere, made several journeys to Kendal to buy his furniture, and engaged a servant to keep house for him. The frequent visits that she had now to pay to the Cottage gave her great delight. 'It is quite a pleasure to us', she wrote to him,[1] 'to go down to the old spot and linger about as if we were again at home there. Yesterday I sate half an hour musing by myself in the moss-hut, and for the first time this season I heard the cuckoos there. The little birds too, our old companions, I could have half fancied were glad that we were come back again, for it seemed I had never before seen them so joyous on the branches of the naked apple trees. Pleasant indeed it is to think of that little orchard which for one seven years at least will be a secure covert for the birds, and undisturbed by the woodman's axe.' Coleridge was to make Allan Bank his headquarters for the next two years. His boys, Hartley and Derwent, were sent to school in Ambleside, but spent their week-ends and part of their holidays with their father. It was a full house, and, with the baby as first claim upon Mary's time, Dorothy was chiefly responsible for its management.

> 'We are regularly thirteen in family,' she says,[2] 'and on Saturdays and Sundays 15. I include the servants in the number, but as you may judge, in the most convenient house there would be work enough for two maids and a little girl. In ours there is far too much. We keep a cow—the stable is two short field-lengths from the house, and the cook has both to fodder and clean after the cow. We have also two pigs, bake all our bread at home, and though we do not *wash* all our clothes, yet we wash a part every

[1] D. W. to T. De Q., May 6, 1809. [2] D. W. to C. C., Dec. 8, 1808.

week, and mangle or iron the whole. This is a tedious tale and I should not have troubled you with it but to let you see plainly that idleness has nothing to do with my putting off writing to you. Besides this we were nearly a week without any servant at all.'

To make matters worse they had

'grievous troubles to struggle with in [their] new, ill-built dwelling —a smoky house, wet cellars, and workmen by the half dozen making attempts, hitherto unsuccessful, to remedy these evils . . . you can have no idea of the inconvenience we have suffered. There was one stormy day in which we could have no fire but in my brother's study, and that chimney smoked so much that we were obliged to go to bed with the baby in the middle of the day, and I, with a candle in my hand, stumbled over a chair, unable to see it. We cooked in the study. . . . Partly on account of smoke and windy weather, and partly because of the workmen, we have been for more than a week together at different times without a kitchen fire. The servants, you may be sure, have been miserable; and we have had far too much labour and far too little quiet.[1]

'The labour of the house is literally doubled. Dishes are washed, and no sooner set into the pantry than they are covered with smoke. Chairs, carpets, the painted ledges of the rooms, all are ready for the reception of soot and smoke, requiring endless cleaning, and are never clean. This is certainly the worst part of the business, but the smarting of the eyes etc. etc. you may guess at, and I speak of these other discomforts as more immediately connected with myself. In fact we have seldom an hour's leisure (either Mary or I) till after 7 o'clock (when the children go to bed), for all the time that we have for sitting still in the course of the day we are obliged to employ in scouring (and many of our evenings also).'[2]

The brightest pages in the annals of Allan Bank are devoted to the Wordsworth children. Like their mother, they 'were not too good for human nature's daily food', and the correct Mrs. Coleridge viewed them somewhat askance, postponing as long as possible the evil day when her little Sara, 'who has nothing about her of the natural wildness of a child', had to pay her periodic visits to her father; 'for she dreads the contamination which her ladylike manners must receive from our rustic brood more than she would dread illness, I may almost say *death*.'[3] But every one else seems to have loved them; and certainly, as we see them

[1] D. W. to J. M., Dec. 4, 1808. [2] D. W. to C. C., Dec. 8, 1808.
[3] D. W. to C. C., Nov. 15, 1809.

through the eyes of their devoted aunt, they are quite irresistible. There is Johnny with 'his shy looks of gladness and beautiful blushes'[1] when anything pleased him, loved by all his play-mates and made up of good and noble feelings; and Dorothy, 'a mixture of wildness and elegance, quick at her book and quick at everything', but wayward and difficult to subdue, not a little, may we say it? like what aunt Dorothy must have been at her age; and Thomas, 'a great chatterer', 'simple, innocent and very loving', who spent so much time in the kitchen that he was known as Potiphar, a nickname which he stoutly resented—'me no Potiphar, me a good boy';[2] and lastly baby Catharine, not quite so hand-some as the others, 'in spite of her blue eyes', but pronounced to be 'the wittiest of the set', and early developing a marked personality of her own, with her bald head—'her father calls her his little Chinese maiden,—and the funniest laugh you ever saw peeping through her eyes'. 'There is something so irre-sistibly comic in her face and movements that it is quite a feast to watch her; and the gravest person and the least disposed to notice children could not help laughing at her sudden turns upon the floor and her speedy journeys with her little bald pate forwards.'[1]

Coleridge and De Quincey had each his favourites among them. Coleridge in his noisy, gamesome moods loved to romp with the quick-witted, high-spirited Dorothy, and would 'repeat to her (altering a line of William's poem 'Ruth') "the wild cat of the wilderness was not so fair as she", to which she replies with a squall, inviting him to some fresh skirmish';[2] but Tom, as he said later, 'is nearest my heart—I so often have him before my eyes, sitting on a little stool by my side, while I was writing my essays; and how quiet and happy the affectionate little fellow would be if he could but touch one and now and then be looked at'.[3] De Quincey slept in the same room with Johnny, and by day made him his constant companion, whilst to Catharine he became romantically devoted, seeing in her the impersonation of the dawn and the spirit of infancy. 'He has made us promise', Dorothy tells Mrs. Clarkson,[4] 'that he is to be her sole tutor, so that we shall not dare to show her a letter in a book, when she is old enough to have the wit to learn; and you may expect that she will be a very learned lady, for

[1] D. W. to C. C., Nov. 18, 1809. [2] D. W. to C. C., Dec. 8, 1808.
[3] S. T. C. to W. W., Dec. 7, 1812. [4] June 15, 1809.

Mr. De Q. is an excellent scholar. If, however, he fails in inspiring her with a love of learning, I am sure that he cannot fail in one thing. His gentle, sweet manners must lead her to sweetness and gentle thoughts. His conversation has been of very great use to John, who is certainly now the finest boy I ever saw.' Dorothy would have found it hard to say which of the four was her favourite, though we suspect that it was the 'noble' Johnny. But each had his separate niche in her heart, and in entering into their lives she found a joyful distraction from the troubles that weighed upon her.

For she had worries enough. With so large an establishment to keep up it was harder than ever to make both ends meet. William, apparently, had put it to their landlord, Mr. Crump, that so far from being charged a high rent for a house with such disgracefully smoky chimneys he ought to be paid for inhabiting it, but the argument does not seem to have carried conviction; and he now thought of adding to his slender income by journalism. He was always deeply interested in national affairs; and never more so than at this time, when by the Convention of Cintra his country seemed to him to have thrown away a chance of freeing Spain and Portugal, and striking a fatal blow at the hated Buonaparte. 'It would not be easy', he said years afterwards,[1] 'to conceive with what a depth of feeling I entered into the struggles carried on by the Spaniards for their deliverance from the usurped power of the French. Many times have I gone from Allan Bank to the top of the Raise Gap as late as two in the morning to meet the carrier bringing the newspaper.' All through this winter he was at work upon that eloquent pamphlet in which he strove to rouse his countrymen to a sense of their duty. A portion of it had appeared in *The Courier*, and he now resolved to write in that or some other journal 'for the sake of getting money, not wholly, however, on that account, for unless he were animated by the importance of his subject and the hope of being of use he could do nothing in that way'.[2] Dorothy could not view without dismay a project which would certainly divert him from his real vocation. 'The misfortune is that he cannot lay down one work, and begin with another. It was never intended that he

[1] I.F. note to *Sonnets Ded. to Ind. and Lib.*, Pt. II.
[2] D. W. to T. De Q., May 1, 1809.

should make a trade out of his faculties'; and yet, she adds,[1] 'I know not how we can go on without his employing some portion of his time in that way.'

Still more disturbing to her peace of mind was the constant anxiety about Coleridge. Was the irony wholly unconscious when she reported that Coleridge had begged William 'that he will not withdraw himself from poetry, for he is assured that there will be no need of it, as he (Coleridge) can get money enough'?[1] One can guess the feelings with which William received this assurance. Only a month before, he had written to Poole, as one of Coleridge's nearest and dearest friends, urging him to come to Grasmere and help to make some arrangements for the future of Coleridge's children. 'I give it you as my deliberate opinion', he said,[2] 'formed upon proofs which have been strengthened for years, that he neither will nor can execute any thing of important benefit either to himself, his family, or mankind. Neither his talents nor his genius—mighty as they are—nor his vast information will avail him anything. They are all frustrated by a derangement in his intellectual and moral constitution. In fact he has no voluntary power of mind whatsoever, nor is he capable of acting under any *constraint* of duty or moral obligation.'

In truth, in this supreme act of their love, by which, receiving Coleridge into their home, they strove to wean him from his evil habits, and make him forget his sorrows 'by applying himself to some grand object of permanent effects', both William and Dorothy knew well enough that they were fighting a losing battle; and if Dorothy fought with the stouter heart, with her, too, fears predominated. 'Troublesome things', she writes in December 1808, 'have happened lately which have robbed me of the confidence of hope'; and the news which from time to time she sent to Mrs. Clarkson is a pathetic record of their struggle. The 'grand object' he had in view was the production of a weekly paper, to be entitled *The Friend*, in which he was 'to assist the mind in the formation for itself of sound, and therefore permanent and universal principles in regard to the investigation, perception, and retention of truth'; and though no one could have been less fitted by natural temper, even in the hey-day of his health, for a work which called for regular

[1] D. W. to T. De Q., May 1, 1809. [2] W. W. to Thomas Poole, Mar. 31, 1809.

and systematic application, they realized that, having undertaken it, his only salvation lay in its accomplishment: another failure would be worse for him than if he had never made the effort. Fully alive to his friends' devotion he had determined not to disappoint them. He reduced his dose of opium to a sixth of what he had been taking, with the result that his general health and mental activity were stronger than he had known them for years past. 'This change' he attributed to 'the blessed effect upon my spirits of having no secret to brood over', and to his resolve 'whatever might be the result, henceforth never to conceal anything from those who loved me, and lived with me.' In this mood he busied himself over the preliminaries to his undertaking.

> 'Dear Coleridge', writes Dorothy (to Mrs. Clarkson[1]), 'is well and in good spirits, writing letters to all his friends and acquaintances, despatching prospectuses, and fully prepared to begin his work. Nobody, surely, but himself would have ventured to send forth this prospectus with no one essay written, no beginning made! but yet I believe it was the only way for him. I believe he could not have made the beginning unspurred by a necessity which is now created by the promises therein made. I cannot, however, be without hauntings of fear, seeing him so often obliged to lie in bed more than half the day—often so very poorly as to be utterly unable to do anything whatever. To-day, though he came down to dinner at three perfectly well, he did not rise till near two o'clock, but however ill he may have been in the mornings he seldom fails to be chearful and comfortable at night.'

But two months passed and no *Friend* was written; and then difficulties arose over its publication. The Kendal firm by whom it was to be issued went out of business, and Coleridge set out for Penrith, to make arrangements with a printer there. 'I cannot but fear', wrote Dorothy,[2] 'that the journey and one thing or other (to use one of his own favourite phrases) will knock him up, and that all will at last end in nothing. I wish he had not gone to Penrith, for we think that by letter he could have managed the matter just as well; and at this critical moment it will be for ever to be regretted if any accident of fatigue, bad accommodations etc. should disarrange his body or mind. If he had been able to stay quietly here, the trial would have been a

[1] Dec. 8, 1808.

[2] D. W. to T. De Q., Mar. 10, 1809.

fair one.' Her anxiety as to what might happen when he was beyond their sphere of influence was not unjustified. Though they wrote to him repeatedly he answered none of their letters, and ugly rumours reached them of his excesses at the Penrith gin-shops. He had left them determined that *The Friend* should appear on April 1, but both April and May passed without a sign of it. Then on June 1 the first number was published, followed punctually on the 8th by the second. Coleridge had fled from the temptations of Penrith to the house of the good quaker Thomas Wilkinson. 'I believe', says Dorothy,[1] 'that at the last, Thomas was the father of *The Friend*. C. was happy in Thomas's quiet and simple way of life, drank no spirits, and was comfortable all the time, and Thomas urged him to his work.'

On June 14 he was back at Grasmere, and spurred on by the sympathy and example of his friends once more made a gallant effort to conquer his failings. On the first morning he was up at six o'clock, and was clearly anxious to get credit for it, for, says Dorothy,[1] 'when I rang the bell to call the maid to fetch Catharine away, he came all alive to my door to ask if he could do anything for me'; and though this was a standard of virtue that no one expected him to maintain, for the next six months *The Friend* appeared frequently, if not always upon the appointed day. 'Coleridge is going on well at present', she reports[2] towards the end of August, 'the 4th essay will come out next week and I know that he has the 5th and more ready. As to its future regularity I dare not speak; . . . at present he is full of hope and has, I believe, made excellent resolutions.'

He always worked by fits and starts: sometimes a week would pass in which he never composed a line. 'The fact is that he either does a great deal or nothing at all; and that he composes with a rapidity truly astonishing, if one did not reflect upon the large stores of thought which he has laid up, and the quantity of knowledge which he is continually gaining from books. Add to this his habit of expressing his ideas in conversation in elegant language. He has written a whole *Friend* more than once in two days. They are never re-transcribed, and he generally has dictated to Miss Hutchinson, who takes the words down from his mouth.' His industry reached its climax in December,

[1] D. W. to C. C., June 15, 1809. [2] To C. C., Aug. 27, 1809.

when, in addition to writing *The Friend*, he sent a series of essays on Spanish affairs to *The Courier*. But early in the next year he began to flag, and to fall back upon any old material that he had by him: and when, even so, he had nothing ready for the press, William came to the rescue with an article. They all did their best to put heart into him, and though the strain told most heavily upon Sara Hutchinson, upon Dorothy it was hardly less. 'His spirits have been irregular of late', she wrote on February 28 to Lady Beaumont; 'He was damped after the twentieth number by the slow arrival of payments, and half persuaded himself that he ought not to go on. We laboured against such a resolve and he seems determined to fight onwards; and indeed I do not think he had ever much reason to be discouraged, or *would have been* discouraged if his spirits had not before been damped.' But a lethargy had now fallen upon him from which no entreaties could rouse him. A week or so later Sara Hutchinson, worn out with her attendance on him, left Grasmere to make a long stay with her brother, who was now farming at Hindwell, Radnorshire, with his cousin John Monkhouse, and Dorothy's next letter[1] is a pathetic tale of their disappointed hopes:

> 'We had a letter from dear Sara last night. She is very comfortable; and happy that she has taken the journey, but her side for a few days was weak and painful. Poor thing, she evidently feels a great want. There is not that life by the fireside that we have—they are sleepy before supper-time, being little interested for anything else but their own domestic or farming concerns, and people must needs languish with no other thoughts from morning till night. . . . I need not tell you how sadly we miss Sara, but I must add the truth that we are all glad she is gone. True it is she was the cause of the continuance of *The Friend* so long; but I am far from believing that it would have gone on if she had stayed. He was tired, and she had at last no power to drive him on; and now I really believe that he also is glad that she is not here, because he has nobody to teaze him. His spirits have certainly been more equable, and much better. *Our* gladness proceeds from a different cause. He harassed and agitated her mind continually, and we saw that he was doing her health perpetual injury. I tell you this, that you may no longer regret her departure. As to Coleridge, if I thought I should distress you, I would say nothing about him:

[1] D. W. to C. C., Apr. 17, 1810.

but I hope that you are sufficiently prepared for the worst. We have no hope of him. None that he will ever do anything more than he has already done. If he were not under our roof, he would be just as much a slave of stimulants as ever; and his whole time and thoughts, except when he is reading (and he reads a great deal) are employed in deceiving himself, and seeking to deceive others. He will tell me that he has been writing, that he has written half a *Friend*; when I *know* that he has not written a single line. This habit pervades all his words and actions, and you feel perpetually new hollowness and emptiness. Burn this letter, I entreat you. I am loath to say it, but it is the truth. He lies in bed, always till after 12 o'clock, sometimes much later; and never walks out. Even the finest spring day does not tempt him to seek the fresh air; and this beautiful valley seems a blank to him. He never leaves his own parlour, except at dinner and tea, and sometimes supper, and then he always seems impatient to get back to his solitude. He goes the moment his food is swallowed. Sometimes he does not speak a word; and when he does talk it is always upon subjects as far aloof from himself, or his friends, as possible. The boys come every week and he talks to them, especially to Hartley, but he never examines them in their books. He speaks of *The Friend* always as if it were going on, and would go on; therefore, of course you will drop no hint of my opinion. I heartily wish I may be mistaken.

'Friday morning. Coleridge is just come down stairs, ½ past 12 o'clock. He is in great spirits and says to me that he is going to get to work in good earnest. I replied it cannot be out this week. "No", said he, "but we will get it out as fast as possible." What will come of this resolution I know not. I only venture to wish or entertain the slightest hope for the 40 numbers, and I do wish that he may go so far. . . . Tell me that you have burnt this letter.

'With respect to Coleridge do not think that it is his love for Sara which has stopped him in his work. Do not believe it. His love for her is no more than a fanciful dream—Otherwise he would prove it by a desire to make her happy. No! he likes to have her about him as his own, as one devoted to him, but when she stood in the way of other gratifications it was all over. I speak this very unwillingly, and again, I beg, burn this letter. I need not add keep its contents to yourself alone.'

But when Dorothy wrote this, the twenty-seventh and last number of *The Friend* had already appeared.

At the beginning of the next month (May) Coleridge went off to Keswick, to stay, he said, for about ten days. Mary was expecting another baby, and he did not intend to return 'till the bustle was over'. Dorothy was not sorry to be relieved of the household work which his presence always entailed; 'for though he does not require near so much waiting on as formerly, he makes a great difference. There is always his parlour to clean, fire to light, sometimes gruel, toast and water, eggs, his bed always made at an unreasonable time, and many other little things which tell in a house.' But he stayed at Keswick five months. Mrs. Coleridge reported him to be 'in better health, spirits and humour than I have found him for any length of time for years before', but though *The Friend* was uppermost in her thoughts she dared not refer to it, knowing that 'to expostulate, or even to hazard one anxious look would soon drive him hence'. He was, in fact, glad to have left Allan Bank. He could face Mrs. Coleridge, for whom he had no affection, with equanimity; but the presence of his friends whom he loved, who had served him with such devotion, from whom he had resolved 'henceforth never to conceal anything', and whom he had failed, he felt to be a continual reproach. At the end of October he went to London, travelling with the Montagus, who were going South from Scotland. On their way they passed through Grasmere and spent a night at Allan Bank. Dorothy was not at home: she was herself at the time returning from a visit to London, so that they must have passed one another on the road. Ten years were to elapse before she saw Coleridge again, and of these the first three were to prove the saddest of her whole life. Coleridge's rejection of the devoted love and service that she and William had lavished upon him was not then her only grief; she was weighed down by almost unintermittent anxieties at home, culminating in the deaths of Catharine and Thomas, and the departure from her beloved Grasmere. But of this the tale must be postponed, in order to follow through its bitter course the story of their estrangement from their dearest comrade.

After a few days with the Montagus Coleridge took up his abode at Hammersmith with his friends the Morgans, with whom, save for a few short intervals, he was to make his home until, six years later, he was to find a last asylum with the Gillmans at Highgate. He sent no word of himself either to Grasmere or Keswick. From the Lambs Dorothy heard in November that he was well and in good spirits. 'He has powdered his head', wrote Charles, 'and looks like Bacchus, Bacchus ever sleek and young. He is going to turn sober, but his clock is not struck yet.' A month later she heard from Crabb Robinson of several pleasant evenings spent in his company; he was in good health and talked in his most eloquent vein. But with no news directly from him, Dorothy became anxious. 'I am going to write to him on business', she tells Mrs. Clarkson. She received no answer. 'Three months and more have elapsed', wrote Mrs. Coleridge in the following February, 'and he has not once addressed any of his northern friends, and we have heard very little of him from other persons. Of course I have passed a very anxious winter.' 'It would pity anybody's heart to look at Hartley', wrote Dorothy, about the same time,[1] 'when he enquires (as if hopelessly) if there is any news of his father.' It was not till May that Mrs. Coleridge was able to explain his silence: on the 11th of that month Dorothy wrote to Mrs. Clarkson:

'. . . We have heard that C. is offended with William. I do not like to begin with such stories nor should I have mentioned it at all, if I had not thought that perhaps Henry Robinson may have heard something of it, and a mutilated tale might so come to your ears. In few words I will tell you, though I am sure you would not be inclined to blame my Brother whatever you might hear from other quarters. You know that C. went to London with the Montagus and that their plan was to lodge him in their own house, and no doubt M. expected to have so much influence over him as to lead him into the way of following up his schemes with industry. Montagu himself is the most industrious creature in the world, rises early and works late, but his health is by no means good and when he goes from his labours rest of Body and mind is absolutely necessary for him; and William perceived clearly that any interruption of his tranquillity would be a serious injury to him, and if to him consequently to his family. Further he was convinced that if Coleridge took up his abode in M.'s house they would soon part with mutual dissatisfaction, Montagu being the last man in the world to tolerate in another person (and that person an inmate with him) habits utterly discordant with his own—convinced of these truths William used many arguments to persuade M. that his purpose of keeping Coleridge comfortable could

[1] D. W. to C. C., Feb. 23, 1811.

not be answered by their being in the same house together—but in vain—Montagu was resolved. "He would do all that could be done for him and would have him at his house." After this William spoke out and told M. the nature of C.'s habits (nothing in fact which everybody in whose house he has been for two days has [not] seen of themselves) and Montagu then perceived that it would be better for C. to have lodgings near him. William intended giving C. advice to the same effect but had no opportunity of talking with him when C. passed through Grasmere on his way to London. Montagu wrote to William that on their road to London he had seen so much of C.'s habits that he was convinced he should be miserable under the same roof with him, and that he had repeated to C. what William had said to him and that C. had been very angry. Now what could be so absurd as M.'s bringing forward William's communications as his reason for not wishing to have C. in the house with him? when he had himself, as he says, "seen a confirmation of all that W. had said" in the very short time they were together. So however he did and William contented himself with telling M. that he thought he had done unwisely—and he gave him his reasons for thinking so. We have heard no more of this or of C. in any way except soon after his arrival in Town by Mr Montagu that he was well in health, powdered etc.—and talked of being busy, from Lamb that he was in good spirits and resolved to be orderly—and from other quarters to the like effect. But in a letter from poor dear Mary Lamb a few days before her last confinement she says she "knows there is a coolness between my Brother and C". In consequence of this I told her what had passed between W. and M. and assured her of the truth that there was no coolness on William's part. I of course received no answer to this letter for she was taken away before it reached London . . . and we heard no more of the matter till the other day when Mrs C. received a letter from Coleridge about his MSS in which he says as an excuse for having written to no-one and having done nothing, that he had endured a series of injuries during the first month of his stay in London—but I will give you his own words as reported to us by Mrs C. She says "He writes as one who had been cruelly injured. He says "If you knew in detail of my most unprovoked sufferings for the first month after I left Keswick and with what a thunder-clap that *part* came upon me which gave the whole power of the anguish to all the rest, you would pity, you would less wonder at my conduct, or rather my suspension of all conduct—in short that a frenzy of the heart should produce some of the effects of a derangement of the brain etc etc"—so I suppose there is a good deal more of this, but she says he mentions no names except Mr and Mrs Morgan. He says "I leave it to Mrs Morgan to inform you of my health and habits," adding that it is "to hers and her husband's kindness he owes it that he is now in his senses, in short that he is *alive*." I must own that at first when I read all this my soul burned with indignation that William should thus (by implication) be charged with having caused disarrangement in his friend's mind; a pretty story to be told —"Coleridge has been driven to madness by Wordsworth's cruel or unjust conduct towards him." Would not anybody suppose that he had been guilty of the most atrocious treachery or cruelty? but what is the sum of all he did? he privately warned a common friend disposed to serve C. with all his might that C. had one or two habits which might disturb his tranquillity—he told him what those habits were, and a greater kindness could hardly have been done to C., for it is not fit that he should go into houses where he is not already known. If he were to be told what was said at Penrith after he had been at Anthony Harrison's—*then* he might be thankful to William. I am sure we suffered enough on that account and were anxious enough to get him away. I say that at first I was strong with indignation but *that* soon subsided and I was lost in pity for his miserable weakness. It is certainly very unfortunate for William that he should be the person on whom he has to charge his neglect of duty, but to Coleridge the difference is nothing, for if this had not happened there would have been somebody else on whom to cast the blame. William wrote to Mrs C. immediately and wished her to transcribe his letter or details of it for C. and told her that he would not write to C. himself as he had not communicated his displeasure to him. Mrs C. replies that she is afraid to do this as C. did not desire her to inform us and that it may prevent him from opening letters in future etc etc. I ought to have told you that C. had a violent quarrel with Carlisle who refused to attend him as a surgeon after C. had slighted his prescriptions. My dear friend you cannot imagine what an irksome task it has been to me to write the above—I would wish it to rest for ever. Time will remove the cloud from his mind as far as the right view of our conduct is obscured, and having deserved no blame we are easy on that score. If he seek an explanation William will be ready to give it, but I think it is more likely that his fancies will die away of themselves.'

But his fancies did not die away; left to itself the wound only festered. For his grievance was not exactly as Dorothy had stated it: it was, as they found out later, that Montagu had said, or, as is more probable, Coleridge in his agitation imagined Montagu to have said, that Wordsworth had definitely *commissioned* him to tell Coleridge that he had been an absolute nuisance in his family, and that he had no hope of him. This, indeed, would have been both cruel and cowardly; but Wordsworth had said nothing of the kind. His error lay solely in trusting to Montagu's discretion; and had he sought at once from Coleridge a plain statement of his grievances he might, perhaps, have dispersed them, as his plain speaking, before Coleridge came to Allan Bank, had dispersed an earlier cloud of delusion. Yet it is no wonder that his patience was at last exhausted; no wonder, either, that Dorothy should share his exasperation. By this last attack upon the brother, whose passionate devotion to his friend she knew, as no other knew it, her eyes were at last opened to facts which for years she had striven to ignore; Coleridge had struck her in her most vulnerable place.

And yet, in her generous nature, the mere sense of personal resentment could not long be dominant:

> 'It has been misery enough, God knows, to me,' she wrote a month later,[1] 'to see the truths which I now see. Long did we hope against experience, and reason; but now I have no hope, if he continues as he is. Nothing but Time—producing a total change in him—can ever make him a being of much use to mankind in general, or of the least comfort to his friends. I am sure I have no personal pain or irritation connected with him. An injury done to my brother, or me, or any of our family, or dear friends, would not now hurt me more than an injury done to an indifferent person: I only grieve at the waste and prostitution of his fine genius, at the sullying and perverting of what is lovely and tender in human sympathies, and noble and generous: and I do grieve whenever I think of him. His resentment of my brother hardly ever comes into my thoughts. I feel perfectly indifferent about it. How absurd, how uncalculating of the feelings and opinions of others, to talk to your father and sister of dying in a fortnight, when his dress and everything proved that his thoughts were of other matters. Such talks will never more alarm me. . . . But enough of this melancholy subject. Only I must add that I fear he slackens at *The Courier* Office, as there has been nothing of his for some days, and he has not written to Mrs C. since the time I mentioned; nor

[1] D. W. to C. C., June 16, 1811.

has he acknowledged the receipt of his MSS which he was in a great hurry to receive, that he might publish them. By the bye, he desired Charles Lamb to write to me about them; therefore, no doubt, he includes me in his resentments. I know not for what cause.'

But six months later the bitterness she strove to master rose once more to the surface.

'I hope', she wrote to Mrs. Clarkson,[1] 'that [your sister] will attend Coleridge's lectures, yet I cannot wish that she should see him; for I have little doubt that he would open out his sore afflictions to her, which could only distress her, whether she believed them justly so called or the delusions of his own self-deceiving heart. If you go to London, you will certainly see him, and the whole will be laid before you; and for this reason, I do sincerely wish that you may not go thither, for I know so well the power of his presence that I should dread the effects upon your health. But perhaps, as I now trust he will, he may have triumphantly concluded his lectures; and in that case he will perhaps be too well satisfied with himself to delight in dwelling upon his supposed afflictions in the presence of one ready to rejoice with him in all good. . . . He has promised to come down to Keswick immediately after the lecture. I wish he may; but I do not think he can resolve to come, if he does not at the same time lay aside his displeasure against William.'

On January 20 Coleridge gave his last lecture; a month later he set off for Keswick. On the way he called at Ambleside to pick up Hartley and Derwent, but to their dismay he passed through Grasmere without stopping even for a moment to greet his old friends. 'Poor Hartley', wrote Mrs. Coleridge to Poole, 'sat in speechless astonishment as the chaise passed the turning to the Vicarage where Wordsworth lives, but he did not hazard one remark—and Derwent fixed his eyes full of tears upon his father, who turned his head away to conceal his own emotions. When they had an opportunity they both carefully asked the meaning of this paradox, and Hartley turned as white as lime when I told him that Mr. W. had a little vexed his father by something he said to Mr Montagu.'

After this clear repudiation of their love Dorothy and William could hardly go to Keswick unless Coleridge gave some sign

[1] Dec. 9, 1811.

that he wished to see them; but to all Dorothy's entreaties, sent through Mrs. Coleridge, he hardened his heart. Persuading himself that he had been cruelly wronged, he seems to have expected, or at least hoped, that they would fall on their knees before him, and beg to be received back into his favour. 'Numerous were the letters and messages', wrote Mrs. Coleridge to Poole,[1] 'I received from Miss W. urging C. to write to her, and not to leave the country without seeing them; but he would not go to them, and they did not come to him; so after staying 6 weeks he returned to give his lecture at Willis's rooms.' Mrs. Coleridge would have been more than human had she been able to repress a little malicious triumph when she saw her husband smarting under the conviction that he had been betrayed by the Wordsworths, whose companionship he had prized so much more highly than her own. 'He has', she added, 'been taught one very useful lesson—that even his dearest and most indulgent friends, even those very persons who have been the great means of his self-indulgence, when he comes to live *wholly* with them, are as clear-sighted to his failings, and much less delicate in speaking of them than his wife.'

Back in town after thus declining to meet the advances made to him from Grasmere, Coleridge continued to enlarge upon the cruelty with which he had been treated; the following extract from a letter which he wrote at this time reveals his bitter mood of self pity and self deception:

> 'And the consummation of all, I had scarcely arrived in London last Octr. 12 months, before the conviction was forced upon me, say rather pierced through my very soul with the suddenness of a flash of lightning, that he had been my bitterest calumniator who to that moment I had cherished in my heart's heart. The benumbing despondency alleviated by no gleam of hope and only alternating with fits of (truly I may call it) mental agony I even now dare scarcely look back on. But in the last worst affliction the case was included. I gradually obtained [control] over my own feelings and now dare call myself a Freeman, which I did not dare to do till I had been at Keswick and satisfied myself that no possibility remained of my being deluded. The effect of this conquest on my health, on my mind, and on my outward appearance have been such that the amiable family under whose roof I have been

[1] MS. letter in Brit. Mus. 35, 344.

sheltered since Oct 1810 declare that till now they have never seen me as myself.'

And so the trouble grew, gossips in London literary circles making the most of it, until in the following April William, urged by Mrs. Clarkson, who wrote to him that 'there has been downright lying somewhere, not mere misrepresentations and and dressing up of facts, but inventions against you', resolved to go up to town, and 'to confront Coleridge and Montagu with the whole vile business'. How much misery might have been avoided if he had taken this step eighteen months before! Among other things he gained a sight of Coleridge's letter which has just been quoted, and he duly forwarded it to Dorothy. At the patent insincerity of Coleridge's reference to his recent stay at Keswick her anger blazed out:[1]

' "At *Keswick*, forsooth! he satisfied himself that no possibility remained of his being deluded"—At *Keswick* where nothing *was* done, nothing *could be* done to increase the offence—whence the insult of total neglect was heaped upon us and received without murmuring. This only proves what we have long been sure of, that he is glad of a pretext to break with us, and to furnish himself with a ready excuse for all his failures in duty to himself and others. Mr Wedgwood is the properest person to be present at your meeting—at all events I hope you have had one or more steady respectable persons—for he ought to be put to confusion after speaking of you as he has done. You were his "vilest calumniator" when you only told a common friend of some part of his failings, in order to prevent his putting himself into a situation through which he would expose them all in a tenfold greater degree. We long for a letter, dearest William. I fear this business will harass you very much, in addition to the first flutter of London—pray tell us all particulars—consider how much we need your letters.'

A week later she wrote:[2]

'I did not get yours till this morning—how happy I am that your mind is going to be settled about Coleridge. You have in every part of the arrangement acted wisely and becomingly—and I hope that such intercourse will henceforth take place between you as will be satisfactory to both parties. When you see him give my love to him. I suppose he will now receive it, though he has acted indeed to us all (and Sara and I could not possibly have offended him) as if he intended to insult us. I am sure he does not know the

[1] D. W. to W. W., May 3, 1812.

[2] D. W. to W. W., May 10.

depth of the affection I have had for him. . . . For God's sake, write as often as you can and I will write again at leisure. God bless thee my dearest William, thine evermore D.W.'

Before William received this letter the reconciliation had been effected. There had been many preliminary difficulties to overcome. Coleridge rejected the proposal that Wedgwood should be called in as arbitrator; he also declined to meet Montagu, though he was willing to meet Wordsworth either alone or in the company of some other friend; and he offered, through Lamb, to send his version of the story as he had stated it, months before, in a letter to Sara Hutchinson, which he had not posted because he heard that Sara had already decided against him. But Wordsworth was unwilling to meet Coleridge alone: he was fearful of those outbursts of passion, or rather weakness, of which Coleridge was capable, in which facts would inevitably be lost in hysteria; and for a similar reason he declined to read the letter to Sara: he wanted a dry statement of facts and not an emotional commentary upon Coleridge's impression of the facts; he also declined to read a letter written directly to him unless Coleridge would assure him that it contained nothing but a plain statement of what Montagu had said, which he could then send to Montagu for his comments. But Coleridge was deeply offended at the suggestion that his letter should be sent to Montagu, and it seemed as though matters had reached an impasse. Then Crabb Robinson stepped in as intermediary; he obtained from Coleridge the plain statement for which Wordsworth asked; and Wordsworth, waiving all inquiry as to whether the initial error lay with Coleridge or Montagu, expressed his belief in Coleridge's sincerity, and met the charges against himself in a manner which convinced Coleridge that the 'monstrous words' attributed to him had never been spoken. For the next few days they saw something of one another, without, however, making any reference to the subject of their correspondence; and their friendship was resumed. But it was with a difference; the division between them had been too deep, and had lasted too long, for it to be ever wholly healed. They could never again be upon the old intimate footing.

'I am glad to think that you will see Coleridge', wrote Dorothy to Mrs. Clarkson early in the next year. 'Poor soul!

I only think of him now with my wonted affection, and with tender feelings of compassion for his infirmities. We have had several letters from him. . . . He talks of coming down as soon as possible, if his play succeeds. I hope it will, and then I am confident he will come.' But Dorothy's confidence was misplaced. The play was successful, but Coleridge broke his word, adding to his offence some act of ingratitude to Mrs. Clarkson, who was doing her best to befriend him:

'My dear friend,' wrote Dorothy,[1] 'as to Coleridge you have done all that can be done, and we are grieved that you have had so much uneasiness, and taken so much trouble about him. He will not let himself be served by others. Oh, that the day may ever come when he will serve himself! then will his eyes be opened, and he will see clearly that we have loved him always, do still love him, and have ever loved—not measuring his deserts. I do not now wish him to come into the North; that is, I do not wish him to do it for the sake of any wish to gratify us. But if he should do it of himself I should be glad, as the best sign that he was endeavouring to perform his duties. His conduct towards you has been selfish and unfeeling in the extreme, which makes me hope no good of him at present, especially as I hear from all quarters so much of his confident announcement of plans for this musical drama, that comedy, the other essay. Let him doubt and his powers will revive. Till then they must sleep. God bless him. He little knows with what tenderness we have lately thought of him, nor how entirely we are softened to all sense of injury. We have no thoughts of him but such as ought to have made him lean upon us with confidential love, and fear not to confess his weaknesses.'

Unable themselves to do more for their friend, they showed their devotion in a constant care for his children. 'The boys', writes Dorothy,[2] 'come to us almost every week. . . . William will now be enabled to assist in sending Hartley to college; but of course this must not be mentioned; for the best thing that can happen to his father will be that he should suppose that the whole care of putting Hartley forward must fall upon himself.'

And so, though frequent reference to Coleridge in the later correspondence bears witness to the eagerness with which they still followed his concerns, and though William from time to time saw something of him in London, he passed from the forefront of their lives.

[1] D. W. to C. C., Apr. 8, 1813. [2] Ib.

XIV

VISITS TO COLEORTON, BURY, AND LONDON. REMOVAL TO THE RECTORY. THE DEATHS OF CATHARINE AND THOMAS

1810–1813 (aet. 38–41)

WE must now retrace our steps to the May of 1810, when Coleridge left Allan Bank. On the 12th, Mary gave birth to her fifth child, William, and Dorothy again undertook the duties of sole nurse: at the beginning of July she left Grasmere with her brother for a much needed holiday. It was long since she had enjoyed any respite from household cares, and the strain of the last few years must have told heavily upon her. But up to the point of starting she was uncertain whether she would be able to go, for though both Mary and the baby were thriving, little Catharine was causing them grave anxiety. Left on the floor to play while Sally Green was stirring the porridge, she had swallowed a large quantity of raw carrot, out of which the older children had been making pellets; violent convulsions had followed which left her paralysed down one side of her body, and though some months had now elapsed since her first attack, she had shown little signs of regaining the full use of her limbs. The two travellers left home with many forebodings, half expecting to be recalled; but after a night spent with the Cooksons[1] at Kendal they received a cheering report from Mary, and they pursued their way in better heart. On the 9th they reached Coleorton, after a pleasant journey through Dovedale.

They stayed with the Beaumonts about a month, and Dorothy

[1] The Cooksons of Kendal were not related to the C.s of Penrith, from whom the W.s were descended on their mother's side. They became friends of the W.s through Sara H., who had spent her youth at Kendal, and was already intimate with them when she joined the W.s at Grasmere. From about 1805 on, the two families often visited each other, and in passing through Kendal to and from the South the W.s would spend a night or two with them. Late in life Mr. C. suffered financial losses and went to live in the Isle of Man, where W. W. visited him (*v. Itinerary Poems* of 1833, Sonnet XX). On his death in 1833 his widow and two of his daughters settled at Grasmere; they were constantly at Rydal Mount, and took a share in the transcription of W.'s poems. Of the two sons, H. Wilkinson C., and W. Strickland C., the one became Master of Pembroke College, Cambridge, and the other a prominent London solicitor: the W.s consulted him on legal matters, and he was one of W. W.'s executors.

delighted in the society of her host and hostess and in visiting the tenants, among whom she had made many friends during the winter she had spent at the house farm. Then William left her to meet Sara Hutchinson in Wales, and a few days later she joined Mrs. Clarkson at Bury St. Edmunds. The letter[1] in which she recounted to William and Sara the details of her journey gives a vivid picture of cross-country travel in the early nineteenth century (to cover the 92 miles between Ashby de la Zouche and Cambridge took her 21½ hours) and by the way throws many a light upon her character—her little economies where her own comfort was concerned, her friendly bearing with chance companions, above all, the way in which, wherever she might be, her beloved brother was constantly in her thoughts:

> My dearest William,
>
> After I had parted from you I was so low-spirited that I hardly knew what to do with myself, so I went to Ashby to put aside my thoughts . . . on Wednesday Sir George arrived with good accounts of you, and he himself delighted with his journey, and not at all the worse for it. Just as I wrote the last word the cook brought me in your letter, dearest Sara and dear William. I have been at least an hour in reading it, first to myself and then to Mrs Clarkson.

No one, it may be remarked, who has attempted to decipher William's handwriting will be surprised at the time which she took over the letter. After speaking of her farewell visits to the farm-house, and her sorrow at saying good-bye to so many good friends, she continues:

> In my way to Ashby I cheered up and Colly[2] and I had some friendly talk. He left me in the snug parlour with one small candle; this will give you a notion that it was but a third rate Inn. It suited me, however, the better, for the woman was very civil. I took my Book out, but could not attend to it, so after writing a few lines to Lady Beaumont I went to bed but did not take off my clothes. I found myself much refreshed when I was called at 12 o'clock though I had not slept; but what was my disappointment on finding that there was no inside place. I must either mount the Coach or take a Chaise. I chose the former, but alas! the Landlady had no cloak to lend me, so I wrapped myself up as well as I could in Mary's thin blue coat and my shawl, and seated

[1] D. W. to W. W. and S. H., Aug. 14, 1810.
[2] Colly was one of Sir George's man-servants.

myself in the front between a quiet old man and a civil young gentleman-like man from Liverpool. It was a beautiful night and mild at Ashby, but very cold upon the Forest. We reached Leicester at half-past three, and after warming myself by the Kitchen fire I went to bed again in my clothes and dropped asleep a little before 6, when I was called again. Breakfasted with a Gentleman who was going to Cambridge, and the morning was so fine that I resolved to go on the outside as he promised to protect me. A gentleman's servant with 3 dogs, two in a hamper, and one who served to keep my legs warm, were my other companions. The servant was very pleasant and polite, and both most delicate in their attentions to me,—if they had been my Brothers they could not have been more attentive and delicate in helping me to and down from my seat. Afterwards we took up two well-behaved young women, better dressed than I was and very modest. I breakfasted again with the Passengers, being determined to take care of myself. We changed coaches at Stamford and I shared my sandwiches with one of the women and she gave me of her cakes. So I saved a dinner—and did not drink tea at Huntingdon, where the rest had tea.[1]

I was pleased to find at Stamford[2] so many new pleasures in store for our latter years. I used to think it an ugly town—and wherever I looked I saw something to admire—the churches—the old houses—the forms of the streets. In short it seems to me a very fine town for a Painter. To be sure the sun-shine and the cleanliness of the streets set it off to the best advantage. I got into the coach at Huntingdon, for the evening was cold. By the bye, I must not forget the Coachman who is one of the nicest men I ever met with; I might have ridden in the inside whenever I liked.

Dear William, we stopped at the gate of St John's to set down the Professor of Arabic, who I afterwards learned was a Cockermouth man. I was awe-stricken with the venerable appearance of the gateway, and the light from a distance streaming along the level pavement. Thy freshman's days came into my mind and I could have burst into tears. I found dear Mr Clarkson at the door of the Inn—I was sick and giddy when I got out (it was half past 9); this

[1] In her letter to Lady B. describing the journey she says, 'I had the offer of tea, but though it would have been very refreshing, I thought it was too expensive a luxury, being only one stage from the end of my journey: therefore I walked about in the town.'

[2] She writes of Stamford to Lady B. in much the same words, and of Cambridge she tells her that at King's College 'and everywhere else at Cambridge I was even much more impressed with the effect of buildings than I had been formerly; and I do believe that this power of receiving an enlarged enjoyment from the sight of buildings is one of the privileges of our latter years'.

I had never been when I was on the outside. . . . Rose at a quarter before 8 and went to Trinity Chapel, and I stood in silence while the organ was played for many minutes before the statue of Newton.[1] It is the most beautiful statue I ever beheld, and before this time I had comparatively viewed it with indifference. The silent face gave me feelings that I am sure were sublime, though dear Mr Clarkson did now and then disturb me by pointing out the wrinkles in the silk stockings, the buckles etc. etc., all which etceteras are in truth worthy of admiration. I was charmed with the walks, found out William's ashtree,[2] visited King's Chapel after dinner—set off at a quarter past 4, drank tea at Newmarket—reached Bury at 9 o'clock. . . .

God bless thee dearest William and dear Sara—write often I pray you—I have yet a hundred things to say.

Dorothy stayed some six weeks with Mrs. Clarkson; the remainder of her holiday she divided between London and Binfield, near Windsor, where her uncle, Canon Cookson, was now the rector. At Bury she was entirely happy; she felt at home in the house and garden, and the little town that was more like a village; after five years' separation she was once more with the friend with whom she was in deepest sympathy, one, too, who was the centre of a large family circle, all of whom seem to have taken her to their hearts. Before she left, Henry Crabb Robinson had joined the party, and he was quick to discern that 'without her brother's genius and productive power [she] had all his tastes and feelings'.[3] As for Dorothy, 'I should feel disposed', she had told Mrs. Clarkson,[4] 'to like your cousin Henry Robinson for his love of William's poems, if I had not already been prepossessed in his favour from your having spent many happy hours of your youth in his society. I am not more confident of any truth than of this, that there must be something good in the heart that is much attached to my brother's poems, and I trust too that they make better the heart that loves them.' But she found that a good heart was not Crabb's only merit: he was also a kindly and interesting companion. He travelled with her to London and gave up his mornings to acting as her cicerone; and when she was at home again she

[1] *V. Prelude* (1805), iii. 57–9.
[2] Ib., vi. 90–109.
[3] *Correspondence of H. C. R. with the W.'s*, ed. E. J. Morley, i. 60.
[4] D. W. to C.C., Dec. 28, 1807.

recalled to him[1] the enjoyment of 'our long journey side by side in the pleasant sunshine, our splendid entrance into the great city, and our rambles together in the crowded streets'. She had gone to London with some misgivings. 'I seem', she said,[2] 'to be constitutionally framed to be uncomfortable when I am there; my health always suffers and I am distracted by noise, and the multitude of objects so different from those among which our lives are spent.' But her fears were soon dispelled. Like her brother William she was an indefatigable sight-seer, and in addition to her morning rambles with Crabb went, among other places, to the British Museum, and with Mary Lamb to an opera at Covent Garden. She stayed with the Lambs at Inner Temple Lane. 'The kindness of Charles Lamb and his sister was unbounded. I was never the hundredth part so comfortable in London . . . there is nobody in the world out of our own house in whom I am more deeply interested.'[3] But her company proved too exciting for Mary Lamb, and after her departure she was distressed to learn that her hostess had paid for her visit by a serious attack of illness. 'I feel', she reproached herself,[4] 'as if I *ought* to have perceived that everything out of the common course of her daily life caused excitement and agitation equally injurious to her.'

From all at Binfield she received a hearty welcome. 'I could not have forgiven myself', she says,[5] 'if I had not come hither, for it is impossible to describe my uncle's kindness to me, my aunt's and everybody's. The old nursemaid who has lived with them 17 years received me with tears in her eyes.' The children whom she had known at Forncett as babies pleased her greatly; Mary, the eldest, was 'an angel in temper sweetness and innocence', Eliza she thought 'very beautiful', Christopher, just down from Cambridge, was 'manly, tall and affectionate'; the two younger boys who were at Eton made a special visit home, 'for, Mary says, "it would break their hearts not to see me"'. Altogether she felt that she 'had never seen people more happy in each other'.

She had intended to stay a fortnight with them and then take another week in London, but her time was cut short by hearing

[1] D. W. to H. C. R., Nov. 6, 1810.
[2] D. W. to Lady B., Aug. 7, 1805.
[3] D. W. to C. C., Oct. 30, 1810.
[4] D. W. to H. C. R., Nov. 6, 1810.
[5] D. W. to C. C., Oct. 15, 1810.

from Grasmere, on October 16, that the children had whooping cough and that Catharine was dangerously ill. She knew that William was by nature over-anxious, and hoped that things were not as serious as he made out, but she returned at once to town, and after three or four days—she was delayed twenty-four hours by failing to secure a seat on the coach—started for the North. She reached Grasmere on the 23rd.

'John was the first to meet me. He ran bounding down the field and almost bursting with joy—then came the two Williams, and last of all Mary with Catharine in her arms. And then I was cut to the heart, for I never saw so deplorable an object as this poor sweet child, worn to a skeleton, and, as it seemed, no traces left of what she had been. William and Mary, seeing my distress, did their utmost to console me, by assuring me that she had mended daily since the day after William had written to me, and that they had now no doubts about her well-doing . . . oh, my dear Friend, if I had known what her mother had to suffer and what the child had to suffer also I should never have gone further than your home. Not that I regret that I did so. . . . I have many kind acts of many kind friends to remember, much that I have done and seen, and I am come home in time to be of the greatest use in assisting Mary to attend upon Catharine and the infant in their restoration to health.'[1]

Tom and little Dorothy had already gone for a change of air to Hackett, the home of their servant, Sarah Yewdale, and the rest of the family except Johnny joined them there the next day.

'It is as poor a cottage as ever you saw, standing upon a hill-top overlooking little Langdale, Tilberthwaite, Colwith, and the vale of Brathay; warm because it fronts the south, and sheltered behind by crags, and on one side and in front by the barn and garden wall, which exclude all prospect from the windows. But at the door, choose to the right or to the left and you have mountains, hamlets, woods, cottages and rocks. The weather was heavenly when we were there, and the first morning we sat in hot sunshine on a crag, twenty yards from the door, while William read part of the 5th Book of *Paradise Lost* to us. He read *The Morning Hymn*, while a stream of white vapour, which coursed the valley of Brathay, ascended slowly and by degrees melted away. It seemed as if we had never before felt deeply the power of the poet "Ye mists and exhalations" etc, etc,!

[1] D. W. to C. C., Oct. 30, 1810.

'That evening William left us, and I went a part of the way with him. The darkness came on before I reached the house, which stands at a great distance from the road, and the way to it is over a peat moss and through trackless fields. I lost myself got into a wood, climbed over high walls that I should have trembled at by day, at last found myself again on the peat moss, and stumbled on, often above the knees in mud, till I came to a cottage. All this time I had been quite composed, and was planning what I should do if I were forced to stay out all night; but, when I laid my hand upon the latch of that cottage-door my heart overflowed, and when I entered I could not speak for weeping and sobbing. I sat a few minutes, put on a pair of the woman's stockings, and her husband guided me to Hackett; and I then perceived that it would have been impossible for me ever to have got thither alone, after the daylight was gone. I found poor Mary in a wretched state with her bairns—Sarah and her father had gone out half distracted to seek me; and Mary was trembling from head to foot. The next day the woman of the house called to see me, and declared she was "never so *wae* for anybody in her life", I was in such a wretched case the night before. Well! it is over, and this good is come of it, that I shall never again go alone in rough places, and on unknown ground late in the evening.'[1]

A few days after their return to Grasmere the fear of scarlet fever, which had broken out in the village, drove them away again, 'for poor William's anxious mind was harassed past enduring'.[1] This time they took refuge with the Wilsons at Elleray. The weather was still delightful and Dorothy was enchanted with the beauty of the situation. 'Oh', she wrote,[1] 'could you see the glittering lake of Windermere which lies before me—bays, islands, promontories. It is paradise itself, and if I go two yards from the door I can behold Langdale Pikes and the range of Grasmere and Rydal fells with the Lake and all the intermediate country.' They only returned to Allan Bank just in time for Christmas. With seven children in the house, for little Jane and Mary Hutchinson joined them for the holidays,

[1] D. W. to C. C., Nov. 12, 1810. While at Elleray, D. W. wrote some of the descriptions which form Section II of W. W.'s Introduction to *Select Views of Cumberland, Westmoreland, and Lancashire, by the Rev. Joseph Wilkinson*, 1810. W. had finished the main part of the Introduction in the previous November (*v.* D. W. to C. C., Nov. 18, 1809): the completion of the work awaited his receipt of the sketches. But when he saw them he lost heart, and called in D.'s assistance. Section II was afterwards rewritten to form the *Directions and Information for the Tourist*, with which the *Guide to the Lakes* opens.

they had a lively time, and the festivities included a large Christmas party in the kitchen, attended by the servants from Elleray, and, a few days later, a dinner with De Quincey at Dove Cottage. The invalids had all recovered, and even Mary, despite what she had gone through, was 'stronger and fatter than she had been for years'. Dorothy laid aside anxious thoughts, and felt 'happy in the company of her beloved friends and the dearest of children'.

Their three years' tenancy of Allan Bank came to an end in the following May; some twelve months before this they had arranged to rent the rectory, which stood opposite the church. Dorothy could not leave Allan Bank without regrets. The house itself had never appealed to her, with its smoky chimneys, 'its plastered walls, half carpeted floors and half furnished rooms, its long passages and clashing doors', but, 'Oh, my dear friend', she wrote to Lady Beaumont,[1] 'this place—the wood behind it, the rocks, the view of Easedale from them, the lake, and church and village on the other side—is sweeter than paradise itself'. The rectory needed much renovation before it would be habitable, and Dorothy felt some doubt whether it would be ready for them in time, for William had undertaken the charge of getting the business done, 'and you know how unfit he is for anything of that kind. Mary and I, however, are determined not to enter upon it till it is finished completely, for we were thoroughly sickened of workmen when we first came hither'.[2] But towards the end of May they moved in, though the workmen were still in the house, making an incredible mess and 'seeming to take delight in scattering lime about wherever they went'. In justice to William it should be stated that bad weather, and not his incompetence, had been responsible for the delay. By the middle of June Dorothy was able to report that the house was more or less tidy and that they all liked it. True, it had three drawbacks: it faced the east so that the sitting rooms lost the sun very early; it was too near the road and lacked privacy; and the field in which it stood was wet and no fit playing place for the children. But inside there seemed no comfort wanting: it was more like a large cottage than a house, and the furniture 'took to its places much better than at Allan Bank'; altogether she saw no reason why it should not 'be made a very canny spot'.

[1] D. W. to Lady B., May 10, 1810. [2] D. W. to C. C., Dec. 30, 1810.

It was a coincidence, and not the result of their occupation of the Rectory, that during this spring the family became regular attendants at the Grasmere parish church. Since the Forncett days Dorothy's visits to church had been only occasional: in this, as in so much else, she was at one with William, who stoutly defended the Church Establishment—he even said he would shed his blood for it, but confessed he knew not when he had been to church in his own country. 'All our ministers', he said,[1] ' "are so vile".' And their experience at Grasmere, where the rector was an imbecile and the curate a drunkard, lent some support to his contention. During their stay at Coleorton, perhaps out of consideration for their hosts, they had modified their practice, but somewhat perfunctorily. 'I wish', wrote Dorothy to Mrs. Clarkson from Coleorton,[2] 'you would not go to church so often, (I am not going to disturb your religious sentiments, or to argue against going to Church in general; for we are become regular churchgoers, that is, we take it by turns, two at a time, and always two every Sunday when the weather will permit); but I do think that you have no business at Church in winter, and that you are more likely to catch cold there than anywhere else.' And when they returned to Grasmere, and found Mr. Jackson installed as rector, 'a worthy man, very good as a steward and a farmer, but totally unfit to preach or read prayers',[3] they were not encouraged to continue. But in 1811 Mr. Jackson secured a curate of a very different stamp in Mr. Johnson,[4] whom Dorothy found both amiable and inspiring. They felt, too, that church would be good for the children. 'Mary', she writes on May 12, 'went with the troop in the morning and I in the afternoon, and a pretty show we make, I assure you.' A few weeks later Mr. Johnson had even induced them to teach in the Sunday school. 'Do not think', she protests, 'that I am going to set myself up as a regular teacher; at present we have too much to do all the week to make us take upon ourselves this voluntary labour as a regular duty, but our curate is very earnest in his attentions to Sunday schools, and

[1] H. C. R. *Diary*, ed. Sadler, i. 203.

[2] D. W. to C. C., Feb. 17, 1807.

[3] D. W. to J. M., July 26, 1812.

[4] William Johnson (1784–1864). In 1812 Dr. Bell took him to London to be head master of a new school which was to be conducted on the 'Madras system'. In 1820 he became rector of St. Clement's, Eastcheap.

wished my sister and me to encourage them by our occasional presence, so as often as we may without inconvenience, we intend, one of us, to go in the mornings.' It is evident that at this time the Church held no vital place in her religious life; her own deepest spiritual needs were still satisfied by worship in temples not made with hands, her natural piety found its true expression in glad response to the daily calls upon her love and service in the home, and she felt an instinctive suspicion of anything that savoured of pietism. Books 'full of indefinite breathings of godliness, exclamations without end, and "God" in every fourth line of a page' were her abhorrence: of an acquaintance who inclined to withdraw from her practical duties into a kind of pious invalidism, she wrote shrewdly,[1] 'I cannot but think it unfortunate that her mind should have taken such a decided turn towards religious contemplation: surely she has sensibility enough to have been good and happy in another way'. But these visits to church and Sunday school, made for the children's sake and to please Mr. Johnson, mark the beginning of a gradual revolution in her point of view. Many causes contributed to bring it about—the general awakening of the Church itself to its responsibilities, a closer intimacy with men, like Mr. Johnson and her brother Christopher, who found in an orthodox faith and practice a real spiritual inspiration, the growing consciousness which she shared with William of the support that such a faith had to give. She came, at last, to look back upon her earlier attitude with an almost pathetic disapproval. In 1832, turning over the pages of her *Recollections of a Tour in Scotland*, she added a solemn note: 'I find that this tour was both begun and ended on a Sunday. I am sorry that it should have been so, though I hope and trust that our thoughts and feelings were not seldom as pious and serious as if we had duly attended a place devoted to public worship. My sentiments have undergone a great change since 1803 respecting the absolute necessity of keeping the Sabbath by a regular attendance at a Church.'

But, quite apart from her busier Sundays, the summer of 1811 was fully occupied. No sooner were they settled into the rectory than haymaking began, and with the servants at work in the fields, Dorothy had to make beds, cook, and attend to the

[1] D. W. to C. C., May 12, 1811.

children. Then Sissy's clothes had to be got ready for her to go to Miss Weir's boarding school at Appleby. The little Grasmere school had not improved her manners; her mother and aunt had long felt that, quick and excitable as she was, she needed a sterner discipline than home could offer; they hoped that the example of other girls would help to steady her, and William had reluctantly been brought round to their opinion. But they parted from her with many fears. 'There is no reason', wrote Dorothy,[1] 'to dread gross vice at Miss Weir's, and all the girls are young and their number is only twelve, so that it is more like a large family than a school; yet when such a number even as that are together there is always cause to apprehend little artful tricks among them. Much good, we are sure, she will get . . . there was never a girl in the world who would more easily be led to industry by following others, or to whom it would be more difficult to learn to sit still when she has no companions.'

Three days after she was gone William and Mary left for the seaside with Thomas, Catharine, and one of the maids; it was hoped that bathing might help to cure little Catharine's lameness. In their absence Dorothy went for a few days to Hackett with John and Willy, and for the first time for months she enjoyed a little leisure. William came over to join her, and they had delightful walks together, for the old couple at the cottage took a great fancy to little Willy; Betty minded him all day except when she was milking, and when her 'husband came home from his work at the quarries' they made a group round the fireside which, as Dorothy presents it,[2] might have inspired a Dutch painter: 'Willy took his place on the quiet man's knee, never wishing to stir, Jonathan smoked his pipe, Betty smoked hers, and the child smacked *his* lips imitating them.'

The event of the winter was little Dorothy's return from her first half year at school; it is characteristic of her aunt, that though she longed to see her again, she arranged to be away at Keswick when she arrived, so that her family, and above all her father, should have her to themselves. They were pleased with the progress she had made, and decided to send her back to Appleby for one more half year. She was still wayward, but 'tender hearted, affectionate, and very lively as ever. . . . I wish you could have seen the animated countenance with which this

[1] D. W. to C. C. Aug. 14, 1811. [2] Ib.

instant she looked up at me when she came to something in her book which amused her'.[1] And when the village fiddlers were paying their annual rounds she was in her true element, and aunt Dorothy was called into the kitchen to join the dance. As far as all the children were concerned it was as happy a Christmas as could be.

But with the return of winter they had found that the rectory was not the 'canny spot' they had pictured it. The surrounding field was a perfect bog, and their landlord was so dilatory in attending to it that they feared it would be another six months before they were clean and decent even at their doors. And within, the parlour fires smoked as badly as at Allan Bank. Sara drew for Mary Monkhouse[2] a melancholy picture of their woes. 'It is a hateful house . . . it is really deplorable to think how much of William's time has been taken from him by these petty inconveniences. Sometimes within the last months we have had no room to sit in but Dorothy's bedroom, not another chimney would carry the smoke. Then the sun never shines upon the house except when we are in bed, so that we need more fires than anybody else. The other day the sun shone so hot that you were almost oppressed by it, and when we came in, the house was like a well and made us shiver.' It was not a place for delicate children to thrive in, nor did it suit Mary, who, as spring came on, had grown so alarmingly thin, that in April they packed her off for a visit to her brother Thomas at Hindwell. On the night of June 3, while she was still away, and when William was in London effecting his reconcilation with Coleridge, little Catharine was seized with convulsions; early the next morning she was dead.

The shock to Dorothy was all the greater because Catharine had seemed in perfect health.

> 'For several days,' she says,[3] 'the child had been in the most joyous spirits . . . that very night on which she was seized she ran up to bed, in such glee striving to get before William and proud that she was going to sleep in her *Mother's* bed, an unusual treat. We returned from our walk at a little after nine, and John called me to her at about ¼ before ten; he was going to bed and found that she had been sick. She was lying with her eyes fixed, and I

[1] D. W. to C. C., Dec. 27, 1811.
[2] S. H. to Mary Monkhouse, Mar. 1812.
[3] D. W. to C. C., June 23, 1812.

knew what was going to happen and in a fright called Sara. She would have persuaded me that the child was only overpowered by sickness, but I had seen her before and knew too well. We lost no time in sending for Mr Scambler and in the meantime applied the remedies used before. Mr Scambler gave us no hope and . . . we only prayed for her release in death; for it was plain that had she lived she could not have recovered the use of her limbs nor probably of her senses, and what a sorrow this would have been for her mother and every one of us! We know not how soon we may be deprived of one of the other children, but there is great cause for thankfulness that if one was to be taken away it was this sweet innocent: for we now find that there was the greatest reason to fear a return of the paralytic affection . . . and oh how merciful this heavy stroke compared with one that might have left her helpless and deprived of her understanding!'

But by dwelling upon this and 'other reasons for thankfulness', Dorothy could not stem a grief which was intensified by the thought of poor Mary, away from home and separated from William, who alone had power to console her. Willy was ailing, and she exaggerated to herself his danger: Johnny seemed never tired, 'a proof that he is very strong: this thought strikes suddenly upon me many and many a time and my heart is humbled, and I fear the more because he is so strong'; for was not Catharine in health when she was struck down? Jane Marshall, who knew what Dorothy must be suffering, begged her to come over to Watermillock, if only for a few days. But she could not be persuaded. 'I cannot', she said,[1] 'leave home till after my Brother's and Sister's return. I *cannot* do it . . . I could not be easy to leave the children for a single night to the care of any others than their Parents. You will say perhaps, "Miss Hutchinson is here, and what can you do more than she can do?" That is very true, and more I cannot do; but I could not bear to leave them.' And when Mary arrived, outwardly calm, but looking terribly thin and worn, and her face drawn with suffering, Dorothy had many a struggle to control her own grief.

A few days later she left for a short visit to Watermillock. She found it hard to go, but a change was necessary for her; and aunt Rawson, now old and ailing, was staying with the Marshalls and was anxious to see her. On July 23 William came to fetch her

[1] D. W. to J. M., June 21, 1812.

back, and they returned over Dove Crag and Fairfield. It was a stiff climb, and in the steepest part of it she looked back, turned giddy, and would have fallen over a precipice had not her brother caught hold of her. But she was rewarded by a superb view from the top, and save for a bad cold and a swollen face she was none the worse for the fatigue.

In her grief for Catharine, 'the sweetest and mildest tempered child that ever was born, and the freest from all bad passions', Dorothy watched more intently than ever the mental and moral growth of the other children. Sissy was a puzzle to her. She had always been devoted to little Catharine and was much afflicted when Miss Weir broke to her the news of her death: but she was of so 'volatile a nature that the next day she was as happy as ever'. When she came home 'we were surprised at her joyfulness; at night when she went to bed she knelt down before me to say her prayers, and as usual prayed for her brothers and sister. I said to her when she had done, "My dear child, you have no sister living now, and our religion does not teach us to pray for the dead. We can do nothing for them, our prayers will not help them. God has taken your sister to himself." She burst into a flood, an agony of tears, and went weeping and silent to her bed, and I left her after some time still weeping, and so she fell asleep'.[1] All through the summer she gave them trouble. 'She *can* do anything, but she is extremely wayward and is desirous to master everybody. It is a woful thing that so sweet a creature should be capable of seeking the perverse delight of making those who love her unhappy . . . sometimes we have terrible battles and long confinements. I hope that perseverance may conquer her, and that the sense will in time come that it is wiser not to make herself miserable.'[2] With Johnny her perplexity was of a very different kind. On Catharine's death his thoughtfulness, good sense, and delicate feeling had made them all lean on him for support, and when he returned from school at Ambleside 'with a bottle over his shoulder and a basket in his hand', he always met them with smiles. But he seemed to learn nothing at school and was terribly backward; and yet she was sure that he was 'not a dunce in soul'; though his sister was much quicker and forwarder than he, when you 'read to them both—poetry, history, natural history, stories,

[1] D. W. to C. C., June 23, 1812. [2] D. W. to C. C., July 31, 1812.

whatever it is, she yawns and grows sleepy, and his attention would be kept continually awake if you read till midnight'.

Happily for all of them the summer brought many friends to Grasmere. Mary Monkhouse, whom they all loved, was with them again for two months; De Quincey returned to Dove Cottage. He was in London at the time of Catharine's death and he had been the first, after William, to whom Dorothy had sent the sad news, telling him by way of comfort, that the little one 'never forgot Quincey'; and his love for their lost child made his company especially dear to them. William found distraction in the society of the poet Rogers and his old friend 'conversation' Sharp: two young clergymen from Cambridge, Bloomfield[1] and Tillbrook, were in Robert Newton's lodgings, and the eccentric Dr. Bell was in the neighbourhood.

Andrew Bell, the tireless expounder of his Madras system of education, was in high favour at Keswick and Grasmere. Southey lauded his theories in the press; Coleridge, when he had been with them, had talked of him as insistently as of Sir Alexander Ball. 'Bell and Ball, Ball and Bell', says De Quincey, 'were two of his pet subjects, he had a craze about each of them'; William had shown his enthusiasm in the previous autumn by teaching in the village school on Bell's method; and though to the world at large Bell was known as both quarrelsome and irascible, to the ladies at the rectory he was 'dear Andrew'; Dorothy gave much time during the summer to helping him collect his stray articles into a connected book; and he was on terms of such intimacy with her as to address her in his letters as 'my dear antelope';[2] he missed her badly, for, as he said, 'nobody scolds me as you do'. Bloomfield was a native of Bury, and both he and Tillbrook were heartily welcomed as friends of Mr. Clarkson's. Bloomfield was the abler of the two, and could 'preach a good sermon of his own composing', but Tillbrook was their favourite. Dorothy found Bloomfield a little irritating. 'His views of everything', she says,[3] 'are contracted by his love of the picturesque, he has yet to learn there is a wider range of enjoyment than he at present realizes'; but Tillbrook,

[1] C. T. Bloomfield (1786–1857) of Trinity Coll., Cambridge, a pupil of Porson's, who spoke of him as 'a very pretty scholar'. He was ordained in 1810, became Bishop of Chester in 1824 and Bishop of London in 1828.

[2] S. H. to Mrs. Thos. Hutchinson, (Mary Monkhouse), Nov. 19, 1812.

[3] D. W. to C. C., Aug. 10, 1812.

though at first she had noted in him 'a coarseness and want of polish that might be smoothed away with advantage',[1] had wider sympathies, and he delighted them all with his blunt plainness and honest sincerity, and 'his droll way of telling things for and against himself'. In their company they took many pleasant walks, best of all one to Hackett, where old Betty provided them with tea. 'Mr Sharp was of the party and was very entertaining, and Tillbrook stationed himself upon a rock and sounded his flute[2] to the great delight of our party, the cows in the field, and a group of rustic children. Dear Mary was the only one who remained at home. She *could* not go to Hackett, which had been so dear to her as that place where Catharine first began to recover after the whooping cough.'[3]

The children were made much of by all their friends; but the visitor to whom they gave the most uproarious welcome was a pig sent them by their relative Captain Wordsworth.[4] 'And their joy was tenfold when they heard that the pig was to be kept to have young ones. The pig was set down upon the kitchen floor, and it was impossible to say whether the voice of Willy's raptures or of the pig's fears was louder.'[5]

On November 2 they had the excitement of a wedding in which they all rejoiced, for Mary Monkhouse was married in Grasmere church to her cousin Thomas Hutchinson, the children's uncle. But a month later they were once more plunged in bitter grief. Little Thomas took the measles, and on December 1 he died, almost as suddenly as Catharine had done only six months before.

Dorothy was away at the time, staying with the Marshalls at Watermillock. In a long letter to Mrs. Clarkson,[6] written at three sittings, she told the whole story of their sorrow. She wrote on their return from Ambleside, whither they had gone a week after Thomas's death, so that the children, who had all caught the infection, might be nearer to Mr. Scambler:

'It was a dismal coming home for all of us; but Sara and I had

[1] In August 1809, when Tillbrook had made their acquaintance on his first visit to Grasmere.

[2] Cf. Sonnet 'The fairest, brightest, hues of ether fade' (*Oxf. W.*, p. 252).

[3] D. W. to C. C., July 31, 1812.

[4] Captain Wordsworth was the son of W.'s and D.'s uncle, Richard W. of Whitehaven.

[5] D. W. to J. M., July 26, 1812.

[6] Jan. 5, 1813.

exerted ourselves to the utmost, yet in spite of all we could do, the very air of the place,—the stillness—the occasional sounds—and above all the view of that school, our darling's daily pride and joy—that Churchyard his playground—all oppressed us and do continue to oppress us with unutterable sadness, and his poor mother seems almost to give herself up to it. She is as thin as it is possible to be except when the body is worn out by slow disease, and the dejection of her countenance is afflicting; insomuch that though we force ourselves into seeming chearfulness whenever we can, I feel that it knits about the heart strings, and will wear her away if there is not a turn in her feelings. When I came home (I surely must have told you that I was from home when the child died) she received me with the calmness of an Angel—she comforted me—and in truth I was ashamed of my own weakness, and bitterly reproached myself that I could not bear the sorrow as she did. After this came on the anxiety for the other children. *This* I believe supported her, but that is now over—and the day through she is dejected—weeps bitterly at times—and at night and morning sheds floods of tears. All this I could bear to see in another—I should trust to time and to the power of that resignation to the will of God, which at length would become a habit of the mind . . . and I would gladly sympathize in the sorrow to its full extent; but in her case it must be struggled against, or it will destroy her. When Catharine died she was terribly shaken, for her body was not strong enough to bear up against the shock of the mind and that corroding sorrow which followed. She was beginning to recover, when this second shock came, and now she seems more feeble than ever.

'We are determined to quit Grasmere and have every reason to expect that we shall get that house called Rydale Mount. . . . It is most delightfully situated, the very place which in happier days we longed for. There is no objection to it but that from the garden we shall view the Grasmere hills, yet on the other hand we should wish to be within a walk of Grasmere, and should wish to keep up the Bond betwixt the living and the dead by going weekly to the Parish Church, beside which their bones are laid; and I do not think there will be anything unkindly in the sadness produced by the sight of those dear hills, except in Mary's mind, and I am not sure that it will be so in hers; I would fain hope not; and that her chearfulness may return when those familiar objects connected with the daily goings-on of the children are no longer before her eyes; objects which are to all of us perpetual sources of melancholy and of frequent anguish. Thomas was the darling of the house and of everyone who looked at him. . . . Oh! my dear Friend! he is an unutterable loss to all of us . . . as you rightly say, it is a selfish grief when we pine after the pure spirit of a child returned to the Heaven from whence it came—pure and unspotted as when it first came from the presence of its Maker. Yet this child seemed so peculiarly fitted to give and to receive happiness, to calm the thoughts of those who looked upon him, and to enjoy the best things of this life from the virtuous ardour which he possessed, that it is most hard to think upon his grave without the anguish of regret, which nothing can ever wholly repress, save the Christian's faith in another world, and in the mercy of God which always works for our good, though we are too blind to see *how* this is accomplished. I trust the time will come when his dear Mother will so be comforted. If not I am sure she will sink away, her constitution will be gradually undermined. It has been a cruel stroke for William. He loved Thomas with such a peculiar tenderness. . . . But I said I would retrace the last 5 weeks. A painful task for both of us, me to write and you to read, but I would fain have you know all that you can ever now know about this darling child. I had been at Watermillock a fortnight, and on the evening preceding my departure I received a letter from Sara, telling me that all were well except Thomas who had been confined to the house since Thursday, and had a cough, and that they were looking out for the measles. I read the letter among a company of chearful friends, and an unconquerable sadness overcame me, and poor Innocent I shed tears for him, little thinking that at that very moment he was lying a senseless corse. My friends chid me and in vain I strove to get up my spirits. I answered them. "If I were sure it were the measles I should have no fears, but I dread that cough which he had two years ago, and we always believed that he had had the measles." The next morning with the morning light my fears vanished. I went in Mr Marshall's carriage to Penruddock and proceeded towards Keswick on the outside of the Penrith coach, intending if I had good news from home to stay a few days at Mr Calvert's,—but at Threlkeld I met my Brother.

'After I had come a little to myself I was told that a Grasmere cart was going home and I might either be conveyed in it or send for a chaise. I chose the cart, and there I lay upon some straw—William beside me part of the way, and part of the way he walked. It was dark when I reached home and I was roused by the light of candles at the door from a kind of stupor. I have told you how I found Mary, and you may guess the rest. . . .

'We all except Sara followed him to the grave—Poor thing! she has suffered and still suffers greatly. . . . These have been hard trials for her, but inexpressible is the comfort which she has been to me in both cases, and to all of us, but to me especially. I know not how I could have borne up if I had not had her when Catharine died, and I could never have kept up without her against Mary's depression of mind. God bless her, poor thing! . . . William has begun to look into his poem, *The Recluse,* within the last two days, and I hope he will be the better for it. He looks better. . . . It would have pitied the hardest heart to witness what he has gone through—he went for Mr Scambler to the child without fear of danger—he returned and found him dying. That miserable night they went to bed but slept not—and early the next morning he set out to meet me, and what a task he had to perform!'

To Jane she wrote[1] about three weeks later, still weighed down by her grief:

'Do not be uneasy about me. I walk daily and strive against sadness, but I cannot conceal from you that this is a hard trial—the hardest I have ever had, except when my Brother John died. . . . My tears will flow, I cannot help it. The image of him, his very self, is so vivid in my mind; it is like a perpetual presence, and at certain moments the anguish of those tender recollections is more than I can bear . . . at times when I muse on a future life and on his blessedness in another world I lose all thoughts of anguish; the child becomes spiritualized to my mind. I wish I could have such musings more frequently—and longer, but alas! the image of the boy disturbs me and I weep again. . . . My Brother is grown very thin, and at times I think he looks ten years older since the death of Thomas.'

Letters from Coleridge brought them a short-lived comfort. 'Our sorrow', said Dorothy,[2] 'has sunk into him, for he loved the darling the best of all our little ones.' And both she and William replied that nothing would do them as much good as his company and presence. Surely, they thought, they would be drawn together as of old by the bond of this common sorrow. But Coleridge, as Mrs. Clarkson told Crabb Robinson[3] with burning indignation, 'has taken no notice whatever of these letters, and they have heard by a letter from Mr Morgan to Southey or Mrs C.—that C. is going out of town to the sea-side!!! imagine them in the depths of their sorrow receiving this

[1] D. W. to J. M., Jan. 19, and Jan. 24, 1813.
[2] D. W. to C. C., Jan. 5, 1813. [3] C. C. to H. C. R., Mar. 10, 1813.

cutting intelligence. . . . The account of the state of the family at Grasmere would make your heart ache. . . . And, after all, what has C. suffered compared with the misery which he has inflicted? He does not, I know, give pain for the sake of giving pain. But who does except the Arch-fiend?'

No wonder that they longed to get away from Grasmere with all its painful associations. Rydal Mount was empty early in March, and William begged Mr. North, its late occupant, to give them entry. But the Norths were not inclined to be accommodating—possibly Mrs. North still resented the way in which Dorothy had stood up to her on the committee which looked after the little Greens. Anyhow the request was refused upon the hollow excuse that nine cart-loads of wine were still locked up in the cellars. Were they afraid that the Wordsworths would prize open the cellar door? So Mary and Dorothy had to occupy themselves as best they could in preparations for the removal, whilst William, who had just received, through the influence of Lord Lonsdale, the post of Distributor of Stamps for Westmorland, was busy with arrangements connected with his new office. Relieved as they were by this accession to their income (they reckoned that, when all expenses incidental to it had been paid, it would bring them £400 per annum) they were not yet in a mood to rejoice at it. 'We are very thankful', Dorothy wrote later,[1] 'for the prospect of an entire release from care about spending any money for any little luxuries that we may desire or providing against future wants for the children, but at first we hardly seemed to be glad, glad we were not—we hardly thought about the change.'

On May day they moved in; on May 2 Dorothy wrote to Jane:

> 'We are all well, though some of us, especially my Sister, jaded with our fatigues. The weather is delightful, and the place a paradise: but my inner thoughts *will* go back to Grasmere. I was the last person who left the House yesterday evening. It seemed as quiet as the grave; and the very churchyard where our darlings lie, when I gave a last look upon it, seemed to chear my thoughts. There I could think of life and immortality,—the house only reminded me of desolation, gloom, emptiness, and chearless silence—but why do I turn to these thoughts? The morning is bright and I am more chearful to-day.'

[1] D. W. to C. C., Apr. 8, 1813.

XV

RYDAL MOUNT. *THE EXCURSION*. PROJECTED VISIT TO PARIS

1813–1816 (aet. 41–44)

'MANY employments and a little bustle have been no evil thing to any of us', wrote[1] Dorothy, a month or so after they had moved into Rydal Mount; and though they sometimes 'impatiently wished it to be over', she knew that it was 'far better for them than perfect stillness would have been'. The loss of Thomas had inflicted wounds upon them all that were slow to heal. 'The thought of him rends my heart', she wrote,[2] 'and hard work I have had to bear up often and often'; but with her natural buoyancy of spirit she threw herself whole-heartedly into all the little incidents of their removal. Rydal Mount was a larger house than the Rectory, and needed much extra furniture; and, as luck would have it, there were several sales in the neighbourhood, at which they could make the necessary purchases at a low cost and with much entertainment. The Westmorland sale was not merely an occasion for buying and selling: it was among the most popular diversions of the countryside. Here all classes of society would foregather on friendly terms to pass the time of day; and in addition to the ordinary topics of local gossip, the goods offered for sale afforded an inexhaustible theme for voluble discourse; there was also the mild excitement of bidding, and then the eager discussion of the wonderful bargains they had secured, or just failed to secure. From one of these sales William returned in triumph with 'six buff chairs with cushions and cane bottoms for the study at 9/-';[3] a purchase of which he was still prouder consisted of 'drawing-room curtains with a grand cornice the length of the room'; he thought them much handsomer than the curtains which Dorothy and Mary had already made with much labour, but they thought otherwise, and decided, no doubt secretly, to cut them up for sofa-covers. A few days later they were all at a

[1] D. W. to C. C., June (?), 1813.
[2] D. W. to S. H., Aug. 10, 1813.
[3] D. W. to S. H., *Fair Day* (i.e. Sept. 1), 1813.

sale at Coniston, and, says Dorothy, 'fully entered into the spirit of it'. Beds and pillows, a sofa, chairs, knives, and glasses were only some of the articles that were knocked down to them. 'We stayed the sale out to the very last and the beds were sold by candle light, and all walked home in the bright moonshine, I with a decanter and glass in my hand and William and Mary with a large looking glass—oval with a gilt frame—to be hung in the best lodging-room, very cheap, £1 13*s.* Fanny went home with a full cart, and John is gone to-day with one which will be half loaded.'[1] And when they reached home there was much pleasant talk of their own astuteness, and the folly of their neighbour Mrs. Green, who, like them, was furnishing a new house, and 'laid out so much money in buying bargains she did not want and wonders at the cheapness of them' that she 'could not find it in her heart to buy a bed or mattress for her maid's bedstock', and came to borrow one from Rydal Mount. 'She snorts, and nods, and chatters—chatters, oh me! till I am weary, about her marvellous bargains.' But on the arrival of their own purchases they realized that they, too, had been a little reckless. 'We are quite bewildered', says Dorothy, 'amongst our furniture. This comes of buying pennyworths. We have far more chairs than we know what to do with, and the dining-room will not be at all nice with the sofa.'[2]

Their only extravagance was in carpets, which Tom Monkhouse was commissioned to buy for them in London. 'I must tell you', she writes to Mrs. Clarkson,[3] 'we are going to have a Turkey!!! carpet in the dining-room and a Brussels in William's study. You stare, and the simplicity of the dear Town-End Cottage comes before your eyes, and you are tempted to say, "Are they changed, are they setting up for fine Folks? for making parties, giving Dinners etc. etc?" No, no, you do not make such a guess, but you want an explanation and I must give it you.' Her explanation is one with which we are all familiar—that the most expensive articles are cheapest in the

[1] D.W. to S.H., Sept. 1, 1813. Fanny was one of the maids. The John referred to is not Johnny Wordsworth but John Carter, a young man whom William had engaged to assist him in the clerical duties connected with his Office of Stamp Distributor, and to act as gardener and general handyman about the house. He remained in the employ of the family for more than forty years.

[2] Ib.

[3] D. W. to C. C., June (?) 1813.

RYDAL WATER ('THE OPPOSITE SHORE')

from an oil painting by

FRED YATES

end. They had all, she says, agreed at once to the purchase of the Turkey, but at first 'Mary and I were rather ashamed of the thought of a Brussels for the study, and inclined' to a cheaper carpet 'as looking less ambitious and less like setting up on the model of our neighbours the Ambleside gentry', but 'our Master was all for Brussels, and to him we yielded—a humour took him to make his Room smart'. When the house was in some order the garden had to be attended to. Sara was to be head gardener, but the rest were all to give a hand. 'I', says Dorothy, 'am contented to work under her, and Mary does her share, and sometimes we work very hard, and this is a great amusement to us, though sad thoughts come often between' [1] Little Thomas had been especially happy digging in the swamp that surrounded the Rectory. But the garden at Rydal was very different. 'You must, indeed you must, come next year'. she tells her friend. 'It is the place of all others for you, so dry that you need never have a wet foot after the heaviest showers; and the prospect so various and beautiful . . . we have such a terrace for you to walk on, and such a seat at the end of it. And, as Sara tells us, the time that could be spared from house and garden was spent upon the lake. 'We have two nice boats on Rydale at command, and it is a sweet lake to fish upon. We take our tea, tackling etc. and drink tea on the opposite shore where on an evening we have the most beautiful scene among the lakes.'[2]

As soon as they were settled, the Ambleside gentry, who had all expressed their intention of calling, began to pour in on them. For William was in high favour with Lady Fleming of Rydal Hall, from whom the Mount was rented, and the Wordsworths were now to be regarded as members of the county society. 'Our neighbours the Ladies', says Dorothy, 'are very fond of us . . . we have unrestrained right to walk in the grounds as if they were our own, and Lady Diana[3] pops in and takes a

[1] Ib. [2] S. H. to Mrs. Thos. (Mary) Hutchinson, Aug. 1, 1813.

[3] Lady Diana le Fleming, only child of the 14th Earl of Suffolk and Berkshire, died in June 1816; her husband, Sir Michael, had died ten years earlier. But she often stayed at Rydal with her daughter, Lady Anna Frederica Elizabeth le Fleming, who had married her distant cousin, Sir Michael, the heir to the baronetcy. On Lady Diana's death S. H. wrote to Tom Monkhouse, 'Poor Lady Fleming has lost her only friend, the poor a most benevolent one, and we and the country round, an excellent neighbour!'

friendly cup with great pleasure.' Even the Lowthers of Lowther Hall notified that they were coming over, and Dorothy was highly amused at Mrs. Green's annoyance when she angled, without success, for an invitation to meet them. There were many visitors, too, from among their old acquaintances, who as she shrewdly observed 'came to see the new place almost as much as to see us'.

In October she was already looking eagerly forward to 'long evenings and winter's quiet'.[1] For the first time all the children would be at school—even little Willy, who was hardly more than three years old, was to go. Sissy, still a problem, was to try a new school at Ambleside, Johnny was to leave the village school and make an effort to conquer his laziness and shyness among boys of his own class, at Mr. Dawes's. Earlier in the year his friend Quincey had undertaken to prepare him for this ordeal, but his aunt was a little sceptical of the result. 'He goes', she had said,[2] 'to Mr De Quincey for a *nominal hour* every day to learn Latin upon a plan of Mr De Quincey's own "by which a boy of the most moderate abilities may be made a good Latin scholar in six weeks"!!! This said nominal hour is generally included in the space of twenty minutes; either the scholar learns with such uncommon rapidity that more time is unnecessary, or the Master tires. Which of these conjectures is the more probable I leave you to guess.' But anyhow the children would now be off their hands, and their aunt would have a little more time to cultivate her own mind and to 'call her heart home to quietness'.

Dorothy felt the need for it. She had the common experience of middle age, that much of the knowledge she had gained from books was slipping from her; 'the sorrows of this life', she said,[1] 'weaken the memory so much that I find reading of far less use than it used to be to me; if it were not that my feelings were as much alive as ever, there would be a growing tendency in the mind to barrenness.'

But books had always been of less account to her than her fellow creatures, and with her feelings 'as alive as ever' there was no danger that she would stagnate. Whilst the loss of Thomas and Catharine had, if possible, strengthened the tie which

[1] D. W. to C. C., Oct. 4, 1813.
[2] D. W. to Mrs. Thos. (Mary) Hutchinson, Feb. 1813.

bound her to William and his family, the circle of her friends was always widening. A late addition to these was Miss Barker, who had settled at Keswick some years back in order to be near Southey. There was much in Miss Barker to appeal to Dorothy, who describes her as a woman of great social gifts and of a fresh downright character, an enthusiast for the country and an assiduous amateur painter, fond of music and reading, and of a reflective mind; but it is hardly surprising to learn that she was less popular with the ladies at Greta Hall. Early in 1814 Dorothy went over to Keswick to help her nurse Basil Montagu, who was slowly recovering from a haemorrhage; she had intended to stay a week or two, but her visit was prolonged for nearly three months; for no sooner had she arrived than a bitter quarrel broke out between her hostess and the ladies Southey and Coleridge, and 'while things were so unpleasant for Miss Barker' she could not bring herself to leave.

> 'Almost at the very first day of my coming hither', she writes,[1] Miss Barker 'had a dispute with the Females of the other house, which unfortunately, and I think very injudiciously, Southey took up, and though he comes to this house to sit with Montagu he takes care that Miss Barker should know that his visits are not to *her*, yet they talk to each other as pleasantly as can be, and each has a high esteem for the other. But the ladies "cannot possibly enter Miss B.'s house" and there is no free intercourse except with the children whom Miss Barker loves very much and has always been excessively kind to, and they run in and out at their pleasure. I go to the other house as usual, and I assure you the part I have had to play has not been agreeable; for between my zeal for Miss Barker, and the hotness of their tempers, with the utter impossibility of *making* them look coolly either upon her supposed faults, or her virtues, I have had much ado to prevent quarrels with me also. These however I determined to avoid, and when irritation of mind bubbles over I am obliged to desire that the subject might be dropped.'

Dorothy returned to Rydal none too soon. Without the distraction of her lively company William and Mary were fretting badly for their lost children: Mary in particular gave her anxiety; she was thinner than ever and evidently weak, and Dorothy feared that 'she will never be the same chearful creature

[1] D. W. to C. C., Apr. 24, 1814.

as heretofore. The worst of it is', she adds,[1] 'that she has a bad appetite, and the habit she has always had of disregarding herself makes her unwilling that any little things not going in the family should be provided for her.' And Dorothy plots with Sara to circumvent Mary's unselfishness, by giving the cook a commission 'to cook all sorts of nice things for Mary; to which Mary will not object; for (strange it is) Mary in these little things would be far more easily ruled by a servant than by us. Thus extremes meet. The more she loves people the less attentive she is to their happiness in trifles which make up so much of human life; but her own health is not a trifle, yet that disposition of hers to self-sacrifice, which has characterised her through life, prevents her from taking any care of herself, though she sees and knows how uneasy she makes us.'

This is the only criticism of Mary to be found in all the family correspondence.

The great event of the summer was the appearance, in August, of *The Excursion*, the first instalment of William's projected masterpiece; it was published in an edition of 500 copies, in magnificent quarto, at the price of two guineas. For years Dorothy had followed the progress of its composition, and had often acted as amanuensis; and it was a real disappointment to her that her attendance on Miss Barker had prevented her from helping to make the final copy and to correct the proofs. With its reception she was bound to be disappointed.

'I think,' she wrote six months later,[2] "that so small an Edition *must* sell, though I see clearly that the effect of the publication has not been such as I expected. I thought that a powerful band of fresh admirers would have been immediately formed, though I did not expect that it would escape ridicule or severe censure. All I care about—the sale or anything else—is here bounded. I should wish the present Edition to go off, and quickly, that it may be printed in a cheaper form; and that we may have some small pecuniary advantage from it. As to the permanent fate of that poem or of my Brother's collected works I have not the shadow of a doubt. I know that the good and pure and noble-minded will, in the days when we sleep in the grave, be elevated delighted and better for what he has performed in solitude for the delight of his

[1] D. W. to C. C., Apr. 24, 1814.
[2] D. W. to C. C., Dec. 31, 1814.

own soul, independent of lofty hopes of being of service to his fellow creatures.'[1]

In the meantime she was following the fortunes of the book with excited interest. She urges the Clarksons to press its sale among their rich Quaker friends. 'There are few persons', she admits, 'who can afford to buy a two-guinea book merely for admiration of the book. The edition has no chance of being sold except to the wealthy, and they buy books for fashion more than anything else, and alas! we are not yet in the fashion.' Lady Beaumont was their only friend who answered to that description, but, she says,[2] 'I am afraid her zeal will outrun her discretion, and prevent her from aiding the sale of the work as, were she moderate in her expressions, she might do.' More was to be hoped from the approval of the Duke of Devonshire, who 'had made *The Excursion* his companion during a tour in Ireland, and had been greatly pleased with it. . . . I think that the more friends William has either of rank, or talents, or notoriety the better; that they may *talk* against the writers, for the more that is said about the work the better.'[3]

Naturally enough, she shared with the fraternity of authors a hearty contempt for the rich man who borrows books.

> 'I could be half angry with you', she wrote to Mrs. Clarkson,[4] 'for leaving *The Excursion* with William Smith. Who *is* to buy two guinea books if not people with such fortunes as his? William gave Charles Lloyd a copy with this charge that he should lend it to no one who could afford to buy it, and accordingly upon the application of our summer neighbour Mrs Green (a widow with 1500£ per annum of whom you must have heard us speak—a blue stocking dame) he refused, giving his reasons. She had before exclaimed with horror "Two guineas! and for a *part* of a work!" and she then pettishly told him that she must wait till her return to York when she could have it from a circulating library; for she never bought books unread! This lady has stayed under our roof and has been extremely anxious to number William in the train of her friends.'

[1] This passage is clearly a reminiscence of what William had written of the fate of his poems to Lady Beaumont in May 1807.

[2] D. W. to S. H., Feb. 18, 1814.

[3] D. W. to C. C., Oct. 9, 1814; *writers, viz.* the reviewers who had damned *The Excursion.*

[4] D. W. to C. C., Dec. 31, 1814. William Smith, M.P. for Norwich.

But all their acquaintances were not like Mrs. Green.

'William and Mary and little Willy paid a visit to old Mrs Knott yesterday with *The Excursion* in hand, William intending to read to the old lady the history of the Grasmere Knight. She could not hear his loud voice but understood the story very well when her niece read it, and was greatly delighted. To-day they have returned the book and poor Mrs K. has written a complimentary but alas! unintelligible note—unintelligible but by courtesy. She must have been in a strange ruffled state of mind; she concludes however by saying in plain words that she has written to Kendal to order the Book. She says she has been told by Mrs Green and others that it was above their capacity, and of course above hers, but what she has read had given her infinite delight. I tell William that the family made a trading voyage of it. Certainly the Book would never have been bought by Miss K. if Willy and his father and mother had stayed quietly at home.'[1]

Praise, from whatever quarter it came, was balm to her, and was duly handed on to her friends. Charles Lloyd's old mother, she tells,[1] 'is enraptured with it', whilst a Mr. Edwards of Derby has written that 'he would not be without the book for twice its value,'[2] adding that the poet Montgomery regarded it as 'incomparably the greatest and most beautiful work of the present age of poetry, and set Mr W. beyond controversy above all the living and almost all the dead of his fraternity'. And when Mrs. Clarkson informs her that her son Tom sat up all night reading it, she longs to renew her old acquaintance with him. 'It shews', she says, 'that he has very strong sensibility.'

Her statement, in the following February, that they had seen none of the reviews must be accepted with some reserve: they had certainly read the first of them, Hazlitt's articles in *The Examiner* of August 21 and 28.

'I did not think them nearly so well written as I should have expected from him, though he praised *more* than I should have expected. His opinion that all the characters are but one character I cannot but think utterly false, there seems to me to be an astonishing difference considering that the primary elements are the same —fine talents and strong imagination. He says that the narratives

[1] D. W. to S. H., Feb. 18, 1815: 'The Grasmere Knight', *v. Excursion*, vii. 911 ff., and I.F., note. The Knotts were traditionally descended from the Grasmere Knight—hence W.'s choice of this passage, and, perhaps, Mrs. K.'s delight.

[2] D. W. to S. H., Mar. 16, 1815.

are a clog upon the poem. I was not sorry to hear that, for I am sure with common readers those parts of the poem will be by far the more interesting . . . . The last part of Hazlitt's Review' she reports,[1] 'is more a criticism of country life and its effects than upon the poem, and amongst other evils he has the audacity to complain that there are no courtesans to be found in the country. He makes another bold [assertion?] that all people living in retirement hate each other.'

How, she implies, can a man capable of such remarks enter into the spirit of *The Excursion*?

But if they did not actually see the other reviews their friends must have supplied them with copious extracts:

'The Eclectic, we are told, is highly encomiastic, and probably it may be of use towards promoting the sale of the Excursion amongst the serious and religious part of the reading public; but I am convinced, notwithstanding the zeal of a whole body of admirers of the Edin. Rev., that Review will do less harm than the feeble praise of the Quarterly. An injudicious and malignant enemy often serves the cause he means to injure; but a feeble friend never attains that end. By the bye the history of that same criticism in the Quarterly is very provoking. It was originally drawn up by Charles Lamb at the request of Southey; but so deformed by the lopping knife of Gifford, and by the substitution of his own flat phrases, that not even the skeleton of Lamb's production remains, which, Lamb says, was pronounced by his sister "the best piece of prose he ever wrote". From this we have learned one lesson, never to employ a friend to review a book unless he has full command of the Review; so that the master critic can neither add to nor diminish it.'[2]

One less greedy of praise for her brother might have been satisfied with Lamb's review, even in its altered form, but she was hard to please. As for 'that ignorant coxcomb Jeffrey', she tried to persuade herself that he would do more good than harm. 'From all hands we hear the same story, that Jeffrey has played the fool, has suffered his malignity to cheat him into producing passages as fit matter for ridicule which are so beautiful that even the eyes of his [i.e. Jeffrey's] worshippers must be opened.'[3] Of this she had welcome proof from De Quincey, who reported from Bristol that William had 'made a

[1] D. W. to C. C., Oct. 9, 1814.
[2] D. W. to Priscilla W., Feb. 1815.
[3] D. W. to S. H., Feb. 18, 1815.

conquest of holy Hannah'[1]—though she had seen nothing but the extracts in the *Edinburgh Review*—'yet she is determined to buy it, but is waiting for the octavo edition!'

As a counterblast to Jeffrey she joined with William in urging Mrs. Clarkson to get a favourable review into *The Philanthropist*, for, said William, 'as the evil spirits are rouzed it becomes the good ones to stir.'[2]

> 'There is no one better fitted for the task imposed than you, in case Mr Clarkson is not inclined to it or has not sufficiently studied the book to perform it himself. We pray you earnestly to do the work yourself, for there is no body here who *can* do it. It would be too impudent in *us* to set about it, and Mr De Quincey, notwithstanding his learning and his talents can do nothing; he is eaten up by the spirit of procrastination, but if once in two or three years he actually does make any effort, he is so slow a labourer that no one who knows him would wish to appoint him to it, if it might not as well be 3 months in hand as 3 hours, though in itself but the work of one sitting for another person. If it is not very irksome to you I entreat you that you will resolve to write, and not be over nice yourself. You cannot but satisfy others, and will do the sale of the Excursion service. That is all we care about. If this edition were once sold I should not have a moment's anxiety afterwards.'[3]

But the sale was slow; though by March 300 copies had gone, the last 200 hung fire, and the cheaper edition did not appear till 1820.

Dorothy's mind was never wholly absorbed in family concerns; it would, indeed, have been impossible for her to share William's life had she not entered, with some of his passionate interest, into the progress of national affairs. Her excitement on hearing of the Battle of Trafalgar has already been noted, and all through these years she had watched with intense anxiety the struggle against the hated Buonaparte, re-echoing in vivid and often unmeasured language what we know to have been her brother's sentiments. The English successes in Spain during the spring of 1811 had called from her the ejaculation 'God be thanked the tide is turned against Buonaparte, and we shall see, I trust, the delusion speedily vanish which even in England has

[1] *holy Hannah*—a somewhat disrespectful reference to Hannah More. D. W. to C. C., Mar. 16, 1815.

[2] W. W. to C. C., Dec. 31, 1814.

[3] D. W. to C. C., Apr. 15, 1815.

spread too widely, that he was a great genius and a great hero.' In 1814, when the news of his abdication reached Rydal, she wrote:

'To the last page I am come, and not a word of the Emperor Alexander, the King of France or the fallen monarch! surely it must seem to us, encircled by these mountains, that our own little concerns outweigh the mighty joys and sorrows of nations, or I could not have been so long silent. It is not so; every heart has exulted, we have danced for joy! But how strange; it is like a dream—peace—peace, all in a moment—prisoners let loose—Englishmen and Frenchmen brothers at once; no treaties, no stipulations. I am however vexed beyond my strength that Buonaparte should have been thus treated: the power was in the hands of the Allies. If he would have stood but with a few of his Miscreants they should have fought him to the death and yielding him a prisoner he should have been tried for the murders of the Duc d'Enghien, of Pichegru, of Captain Wright, of Palm—of one or all; and what a pension they have granted him! This is folly, rather than liberality; for of what use can a large income be in an island without luxuries, and without company? He can have no wants beyond a mere maintenance. Therefore if the [?] be used it must be for the purposes of intrigue or the support of bad people. In short he ought not to be suffered to live except utterly deprived of power, and while he has so much money he will certainly contrive to convert it into power.'[1]

Among the prisoners let loose was Eustace Baudouin, a young French lieutenant, who had been captured in Spain three years before, and during his residence in England had paid several visits to the Wordsworths. How the acquaintance sprang up is uncertain, but it seems probable that he was introduced to them by Annette; for, like her, he was of royalist sympathies. Anyhow, he returned to France with special injunctions from Rydal to send news of Annette and Caroline, and the next they heard was that Baudouin's elder brother, Jean Baptiste, had sought Caroline's hand in marriage, and that both she and her mother were urging Dorothy to come over for the wedding. Their meeting at Calais in 1802 had evidently strengthened Annette's affection, which had been awakened by Dorothy's loving sympathy with her in her trouble ten years before. Whether she now suggested that William should come with her we do not know, but it was decided that Sara should be her companion.

[1] D. W. to C. C., April 24, 1814.

Mr. and Mrs. Clarkson were among the many English people who took advantage of the peace to visit Paris; and Dorothy wrote to her anxiously for news that might help her in making her plans. It is noticeable throughout the letters that follow how the protracted war had prejudiced her mind against France and all things French:

'I cannot help very much regretting that you forgot to tell me where to address you while you were (in Paris) as I should have been exceedingly glad that you had seen the young woman whom I mentioned to you, the more so as a treaty of marriage is now on foot between her and the brother of the officer Baudouin whom I mentioned to you as having been at Rydal, and she and her mother are extremely anxious that I should be present at the wedding, and for that purpose pressed me very much to go in October. This, unless such good fortune had attended us as being taken under your and your husband's protection, we could not think of at this season, and therefore I wish that the marriage should be deferred till next spring or summer, because I desire exceedingly to see the poor girl before she takes another protection than her Mother, under whom I believe she has been bred up in perfect purity and innocence, and to whom she is life and light and perpetual pleasure; though from the over-generous dispositions of the mother they have had to struggle through many difficulties. . . . I particularly wished that you had seen them at this time as through you I should have been able to enter into some explanations, which, imperfectly as I express myself in French, are difficult, and as you would have been able to confirm or contradict the reports which we receive from Caroline's mother and Mr Baudouin of her interesting and amiable qualities. They both say that she resembles her Father most strikingly, and her letters give a picture of a feeling and ingenuous mind. Yet there must be something I think very unfavourable to true delicacy in French manners. Both C. and her mother urge my going in October on the account that after a young person is engaged to be married, it is desirable that the delay afterwards should be as short as possible, as she is subject to perpetual scrutiny and unpleasant remarks, and one of the reasons which they urge for marriage in general, is that a single woman in France unless she have a fortune is not treated with any *consideration*. . . . We are delighted to hear that you are so much pleased with Paris and the French people, now we venture in our little way to expect pleasure and amusement. All the accounts we have received from other quarters have been unfavourable, that neither provisions nor anything else was much cheaper than in England, which, allowing for the exchange we thought would make things dearer—and the people rude and brutal in their manners. Now I guess there must have been some fault in the manners of the Reporters, yet we cannot help thinking at the same time that your judgment is formed from the best of the people, to whose society the recommendations which you carried with you naturally introduced you. There are many things we want to know. . . . With respect to the mode of travelling we of course must go as cheaply as possible consistent with tolerable comfort, and in an open carriage, because Sara cannot ride in a closed one. Are any of the diligences so constructed? and supposing we can meet with no eligible companions from England, do you think we might venture to go alone? *I* think I should have no fears, but Sara would fain have a gentleman, and we can, at all events, desire Mr Baudouin to come from Paris to meet us at Calais; the expense however makes this last plan somewhat objectionable. Oh that Henry Robinson were going again! you know I like him well as a companion. And still a thousand times better Oh! that you were going! We should wish to convey presents of English manufacture; can this be done without much risk or disagreeable trouble? When William and I were at Calais our trunk was simply opened—we paid half a crown or three shillings and the trunk was closed again. In returning also we should like to bring back some things of French manufacture, under what sort of management is this practicable? Of course it would be easy enough to hide lace and such small articles, but can silks be brought unmade up—or if made up is there any danger of their being siezed?'[1]

In November she writes that April has been definitely fixed for their visit, but on New Year's Eve she is more doubtful:

'I find the King is to be anointed in June,—all France will be gathered together and I fear there may be disturbances; for though all is quiet at present it is evident enough that the party of discontented and turbulent spirits is very strong. On this account (as we cannot think of staying less than 9 or 10 weeks) I should wish our journey to be *after* June if it be at all. But I never, never, dreaded so much to leave home as now, so deeply am I impressed with the image of what William and Mary have lately suffered in my absence, and with the uncertainty of all things. Besides, the journey will be very expensive, which we can ill afford, and the

[1] D. W. to C. C., Oct. 9, 1814.

money would be better spent in augmenting my niece's wedding portion. To this effect I have written to her, she would not consent to marry without my presence, which was the reason that April was fixed. A few weeks will decide whether we go to France or not. . . . This is a plaguy business that I have teased you about. If it were not for my fears for what may happen at home I could think of it with satisfaction, nay with delight for that dear young woman's sake, whom I believe to be thoroughly amiable. Oh! that you were going to France! Do you know of anybody going?'

As time went on she looked forward to the journey with a growing uneasiness, and if it had not been for Caroline's entreaties she would have dropped the idea altogether. 'I fervently wish', she wrote to Sara on February 18, 'it may be given up for this year. If, however, we find that we shall have no peace or rest without it I must try to imitate your good example and make a pleasure of it. A fortnight or little more must settle the point.'

And a fortnight did settle it, at least for the time; for on March 1 Napoleon had landed from Elba, and on the 20th had entered Paris. Dorothy's letters throughout these months of national anxiety have not merely a personal interest; they reflect what must have been the general state of English feeling and opinion. On March 16 she wrote to Sara:

'On Monday the tidings of the Buonapartist entrance into France would reach you. As Dorothy [i.e. her niece] said, "why did they not kill him when they *had* him?" So you would say, with many an indignant reflection upon the childish folly of the Allies. I wrote to poor Annette on the Thursday, and on Monday morning Mr Scambler brought us the news. He had not read the papers, so William posted off to Ambleside; for we felt that seeing only was believing. At first he considered our French journey entirely put a stop to; but if no great body of adherents rise up he may be crushed at once, hanged and jibbeted, in which case the government would be stronger than ever. The report was that Toulon had surrendered to him; but that appears to be false; but one can hardly suppose that he would be so mad, notwithstanding the ludicrous and ragamuffin way in which he has proceeded, to venture unless he had had some encouragement from France. If that encouragement be not very powerful he will attempt to fall back to Italy, and there William thinks Murat and he may be very troublesome; but God grant that his insane mind may push him on till he is surrounded and captive! At all events we have nothing to do at present but to be thankful that we are not already in France; and it is very unlikely that it will be prudent for us to think of going as soon as we had intended. . . . I am exceedingly distressed for poor Annette and Caroline—especially Annette; Caroline is young, fresh hopes will spring up for her—but her Mother! so near happiness and again to lose it! This is a very hard case and hard to be endured. Only in her last letter she spoke (like one who had been worn out with anxiety and exertion during the reign of the tyrant) of present happiness and peace for all France, and said that even those who had been warm admirers of Buonaparte were satisfied and perceived the wickedness and misery he had caused. I hope we shall have letters from her very soon. I am sure she will write as soon as she can perceive anything like comfort. It is very fortunate that I wrote to say that we were going. She will at least have the satisfaction of being assured that we were prepared to fulfill our promise, and it will serve as an earnest that we shall take the first opportunity of so doing. . . . The French people are not worth grieving for, if they do not rise en masse to destroy the tyrant, and my griefs are all for our friend and other good quiet people who have fancied themselves at once released from their misery.'

On April 4 she writes to Mrs. Clarkson:

'In common with you our minds have been occupied continually by the tremendous changes in France. Till we heard of the arrival of B. in Paris I never slept without dreaming of troubles connected with his fiendish ambition, and every night I was kept awake for hours. After he had entered the City, having passed through France without opposition, I was at first in despair; but this lasted for a very short time; and now I am confident that we shall be more secure than ever, provided the Allies act promptly and with unanimity. There seems to be no doubt that the middle ranks of society are almost universally against Buonaparte, and when they have military force to aid them they will act with voice and hand. Our military must be much stronger than B.'s and the mob will side with the strongest. The infatuation of governments in not being warned by the information given of the conspiracy, and of the French government in particular, argues an inconceivable weakness. If they had exercised half the understanding and zeal which the wicked have shewn in conducting their plots things could never have been in this state. Refer to the 4th book of the Excursion[1] and you will find an admirable comment upon the

[1] *Excursion*, iv. 295–319.

conduct of the Allies from beginning to end. God grant that if they have once again the Sword and the Victory in their hands no puny relentings of mercy may stop the slaughter till the Tyrant is taken and his wicked followers completely subdued. To this result I look forward with hope. Nay, I may almost say with confidence, but let them begin quickly, there is no time for pondering. The people of England in general are eager to begin. At Kendal this spirit is almost universal. We had given over taking a Newspaper (except *The Courier*, which came from Keswick,) but we could not exist without one sent directly to us; and every post-day, though till the warfare actually begins we can expect nothing of much importance, we are full of anxiety and catch at every favourable omen. . . . Pray let us have all the private information that you receive. Everybody here is anxious but none a hundredth part so much as we are. We had a long letter from France written on the 19th or 20th. The letter was concluded at midnight and my friend says "I hear troops entering the City. I think it is the avant-garde of Buonaparte. Good God! what is to become of us!" We have had another letter written the next day in miserable dejection, but she says "All is quiet." . . . Poor creatures! they say they are shipwrecked when just entering into port. Indeed it is a distressing situation, but I trust that we shall see them in Paris before the end of another twelve-month.'

To Sara she wrote a few days later[1] in much the same vein:

'Buonaparte's conduct, in direct contradiction to former practice and profession, proves his weakness. Did you not smile with scorn when you read his decree of abolition of the slave trade and liberty of the Press? Then his fine professions of renouncing conquest after his first declaration that he was come to avenge the cause of France stripped of her Conquests! Those villainous Sunday newspapers are my abhorrence—I read in one the other day the following sentiment. "Surely it would be wise that the allies should at length give Buonaparte time to show whether he is sincere or not!" In other words give him time to be quite prepared to fence himself in in his wickedness. Then that impudent assertion follows, so often repeated, that *we* shall be the aggressors if we meddle with the internal government of France.'

And after telling of the letters just received from Annette she adds the comment:

'Oh! with what bitter anguish must Annette have lighted her

[1] D. W. to S. H., Apr. 8, 1815.

candles for the illuminations! . . . Eustace B. had been with them the day before when they received my letter. He was to take leave of them and was going into camp near Paris. He parted from them in tears, but said he hoped yet to be our "Chevalier". She says "he is honorable, he has high duties to perform and he will perform them," but in the next letter, not daring to speak out she gives us to understand that he is returned to Paris by saying, with a stroke under the word, "*Messieurs* B. send their regards". I cannot be angry with him, knowing that the virtue of an Abdiel was more than could be expected, especially from one who no doubt is still dazzled by his youthful recollections, whatever change his year's service with Louis may have brought about in his opinions.'

But Dorothy was unjust to young Baudouin. From the Archives of the Minister of War, Professor Legouis has unearthed documents which prove that he was working with Annette, both of them with 'the virtue of an Abdiel', for the Royalist cause. 'During the last events which plunged France into mourning, she performed acts of courage with no interested motives. Conscious only of her attachment to the legitimate dynasty, she posted proclamations at night, distributed them in the daytime, favoured the escape of the brave men who wanted to devote themselves to the king's service', whilst Eustace Baudouin 'was entrusted with the exhibition of all posters destined to bring back the people to their king'.[1]

For the next two months there is a break in the correspondence: on June 28 Dorothy writes to Mrs. Clarkson:

'Strange it is that I can talk so long of private concerns when I have so much cause to be anxious for the arrival of this night's post which is to bring tidings of the fate of Nations. Upon the Ambleside coach this morning was affixed a paper "Great News, *Abdication of Buonaparte*," but no particulars. Now I do not like the word *abdication*. What right has he to abdicate, or to have a word to say in the business? I am only afraid that the armies have stopped too soon, as they did before. A few hours will explain all, but I confess I dare not hope that matters will not be again mismanaged. The particulars of the battle of the 18th are dreadful. The joy of victory is indeed an awful thing, and I had no patience with the tinkling of our Ambleside bells upon the occasion, nor with the Prince Regent's message, the passage dictated, as he says, by "serious consideration", recommending that further proofs of

[1] Legouis, *William Wordsworth and Annette Vallon*, pp. 98, 137–40.

the munificence of the people should be shewn to the Duke of Wellington. It is perfectly childish to be in such a bustle while even his own family ought to have been *at least* paying the tribute of respectful tears to the memory of the gallant Duke of Brunswick.

'11 o'clock. Before I go to bed I must tell you that, saving grief for the lamentable loss of so many brave men, I have read the newspapers of to-night with unmingled triumph; and now I wait anxiously for Friday's post, to know how our armies will proceed. So the abdication was made to his own people! that is as it should be: and I hope he is now a safe prisoner, somewhere.'

But the conduct neither of the armies nor of the diplomats satisfied her almost bloodthirsty hatred of Napoleon, and two months later she wrote[1] in bitter invective of

'these days when French impudence and French vice seem to have dazzled the judgments and vitiated the feelings of one half of the nation. . . . Oh I am sick of the adulation, the folly, the idle curiosity which was gathered together round the ship that held the dastardly spirit that has so long been the scourge of all whom he *could* injure. *He* kill himself! No, he is too much of a coward, and we can be so dull of perception, so insensible to the distinctions between vice and virtue, as to bend, to bow, to take off our hats to him and call him great. His looks! fancy them filled with magnanimity,—but he is not worth talking about, and how I go on so far I do not know. As to the French Government and the French people they too would not be worth a thought, if it were not that, left to themselves, they would soon plague us and the rest of the world. Would that all the English had Prussian hearts and that our Generals and Councillors had the will of Blucher! Then we should not have seen the Jacobins lift up their audacious heads—there would have been no fear, no affected magnanimity in our counsels.'

Dorothy goes on to say that she had received letters from Annette written just after the return of the king, that they were in great joy at the event and urged her to come, all being safe and quiet; but, she adds, 'it is impossible for me to think of going to Paris this year'. There were equal difficulties about a proposed visit of Caroline to England; and in the following February the marriage took place without her presence. 'Her mother's details of the wedding festivities', writes Dorothy,[2] 'would have amused you. *She* was to give the fête, she who per-

[1] D. W. to C. C., Aug. 15, 1815.

[2] D. W. to C. C., Apr. 4, 1816.

haps for half a year to come will feel the effects of it at every dinner she cooks. Thirty persons were present to dinner, ball, and supper. The deputies of the department and many other respectable people were there. The bride was dressed in white sarsanet, with a white veil—"was the admiration of all who beheld her, but her modesty was her best ornament". She kept her veil on the whole of the day. How truly French this is!'

The undertone of mockery, so unworthy of her, which Dorothy gives to her account of her niece's wedding, can only be accounted for by the blind prejudice with which, at this time, she viewed anything 'truly French'. Her affection for Annette and Caroline was warm as ever, and she still clung to her plan of visiting them.

> 'You ask me', she says in the same letter, 'if I mean to go to France this spring or summer. I wish it very much, but William and Mary are unwilling that I should venture so soon. For my part I believe that there is nothing to fear for an obscure individual like me, and I believe William would consent provided I could hear of proper companions for the journey. . . . I do not like to put off year after year. Another war would make it impossible, and if I do not go when I can I think it may be out of my power to go at all, and my motives for the journey are very strong. . . . We have just had a letter from them both, written a month after their marriage. I believe him to be a noble-minded, excellent man, and she seems to have well-grounded hopes of happiness, provided poverty can be kept out of doors.'

But four years were to pass before Dorothy got to Paris. William, always an alarmist, was convinced that another war was imminent; and apart from this, the Wordsworths were a byword among their friends for a constitutional inability to make plans, or to keep to the plans they made. But Annette and Caroline bore them no ill will for Dorothy's failure to keep her promise. On December 27, 1816, when Caroline gave birth to her first child, William was godfather, and the baby was named after her great-aunt, Louise Marie Caroline Dorothée.

XVI

HINDWELL. ILLNESS OF LLOYD. DEATHS OF PRISCILLA AND RICHARD WORDSWORTH. HALIFAX. DE QUINCEY'S MARRIAGE. THE 1818 ELECTION. THE WILBERFORCES AT RYDAL. ASCENT OF SCAFELL PIKE. LONDON

1814–1820 (aet. 42–48)

THE years during which Dorothy's trip to France was being discussed and continually postponed were full enough of other family concerns. For two months in the summer of 1814 she was left in charge of the children whilst William, Mary, and Sara took holiday in Scotland; on September 16, less than a week after their return, she and Sara were off on a visit to Tom and Mary Hutchinson at Hindwell near Radnor. They took the journey in leisurely fashion, for much of the country was new to them, and there were friends to see upon the way. A night was spent with the Cooksons at Kendal, three at Liverpool with their old landlord of Allan Bank, Mr. Crump, with whose family they were now on terms of friendship, two at Chester with a cousin, and two more at Shrewsbury. Here Tom Hutchinson met them with a gig, and after a night at Ludlow, they reached Hindwell on the tenth day from their setting out. They were in Wales for nearly three months and thoroughly enjoyed the holiday. It was always a pleasure to be with the vivacious Joanna and with their friend Mary, now so happily married; and Dorothy could not stifle a regret that Mary was living in so secluded a spot, 'where her merits are hardly seen and felt except by her own family'.[1]

Dorothy's passion for her native soil did not blind her to the beauties of the west country. 'You could hardly believe it possible', she says,[2] 'for anything but a lake to be so beautiful as the pool before this house. It is perfectly clear and inhabited by multitudes of geese and ducks, and two fair swans keep their silent and solitary state apart from all the flutter and gabble of the inferior birds.' The weather was fine, she was seldom kept indoors, and not only had many walks, but Tom gave her lessons

[1] D. W. to C. C., Nov. 11, 1814.

[2] D. W. to C. C., Oct. 9, 1814.

in riding. 'By little and little I have become a tolerable horsewoman,' she writes,[1] 'I have no fears, and that is a great point, but I cannot attain the power of managing my horse; I can however ride for four or five hours without fatigue, and at a pace which was torture to me when I first began.' Thus she was able to go farther afield than her legs could carry her, visited Mary's brother John Monkhouse, who was now farming near Hay, some twelve miles off, and with him went over to Hereford. But, best of all, Thomas Hutchinson took her for a few days' expedition down the Wye, to revisit scenes that were crowded for her with precious memories.

Early in the next summer (1815) she was again left in charge at home, for Mary and William went south to stay with the Clarksons and with their brother Christopher. In their absence she was thoroughly wretched, for both she and the children were ill, and she simply dared not break the news to their parents, knowing only too well the forebodings which had haunted them continually ever since their loss of little Thomas.

> 'If,' she wrote to Mrs. Clarkson,[2] 'I had told what was to my mind the truth it would not have been the truth to theirs. They would have magnified the evil a thousand fold and would either have come home immediately or have spent an anxious and miserable time of absence . . . and though I was not very fearful for the present evil . . . yet all *tranquillity* and power of *free* enjoyment was destroyed. In short I had a most anxious time, yet I had far less of unhappiness than if William and Mary had been at home. In the first place I was glad they were spared the anxiety, and for the second I always suffer a thousand times more from my brother's unconquerable agitation and fears when Willy ails anything than from any other cause.'

Fortunately all the invalids had recovered before the travellers returned, and in August there was their usual inroad of visitors, among them John Monkhouse and the Beaumonts, who 'were enchanted with the place'; in the autumn Dorothy was counting on a little holiday with the Marshalls at Ullswater, when her plan was frustrated by the complete mental breakdown of their neighbour Charles Lloyd.

[1] D. W. to C. C., Nov. 11, 1814.
[2] D. W. to C. C., June 28, 1815.

Lloyd had never been a favourite with the Wordsworths, but the marriage of his sister Priscilla with Christopher Wordsworth had necessitated some friendly intercourse with him, and their dislike did not extend to Mrs. Lloyd. Years before this William had written[1] that she 'has long been living in hourly apprehension that he will be obliged to be confined in a mad-house or he will destroy himself; . . . the women of my family have in compassion given to Mrs. Lloyd something of their company; she has no sympathy or advice from any other quarter'; and the cheerful courage with which she faced her troubles had won from Mary and Dorothy an affectionate admiration; now that her husband's mind had completely given way Dorothy could not 'bear the thought of poor dear Mrs Lloyd, with her family of eight children, nearly worn out with sorrow and watching.' She and Mary were 'the only persons apart from his wife whom Lloyd could bear to see or have sitting near him. To me,' she says,[2] 'he has never objected—he liked me when he was well and the same liking has continued during his woeful depression'. And when Mrs. Lloyd decided to move him to his old home at Birmingham, where he could get proper medical attendance, William gave them his escort as far as Manchester, while Dorothy went to Brathay to look after the children. 'I shall be mostly here', she tells Jane, 'through the day and always at nights to gather the stragglers together and keep them to their business round a warm fireside. Poor things! they are happy, chearful, tractable children, and I find a melancholy consolation in being of some little use to their dear mother. Perhaps, too, after her return she may wish me to stay, and I cannot leave the house as long as I can do any good here.'

The day before Lloyd left Brathay,[3] news came of the death of his sister, Priscilla Wordsworth, and Dorothy held herself in readiness in case she should be summoned to console her bereaved brother.

[1] W. W. to S. T. C., early summer, 1808.

[2] D. W. to J. M., Oct. 13, 1815.

[3] Lloyd never returned to live at Brathay. After a short stay at Birmingham he was sent to an asylum at York; in 1818 he escaped, and De Quincey has left a vivid description of how, one night, he burst in upon him at Dove Cottage. In 1819 he recovered his sanity and for some years lived in London, where the Wordsworths visited him in 1820. A little later his wife took him abroad, and he died at Versailles in 1839. There is little information as to his last years, but we know that they were clouded by periodic mental delusions.

'Of course,' she writes,[1] 'I have no thoughts of residing with him. I could not give up my present home for any other, but perhaps he will find comfort in me in his present desolation: and I am glad that it is in my power to offer him my feeble support. My first impulse would have led me to go immediately . . . but on mature consideration I thought it best to wait for a summons. . . . My dear Jane, I am sorry to distress you with this woful history. Death is nothing to the misery of living as poor Charles Lloyd lives now, in the wofullest agonies of utter depression, and his wife's sufferings are a hundred-fold more difficult to support than the final separation by Death.'

But as it turned out Christopher did 'not seem to want anyone to lean upon, even for a time', and Dorothy was not summoned to Bocking; in December she started with William for a week's holiday of the kind she most enjoyed. 'The weather was frosty without snow, and I never in my youngest days, in the summer season, had a more delightful excursion; except for the intervention of melancholy recollections of persons gone, never to return. We set off at one o'clock, walked over Kirkstone, and reached Patterdale by daylight; slept there, and rose early the next morning, determined to walk to Hallsteads (Mr Marshall's new house, built upon Skelly Nab) before breakfast—the lake was calm as a mirror, the rising sun tinged with pink light the snow-topped mountains, and we agreed that all we saw in the grander part of the scene was more beautiful even than in summer.' The next two nights she spent at Penrith, after which they 'walked to Lowther, stayed all night and walked to Sockbridge to dinner'. The next day 'we left Sockbridge, slept at Hallsteads, were conveyed to Brother's Water in a Car and reached home at 5 o'clock. I was just as fresh as on that day week when we began our journey. My dear friend, have I not reason to be thankful that my strength is thus continued to me, and that my pleasure in walking remains as keen as ever?'[2]

The object of their visit to Sockbridge was to see Richard on business, and to make the acquaintance of his wife and baby. Some eighteen months before this, to their great consternation, he had married his servant, a woman less than half his own age. Dorothy was relieved to find that she liked her new relative 'very well, the circumstances of her education—her rank in

[1] To J. M., Oct. 13, 1815. [2] D. W. to C. C., Dec. 23, 1815.

Society—her youth etc. being got over. . . .[1] She is not vulgar, though she has nothing of the natural gentlewoman about her. Her face is very comely and her countenance excellent.' The little boy captured her heart at once, for he was 'very pretty and most intelligent and engaging'. Their business with Richard was to try and get him to put the family finances upon a proper legal footing. Though twelve years had passed since Lord Lonsdale had repaid the debt due to their father's estate, he had not yet drawn up the necessary documents assigning the money to the several heirs, and William was informed that if his brother died before this was done, neither he nor Dorothy could touch a penny of their portion until Richard's little boy came of age. 'Richard', says Dorothy, 'was as usual very kind and affectionate, and will, I dare say, be as glad as we when the settlement is made. At present we have neither accounts nor security of any kind whatever.' But despite all efforts to bring their procrastinating brother to the point it is uncertain how much they actually achieved; for when Richard died, in the following May, William, as one of his executors, was threatened with a Chancery suit, and had months of distracting anxiety before him. 'He is so little fit for business', wrote Sara to Tom Monkhouse in February 1817, 'that it worries him beyond all measure; the affairs of his brother and some plaguy Stamp concerns have deranged him in a piteous manner; when he is thus employed he is in a fever the whole time and unable to sleep.' To Dorothy this waste of William's precious time and energies was deeply distressing. 'One can see no end to it,' she wrote two months later,[2] 'but I think he begins to take things more quietly, and for the first time during more than a year and a half he has taken to his old employments. To-day he has composed a sonnet, and in our inner minds we sing "Oh, be joyful!" It has indeed been most melancholy to see him bowed down by oppressive cares, which have fallen on him through mismanagement, dilatoriness, or negligence. Nothing can exceed the apathy which our poor deceased brother must have lived in, nor his irresolution and weakness.'

During the summer of 1816, while William was still in the thick of his financial troubles, the Beaumonts were again at

[1] D. W. to C. C., Dec. 23, 1815.
[2] D. W. to C. C., Apr. 13, 1817.

Rydal, and Tillbrook, who for some years had spent much of his holiday there, took a lease of Ivy Cottage, a little house at the foot of the hill leading to Rydal Mount, and 'edified' it for use as a long vacation residence. In September Crabb Robinson paid his first visit to the Lakes, and in addition to long expeditions with William had a wet walk to Kendal with Dorothy, who, he says,[1] 'rendered the day as comfortable as good company possibly could'. Crabb also visited Southey at Keswick and saw Hartley Coleridge, and he renewed his acquaintance with De Quincey at Dove Cottage. These two were now causing much worry to their old friends. 'Hartley', wrote Sara Hutchinson to Tom Monkhouse, 'has come from college in very bad spirits and full of fantastic sensibilities, which I fear will stand greatly in the way of his well-doing. He is far too much like his father in many points, and consequently we are very anxious about him.' Of De Quincey they had seen little for some time. In the previous November Sara had reported that the return of the boisterous Wilson[2] for a fortnight at Elleray had done him no good. 'Wilson', she says, 'was tolerably steady, though De Quincey was often tipsy. We believe that he will marry Peggy S. after all. He doses himself with opium and drinks like a f[ish] and tries in all other ways to be as great a g[un] as Mr Wilson.' The attentions that De Quincey was paying to Peggy Sympson, the daughter of the farmer at the Nab Cottage, was a fruitful theme of gossip in the neighbourhood, but though he was very sensitive on this score, he could not bring himself to decide whether he would marry her. On a visit to London he had amused Lamb by his hesitant allusions to the affair: 'O how funny he did talk to me about her, in terms of such mild quiet whispering speculative profligacy.'[3] When Crabb Robinson called at Dove Cottage he found him 'in a sore state',[4] admitting an estrangement from the Wordsworths and resenting their 'imagined comments' on his behaviour. He had got it into his head that Wordsworth was condemning him, and years later made this an excuse for the malice of his gossip in *Tait's*

[1] H. C. R. to Thomas Robinson, Sept. 29, 1816.

[2] Wilson had lost a large part of his fortune in 1815 and left Elleray for Edinburgh, when he was called to the bar and took to literature as a profession. But he still kept on for many years his house at the Lakes and paid occasional visits.

[3] Charles Lamb to D. W., Nov. 21, 1817.

[4] H. C. R. to W. W., Oct. 1816.

Magazine; but all the evidence goes rather to show that it was the ladies at Rydal who were his censors; and, after all, it was natural enough not only that they should regard his too protracted courtship with some disfavour, but that, knowing as they did his intellectuality and refinement of manners they should view with gloomy forebodings his marriage with a small farmer's daughter of no education. The wedding took place on February 15, 1817, and Dorothy thus reported it to Mrs. Clarkson:[1]

> 'Mr De Quincey is married; and I fear I may add he is ruined. By degrees he withdrew himself from all society except that of the Sympsons of the Nab (that pretty farm house between Rydal and Grasmere). At the up-rouzing of the Bats and the Owls he regularly went thither, and the consequence was that Peggy Sympson, the eldest daughter of the house presented him with a son ten weeks ago, and they . . . are now spending their honey-moon in our cottage at Grasmere. This is in truth a melancholy story! He uttered in raptures of the beauty, the good sense, the simplicity "the angelic sweetness" of Miss Sympson, who to all other judgments appeared to be a stupid heavy girl, and was reckoned a Dunce at Grasmere School, and I predict that all these witcheries are ere this removed, and the fireside already dull. They have never been seen out of doors, except after the day was gone. As for him I am very sorry for him—he is utterly changed in appearance and takes largely of opium.'

But in the event, Dorothy's melancholy predictions proved as false as the verdict of the Grasmere school. For Margaret De Quincey was a woman of character and natural refinement; under the tuition of her husband she acquired no little culture, and she made him an admirable wife.

In October 1816 Dorothy went on a visit to Halifax, dividing her time between two aged relatives, Mrs. Threlkeld and Mrs. Rawson—both of them over seventy; and she was not back in Rydal till the middle of February, for though she received from home many reproaches for her long absence, and herself wished to return, she could not resist the fervent entreaties of the dear aunt who had been a mother to her in her girlhood. Here she saw something of the poverty and the distress which were rife

[1] Mar. 2, 1817.

throughout the country, but of which at Rydal she was hardly conscious.

'Cotton and worsted mills', she writes,[1] 'and steam engines are no better than incumbrances on the ground, trade being so bad. The wealthy keep their mills going, chiefly for the sake of employing workmen, and few get more than *half* work—great numbers none at all, so that really a great part of the population is reduced to pauperism, a dreadful evil. Things cannot go on in this way. For a time whole streets,—men women and children may be kept alive by public charity; but the consequences will be awful, if nothing can be manufactured in these places where such numbers of people have been gathered together. It can never be expected or even *wished*, I think, that the state of our manufacturers should again be what it *has* been; but if there be not a revival of trade in a smaller way people and things cannot go on as they are. Looking round now I see "many rich sink down as in a dream among the poor",[2] and I daily hear of families accustomed to a plentiful maintenance through labour completely "broken down,"—that is their expression. It is a great comfort to me that my home is out of the way of these dismal sights and sounds. We see little of distress in our neighbourhood that we cannot in some degree diminish either by sympathy or help, but if one lived here it would be far otherwise.'

On March 2 she wrote from home:

'It was a fortnight yesterday since my arrival; and I have had so many employments and above all such a succession of happy, I may say joyous feelings, that the time seems to be twice as long. . . . I never had this feeling before after any absence from home, and I attribute it to the contrast in all respects between my manner of spending my time here and at Halifax, and the perfect opposition, if I may so speak, in all domestic manners and arrangements. There I was in a large house with two old people, servants to perform the work as by magic,—no child's voice—all perfect stillness. True it is that they are the most chearful and happy old people I was ever acquainted with, yet how different the chearfulness of their fireside from the chearfulness of ours, and how different the seriousness! I was very happy there, yet now that I am placed again in the perfect freedom of home, I rejoice many times in every day that I am here, saying, "How glad I am that I am among you again!" Then I have had so much delight in the

[1] D. W. to C. C., Jan. 10, 1817.

[2] *Excursion*, i. 544 (from the 'Tale of Margaret').

beauty of the country. . . . When I was there I thought the hills and vallies beautiful, and so they are, and they reminded me of our mountain regions; but when I came *home* again I was even struck with *surprize* at the excessive loveliness of the objects before my eyes, the exquisite proportions, combinations of forms, and richness and harmony of colours.'

For the rest of the year there is little record of her doings, save of a few days early in June, spent with William at Hallsteads, whence she returned to Rydal over the summit of Helvellyn. 'Never', she tells Jane,[1] 'have I walked with more spirit in my life than on the lofty terraces of Helvellyn.' In a letter to Thomas Monkhouse in the following January (1818) we have a pleasant picture of her looking after the children while Mary and William were staying with him in London. 'I have often wished I could be with you in an evening in Queen Anne Street and back again to Rydal Mount; but as that is impossible believe me I have had no painful regrets that I could not be of your joyous party. We have had our own pleasure and not the merriest were merrier than on Christmas day, when we drank a bottle of Cowslip wine to the healths of Father and Mother, Aunt Sara and all absent friends—with a single toast to me, being mistress of the ceremonies on my own birthday.' And she goes on to tell how, in the new year, they invited their old friends from Hackett to a whist party. 'It consisted of Jonathan, Betty, Miss Smith and Dorothy.[2] D. instructed Miss S. for the first time in the rudiments of whist during the ½ hour before we lighted candles, D. playing three hands and directing Miss S. at the same time. It was a very droll scene. D. was so clear-headed and so sharp, confounding neither the order of the cards nor the laws of justice and strict honour, which I thought she had some temptation to do. After this one lesson, Miss S, with my overlooking her, performed her part to the satisfaction of Betty and Jonathan, and he, good creature, after cards were laid aside, listened enraptured to the duets which they played; hanging over the piano, and looking up now and then at his wife in wonder and delight.'

For the next six months Dorothy could think of little else but politics. Brougham was making his first attempt to wrest the county of Westmorland from the Lonsdale interest and the Tories. William was among his foremost antagonists, and in

[1] D. W. to J. M., June 25, 1817.

[2] i.e. niece Dorothy.

February and March wrote his addresses to the Freeholders of Westmorland; Dorothy took her opinions from him, and without his cogency of argument had all his passionate conviction. In Easter week, when Brougham came to Kendal to address the electors, she walked over with Henry Hutchinson 'not, you may be sure, to do honour to Mr Brougham, but to see him, the man, and to hear him speak (I had never before heard a Parliament man), to speculate upon a Kendal mob and to note the stirrings in all ranks.'[1] But the account of the proceedings which she sent to Sara[2] does more credit to her vivacity than to her powers of disinterested speculation:

> 'At a little after one we stationed ourselves at Mrs Strickland's windows, and at about two, in the midst of a bitter snow shower, B. and his attendants, with music and banners, halted before the Bank. . . . The Hero of the day had been dragged by a set of raggamuffins in blue Ribbands from within 3 miles of Burton, and when he drew up towards the door with music, Banners, horsemen, and the immense multitude on foot all joining in one huzza, fearless of the driving storm, the spectacle was grand. To my feelings it would have been sublime if the cause had been a good one. The candidate for the favour of that mob assembly was distinguished by a large blue handkerchief which hung from his neck to the bottom of his waist. He appeared at the window—face to face with us. Silence was proclaimed and the oration began. But if such be House of Commons eloquence, commend me to a mountebank Doctor. Mrs Strickland, whose faculties are as lively as they were at 20 years of age, says that when Dr Green used to speak it was something like. *He* appeared like a gentleman and what he said was worth listening to. But Mr B.'s speech was addressed *to* a mob, intended *for* a mob; and that mob he invited to meet him at Appleby. He never once addressed himself to the Freeholders, never but once used the word (and he spoke for ¾ of an hour) and that was incidentally. In short you might have thought he was ashamed of claiming any connexion with that respectable body. But I have already once written down the substance of his speech for Rydal, and cannot set about it again. So you must be contented with one part of it. But first conceive John and me stationed side by side in the window right before him, E. Cookson's head above mine, Henry's above John's; and cousin Crackanthorpe and two or three of the Thompsons at the next window to Brougham. His first words were words of gratitude to

[1] D. W. to C. C., Mar. 29, 1818. [2] D. W. to S. H., Mar. 24, 1818.

that goodly assembly, next of lamentation and sympathy on account of the bad weather which was indeed a contrast to the weather on the memorable 11th, a day which none of them could forget if they were to live a hundred years, but in all other respects how much the contrast was in *their* favour! (Loud applause.) and here he impudently styled them the Lowther Riots and in plain language charged the Lowther party with being the Authors of them (which by interpretation was saying that they were so silly as to incite a mob to do its best to destroy themselves!) Then he began to describe the arts used by the party to mislead the people. Their agents were anonymous writers, or writers under false names. One of these, the first who descended to personality in this contest, had taunted him with his poverty and the county of Westmorland with a like charge (he quoted the words of a friend of yours about Westmorland) "That man held a *sinecure* in the county, and he had nothing else, or very little else, to live upon. *He* was the most active of the secret agents of the cause, and to be sure it was much harder work to read his writings—"understand me I do not mean his *poetry*, but those other writings which he now pours out—than any the duties of his office impose upon *him*." There was much more of the like, and I determined to face it out. In the beginning of this part of the harangue Crackanthorpe cast a good-humoured and significant look at me, which I returned, and a short time after the end of this part of the subject I pushed E. Cookson to my place and took hers. No doubt he expected that the mob would at once understand whom he alluded to, and looked for a triumphant laugh of sympathy; but no, it fell a dead weight upon the ears of all except the Faction at his elbow. However, not daunted by this rebuff he turned to the subject again. "In the words of our immortal Poet (you are not to suppose I mean that poet of whom I have spoken to you before (pointing towards the Windermere road) no, in the words of our immortal poet"—and here, poor man, his memory failed him, and he blundered out some garbled lines which I could not hear distinctly—no doubt they had been *intended* for the words of Shakespear—but enough of this. The speech had not even the merit of producing much effect even upon the mob to whom it was solely addressed, and I must say that I could perceive no merit in the man as an Orator, except words at will when he did not pretend to quote from others,—and a very distinct utterance. The utmost attention was paid by the auditory; but when all was over they looked heavy and stupid, as if they had expected something which they had not found. . . . Brougham had been galled by nobody's writings but William's, and they have cut to the quick. Depend on it. . . . You will think, dearest Sara, that my head is turned with this election, that I can think of nothing else, and true it is, the tendency of all these proceedings is evidently so dangerous, that we are interested far more than it is even possible for *you* to conceive at a distance.'

In truth, no sensible woman ever lost her head more completely than Dorothy in the prejudices and passions of the Brougham election. Her cousin Crackanthorpe, the son of Uncle Kit of Newbiggin Hall, was a leading supporter of Brougham, and she saw much of him at Kendal; and 'to be sure', she says, 'we were the most good-humoured disputants that ever met'; but for this the credit must clearly be given to Crackanthorpe, for 'many a plain truth did I tell him and poured out some shameful lies which I heard uttered by Mr B'. It seems to her quite natural that Lord Lonsdale's tenantry should vote tory, but when she hears that Crackanthorpe's tenants and neighbours intend to support Brougham, she 'cannot believe it is through the free use of their understandings convincing them that it was for the general good; but they were swayed by many motives—gratitude and personal respect and belief that he knew better than they, and the like'. Crackanthorpe was especially delighted at receiving from Mr. Clarkson a letter in support of Brougham. 'Well', says Dorothy,[1] 'may he be proud of his prize. They never *had* such a feather in their caps before, and never will have again.' She admits to Mrs. Clarkson that the letter is 'a faithful picture of her husband's noble mind,' but, she adds, 'I cannot but lament that he has thought it right to lend his help to such a cause. He is little aware of the rebellious spirit stirred up in this county, or I am sure he would not have done it. The majority of the populace of Westmorland are ready for revolution, I firmly believe, and that they would be set to work before many years are over, if a majority of county members such as B. in political conduct and principles were returned to Parliament.' That there was no rioting during Brougham's visit to Kendal she attributed solely to the wonderful forbearance of the Lowther party, 'who took the utmost pains to prevent any interference', but there certainly was much 'odious coarseness'. The contempt with which she viewed the rank and file of her opponents shows

[1] D. W. to C. C., Mar. 29, 1818.

nothing of the democratic sympathies which characterized her normal life, and with which she had entered into the distress of the workers at Halifax. In the motley group that accompanied Brougham to Kendal 'there was not one,' she says, 'except Towers the apothecary, who looked in the least like a gentleman'; his enthusiastic supporters are 'a set of dirty lads and vagrant-like men,' and 'girls working at trades, comb-makers, straw hat makers etc.—and really walking Kendal streets of an evening of one of these bustling days of Easter week the number of disgusting females shouting B. and independence were so great you might have supposed the whole of the female populace had turned out. I could not have believed that so many impudent women and girls were to be found in Kendal.'

The election took place at the end of June; on the 27th, when all the Wordsworths were at Kendal, canvassing for the Lowthers, Keats, on his way to Scotland, called at Rydal Mount. 'I was much disappointed,' he wrote to his brother, 'I wrote a note for him and stuck it up over what I knew must be Miss Wordsworth's portrait.'[1] We share his disappointment, and could spare some of Miss Wordsworth's comments on the disgusting females who supported Brougham if, in their place, we could have had from her pen an impression of a poetic genius in whom she could not have failed to recognize a spiritual kinship. For had he not pronounced *The Excursion* to be one of the three wonders of the age, and was he not, at this very moment, in the first flush of enthusiasm for those lakes and mountains that were her daily inspiration? Of that favourite walk of hers from Windermere to Ambleside he had just sent his brother Tom an account as sensitive and discerning as any of her own. 'The views of the lake', he had felt,[2] 'were of a noble tenderness—they can never fade away—they make one forget the divisions of life; age, youth, poverty and riches. . . . I shall learn poetry here and shall henceforth write more than ever. . . . I live in the eye, and my imagination, surpassed, is at rest.'

'I really think', she wrote[3] in September, 'that our Party have carried themelves with moderation on their triumph, and it may

[1] John Keats to George Keats, June 27, 1818. One would be glad to know more of this portrait. Was it really of Dorothy? There is no record of one having been in existence at this time, and if there was, all trace of it is lost.

[2] John Keats to Thomas Keats, June 25, 1818.

[3] D. W. to C. C., Sept. 18, 1818.

be hoped that private enmities are subsiding . . . . We gained some new friends and I do not think we have lost any of our old ones—at least we have had no sparring, and have met one another at all times with "accustomed cordiality".' Their zeal for the Tory cause had raised their status higher in the eyes of the county than a wilderness of *Excursions*. Even the Norths, their snobbish and disagreeable predecessors in the tenancy of Rydal Mount, who, says Dorothy, 'formerly never looked upon us with a friendly eye, give us always a cordial greeting'. Lord Lonsdale spent a few days with them as their guest, Colonel Lowther, the newly elected member, and Lady Elinor, his wife, paid a friendly call. Colonel Lowther struck her as a 'fine brave fellow,' but 'painfully shy! The first time he spoke to Mary and me' (during the election) 'he was quite daunted—like a rustic from one of our mountain vales—but he had gained courage during the late struggle, for his shyness seemed to have much worn off.' But Mrs. Clarkson could not help regretting to find her friends the Wordsworths 'so thoroughly torified', and after their next meeting she admitted to Crabb Robinson,[1] 'though I *will* not acknowledge it to my husband, it is a little drawback upon the pleasure of our intercourse even to me'.

Later in the summer the Wilberforces spent six weeks at Rydal. Dorothy had not seen Mr. Wilberforce since he had come, a young college friend of her uncle's, as a visitor to Forncett. He was now a famous man, among the most eminent of politicians, a man of wealth with a great establishment; and to accommodate his party of nineteen, two houses were secured at the bottom of the hill opposite the turning to Rydal Mount, and five extra beds had to be taken at different houses in the village. 'The arrangements', says Dorothy, 'were first begun by letters between Mr W. and my Brother, but the business was soon given up by William to me, and innumerable were the letters that passed between me and Mr Wilberforce.'

Two of his epistles have survived, written with that rotundity of style in which he must have addressed the House of Commons. In the first[2] he alludes to the changes that had come over the district since he knew it more than thirty years before. 'But how great must be the encroachments of civilization in these

[1] C. C. to H. C. R., Mar. 31, 1821.
[2] Samuel Wilberforce to D. W., July 1, 1818.

recesses of nature! a daily coach between Kendal and Whitehaven! I almost envy the coachman his office, but he, I suppose, cares no more for the prospect than Cowper's Postman for his news. I little intended being so prolix, but the very idea of the Lakes intoxicates me.' In the second[1] he recalls their earlier acquaintance at Forncett: 'I really quite delight in the idea of the occasional coincidence of our orbits after so long a period, and to find it attended with the same friendly dispositions as before.' Then, condescending to matters of more practical concern, 'would there be shade in the garden, as Mrs Wilberforce is not a good walker? . . . It is supposed that my eldest son and his young mentor will study better if they are in a lodging by themselves. I should hope it would not be difficult to hire at Ambleside a sitting room and two comfortable bedrooms with the necessary apparatus, and as it is for young men the people should be solid good sort of people. I was never more sensible of the wisdom of Dr Paley's remark on the advantages resulting from a right constitution of habits. We so overflow with conveniences and comforts that we are absolutely obliged to send by waggon the greater part of our baggage. It is actually as necessary as to——But I have no time for comparisons—I will only add that I am with best remembrances to Mr Wordsworth my dear Madam, yours very sincerely.'

In the last days of August these imposing visitors descended upon the village of Rydal.

> 'First of all', says Dorothy,[2] 'I had to receive 7 servants, (William and Mary were at Keswick at the time) and on their arrival I was a little out of heart. With 7 servants came 5 horses,—and there was no provender for them—and the Inns at Ambleside could not take them in—and packages and servants upon a wet and dirty day seemed at once to fill the small rooms—and when I said "the family will, I fear, be sadly crammed!", I assure you I was not encouraged to dissipate my fears. "Aye, if you saw our house! the first floor would far more than hold both these two houses." Add to this, the old Cook's observation upon my answering to one of her questions "such and such things must be sent for to Ambleside," "Our men dont like going errands, they are not used to it"—and her exclamation "what an inconvenient place!" when she found

[1] Samuel Wilberforce to D. W., Aug. 10, 1818.

[2] D. W. to C. C., Sept. 18, 1818.

they could not get a "drop of beer" nearer than Ambleside—besides objections of the housemaid and kitchen maid to sleep upon a mattress, and you will not wonder that I was rather afraid that our good friends might find themselves not a little uncomfortable on their arrival. But I assure you it was a pleasing contrast when they *did* come—all joy, animation and thankfulness. The rooms were larger than they expected—and so *many* sitting rooms, it was quite delightful, and as to the garden, the situation, everything was to their minds. I desired the servants to send for me when the Family came. I found all at dinner except Mr W. and his two youngest sons who were not come. Mrs W. looked very interesting, for she was full of delight and talked as fast as any of the young ones—but I must say that she has never since appeared to me to such advantage. Yet I like her very well—admire her goodness and patience and meekness—but that slowness and whininess of manner, tending to self-righteousness, I do not like. Not a particle of this was visible that first day, when they were all rejoicing over their dinner of mountain mutton and Westmorland beef—and each telling, and all at once, his or her separate feelings. Then came Mr Wilberforce himself and all ran to meet him—and *I* must go too,—and then indeed I was much affected, seeing his feeble body, which seemed to me completely worn out. This was the more affecting as I perceived at the same time that his mind was as lively as ever.'

The Wilberforces did not leave Rydal till the middle of October, 'and truly', says Dorothy, 'we were sorry to lose them. There never lived on earth, I am sure, a man of sweeter temper than Mr Wilberforce. He is made up of benevolence and loving kindness. . . . His children very much resemble him in ardour and liveliness of mind.'[1]

Towards the end of their visit Sir George and Lady Beaumont were at Rydal Mount, and they all made an expedition together into Borrowdale. Miss Barker, who had found her close proximity to the ladies of Greta Hall too serious a strain, was now living up the valley six miles from Keswick; and the whole party dined with her, bringing their own more solid provisions while she provided the vegetables. All but Dorothy returned to Keswick in the evening, but she stayed on, and the next day, October 7, she ascended Scafell Pike. For her friend Mr. Johnson, the former curate of Grasmere, but now master of the Central

[1] D. W. to J. M., Oct. 1818.

School in London, she wrote an account of her expedition which William printed as an Appendix to his *Guide to the Lakes*.

With Miss Barker and her maid, a shepherd 'statesman' to guide them, and a man to carry their provisions, they drove to Seathwaite, and then started the ascent to Eskhause.

> 'From the top of Eskhause we beheld a prospect which would indeed have amply repaid us for a *toilsome* journey, if such it had been; and a sense of thankfulness for the continuance of that vigour of body, which enabled me to climb the high mountain, as in the days of my youth, inspiring me with fresh chearfulness, added a delight, a charm to the contemplation of the magnificent scenes before me, which I cannot describe. Still less can I tell of what we saw. Three views, each distinct in its kind, we saw at once—the vale of Borrowdale, of Keswick, of Bassenthwaite—Skiddaw, Saddleback, Helvellyn, numerous other mountains, and, still beyond, the Solway Firth and the mountains of Scotland. Nearer to us on the other side, and below us, were the Langdale Pikes—then our own vale below *them*,—Windermere—and far beyond Windermere, after a long, long distance, Ingleborough in Yorkshire. But how shall I speak of the peculiar deliciousness of the third prospect? At this time *that* was most favoured by sunshine and shade. The green Vale of Esk—deep and green, with its glittering serpent stream, was below us, and on we looked to the mountains near the sea—Black Comb and others,—and still beyond, to the sea itself in dazzling brightness. Turning round we saw the mountains of Wasdale in tumult; and Great Gavel, though the middle of the mountain was to us as its base, looked very grand.'

They had intended to go no farther than Eskhause, but the beauty of the day tempted them on: at first they thought of Scafell, then, realizing that it would entail a great dip, and take too long a time, they decided on Scafell Pike.

> 'The sun had never once been overshadowed by a cloud during the whole of our progress from the centre of Borrowdale; at the summit of the Pike there was not a breath of air to stir even the papers which we spread out containing our food; we ate our dinner in summer warmth, and the stillness seemed to be not of this world. We paused, and kept silence to listen, and not a sound of any kind was to be heard. We were far above the reach of the cataracts of Scaw Fell; and not an insect was there to hum in the air. The vales before described lay in view; and side by side with

Eskdale, we now saw the sister Vale of Donnerdale terminated by the Duddon Sands. But the majesty of the mountains below and close to us is not to be conceived. We now beheld the whole mass of Great Gavel from its base, the Den of Wasdale at our feet, the Gulph immeasurable—Grassmore and the other mountains of Crummock—Ennerdale and *its* mountains; and the sea beyond.

While we were looking round after dinner our Guide said that we must not linger long, for we should have a storm. We looked in vain to espy the traces of it; for mountains, vales and sea were all touched with the clear light of the sun. "It is there," he said, pointing to the sea beyond Whitehaven, and, sure enough, we there perceived a light cloud or mist, unnoticeable but by a shepherd, accustomed to watch all mountain bodings. We gazed abroad again and yet again, fearful to lose the remembrance of what lay before us in that lofty solitude; and then prepared to depart. Meanwhile the air changed to cold, and we saw the tiny vapours swelled with mighty masses of cloud which came boiling over the mountains. Great Gavel, Helvellyn, and Skiddaw were wrapped in storm; yet Langdale, and the mountains in that quarter were bright with sunshine. Soon the storm reached us; we sheltered under a crag; and, almost as rapidly as it had come, it passed away, and left us free to observe the goings-on of storm and sunshine in other quarters. Langdale had now its share, and the Pikes were decorated by two splendid rainbows, Skiddaw also had its own rainbows. . . . We were hardly at all wetted, and before we found ourselves again upon . . . Eskhause every cloud had vanished from every summit.'

Instead of descending by the direct route they made a detour by Ruddle Gill and Sprinkling Tarn to the head of the Stye Head Pass, in order to enjoy the view of Wastwater, and thence by Stye Head Tarn to Seathwaite.

'Before we reached Seathwaite a few stars had appeared, and we travelled home in our cart by moonlight. . . . I ought to have described the last part of our ascent to Scaw Fell Pike. There, not a blade of grass was to be seen—hardly a cushion of moss, and that was parched and brown; and only growing rarely between the huge blocks and stones which cover the summit and lie in heaps all round to a great distance, like skeletons or bones of the earth not wanted at the creation, and there left to be covered with never-dying lichens, which the clouds and dews nourish; and adorn with colours of the most vivid and exquisite beauty, and endless in variety. No gems or flowers can surpass in colouring the beauty of some of these masses of stone which no human eye beholds, except the Shepherd as led thither by chance, or the Traveller by curiosity; and how seldom must this happen! The other eminence[1] is that which is visited by the adventurous traveller, and the Shepherd has no temptation to go thither in quest of his sheep, for on the Pike there is no food to tempt them.'

What with the election, the visit of the Wilberforces, and the ascent of Scafell, 1818 had been an eventful year for Dorothy: 1819 passed more quietly. But it added a new friend to the Rydal circle in John Kenyon,[2] who, as Sara tells Tom Monkhouse, 'ever since his visit to Keswick fifteen years before has been, as he says, *bit* by W.'s poems, and indeed seems to have a better verbal knowledge of them than the author himself. He has been four years on the continent, is full of anecdote, and tells his stories in the most agreeable way. He is a man of fortune, without profession, a scholar.' And during the summer Mary Hutchinson brought her small family from Hindwell to visit their cousins at Rydal Mount. 'We were very sorry when they left us,' wrote Dorothy to Mrs. Clarkson.[3] 'The house was quiet even to dulness. Rydal Mount is the nicest place in the world for children. You will almost long to be young again, as I do, when you see it; for the sake of trotting down the green banks, running and dancing on the mount, etc. You must come and see us, indeed you must, before it is too late for you and all of us.'

Mary Hutchinson seemed to Dorothy a model parent. 'She is playful and tender with her children, yet resolutely guards against all foolish indulgence.' How different, she thought, from William! She was herself something of a disciplinarian, but ever since the loss of Thomas and Catharine William's nervous anxiety about his children had troubled her, and not least because it led him to pet and pamper them in a way of which she strongly disapproved. The worst sufferer was Willy, who was his father's darling. 'Willy', he said,[4] 'is the delight of my eyes; pray heaven that I may not have to say with Ben Jonson "My sin was too much hope of thee, loved boy!"' To Dorothy

[1] i.e. Scafell.

[2] John Kenyon (1784–1856), the friend of many literary men of the time, among them Southey, Landor, and later the Brownings.

[3] Aug. 1, 1819.

[4] W. W. to C. C., Dec. 31, 1814.

William's sin was too much indulgence. 'Oh Sara,' she had written,[1] 'it is ten thousand pities he should be so spoiled! it is impossible, unless you have seen it, to have an idea of the father's folly respecting this child—we strive against it as much as possible, but it is all in vain.'

As the years passed William did not grow any wiser. After her five months' absence at Halifax in 1817, she was 'astonished at Willy's babyishness—and really his father fondles over him and talks to him just as if he were but a year old'.[2] She can only hope that in time he will recover from 'being treated as the little pet, "the little darling", for when he is amongst his school-fellows none is more active independent and manly than he, and he disdains all notice from Father, or Mother, or any of us at such times'. But now at last Dorothy had prevailed upon them to send Willy away to school, and in September the good Tom Monkhouse, who was staying at Rydal, undertook to conduct him to London and deposit him with their old friend Mr. Johnson, master of the Central School, Baldwin Gardens, to be prepared for Charterhouse. '*I* had long been convinced', wrote Dorothy in December,[3] 'that nothing but a removal from home could save the Boy from ruin, but his Mother could not be brought to this conviction till it was forced upon her; and long did his Father waver and despond from fears for his health; but happy am I to be able to tell you that his health and his looks have visibly improved; and this I believe to be solely owing to a chearful submission to unbending laws, and activity of mind *fixed*, not wandering, as it ever used to be.'

But Dorothy, for all her sternness, was fully as anxious about Willy as either his father or mother, and she read with a like eagerness any news of him that friends in London could send them. Late in November came this inimitable letter from Charles Lamb:[4]

> Dear Miss Wordsworth, You will think me negligent, but I wanted to see more of Willy, before I ventured to express a prediction. Till yesterday I had barely seen him—Virgilium tantum vidi—but yesterday he gave us his small company to a bullock's heart—and I can pronounce him a lad of promise. He is no pedant nor book-worm, so far I can answer. Perhaps he has hitherto paid too little

[1] D. W. to S. H., Apr. 8, 1815.
[2] D. W. to C. C., Mar. 2, 1817.
[3] D. W. to C. C., Dec. 19, 1819.
[4] Nov. 25, 1819.

attention to other men's inventions, preferring, like Lord Foppington, the "natural sprouts of his own". But he has observation, and seems thoroughly awake. I am ill at remembering other people's bon mots, but the following are a few. Being taken over Waterloo Bridge, he remarked that if we had no mountains, we had a fine river at least, which was a Touch of the Comparative, but then he added, in a strain which augured less for his future abilities as a Political Economist, that he supposed they must take at least a pound a week Toll. Like a curious naturalist he inquired if the tide did not come up a little *salty*. This being satisfactorily answered, he put another question as to the flux and reflux, which being rather cunningly evaded than artfully solved by that she-Aristotle Mary, who muttered something about its getting up an hour sooner and sooner every day, he sagely replied, "Then it must come to the same thing at last", which was a speech worthy of an infant Halley! The Lion in the 'Change by no means came up to his ideal standard. So impossible it is for Nature in any of her works to come up to the standard of a child's imagination. The whelps (Lionets) he was sorry to find were dead, and on particular enquiry his old friend the Ouran Outang had gone the way of all flesh also. The grand Tiger was also sick, and expected in no short time to exchange this transitory world for another—or none. But again, there was a Golden Eagle (I do not mean that of Charing) which did much *arride* and console him. William's genius, I take it, leans a little to the figurative, for being at play at Tricktrack (a kind of minor Billiard-table which we keep for smaller wights, and sometimes refresh our own mature fatigues with taking a hand at) not being able to hit a ball he had iterate aimed at, he cried out, "I cannot hit that beast." Now the balls are usually called men, but he felicitously hit upon a middle term, a term of approximation and imaginative reconciliation, a something where the two ends, of the brute matter (ivory) and their human and rather violent personification into *men*, might meet, as I take it, illustrative of that Excellent remark in a certain Preface about Imagination, explaining "like a sea-beast that had crawled forth to sun himself". Not that I accuse William Minor of hereditary plagiary, or conceive the image to have come ex traduce. Rather he seemeth to keep aloof from any source of imitation, and purposely to remain ignorant of what mighty poets have done in this kind before him. For being asked if his father had ever been on Westminster Bridge, he answer'd that he did not know.

It is hard to discern the Oak in the Acorn, or a Temple like St. Paul's in the first stone which is laid, nor can I quite prefigure what destination the genius of William Minor hath to take. Some few hints I have set down, to guide my future observations. He hath the power of calculation in no ordinary degree for a chit. He combineth figures, after the first boggle, rapidly. As in the Trick-track board, where the hits are figured, at first he did not perceive that 15 and 7 made 22, but by a little use he could combine 8 with 25—and 33 again with 16, which approacheth something in kind (far let me be from flattering him by saying in degree) to that of the famous American boy. I am sometimes inclined to think I perceive the future satirist in him, for he hath a sub-sardonic smile which bursteth out upon occasion, as when he was asked if London were as big as Ambleside, and indeed no other answer was given, or proper to be given, to so ensnaring and provoking a question. In the contour of scull certainly I discern something paternal. But whether in all respects the future man shall transcend his father's fame, Time the trier of geniuses must decide. Be it pronounced peremptorily at present, that Willy is a well-mannered child, and though no great student, hath yet a lively eye for things that lie before him. Given in haste from my desk at Leadenhall. Your's and your's most sincerely

C. LAMB.

We can imagine the delight with which Dorothy read and re-read this letter; it was, indeed, largely the intensity of her life in the children that kept her spirit young despite the ravages of time. 'Think', she wrote to Mrs. Clarkson,[1] 'how years go by—how the children are coming forward to take their place in active life, and we are going down the hill. Thank God, your health being amended, you are stronger than you were years ago, and perhaps not one of *us* is very much failed in point of strength; and for my part I have as much enjoyment in walking as when I first came into Westmorland twenty years ago, yet you will be surprised when you see me, in face a perfect old woman. . . . My teeth are all gone but three above and three below, and I have now a true old woman's mouth and chin. My profile is 70. Shall I get a set of new teeth? We talk of it, yet I do not altogether like the experiment.'

Fortunately both for herself and all her friends she screwed up her courage, and a 'true gossiping letter' to Mary Hutchinson, dated from her brother Christopher's house at Lambeth in the

[1] D. W. to C. C., Aug. 1, and Dec. 19, 1819. According to Lamb, Dorothy had 'mounted spectacles' three years before (C. L. to W. W., Apr. 9, 1816).

following May, shows her facing the ordeal. Fifty guineas, the charge of Mr. Dumergue, the dentist recommended to her, seemed a terrible sum, and she only consented to go to him after a fortnight spent in inquiries about other practitioners. But the horrors of the dentist's chair and the 'ten days when she could not show herself' did not spoil her enjoyment of all that London had to offer. Nearly all her friends seemed to be collected there, and some of them she had not seen since her visit ten years before. Mrs. Clarkson was staying with her son Tom, now a lawyer's clerk: 'You will be glad to hear', Dorothy writes, 'that she looks much better than 11 years ago, and, I think, hardly a day older. . . . She tells me I am not so much changed by the want of teeth as she expected; but how this is I know not; for now my mouth is drawn up to nothing, and my chin projects as far as my nose; but I look healthy enough, though I have lost 8lbs since I was last weighed, being now only 6 stone 12 lbs. Miss Lamb is quite well and has been so for above a year. She is little altered in the face except for the loss of a tooth' (teeth were very much on poor Dorothy's mind) 'but is sadly fat and she dresses so loose that she looks the worse for it, yet she is still a good walker.' The Marshalls were in town, and Southey, who often came to breakfast at Lambeth, and Derwent Coleridge (there is no mention of his father), and the young Cooksons. To her friends she now added Mrs. Hoare of Hampstead, an intimate of Tom Monkhouse and her brother Christopher, and at her table she met Joanna Baillie. Some years before this Miss Baillie had called at Allan Bank when, as she wrote to Scott, she 'was very much pleased with the sweetness and modesty of Miss Wordsworth's appearance—the shortness of our visit to the house not permitting us to be further acquainted with her'. Dorothy was delighted to see Miss Baillie again, knowing William's opinion of her as 'the model of an English gentlewoman', and she reports her to be 'one of the nicest of women, very entertaining in conversation, without the least mixture of the literary lady'.

Of course she saw much of Willy, who had just left Mr. Johnson's for the Charterhouse. He was 'very sweet and interesting—in all respects wonderfully improved—no better boy can be—and he can well take care of himself among the 400. I went once to him at school. The boys were at play without hats and he and I wandered about the large Square like two forlorn things—nobody noticing us—but I doubt not he is quite at home there when he is playing with the rest.' She took him one day to Kensington Gardens, and for a week of his holiday had him to stay with her at Lambeth; but much as she wanted to be with him she 'thought it better to deny herself at present for fear of unsettling him at his first going to Charterhouse; and I assure you,' she adds, 'I have no disposition to spoil him.'

Tom Monkhouse, who was soon to be married to Miss Horrocks of Preston, evidently found Dorothy a sympathetic friend and confidante, for he was unremitting in his attentions to her. 'Your dear and good kind brother', she tells Mary Hutchinson, 'is my companion almost daily'; and with him she visited the sights of London, 'gazing about the streets, seeing panoramas, pictures, Exeter Change etc etc' as with Crabb Robinson ten years before; and when Tom was busy she wrote him affectionate letters.[1] 'I could thank you a hundred times for all your kindness to me, but that I know you would not like it. It does me good to think that I have such a kind friend near me'; and again, 'without seeing you now and then I find such a want of you as I can hardly give you a notion of'.

And when she was alone she could still enjoy the beauty of London. It is pleasant to see it with her eyes, as it was a hundred years ago:

> 'I am exceedingly comfortable and happy at Lambeth. I have a nice drawing room which overlooks the Archbishop's garden grounds—a beautiful green field with very fine trees and not a building to be seen except one rustic cattle shed. I left my writing to take a solitary walk—solitary though in a crowd, for I came up the Strand having crossed Waterloo Bridge. The river was most beautiful to-day and beyond Vauxhall Bridge all was as clear and bright as among the Lakes. . . . Though I walked in the morning, I must go out again to look at the sunset. The trees are casting their long shades over the green field, and the sparrows are making no unpleasant chirping—and I do assure you that I sometimes hear the notes of the thrush and blackbird from these trees— . . . (*Evening.*) I am just returned from walking in a little garden of the Archbishop's. It is about 50 yards long or more—close to the

[1] D. W. to Thomas Monkhouse, May 9 and 16, 1820.

Thames, being only separated from the water by a wall from which you look down upon the water, which is for ever varying with boats perpetually enlivened. The Abbey is right before us and we look down to Westminster Bridge and up to Vauxhall, and are shut out behind from all houses except the Palace Towers which overtop the garden wall. . . . There I have walked before and since sunset—and only wanted some friend by my side for perfect enjoyment. Before, I treated myself to a shilling's worth on the water; I am delighted with the water and often tempted to extravagance. Whenever my walk is likely to be too long I take a boat, preferring it greatly to paying the same money or more for a coach.'

Thus pleasantly she spent nearly three months in London: in June William and Mary joined her, and all three were present at Tom Monkhouse's marriage on July 8; on the morning of the 10th they took coach to Dover, where Tom, his bride, and sister-in-law were awaiting them. The Wordsworths were to accompany them on a continental tour; this was the third honeymoon in which Dorothy was to participate.

XVII

TOUR ON THE CONTINENT

July—November 1820

SOON after nine o'clock on July 12 they set off from Calais in two stout carriages, which they had bought for 1,000 and 900 francs apiece, Thomas Monkhouse, his bride, her sister and maid in one of them, William, Mary, and Dorothy in the other. 'Off we drove', says Dorothy, 'preceded by our friends, each Postilion smacking his whip along the streets with a dexterity truly astonishing. Never before did I know the power of a clumsy whip in consort with the rattling of wheels upon rough pavements. The effect was certainly not less upon the spectators as we jolted away as merry as children,—showed our passports, passed the gateways, drawbridges and shabby soldiers, and fresh to the feeling of being in a foreign land, drove briskly forward, watchful and gay.'

Their route was by Dunkirk to Bruges, where they arrived on the 14th; here they put their carriages on the packet-boat and sailed to Ghent, then drove to Brussels and so by easy stages to Namur, Aix-la-Chapelle, Cologne, Bonn, Coblenz, Frankfurt, and Heidelberg. Shaffhausen was reached on August 1, and after visiting the Falls they made first for Zürich and then for Berne, where they passed the nights of August 5 and 6. Here they left their two carriages, and hired another to convey them all to Thun; rowed down the Lake to Unterseen and there hired a char-a-banc,[1] in which they drove to Interlaken. The next morning they breakfasted at Lauterbrunnen, and then proceeded to Grindelwald, Mrs. Monkhouse and her sister by carriage, Monkhouse and the Wordsworths crossing the Wengern Alps with three mules between them. The

[1] The char-a-banc was apparently unknown in England at this time, for both Mary and Dorothy think it necessary to define it. Dorothy says of it: 'The name tickled our fancy and (blundering between the Swiss pronunciation and our stupid ears) we called the carriage a Sharaban, and thence derived our own Shandrydans. The carriage itself, not less amusing than the name, was a long narrow waggon with cross benches where all could sit (seven in number) with the postilion, who was the owner, in front.' Mary calls it 'a long-bodied car with benches slung across, each to hold two persons, with five rows', and adds, 'a curious shadow it cast, as we flew through these delicious lanes'.

honeymoon now suffered a six weeks' interruption, for the bride, deciding that the tour was becoming too strenuous for her, returned by carriage with her sister to Berne, whilst the bridegroom, with his stouter friends, took guide and mules over the Scheidegg ridge to Meiringen, and thence to Sarnen. From Sarnen they drove in a char-a-banc, by way of Engelberg, to Stansstad, and thence took a boat to Lucerne. Here, on August 16, they were joined by Crabb Robinson, and on the 18th left by boat for Kusnach, ascended the Rigi to see the sunrise, and sometimes walking, sometimes by boat, made their way to Altdorf at the foot of the Lake, and so by char-a-banc to Amsteg. They crossed the Alps on foot by the St. Gothard Pass, spending the night of the 24th at Hospenthal, of the 25th at Airolo. They walked to Faido, drove thence to Bellinzona, and walked on to Locarno. After eight days spent in wandering on foot and by water about the lakes of Maggiore, Lugano, and Como, they passed three nights at Milan, three more on Como, thence to Baveno on Lake Maggiore, and so by carriage to Domodossola. From Domodossola they started on the morning of September 10 to cross the Simplon Pass, the Wordsworths on foot, Monkhouse and Crabb Robinson in a carriage: sometimes walking, sometimes driving, or on horses or mules, made their way via the Gemmi, the Baths of Leuk, Martigny, Chamouny to Lausanne, and thence to Geneva, which they reached on September 22. Here they found Mrs. Monkhouse and Miss Horrocks and their carriages awaiting them; and after four days spent in exploring the neighbourhood, started on their homeward journey. Passing through Dijon, Ancy, Sens, and Fontainebleau they were in Paris on October 2. Here they stayed a month: and after selling their *voitures* for half of what they had paid for them, they took the diligence to Boulogne, spent ten days there, and were in London on November 9, just four months after their setting out.

There is no lack of information regarding the tour. All the travellers, except William, kept diaries, and those of Crabb Robinson, Mary, and Dorothy are extant, as well as several journal letters sent to friends at home. Mary's narrative extends to nearly three hundred closely written quarto pages: Dorothy's more elaborate account to seven hundred and fifty.[1] As, during

[1] Of Dorothy's *Journal* rather less than a fifth has been published (*Journals of*

the following winter, she sat at her bedroom window at Rydal, muffled up in her fur cloak, 'copying that enormous journal which I can never expect anyone, except a few idle folk, ever to read through', she was herself a little appalled at its length, and had no exaggerated opinion of its value. 'It is', she said, 'a mere transcript of hasty notes, taken by snatches, during our journey.' And certainly it has not the fine artistic perspective of the *Memorials of a Tour in Scotland*. It is far too long. Though one day was never exactly like another, many of them were too similar in incident and experience to justify so copious a treatment. Yet it is full of matter both good in itself and worthy of the writer of the *Grasmere Journal*. A traveller in the Alps to-day could take with him no better supplement to his *Baedeker* or his *Blue Guide*.

For Dorothy this journey through Switzerland was the tardy fulfilment of one of the dreams of her life. 'The first sight of that country, so dear to the imagination, though of no peculiar grandeur, affected me with various emotions. I remembered the shapeless wishes of my youth—wishes without hope—my brother's wanderings thirty years ago and the tales brought to me the following Christmas holidays at Forncett, and often repeated while we paced together on the gravel-walk in the parsonage garden by moon or starlight.' Her excitement when she caught her first glimpse of the snow-clad Alps is told by Mary. 'About five or six miles from Zurich we first came in sight of the snowy mountains. I had been asleep and was now pondering at the appearance, when D. (who had beheld it for some time, but only at that instant had satisfied her own mind that what she saw were not clouds but the Alps) gave a scream that made us think something had happened.' For Dorothy, indeed, something *had* happened. During all their journey through Belgium and Germany she had shared William's 'habitual eagerness to be in Switzerland'. The excessive heat, the change of diet, continual carriage-travelling had combined to knock her up. For the first fortnight, Mary tells us, 'she was very ill in her usual way', and was obliged to keep her bed or otherwise rest indoors while the others went sight seeing. But she did not allow ill health to damp the ardour of her

Dorothy Wordsworth, ed. by W. Knight, 2 vols., Macmillan 1897): Mary's Journal is still in manuscript.

anticipations. 'Sick and weary as I was', she wrote of her feelings on the way through Germany, 'I felt as much of the eagerness of hope as when I first visited the Wye, and all the world was fresh and new'; after a day or two in Switzerland 'the change was marvellous; for when I began to climb the mountains the full possession of health and even youthful vigour seemed to have returned, and never again did I suffer a moment from pain or weakness, hardly from fatigue'. The heat no longer troubled her: the others might flag, but she felt that 'the peculiar lightness of the air prevents oppression'. 'Let no one speak of fatigue in crossing the Alps who has climbed Helvellyn,' she wrote to Mrs. Clarkson. 'It is nothing in point of exertion to that ascent. Would you believe it? I am grown fat in the journey, and we are all perfectly well.'[1] Cooped up in a carriage she was never completely at her ease: walking suited her body and spirit alike. As they drove by the Rhine 'we rolled along', she says, 'ah! far too swiftly! and often did I wish that I were a youthful traveller on foot'. Up the valley of Lauterbrunnen 'we travelled pleasantly enough in the char-a-banc; yet I thought how much more delightful were pedestrian liberty, . . . the sounding torrents undisturbed by rattling wheels'. When walking she felt that 'fresh society was always ready and solitude could be taken at will. . . . Then everyone followed his or her devices. My scheme was always the same, pushing onward right till tired limbs made rest delightful, and I rose a hundred times with morning freshness. Mary, on the other hand, moved on perseveringly at a slower pace, with fewer intervals of repose'. It was a temperamental difference between them.

Her capacity for enjoyment seemed inexhaustible. Up at five on most mornings, so as to ensure an early start, she was often at her window at midnight, absorbing the moonlit landscape. High as had been her expectations they were always realized. Her brother's description of her girlhood held true of her at fifty years of age:

> She welcom'd what was given, and craved no more;
> Whatever scene was present to her eyes,
> That was the best, to that she was attuned.[2]

[1] D. W. to C. C., Sept. 3, 1820.
[2] *Prelude* (1805), xi. 207–9.

Mary records how on viewing Mont Blanc from the vale of Chamouny 'we all, save Dorothy, felt disappointed'. Descriptions of scenery, as she knew, can be tedious enough: the best of hers are redeemed by the manner in which she suffuses them with her own sentiment. Thus she tells how at Berne, before she had recovered her normal strength, they took an evening walk:

> 'We ascended a hill till we came in view of as magnificent a prospect as can be conceived. The Jung-frau, the Shreckhorn, the Wetterhorn, and many other famous mountains, their summits crowned with snow. I sate upon one of the seats placed under shade of trees beside the broad highway; and the others went further. I should have been ungrateful could I have felt a regret at parting from them, with such a spectacle before me, indeed, it seemed almost a privilege that my weakness removed all temptation to go further. Seeing only one side of the peninsula from my resting place, the City appeared to hang upon the half of a semicircle of the near bank, crowned by the Cathedral and adorned by spires and towers. The green tinted river flows slow, wide, full, and impetuous. I saw the snows of the Alps burnished by the sun about half an hour before his setting. After that, they were left to their wintry marble coldness, without a farewell gleam; yet suddenly the city and the Cathedral tower and trees were singled out for favour by the sun among his glittering clouds, and gilded with the richest light. A few minutes, and that glory vanished. I stayed till evening gloom was gathering over the city, and over hill and dale, while the snowy tops of the Alps were still visible. Before I reached the city gates the stars were beginning to appear.'

And here is part of her account of the descent into Grindelwald:

> 'The vale first opens on the view in the form of a large open basin, at the upper side of which a Glacier appears to be lying upon a gentle declivity at the base of a mountain. We, *long* after this, continued to descend by a steep stony track. It is indeed astonishing how far one must travel in the Alps to reach an object that has appeared close at hand. . . . Soon the vale lay before us with its two glaciers, and, as it might seem, its thousand cabins sown upon the steeps. The descent became so precipitous that all were obliged to walk; deep we go into the broad cradle valley; every cottage we passed had its small garden, and cherry trees sprinkled with leaves, bearing half-grown, half-ripe fruit. In plunging into

this vale I was overcome with a sense of melancholy pervading the whole scene—not desolation or dreariness; it is not the melancholy of the Scotch Highlands, but connected with social life in loneliness, not less than with the strife of all the seasons. When near the bottom of the declivity we were almost stunned by the roaring of the stream—under our feet (as it seemed); and from the centre of the wooden bridge we beheld it issuing from its icy cavern beneath the snow-like roof of the larger glacier. A cold blast following the river blew upon us while we passed over the bridge. I shall never forget the wintery sensation. The blast seemed as if its birthplace were in the icy cavern and thence issuing it would be fed with indestructible power. As I have said, when I first saw this vale from a point sufficiently near to distinguish the objects, the impressions were very melancholy:—the greeting of the river strengthened those impressions; and our ascent from the bridge to the village (distant about half a mile) did not abate the feeling. The sunshine had long deserted the valley, and was quitting the summits of the mountain behind the village; but red hues, dark as the red of rubies, settled in the clouds, and lingered there after the mountains had lost all but their cold whiteness and the black hue of the crags. The gloomy grandeur of the spectacle harmonised with the melancholy of the vale; yet it was a heavenly glory that hung over those cold mountains.'

She was often helped to define her impressions by comparing the scene before her with memories of home:

'Many a streamlet crossed our way, after tumbling down the hills, sometimes as clear as the springs of the Westmorland mountains, but the instant they touched the glacier river of the valley their pure spirit was lost,—annihilated by its angry waters. I have seen a muddy and a transparent streamlet, at a few yards distance hurrying down the same steep:—in one instance the two joined at the bottom, travelled side by side in the same track, remaining distinct, though joined together, as if each were jealous of its own character. Yielding to mild necessity, they slowly blended, ere both, in turbulent disrespect, were swallowed up by the master-torrent.'

At the Fall of the Reichenbach:

'The man unlocked the door and, as in the small summer-house at Rydal, we saw the cataract through an open window. It is a tremendous one; but wanting the accompaniments of overhanging trees and all the minor graces which surround our waterfalls—

overgrowings of lichen, moss, fern and flowers—it gives little of that feeling which may be called *pleasure*: it was astonishment, and awe—an overwhelming sense of the powers of nature for the destruction of all things, of the helplessness of man—of the weakness of his will if prompted by instinct to make a momentary effort against such a force.'

But she was moved most deeply by scenes which she could associate with William's undergraduate tour with Robert Jones; when she saw with her own eyes places that had long been dear to her imagination, from references to them in the *Descriptive Sketches* or *The Prelude*, and from talks far back in the Forncett days. Crabb Robinson noted the eagerness with which she tracked her brother's footsteps, and tells us that the return to Como from Milan was undertaken solely 'in order to gratify Miss Wordsworth, who wished to see every spot which her brother saw in his first journey'. To this Dorothy's narrative bears ample witness. 'Our journey', she writes, 'through the narrower and more romantic passages of the vale of the Rhine was specially endeared to Mary and me by recollections connected with times long past, when my brother and his friend (it is thirty years ago) floated down the stream in their little bark. Often did my fancy place them in a freight of happiness in the centre of some bending reach overlooked by tower or castle or (when expectation would be most eager) at the turning of a promontory, which had concealed from their view some delicious winding which we had left behind. But no more of my feelings, a record of his will be more interesting', and she quotes from the *Descriptive Sketches*. Again, on the road from Shaffhausen, 'I thought of our youthful travellers, thirty years ago, that they might have selected that very track:

> Dear was the forest frowning o'er their head,
> And dear the green sward to their velvet tread.'[1]

At Cadenabbia she rose early to go and explore the vale of Gravedona 'a name interesting to Mary and me for the sake of an adventure of our youthful travellers recorded by my brother in the poem on his own life'; and on the shores of Como, 'though often baffled, it was a constant amusement to attempt to trace that path which my brother had formerly paced, perhaps with

[1] *Descriptive Sketches*, 23–4 (*Oxf. W.*, p. 602).

more delight than any other; and Mary and I often wished we had been pursuing the track of his youthful steps'. One of her greatest experiences was by 'road and river' up the Simplon, past the spital where William had spent that awful night, so vividly described in *The Prelude*[1], to the path at the top of the pass which had misled him into thinking that he had yet higher to mount before he had crossed the Alps. 'William was waiting to show us the track, on the green precipice. It was impossible for me to say how much it had moved him, when he discovered it was the very same which had tempted him in his youth. The feelings of that time came back with the freshness of yesterday, accompanied with a dim vision of thirty years of life between. We traced the path together with our eyes.'

On ascending from Martigny, with the vale of Trientz below them, Dorothy had an experience hardly less precious to her:

> 'I being then alone looked suddenly down from the edge of the steep into a long level verdant and narrow dell, sprinkled with brown wood cottages. While standing upon the brow of the precipice above this shady deep recess, the very image of pastoral life, stillness and seclusion, William came up to me, and if my feelings had been moved before, how much more interesting did the spot become, when he told me it was the same dell, that "aboriginal vale", that "green recess",[2] so often mentioned by him,—the first of the kind that he had passed through in Switzerland. "And now", said he, "I find that my remembrance for thirty years has been scarcely less vivid than the reality now before my eyes!" '

Descending into this lovely valley they took refreshment at the Inn. 'We enter the house by going upstairs, the ground floor being allotted to cows and goats. All looked snug and cleanly, light and chearful—our fare excellent—good wine, butter, cheese, milk, bread and honey—all this for one franc each. Mary and I thought what a rare pleasure would it be to lodge here but for one night!' Two days later they returned, undeterred by the warning of a young priest whom they met upon the road, who told them that they would be very ill accommodated there:

> 'The Mistress of our little Inn welcomed us with surprize and pleasure. . . . Entering the house I was glad of the sight of a chear-

[1] *Prelude* (1805), vi. 573–80.

[2] Ib. 448.

ful fire that lighted up the good woman's kitchen. After supper we went to bed, having first looked round the hills. The new moon cast a gleam over the glacier at the top of the mountain—nowhere else, and itself not visible.

'The sheets were clean—the rooms clean—benches and tables white,—and, as I saw no appearance of want of cleanliness about my bed, I lay down chearfully on the sacking of straw, expecting to sleep. Mary's blankets did not altogether please her; and she was less hopeful; but alas! my state was soon no better than hers;—not because of the incessant tinkling from the bell of a goat, lodged with the cows beneath, and only divided from us by a floor of planks, but for other causes which I need not name:—so, after a few fruitless efforts we found it best to make an amusement out of our singular situation, listening to the streamlet and the jingling bell; and sometimes a rushing breeze. I thought of Loch Ketterine,[1] and that open window at my bed's head (such a one was close to me at Trientz) and rose in the middle of the night to look out upon the mountains. Another Traveller arrived after we were in bed—then followed the bustle of attending to him—all which could be distinctly heard;—and still later, the Master of the house returned from Martigny with provender. Our kind Hostess, I am sure, owes me no grudge though I thought of smugglers and banditti:—the scowling mountains and the deep valley must bear the blame:—it was but a transient fancy taken to amuse a long, but I must not say, *tedious* night, and chased away by images and thoughts of simple and quiet life.

'Rose at 5 o'clock. After a washing in the cold rivulet, hastened back to cower over the fire beside the traveller who came in last night. . . . I chatted by the fire with our hostess and her peasant guest (well contented if I could gather the sense of one half of what was said in their barbarous French—or make a question intelligible after various wordings) and at the same time took a basin of new milk with bread; for which, and our supper (wine, bread, cheese, eggs, milk, and coffee for Mary) we paid six francs. The woman would make no charge, seemed satisfied with what we gave her, and parted from us with friendly handshakings.

'We left the hut of Trientz musing on the strange connexions of events in human life; how improbable thirty years ago, that William should ever return thither! and *we* to be his companions! And to pass a night within the hollow of that "aboriginal Vale" was a thing that the most romantic of our fancies could not have helped us even to dream of!'

[1] *V.* chap. ix, p. 167.

William is, in truth, the pivot of her narrative. In one place she gives us a delightful picture of him lying, asleep in the sun, regardless of a little beggar who stood singing before him, 'the child continuing her song with all the collected might that a youthful voice could muster'; in another she shows him to us lit up with something of his youthful fire:

At Engleburg

> 'we breakfasted in view of the flashing, silver-topped Mount Titlis, and its grey crags,—a sight that rouzed W's youthful desires, and in spite of weak eyes and the weight of fifty winters, he could not repress a longing to ascend that mountain. He had much earnest conversation with the waiter, who had attended an English gentleman on that perilous adventure, and shewed us the snow pattens with which they were shod, described the scarification of their cheeks, and the blinding of their eyes by insufferable light (though they wore black veils), the excessive fatigue of the Englishman, and his resolution never to trust himself again to like perils. But my brother had his own visions of glory, and, had he been twenty years younger, sure I am that he would have trod the summit of the Titlis.'

With his vivid memories of the past and his inborn passion for wandering, William was a most invigorating travelling companion, at least when he could be kept from the fever of poetic composition, and when the business arrangements of the tour were not too harassing, and he was not 'tormented by the knavery of guides and muleteers' and their like. He had, perhaps, too violent a dislike of being cheated. 'At Alost', says Dorothy, 'unreasonable demands were made by the postilions, and William at the Inn door looked as fierce as Buonaparte. When he came bustling up to us after his conflict Mary and I said to each other "They will think that Buonaparte himself is come back again to threaten this poor town!"' But lacking as they did the limitless resources with which the English tourist was credited, they fully sympathized with his resistance of flagrant extortion, though on two occasions it led them into something of an adventure.

When the landlord at Herzogenbuchsee demanded an exorbitant price for lodgings, though they were obliged to engage a room for the frail Mrs. Monkhouse, her sister and maid, the rest of the party decided to pass the night in their *voitures*.

Monkhouse took tea at the inn with his wife, but, says Dorothy, '*we* would not enter the house either for food or rest'. Walking up the steep street they 'came to a cottage in perfect rural seclusion, and quiet, though not a hundred yards from the town. We seated ourselves on a bench under a shed at the door, and the good woman supplied us with nice milk, and ripe cherries in abundance, and fragrant flowers from her orchard garden. (We had bought bread.) After our simple meal we strolled near the Church, which overlooks the little town, and the sylvan country bounded by the mountains of Jura; and when twilight came on took our seats in the carriage, as close as beans in their velvet shell'. But the night that opened so auspiciously did not fulfil its promise.

'Then began the fleas; and, though sleepy, we had little hope of rest. At last, after long and patiently submitting to struggles with sleepiness, intense heat, and the restless fleas, William left us to refresh himself with water from the fountain, and prayed for admission into Mr M's carriage. Never were people more glad to get rid of their worst enemy than we were to part with him. We felt as if a bath of fresh air had come to us with space and liberty. We shook our garments, and sate down in quiet; but alas! soon again began the small tormentors, and we were pleased to while away the time by watching broad flashes of lightning in the distant horizon above the Jura boundary. At length we dropped asleep; but were soon rouzed by a fitful sound of gathering winds—heavy rain followed—and vivid flashes of lightning with tremendous thunder. It was very awful; Mary and I were sitting together—alone—in the open street;—a strange situation! yet we had no personal fear. Before the storm began, all the lights had been extinguished, except one, opposite to us, and another at an Inn behind, where were turbulent noises of merriment, with singing and haranguing in the style of our village politicians. These ceased; and *after* the storm, lights appeared in different quarters;—pell-mell rushed the fountain;—then came a watchman with his dismal recitative Song or Say—the church-clock telling the hours and the quarters—and house-clocks with their silvery tone. One scream we heard from a human voice; but no person seemed to notice *us*, except a man who came out upon the wooden Gallery of his house right above our heads, looked down this way and that, and especially toward the voitures. Mary and I fancied he had some humane feeling for us, thinking of the terrors of the storm; but William and Mr M. gave him credit for no such sympathies.

The beating of the rain, and the rushing of that fountain were continuous; and with the periodical, and the *irregular* sounds (among which the howling of a dog was not the least dismal) completed the wildness of the awful scene, and of our strange situation;—sheltered from wet, yet in the midst of it, and exposed to intermitting blasts, though struggling with excessive heat, while flashes of lightning at intervals displayed the distant mountains and the wide space between,—at other times a blank gloom. Once we were startled by a frightful scream from my brother. He had the night-mare—and no wonder, when sleep could overtake him in such a place and in such a storm! Before four o'clock the thunder had ceased; but not the rain. We laughed heartily on quitting this never-to-be-forgotten place, and vowed to proclaim our wrongs.'

The villain of their other comedy was the Swiss carman who drove them from Engelberg to Stansstad, and

'had the audacity to demand (instead of 18 francs) seven and twenty. Wm refused to give more than the sum agreed for. The man grew impertinent, and Wm desired the Magistrate might be summoned—a woeful resource! the Inn-keeper, who had sided with Wm's opponent, informed him that he himself was the magistrate. Wm paid the 18 francs—refused to give another sous—and the Man would not let us have our cloaks and coats, which (no doubt foreseeing resistance) he had cunningly locked up in a seat of the Char. We, now only anxious to get quietly away, would have prevailed with him to pay the money; but he was resolute. On parting he had asked the man formally, if he *persisted* in the detention, and left him with an assurance that, if justice were to be had in Switzerland he should feel the weight of it. The people (of whom forty or fifty might be gathered round) all sided with the Magistrate in supporting the unjust demand.'

The very next day they were joined at Lucerne by Crabb Robinson and 'our story of the great coats, with all its circumstances, was related. A lawyer ready at our need, and to boot, a master of the German language! It was settled that he should accompany Wm back to Sarnen at day-break'; and on the following evening

'before dinner was ended Wm and Mr R. arrived triumphant. They had obtained ample justice. Wm stated his case in French to the Magistrate at Sarnen—the landlord who had made the bargain and was separately examined, corroborated his statement: Mr R. pleaded in German; and the Magistrate who, Mr R.

declared, had been bribed by a breakfast and I guess plenty of talk, decreed that the man not having returned to his home should be sought after, the coats conveyed with all speed to any part of Switzerland that my brother should appoint, at the expense of the delinquent, and that he should be punished by imprisonment. No witness but the landlord was wanted—no confronting with the accused. Thus summary was this decision of justice in Switzerland.

'Mary and I had retired to our bedroom when our Landlord without ceremony presented himself before us, hung round with coats and cloaks. We hastened down to congratulate the conquerors and give them due praise for the spirit which had carried them through the business, honestly confessing that we, by being willing to submit to imposition, rather than run the risk of losing our coats, should have betrayed our own countrymen, and not done our duty to the Swiss. Wm received afterwards the thanks of the Landmann of Sarnen for the trouble he had taken; and to conclude all, we were informed that our dishonest carman was actually lodged for one month in prison.'

But incidents of this kind were rare, and though they had sometimes to submit to petty overcharges, and to the annoyance of importunate beggars, their intercourse with the natives seldom brought them anything but pleasure. To Dorothy the human pageant which passed before her eyes gave delight as intense as its natural background. As they moved from one place to another she never tired of noting the ever varying peculiarities of dress, fashion, and personal appearance. She was an excellent discerner of persons, and had not lost her happy gift for setting down her impressions. Life at the inns, if not always comfortable, gave plenty of scope to her talent: there was the jolly landlord at Mayence who reminded her of Chaucer's Host of the Tabard, 'with his comfortable visage, eyeing the table before he served the victuals', and arguing so hotly with his guests, that she fully expected a serious quarrel, though all ended in perfect good humour; there was the landlady at Hornberg—'she was fat, merry and Dutch-built; and when she laughed (which she did almost constantly at her own jokes or those of her German guests, with a roguish twinkling of the eye) the thick warm covering of her cheeks, throat, body and arms shook in a manner which was perfectly ludicrous': and the officious inn-keeper who 'with an *excusez* came every two or three minutes to snuff our candles, and ask or inform himself by a glance, if we wanted anything'; and the hostess of 'the pothouse struggling to be an hotel', who 'vain of her cookery, . . . promised a *joli souper* and provided them with meagre fare', and when they disputed her outrageous bill 'regulated the measure of her impertinence by that of her previous servility'. Nor did Dorothy's fellow-guests escape her vigilant eye. At the *table d'hôte* at Baden-Baden she 'was occupied in observing the deliberate composure with which a fat old gentleman and his wife passed from dish to dish, as if appetite grew with what it fed on. Yet the grave how near! and this the highroad to it!'; and at Brientz she noted the 'young lady who in a very loud voice uttered a hundred *vague* exclamations of rapture, telling what she had seen: yet she looked like a clever woman. The mother wore a light coloured wig, was very fair and withered: she must formerly have been handsome, and seemed unwilling to think she had parted from her youth'.

The humbler folk stirred in her a deeper interest, and often drew from her pen pictures of a haunting beauty:

> 'A squalid ragged woman sate alone upon some steps by the entrance of the choir at Calais Cathedral—there she sate with a white dog beside her; no one was near, and the dog and she evidently belonged to each other, probably her only friend, for never was there a more wretchedly forlorn and miserable-looking human being. She did not notice us, but her rags, and her melancholy and sickly aspect drew a penny from me; and the change in the woman's skinny, doleful face is not to be imagined; it was brightened by a light and gracious smile;—the effect was almost as of something supernatural; she bowed her body, waved her hand, and, with a politeness of gesture unknown in England in almost any station in life, beckoned that we might enter the church.'

Equally vivid and as delicate in its portraiture is her picture of the little girl she met on her ascent from Grindelwald:

> 'in a shady and deep part of the lane, a fairy being appeared before us, a child not more than four years old with outstretched arms, reaching almost from one bank of the lane to the other, while in each hand she held a showy nosegay. The little creature had been sent out from a cottage, then unseen by us, in the adjoining field. She walked before us, after giving one of her posies to each, a work performed with a shy struggle (perhaps it was her first effort in barter or begging); she was pleased with our notice,

but ventured not to speak a word. We had not a sous to give her. What was to be done? We were not then so hardened as to leave the child without something to make her glad, so, at last Mary recollected an old needle-book in her pocket. We watched till she had reached the garden fence (whence the mother's eye was upon her) and saw the child make display of her treasure.'

From their ascent of the St. Gothard—'the most delightful day of travelling that Mary and I had ever spent, for we were *crossing* the Alps and in our way to Italy!'—she bore away as vivid a memory of the human beings she encountered, as of their majestic setting: the Swiss peasant, 'stiff-set, rosy-faced, short-bodied', who carried the baggage,

'a load for a horse! and yet was kind enough to wish to rid us of any little encumbrances, basket or umbrella, that we carried ourselves . . . he was sweating under his burthen with face all on fire, and while he halted on a bridge looking down on the raging stream, said to me with a sociable smile "Das Wasser macht es so kühl," '

words, she says, which will come back to her beside her own streams on many a hot summer's day, and bring with them an ineffaceable memory : the

'poor idiot by a way-side image, who with smiles and uncouth gestures placed himself under the virgin and child pleading so earnestly that there was no resisting him. Soon after, when I was lingering behind upon a stone, beside a little streamlet of clear water a procession of mules approached, laden with wine-casks, forty at least—which I had long seen winding like a creeping serpent along the side of the bare hill before me, and heard the stream of sound from their bells. Two neatly dressed Italian women, who headed the cavalcade, spoke to me in their own sweet language, and one of them had the kindness to turn back to bring me a glove, which I had left on the stone where I had been sitting. I cannot forget her pretty romantic appearance—a perfect contrast to that of the poor inhabitants of her own sex in this district, no less than her soft speech! She was rather tall, and slender, and wore a small straw hat tied with coloured riband, different in shape from those worn in Switzerland. It was the first company of muleteers we had seen.'

The landscape was seldom complete for her unless some human figure was in the foreground. Thus she records how on the steep descent into Brennen a maiden overtook her 'with staff in hand, wooden slippers upon her unstockinged feet, and tub of milk in her hand. Fleet of foot, she tripped down the stony path, which *we* could only hobble over, with eyes intent on the ground'. Pictures such as this bring back the thrill of mountain travel far more vividly than pages of ecstasy expended on the view.

But Dorothy was not content only to satisfy her aesthetic sense. She was eager to learn what she could of the habits and characters of those she met, and get into personal touch with them. She spoke French imperfectly, and German still worse, and the jargon of the peasants often baffled her; but she never gave up the struggle. Mary was lost in admiration of the way in which her sister 'dashed at her German'. 'Dorothy', she says, 'is an adept at making her way, for she never hesitates—off into the kitchen, talks to everybody there, and in the villages, on the roads, makes friends and gains information, and jabbers German everywhere. She astonishes us all.' When the Monkhouses wished to visit Baden-Baden, a place that made no appeal to William, the party divided for two days, and Dorothy went with them to act as their interpreter. The next morning, as Mrs. Monkhouse and her sister were too tired to travel, Dorothy ('the best of human beings, always ready to assist others' is Mary's comment) stayed behind with them. They rejoined at Shaffhausen. 'D. in high spirits—had managed so well, given greater satisfaction than any gentleman, and had delighted all parties she came in contact with, and been delighted herself.'

But though Dorothy was glad to be of service to the Monkhouses, the greatest joy that she owed to her gift for language was that it enabled her to talk with the country folk, as she did in her own Westmorland dales. 'Above all', she says, 'we should have liked to have gone into the cottages, made acquaintance with their inhabitants, and brought away some notices of their way of life.' She made the most of every chance she had. While poor Mary, ignorant of any language but her own, could only express her human sympathies by gathering in her arms any babies that toddled across her path—'With these', she said, 'I can converse without difficulty; they speak a common language, the language of all times and all peoples'—her sister conversed freely with men and women. 'Dorothy', says Mary, 'must speak of persons, *I* can make nothing of them.' As she wandered on from place to place, she felt that

if we meet a face
We almost meet a friend.

'Before we came in view of the vale of Grindelwald I (on foot at a distance from my comrades) met several peasant travellers bringing on their backs burthens from the valley. They addressed me with kindly smiles; and often I thought I could have no fears, except from the tremendous powers of nature, if wandering alone among these simple people.' On entering Italy Crabb Robinson warned her that it would not now be safe to walk unaccompanied; and at Airolo some mischievous boys threw stones at her from behind a wall, but she records this as 'the only wanton act of ill-manners towards us during the whole tour. Often', she says, 'as Mary and I have been alone in the roads we never met with the most trifling rudeness—no wonder that we were forgetful of robbers and banditti!'

She spoke to all she met in lonely places, and often before they parted she had drawn from them some details of their simple history, which she treasured alike as an enrichment of her experience and a token of their friendliness. It was her beautiful conviction that 'we meet no one with a stranger's heart'. The following extracts from her *Journal*, in which an exquisite sense of landscape is blended with human sympathies, are characteristic of the spirit in which she pursued her travels:

'Sept 13. *Baths of Leuk*. A delightful walk in fresh morning air down the valley to the village of Inden. I entered one of the cottages to inquire the road to Siders,[1] four leagues distant, in the Valais. The cottage was warm and snug,—a pleasanter winter than summer residence, and much more used in that season, the summer life of the Swiss, both male and female, being chiefly spent out of doors. A young woman happened to be going to Faxen, a league further, on the road to Siders, and we set out together. Leaving the road to Leuk on our left, she led us through fields and shady lanes, looking into the green cleft of the glen, where the Dala pursued its noisy course, *unseen* owing to the great depth below us, and to the irregular scattering of knoll and pastoral glade on the side of the hill where we were. While our attendant was walking by our side, she uttered a startling shout, a protracted hooting peculiar to the Alps,—something between a song and a cry—a morning salutation to her mother, who, she told me, lived in the cottage below, pointing to a roof half hidden by the trees.

[1] *Siders*, better known as Sierre.

The girl, two or three times afterwards, sent forth a like awakening shout, for the ear of some friend or companion whom we could not see. She was a chearful good-natured creature, offered to carry our bags for us, socially stopping wherever we stopped . . . when she could point out the village of Faxen whither she was bound, she made an apology for leaving us. We gave her a few sous, no adequate compensation for her services, but enough to please her. There was so much of chearful simplicity in the manners of this girl, that, in spite of sage admonitions from the Poet and the Lawyer, I could not part with what they called a *delusion*, the pleasant thought that her sociable kindness had proceeded from pure good-will.

'Sept. 28. Joigny. Hereabouts, our journey was enlivened by the business of the vineyards—not yet the chearful gathering-in of ripe fruit—but solitary females—or sometimes a straggling company engaged in propping, or otherwise tending, the laden branches. Cottages sprinkled on the distant slopes. I walked forwards always, while the carriage stopped to change horses, amused, and fearless of missing my way, for there is but one broad road. Sometimes I found the comfort of a track over a surface of turf, beneath a quivering more of sun than of shadow from the slender branches of elm-trees planted by the road-side. Among hundreds of acres covered with vines bearing ripe fruit, I gathered a few branches to slake my thirst, having been unable to purchase any in the village we had just left; and was sharply reproved by a peasant who happened to see me. This I *believe*:—that the French never pluck grapes unbidden, except from their own vineyards. Soon after the reprimand, seeing a party at work among some other vines, I asked them to sell me a few grapes; and they replied that they were working for another, and must not pluck the fruit; but the Mother of the Family, hastening to her dinner-basket, chearfully presented me with her whole stock, brought from their own garden. . . .

'*Joigny*, rather a large town, presents itself sweetly to view on the low banks of the *Yonne*, here a wide stream, bright as silver, inlaying the green meadows or bordered with thin willows and poplars. Crossed a stone bridge of many arches, beyond which lies the main portion of the town. A train of asses on the bridge—their long ears, noses, and feet just discernible under a lading of fresh heather as round as a bird's nest. Leaving my companions at the post-house, I turned back immediately, recrossing the bridge to rejoin the road, which led on between the river and the row of pleasant houses fronting it. Fell into company with an old woman taking an afternoon walk to her vineyard in the country. Her face, unshaded from the sun, was as yellow as a withered leaf, and puckered with wrinkles, her countenance keen and chearful, but when I spoke of Buonaparte and the Revolution it flashed with bitter rage. There was no fighting at Joigny; but every other species of revolution and terror. No one had been in a condition to depend on his own means, but each had aided the other. They lived by their Friends, and those Friends never in security. She told me stories of escapes and concealments in which she had been concerned, saying that she hoped, after all, to end her days quietly at last. I wished I could have spent an hour with this entertaining old woman, in her little vineyard, which she pointed out to me, under the low hills, saying how glad she should have been to entertain me there with the best of her grapes.'

They entered Paris in pouring rain, and Dorothy's first impressions were dreary enough. 'Travelled over rough pavement, black, slippery and plashy—through narrow streets between high grey houses, hung with gaudy symbols—golden balls, painted images, red giant hands (the sign that gloves are sold within) legs of the same hue and fifty other quaint things—but nothing else to be seen that had a touch of gaiety: the only business of the women to ward off splashes from their white stockings: which they did with surprizing address, yet I saw the colour of several pairs of garters.' The Monkhouses took rooms in a fashionable hotel. 'We drove to the Hotel de Toulouse—Rue des bons enfans, a narrow street, near the Palais Royal, indeed all the streets of Paris that we had seen were crooked and ugly, and appeared thoroughly comfortless in the heavy rain. Two tight, smart young ladies, in black aprons and purple silk gowns received us—the same whom, the next morning, we would not have recognised had they been ten yards from the spot, being so transformed by slovenly morning dresses, and hair stuck round with papers. Rain abated—sought out a restorateur in the Palais Royal close at hand. Dined for 3 francs in a small upstairs room—resolved to have no more potatoes "au naturel".'

The next morning the sun shone; and, indeed, for their whole month in Paris they were favoured by the weather. After breakfast, they moved into rooms in the Rue Charlot—'a very pleasant lodging,' says Dorothy, 'the only inconvenience is its distance from the Louvre, but I am so strong that to me it is nothing.'

Here Eustace Baudouin was awaiting them, and took her and William off to see Caroline and little Dorothée. During their stay they spent a good deal of their time with Annette and the Baudouins, but Dorothy's only comment upon them is the tantalizing remark, in a letter to Mrs. Clarkson, 'we have had great satisfaction in seeing our friends whom I have mentioned to you. Of this when we meet.' They paid several visits to Miss Williams, an amiable minor poetess, who presented the ladies with several copies of her 'tender and beautiful verses'; Moore called upon them, and William dined with Canning. They saw all the sights of Paris and went six times to the Louvre. 'The pictures of Raphael, Titian and Poussin rivet me—I cannot like Rubens' fleshy women—his children very sweet' is Mary's entry in her journal. Dorothy's account of her experiences in Paris is of the briefest; she will not, she says, 'attempt describing things lately so well described in books that are in everybody's hands'. Of the journey home she has more to tell, for it provided the most exciting incident in their whole tour. After one night at a comfortless hotel at Boulogne they went to their friend Miss Barker, who was now residing there for her health. 'The sight of old friends made her cast off all discomfort; and we felt as if we were already seated by an English fireside—with Borrowdale Agnes to wait upon us, a little frenchified in exterior, it is true, but retaining her good Cumberland speech.' They intended to stay two days in Boulogne, but were forced to stay ten. On the Tuesday, wrote Mary, 'a boat sailed, but there was no room for us. On Wednesday we stood an hour on the beach with our luggage in heavy rain, but no vessel could get out. On Thursday' —but here let Dorothy take up the tale:

> 'the weather being boisterous, and wind contrary, the Packet could not sail, and we trusted ourselves to a small vessel, with only one effective sailor on board. Even *Mary* was daunted by the breakers outside the harbour, and I descended into the vessel as unwillingly as a criminal might go to execution, and hid myself in bed. Presently our little ship moved, and before ten minutes were gone, she struck upon the sands. I felt that something disastrous had happened; but knew not what, till poor Mary appeared in the cabin, having been thrown down to the top of the steps. There was again a frightful beating and grating at the bottom of the vessel—water rushing in very fast. A young man, an Italian. who had

risen from a bed beside mine, as pale as ashes, groaned in agony, kneeling at his prayers. My condition was not much better than his, but I was more quiet. Never shall I forget the kindness of a little Irish woman, who, though she herself, as she afterwards said, was much frightened, assured me, even chearfully, that there was no danger. I cannot say that her words, as assurance of safety, had much effect upon me, but the example of her courage made me become more collected, and I felt her human-kindness, even at the moment when I believed that we might all be going to the bottom of the sea together; and the agonizing thoughts of the distress at home were rushing in my mind. My brother, thinking it would be impossible to save his wife and me, had stripped off his coat to be ready to swim; but what was our joy and thankfulness when he came into the cabin to tell us that the retreating tide would soon leave the ship bare; and all was safe. No more water came in, and in the course of half an hour, carts were seen on the shore in preparation to come and take us away. A little more time and we were summoned on deck, and very soon the Irishwoman and we were seated with our luggage. How pleasant was the jolting, and the noise of the cart-wheels over the rocky bed of the sea, now dry! Thus we drove rapidly through the streets of Boulogne. Our appearance must have been somewhat extraordinary; for an Englishman (no doubt supposing us fresh from our own country) greeted us in passing with "Well, Ladies, how do you like the French carriages?" and we replied "they are right welcome to us, for we have been shipwrecked!" '

On the next Friday, Mary tells us, 'two packets sailed, but they were engaged by private individuals, and we could not be admitted into the Cabin; and D. suffers so much we could not engage to go upon deck. Yesterday, the wind was fair but no vessel, and to-day here are vessels, fine weather and fair wind, but not a sufficient number of passengers. We should be off to Calais, but the Captain assures William that he will sail to-morrow. I pray that he may, for I am painfully anxious to be home'.

On the Wednesday, eight days after they had made their first effort to get across the Channel, the journey was comfortably effected in seven hours. So hard it was, in the year 1820, to get across the Channel from Boulogne. They left Dover the next morning. 'The day was pleasant and every English sight delightful—the fields sprinkled with cattle—the small snug cottages, the pretty country houses. Many a time we said to each other "what a pleasant country this must appear to the eyes of a Frenchman!" . . . It was to all of us an interesting moment, when we found ourselves crossing Westminster Bridge, the point whence our sixteen weeks' pleasant rambling had begun.'

XVIII

THE QUILLINANS. SECOND TOUR IN SCOTLAND. LONDON. DEATH OF TOM MONKHOUSE. VISITS OF SCOTT AND OF MARIA JANE JEWSBURY

1820–1825 (aet. 48–53)

THE first night in London was passed at a dreary hotel near Charing Cross; then they moved into lodgings in New Oxford Street, just vacated by Kenyon, and enjoyed a busy fortnight among their friends. They saw Johnson of the Central school, Crabb Robinson, Rogers, Sharp, Kenyon, and Haydon, they paid a visit to the Lloyds at Kensington and to the Hoares at Hampstead, and from Hampstead walked across to Highgate to pay a call on Coleridge. Tom Monkhouse, now settled in Gloucester Place, gave one of his famous dinners in their honour, and so princely was his hospitality that before the party broke up Wordsworth, Crabb Robinson, and Monkhouse himself had all fallen asleep, and Lamb talked as though he were.[1] Dorothy had looked forward to the society of the Lambs as 'one of our strongest inducements to linger in London',[2] and five evenings were spent in their company; on one of them Talfourd, a devout admirer of William, took them all to the theatre to see Lamb's favourite actor, Munden. And on Sundays and half-holidays Willy was released from the Charterhouse.

On November 23 they took coach for Cambridge. While they were abroad their brother Christopher had left Lambeth to become Master of Trinity and Vice-Chancellor of the University, and they were naturally anxious to see him while he wore his honours in their newest gloss. They saw him confer degrees in the Senate House and heard the address to the King. A week later Dorothy set off for Playford, an old moated house four miles out of Ipswich, into which the Clarksons had moved some years before; she returned to Cambridge early in January to look after her young nephews; for Willy had joined his cousins John and Christopher for the holidays, and their father was so much occupied with his new duties that he had little time to

[1] H. C. R., *Diary*, ed. Sadler (1872), i. 365.
[2] D. W. to C. C., Oct. 14, 1820.

bestow upon any one younger than an undergraduate. Dorothy, always happy with children, was delighted with their company, though she suffered from her usual anxieties for Willy's moral and physical welfare. His reckless extravagance alarmed her; he had actually spent three and sixpence of his scanty pocket-money on a tiepin; and when he broke it, one of the undergraduates horrified her by buying him another for ten shillings, which she felt it her duty to confiscate; on his leaving for Charterhouse with a slight headache, no unusual conclusion to a Christmas holiday, she wrote off an agitated letter to Tom Monkhouse, urging him to send her minute particulars of Willy's health, to which Tom replied in the proper spirit of good-humoured banter.[1] On the boy's departure she was torn between longings for home and the wish to return to Playford: if only she could be in two places at once! It was nearly a year since she had left Rydal, and yet travelling was so expensive that it seemed a pity, while she was in the South, not to see a little more of her dear Mrs. Clarkson. But at last she decided for home, and after a short stay with the Cooksons at Kendal, whence she paid a visit to Johnny, now at school at Sedbergh, she was back at Rydal early in February.

The day of her arrival Dora came back from school at Ambleside to welcome her; and she was struck at once by the change that ten months had effected. 'She is indeed a sweet girl. I never saw a greater improvement in the time', she informed Mrs. Clarkson.[2] 'She is grown thoughtful, steady and womanly, but is much more lively than she has been used to be since her first going to school. She is *as* lively as when she was ten years old, and has nothing left of her boisterousness or want of gracefulness either in manner or deportment. . . . What a delight do I feel in seeing that dear girl!' She realized that Dora was no longer a child, and an intimacy of a new kind sprang up between them, which was to count among the most precious things in the lives of both.

William was impatient that she should get to work at once upon her Continental Journal, but, naturally enough, it took her some weeks to settle down, 'so much have I to look at, so many old neighbours to see'; and, as William admitted, 'talking is much more easy, and to one party at least, a more pleasant

[1] D. W. to C. C., Jan. 1821. [2] D. W. to C. C., Feb. 15, 1821.

thing than writing'.[1] To her and Mary it seemed a far more serious matter that William, instead of going on with *The Recluse*, gave all his poetic energies to writing sonnets on the Church of England. 'This disturbs us', she wrote.[2] 'After fifty years of age there is no time to spare, and unfinished works should not, if it be possible, be left behind. This he feels, but the will never governs *his* labours. How different from Southey, who can go as regularly as clockwork, from history to poetry, from poetry to criticism, and so on to biography, or anything else. If their minds could each spare a little to the other, how much better for both!'

During the summer both Kenyon and Crabb Robinson were among their visitors, but the chief event of the year was the addition to their intimate circle of Edward Quillinan.

Quillinan was a lieutenant in the 3rd Dragoon Guards, then quartered in Edinburgh, but his tastes and ambitions were literary rather than military. He had long been an admirer of Wordsworth's poetry; and, eager to make his acquaintance, he was taking a holiday at Penrith in the April of this year: a little later he confided to his notebooks a vivid account of their first meeting:

> 'Mr Gillies of Edinburgh had given me a letter of introduction. . . . It was unsealed, for my inspection; and I found it so flattering to me that I was unwilling to present it, though most anxious for the acquaintance of so admirable a genius. I rode over twice from Penrith and back again (50 miles over Kirkstone, that is 25 and back) yet when I approached his dwelling I lost heart; at last I went over a third time, and having made up my mind to quit the army, and settle in this delightful country, I screwed up my courage to the mark, and walked up the steep hill, and passed his gate; rang his door bell, resolved to introduce myself. It so happened that Mr Marshall of Ulswater had heard me say at his house that I had a letter for Mr W., and he had reported to him this fact. Several weeks elapsing without the delivery of the letter, Mr W., little aware of the cause of the detention, was prepared to be offended at my supposed neglect. I was ushered into the library at Rydal. He received me very stiffly, but asked me for the letter. I told him, and it was true, that I had not brought it with me. He seemed quite angry, twirled a chair about, and made short and stiff remarks. I was getting indignant and thought him most

[1] W. W. to Kenyon, Feb. 5, 1821. [2] D. W. to C. C., Mar. 27, 1821.

disagreeable. Presently the door opened, and a young lady about 17, of good figure, not perhaps handsome, but of most engaging innocence and ingenuousness of aspect, stood at the door, seemed surprised at seeing a stranger, and half drew back. Then it was that I saw the Poet's countenance to advantage. All the father's heart was thrown into his eyes and his voice as he encouraged her to come in. She did so, but only staid a few moments. It was a most timely interruption. I have loved that sweet girl ever since. Soon, however, the fine patriarchal expression vanished, and the poet resumed his frigidity and his twirl of the chair. I was about to retire, much disappointed, when in came Miss Hutchinson, who saw at once that there was some awkwardness between us; she relieved me in a moment with that fine tact and benign politeness thoroughly understood only by women. She civilly accosted me, rallied the poet for twirling the chair, took it from him and appropriated it to her own use; made herself mistress of the cause of our restraint, laughed him into a good humour, and sent him out to show me the garden and the terrace. We rambled together for hours; talked of poetry, he taking the lion's share of the conversation to which he was entitled, and Io Triumphe! I returned with him to dinner. That day was the precursor of many and many a happy one under the same roof.'[1]

Quillinan lost no time in following up his success. In a week or two he was settled at Spring Cottage[2] on the banks of the Rotha, only half a mile from Rydal Mount, with his wife and child, his two horses, and his pet spaniel. De Quincey, now living at Fox Ghyll, was his nearest neighbour, and lent him his coach-house and stables; 'I saw little of him,' he says, 'for he remained in bed all day, and only took the air at night, and then was more shy than an owl.'[1] But Quillinan was always welcome at Rydal Mount, and as his horses needed exercise, he had many pleasant excursions with the Wordsworths about the country; with the whole family, indeed, he was soon a great favourite, whilst Dora and Mrs. Quillinan became bosom friends; so that in September, when little Rotha Quillinan was born, Dora was her godmother, and the poet accepted her as his 'spiritual child'.[3]

The friendship thus pleasantly established was still further cemented by the troubles that soon fell upon poor Quillinan. After Rotha's birth his wife's mind became temporarily de-

[1] Quillinan MSS.
[2] Now known as *The Stepping Stones*.
[3] Cf. Sonnet: *Oxf. W.*, p. 274.

ranged; Mary and Dorothy helped to nurse her until she could be removed to Lancaster for special treatment, and in her absence they looked after the children; whilst the poet took off their distracted father for a walking tour in Yorkshire.

By the following April the invalid was restored to health; the Quillinans moved into Ivy Cottage,[1] at the foot of Rydal Mount; and as Tom Monkhouse had also brought his wife and child into the neighbourhood Dorothy looked forward to a cheerful summer. But a few weeks later poor Mrs. Quillinan was the victim of a ghastly accident: her clothes caught fire, and before the flames could be extinguished she was frightfully burned. For some days she hovered between life and death; then she seemed to take a turn for the better; and her husband, summoned to London on urgent business, left her under the care of two nurses, with either Mary or Dorothy in constant attendance. One evening, when Dorothy was on duty, a messenger reached Rydal with the news that her beloved brother had been thrown off his horse at Bampton, near Haweswater. She only heard of it the next morning: 'you may judge', she wrote to Jane,[2] 'of my terror and distress, when I tell you that this intelligence was communicated to me in the most alarming way possible. My wretchedness and anxiety were extreme till 4 o'clock, when I heard from my sister that all was likely to go on well. But the accident might have been terrible indeed! Had the horse been an inch nearer to the wall death would have been inevitable.' On the evening after the accident she wrote to Quillinan;[3] adding to her loving details of his wife's condition the further tale of the anguish she had undergone:

My dear Friend,

I sit by your dear Wife's bedside. She *was* to dictate for me; but I must put it into my own words—"Tell him, she says, I am doing as well as can possibly be expected—" I stop again—and ask her a question. "Have you no message to send?" "Oh yes, about the children. Say they are both uncommonly well—" That is the truth—they give their Mother as little disturbance, and as much comfort as possible. Sunday night was a good one—Monday morning no worse; but in the afternoon there was an accession of fever—and we had a *bad* night—Last night was very good. Today

[1] The property of Tillbrook: now known as *Glen Rothay.*

[2] D. W. to J. M., June 13, 1822.

[3] The letter is undated, but it must have been written late in May.

she has been perfectly composed—and now(at 7 o'clock) is cool and without fever. So far very good. I feel little or no doubt of our now going on with the most perfect regularity. But having told you how we stand at present I must revert to the past. Monday night was indeed a very bad one—not that I was alarmed; but the fever ran so high that I thought it right to send for Mr Carr, which we did at 12 o'clock. He stayed with us till past 3, the fever then almost gone . . . it really now seems that we have nothing to do but to strengthen her to enable her to bear the pain which is yet for her to endure. The Sores give her less pain, and are going on perfectly as they ought to do. . . . A trifling accident befel my brother on his way to Haweswater,—God be praised it was but a trifling one though it might have been very bad. He had got from the back of your pony to go into a Cottage, when within two miles of Bampton, where they intended to halt for the night. In mounting again—fumbling between his portmanteau and umbrella—the horse was frightened and threw him against a stone wall—and the back of his head was cut. Of these particulars I knew nothing this morning—only that he had had a fall—and being at the house of Dr Satterthwaite wanted female attendance,—therefore Mr Monkhouse wrote to desire my sister to set off immediately. The Messenger arrived at a little after 11 o'clock . . . the letter said nothing of the nature of the wound—nothing but that it was in the head—that the Dr had dressed it—and that my dear Brother was very composed. My Sister durst not send down to me for fear of our poor sick Friend's alarm. D. and she set off—and this morning—Miss Horrocks sent for me—attempted to break the force of the tidings by preparations—more frightful than the letter itself—and from the latter I could gather no hope but what was chased away by a frightful fear—all day I lay on a bed at Mrs Monkhouses—and till past 4 o'clock—when the happy news arrived—two letters—one from D.—one from her Mother. Nothing in this world ever made me so happy as D.'s letter. Before she finished she spoke of being at *home* at Lowther, and delighted with Dr Satterthwaite's kindness and hospitality! She said her Father was in good spirits—had no fever and even *wished* to come home in the Chaise; but quiet was necessary.

'I shall urge him to stay till he is quite well. I will not attempt to describe my own wretched state—all this day—my only comfort that I could *rest* upon was the thought that D. was gone with her Mother. Monkhouse and Mr Carr explained away my long absence (which grieved your wife) by saying that I was unwell with the heat—and my sister's by saying that she had been called from home by the sickness of a Friend. My first business, as it was my first duty, when sufficiently composed after the inrush of thankfulness and joy—was to come to see your Wife—who received me joyfully but was anxious for an explanation. I gave it chearfully. She saw that I was happy in my own feelings—and is now as chearful as I am; and was never thrown into agitation. Rotha has just been giving her Mother the evening kiss—before undressing. God bless you, my dear Friend! and bring you safe back again to the Ivy Cottage—we shall be anxious to hear from you. I will write duly—and I trust you will find a great change for the better at your return.

yours truly
DOROTHY WORDSWORTH.

You will not wonder at my penmanship—nor even if my letter is not perfectly coherent. The past is like a horrible dream to me.

But before the return of William and Mary, and while her husband was still in London, Mrs. Quillinan had a sudden relapse. 'It was my lot', Dorothy wrote to Jane,[1] 'to attend her death-bed. . . . It was well that Mary was spared the last awful scene. You will be glad to hear that I, though as you may suppose, much harassed and exhausted when all was over, soon recovered myself, and it was a great satisfaction to me to find how well I have been able to go through the trial, and I pray that I may never, in sickness and sorrow, forget her example of patience and sweetness of disposition under her sufferings.' 'We have', she adds, 'every kind of arrangement to make in this melancholy house.'

During the summer she had little rest. Immersed as she was in Quillinan's affairs, she had no leisure to enjoy a short visit from the Clarksons, to which she had long been looking forward; and only a few days after the Clarksons had left Rydal Willy returned from school dangerously ill. Nor were her labours for Quillinan at an end when he took off his children to their grandfather's home at Lee Priory, Kent. For he left her to settle up his outstanding bills, and to sub-let and manage all the business of Ivy Cottage, which he held on a three years' lease. A letter written on August 6, enclosing a discursive financial statement, gives him the family news of the summer:

[1] D. W. to J. M., June 13, 1822.

My dear Friend,

Truly glad shall I be when we have no more to say to each other respecting money, the most tiresome subject to me in the world, and it has so dried up my brain that I hardly know how to take to any thing better. First let me give you the best news I have, that dear little William's danger has been passed for three weeks; and that he is now in health, strength, spirits—and *shape* nearly as well as we could desire. You may conceive what an anxious time we had after his arrival at home—with death on his countenance—a dry fever on his emaciated body. . . . His dear mother's health has not suffered so much as one might have expected from her constant anxiety and attendance on him; yet I cannot say that she is well. As to my Brother—though *his* anxiety has been much greater than upon any other occasion during the four and twenty years that I have lived with him—his health is not to be complained of—and he is now in excellent spirits, though the inflammation never wholly leaves his eyes[1]—and the slightest exposure to over-heat or cold increases it—so that he is obliged to be constantly on the watch. Dora is neither well nor ill—that is—she complains of nothing; but looks wretchedly, and, when not excited by pleasure, is apt to be dull in spirits, and sluggish in motion—Poor thing! Many a time have I seen her turn away to hide her gushing tears at the mention of your dear Wife's name—or when circumstances have brought her to her recollection at some particular time and place; but she can talk of her not only with composure but pleasure. This brings me back to the time of your departure; and you have scarcely heard of or from us since then. When the Clarksons had stayed their fortnight D and I went into Borrowdale, where we had fine weather—went to Buttermere, Wasdale, and all over the vale of Keswick, so that in spite of herself, D was cheared, returned with amended health and looks, and full of hope,—for her brothers were to come home in three days. You know what followed. For three weeks we had little hope of William's life; and before he was decidedly convalescent two Aunts came from Wales. The one is returned thither—the other remains and will be our visitor in Winter—a chearful old lady 78 years of age, who plays at whist with Willy. In addition to this company we have had a succession of others. Col. Lowther was here last week. . . . Mrs Ellwood is here and Miss Joanna Hutchinson,—so that you see my Brother's number of ladies has increased and is not likely soon to be much diminished. Dr Wordsworth and his Boys are delighted with the Ivy Cottage. The quiet spot

[1] *V.* note, p. 185.

often makes him think of you and yours (though unknown to him) and of what a loss you have had. I think he will stay till the 2nd week of September . . . and in the meantime we expect Mr Jones (*Robert Jones*, the companion of his pedestrian Tour in Switzerland two and thirty years ago) to spend three weeks under our Roof. Thus, you see, the summer—past and to come—is wholly filled up, and I trust I have sufficiently explained to you why you have not heard from us sooner or oftener. When we have been at rest from anxiety our time has been wholly filled up—indeed I can scarcely recollect a period in my life in which I have had so little leisure. . . . Our new rector, Sir Richard le Fleming[1] has had the living for some weeks, and is settled in the Parsonage House. He has given us 3 excellent sermons and two very bad ones—we fear the good are exhausted. . . . We have heard nothing amiss in his conduct hitherto; but reports of the past are so very bad that we cannot but expect some outbreak, in which case I think Mr Barber will represent to the Bishop. . . . John Wordsworth is not to go to College *this* year. He will return to Sedbergh after the holidays. There is to be a Regatta at Low Wood next Thursday and John is to be one of a company of ten (Mountaineers) who are to row against a company of Cantabs now lodging at Ambleside, who have challenged the mountaineers. If *strength* will gain the Victory I think it will be on our side. . . . We long for a letter from you, and shall rejoice in your safe return to England. Tell us what you can about your travels—about your friends in Geneva—and above all tell us, if you write again before your return to Lee Priory, what you have heard concerning the children—and when you have seen them yourself you cannot tell us too much of their ways and their doings. Do excuse this poor scrawl—I have not said half of what I felt I had to say and I am sure you will want to know a hundred things which I have omitted—but you must be thankful and contented that we are all well—we shall never forget you. May God bless you—my dear Friend Ever yours

DOROTHY WORDSWORTH.

In later letters to Quillinan she never forgets to make loving inquiries after his children, or to give some news of interesting neighbours—as, for example, of De Quincey 'shut up as usual—the house always blinded—or left with but one eye to peep out of—he probably in bed',[2] or of Hartley Coleridge, now teaching

[1] Sir Richard le Fleming, Bart., was rector of Grasmere 1822–37, and also of Bowness-on-Windermere. He inherited the baronetcy on the death of his brother, Sir Michael, in 1821. Like his brother he had a very bad reputation in the district.

[2] D. W. to E. Q., Nov. 19, 1822.

at Mr. Dawes's School at Ambleside, and 'very steady: he is the oddest looking creature you ever saw—not taller than Mr. De Quincey—with a beard as black as a raven. He is exactly like a Portugueze Jew'.[1] And there is a later reference to Hartley in the garden at Rydal Mount 'writing a pretty sonnet, and many a run has he had up and down the Terrace while he was composing it—a run such as he used to take at "six years old" '.[2]

After so harassing a summer Dorothy had earned a holiday, and on September 14 she set out with Joanna Hutchinson on her second Scotch tour. It was a trip which had long been planned, but Joanna was a little rash in undertaking it; for she had been for some years a martyr to rheumatism, and after valiant struggles with it was finally laid up in Edinburgh and the neighbourhood; the fortnight which they had allotted to their tour was extended to nearly seven weeks. But despite this misfortune neither of them seems to have regretted the enterprise. They went in a cart as far as Penrith in company with William and with Crabb Robinson, who was spending a few days at Rydal; then they took coach to Edinburgh, went on to Stirling by water and by track-boat to Glasgow. From Glasgow they took the steamer to Dumbarton, the coach to Balloch, and the steamer again up Loch Lomond to Tarbet. From Tarbet they proceeded by carriage and on foot to Inveraray, thence by steamer back to Glasgow, and so to Edinburgh by way of Lanark, Moffat, Langholm, and the Lowlands.[3]

Dorothy found little changed in Scotland since her visit nineteen years before. True, the steamers, which were a recent invention, had brought with them a large number of tourists, and the highland huts had now the refinement of glass windows with sash panes which 'seemed incongruous with the smoke breathing out of the roof and doors'; but if the inns could boast the added luxury of carpets, they were otherwise hardly less primitive. At Tarbet especially, where they had been led to expect comfort, the inn was villainous, 'what for dirt, and litter and damp surely it cannot be surpassed in all Scotland'. For supper they were 'provided with bad potatoes and uneatable mutton chops, made of scraps from the ends of the bones of a

[1] D. W. to E. Q., Nov. 19, 1822. [2] D. W. to E. Q., July 1823.

[3] 'Journal of my Second Tour in Scotland', Dorothy Wordsworth, 1822 (MS.). A few extracts have been published in *Journals of D. W.*, ed. Knight, ii. 263–8.

neck of mutton. We complained: and some chops were brought with a little lean meat upon them, not quite so hard as leather, but so raw that Joanna could not taste them without rebroiling, and in attempting to do this, lost her chop into the fire'. Everywhere in towns or inns or cottages there was dirt. The streets of Stirling were intolerable. 'Talk not of foreign countries! A woman who has been throwing her tea leaves out of an upper window hangs over as long as she can see me, with the teapot handle upon her finger, and the children run after us splashing through the mud, the flesh of their legs cased in mud like black boots.'

As usual, she found much pleasure talking to the country folk, and in observing her fellow travellers. Some of the tourists she met are still upon the roads; such as 'the pert youth' who breakfasted with them at Penrith, 'who was amazingly grand in his style of eating, and on the coach kept up his silence and dignity till past Longtown, and then became troublesome by his loquacity, and affected such raptures that he would never let a single winding of the Esk pass without insisting on our admiration, declaring over and over again that what was before his eyes was "the finest thing he had ever seen in his life", at the same time giving us to understand that he was no ignoramus in scenery'. And who does not know the Scotch doctor 'who enthusiastically pronounced Loch Lomond to be the finest lake in the world . . . [though] it was plain that he had never been out of his own country'?

It was on Loch Lomond and in its neighbourhood, that she spent the happiest days, both because of their beauty and of the memories which they recalled:

'Our entrance to Loch Lomond mild and stately—no marshy flats. We pass at once from the calm river to the gently-stirring wide Lake. Ben Lomond with a shrouded head, and silvery lights on his sides. Opposite hills clear—to the top. A large hilly island before us covered with heather and sprinkled with trees. Great numbers of deer on the island. As we advance, in shape it reminds me of the island on Windermere, though much larger and higher. We pass another large island spotted in every part with fine old yew trees. The wind soon blew cold and fierce—and the waves so large that we might have fancied ourselves out at sea. Sheltered in the cabin, and took a breakfast *à la fourchette*—not at the gentry end—for we had learned by experience that the other was quite as good, and only half price. We saw more of life, and met with more civility and attention. . . . When I returned upon deck we were in calm water. Alas! steamboats are always in a hurry, and take noise and commotion along with them: otherwise we might have sweetly glided among the beautiful islands. We darted through what seemed a wilderness of rocks and woods upon the waters. I could not discover that islet which our fancy (William's and mine) gave to the huts by the wayside, and which charmed us so much on first entering the Highlands.[1] The Bay of Luss even more beautiful than in my imagination. Thatched cottages near the shore—two or three white houses visible and the Chapel and Belfry—the lively brook with its beds of blue gravel. But I have forgotten Inch Devannoc the woody island whence we, (Wm, Coleridge and myself) had so sublime a prospect. I recognized its proud summit. No more islands after Luss. We halted in the Bay to send out passengers, and again at Tarbet, then (rounding the promontory) pass into the narrower part of the lake. Ferryhouse at Inversneyde just the same, but there is now a glass window. A girl standing on the threshold. We are not near enough to distinguish whether her person be awkward or graceful, or her face pretty; but I cannot fancy her so fair as *our* Highland Girl. Poor thing! I ask myself in vain what is become of *her*? . . . The white waterfall drops into the lake as before; and the small bay is calm while the middle of the lake is stirred by breezes; but we have long left the sea-like region of the Isles and low hills. Our Highland musician tunes his pipes as we approach Rob Roy's caves. The grandeur of Nature strangely mixed up with stage effect: but it is good acting—not of the Surrey Theatre. An old Highlander, with long grey locks, bonnet, and plaid, is seated on one of the crags. Boys at different heights with bags of fresh-gathered nuts. Every passenger leaves the boat, and what a scramble among rocks and trees! The piper in his tartan robes is still playing a rousing tune. All press forward to Rob Roy's cave, as it is called, pass through in succession, the cave being so small that not more than two or three can enter at once, and having an outlet at the other side. We flatter ourselves we make a wiser choice in not entering at all; for they profess to have no motive but to *say* they have been in Rob Roy's caves because Sir Walter Scott has made them so much talked about: and when they come out, dashing the dust off their cloaths, the best they can say is "Well, there is nothing to be seen:

[1] Cf. Recollections of 1803 Tour, in *Journals of D. W.*, ed. Knight, i. 220: 'The cottages and the island might have been made for the pleasure of each other.'

but it is worth while, if only to say that one has been there!" An old gentleman, smitten with the same enthusiasm, after being led and supported on the difficult way by his servant, enters and passes through the cave. He must be near eighty. His head is as white as snow. When all were satisfied we were sorry we must quit our seat upon the rocks—climbing woods above us—the shore below—crags and trees intermingled, as richly beautiful as it is possible to imagine, and a charming prospect across the water. One white house near the shore—green field and woods behind it—a cheerful solitude! so it appeared on that fine day. Broad flakes of sunshine on the hills, brightened by intervening and passing shadows.

'Back to Tarbet, where a crazy boat came out to meet us at 3 o'clock. I thought of our coffee and fowls dropped into the water when poor C. was with us, and of our coasting the bay in a vessel even more crazy than this. Quiet, warm, beautiful was now our approach to Tarbet,—up the green field—lasses washing their linen beside the shady burn, their kettle hung from a bough, fire smoking among the trees. Poor Joanna had been sick and weary after a heartful of pleasure at Rob Roy's caves, and was obliged to go to bed, where I left her, and walked to Arroquohar. Having passed between the hills, gladly did I bend my course towards the Inn at A., remembering our descent in the Irish car. My approach was now slower, and I was glad of it. The evening was delicious, the Loch as smooth as a mirror. Sun declining towards the mountains of Glen Croe, yet shining full on the Cobbler's head. Not a touch of melancholy in the scene, all majesty and solemn grandeur with loveliness in colouring, golden and green and grey crags. On returning through the Cradle Hollow, reapers still busy—making haste to finish their day's work, heaping corn upon the carts. Their dogs make a clamorous barking after me, which echoes through the valley. When near Tarbet, again looking back towards Arroquohar, the sun sent forth slanting rays, and a veil of brightness concealed all but the *forms* of some of the mountains; and, when *that* was gone, a pink light rested on Ben Lomond's top till a white cloud hid the pyramid from me, a cloud that seemed to belong to that mountain through pre-eminence. It was stationary; and all the other mountains perfectly clear. I walked half a mile up the Lake—twilight in returning.'

Despite her rheumatism Joanna proved a more lively travelling companion than her sister Mary, but she had not Mary's beautiful composure of spirit, and her nervous excitability proved infectious; in her company the lonely Scotch moorlands bred in Dorothy fears which had never troubled her in the vaster solitudes of the Alps. Thus their journey from Lanark to Moffat was transformed into an adventure:

'At Elvan-foot nothing was to be had but the coach at eleven o'clock. Having paid our attendant whom no entreaties could induce to go on to Moffat, we sate down in a damp dirty parlour to consider how we should proceed. Went to view the bedrooms —worse than the parlour. Joanna durst not expose her rheumatism to such a trial: and places in the coach being uncertain, she determined to walk on—to Moffat, if possible; but if not, to the Toll-bar (6 miles), where we might have as good a chance of being taken up by the coach as at Elvan-foot.

'We cross the Clyde, leave our luggage to be forwarded. Here is a handsome stone bridge and a well-looking old house among tall trees. . . . We turn to the left, from the now little river of Clyde— very solitary—two boys mending the road. The boys left behind, and out of sight. A big strong old man met us, a tramper he must have been for thirty years. "How far to the Toll-bar?" said I. "What, do you mean to *house* there?" was his hasty reply,—and I instantly felt that I had been imprudent in speaking to him; but collecting myself I answered "No, we are only going thither to wait for the coach."

'Poor Joanna went on, not raising her eyes from the ground, till the man, having told us that the Toll-bar was a long way off, was moving forward, and then her looks showed plainly what she had been suffering, and she exclaimed "How could you be so imprudent as to speak to that man in this lonely place?"

'We began, when we thought him at safe distance, to look backwards, and without halting watched till he was out of sight,—the white road for half a mile or more being visible behind us. Twilight was fast approaching, and the moon hidden behind the hills, which appeared very high. The sky clear blue, and one or two stars near the hill-tops. Valley long and narrow, and no house or hut. It seemed I had never been in a place so lonely. While we were trudging on side by side, Joanna talked incessantly to keep away thought, and was most amusing telling stories of times past; and now and then she cast her eyes backward, and in so doing, fancied she spied a man hastily crossing over the side of a hill, *towards* us, though at a considerable distance. After this, I believe she never once looked behind, but went on at a speed for *her* almost supernatural; and ere long we saw a light in the bottom of the valley at a distance. Great joy! for we were assured that it came from the turnpike house: yet after the first gladness, a trepidation came upon *me*, and I felt (as we often do in a dream, when making an effort to escape from danger) as if the space we had yet to travel could never be got over. Poor Joanna was in worse condition; but at length we arrived. One farmhouse was near the Toll-bar, and this we were comforted in discovering: the toll-bar house and the road appeared so very lonesome. In the same moment that we knocked at the door we laid a hand on the latch and opened it, and were cheered by the sight of a woman's kind face and a good fire. We took our seats in the parlour beside the master and his brother, two respectable looking men; but before we were well settled, or had got the accident which led us thither fully explained, the door was opened suddenly, and two travellers came forward, and in a loud voice with very broad Scotch accent, demanded a glass of whiskey. The woman told them she had no whiskey, and that it was not a public house. "But we are tired, have come from Aberdeen, and to-day have travelled far, and you will let us sit by the fire till the coach comes." She looked inquiringly at our faces, and asked in a low voice "Do you know anything of these men?" and, turning to them replied that there would probably be no places for them—these ladies were waiting for the coach, and must be first served—it was a fine moonlight night, and only six miles to Moffat. The men had a rattling wild air and demeanour which would have completely upset us had they overtaken us on the road. They reminded me of the roughest of the Heidelberg students. Each carried a knapsack, with a stout staff in hand, and leather caps on their head. You may judge we were anxious that the house should be cleared of them, especially as we were convinced that it must have been one of these men whom Joanna had seen, and that they had hurried forward to overtake us; and we even *suspected*, from the tenour of their discourse, that they *had heard something* about us. They were surly and abusive when the landlord upheld his wife in refusing to let them stay; at length, however, they moved away grumbling and the door was bolted against them, and we soon began to feel ourselves at ease and thankful for a shelter. The fire was heaped up with fresh peats, we had some boiled milk, and chatted comfortably. . . . By degrees the whole party seemed to become thoroughly acquainted—the landlady pressed us to stay all night—the coach would not come till 12 o'clock. She had a good bed, and would do her best to make us comfortable. We consented, dreading the journey by night for Joanna; and besides, she was only fit to lie down and rest. When the landlady unlocked her cupboard to make preparations for our lodging, we were astonished at her store of blankets and linen, for though the house was well-built, tolerably furnished, and cleanly for a Scotch dwelling, there was nothing that should lead us to expect to see a hoard of that kind; but, as in France, it seems almost universal in Scotland to heap up a store of household linen disproportioned to the other accommodations of the house. Sheets were presently aired, and the family withdrew, after heaping up the fire afresh with peats. We lay down on the bed without undressing, and, shortly after, the landlord and his wife went to their bed in the same room—both beds being within a recess. After the coach had passed (as the clock was striking twelve)I had snatches of sleep, but poor Joanna was wakeful all night—and no wonder—for it was a strange situation into which we had imprudently brought ourselves; and the thought of the wild hills, between which we had travelled so far to this spot (the central point of the lonely road from Elvan-foot to Moffat) and that here we were completely in the power of people entirely unknown to us—these thoughts haunted her the night through. As for me, there was one five minutes during which I was more terrified than ever before in my whole life. I was thoroughly awake, and had heard no sound except the brook at a little distance from the door—no call at the turnpike gate, nor any one on the road—the clock had been striking two—the outer door was opened from within and the landlord's brother went out as I distinctly heard. He had moved very quietly, and my fears cannot be described, for at that moment I was struck with the horrible thought that he had got out of bed to admit the two men who had come in after us in the evening—and, recollecting that both he and his brother, during the parley, had gone out with the men talking about their journey—I thought what if they then settled upon murdering us! Joanna and I lay trembling side by side—the door was again locked on the inside, and what was my comfort when I heard the crying of a child, as if disturbed by his uncle getting into bed. I was then satisfied that he had only risen to open the gate, and two or three times more he got up for the like purpose, which no longer alarmed me. It was a fine moonlight night. We rose at seven, sunshine on the hills: frosty dew, all round the house black cattle pasturing. Departed at eight, with feelings towards those kind people at the Toll-bar the more friendly for the injustice our fears had done them.'

On her return from Scotland Dorothy was less interested in writing up the notes which she had made during her journey than in the revision of her *Recollections* of her tour with William in 1803. Among the enthusiastic readers of that volume, which had been widely circulated in manuscript, was the poet Rogers; Rogers had probably borrowed it on his visit to the Lakes in 1813; and in 1820, when they met again in London, he had urged her to print it, offering to find her a publisher who would give her favourable terms. Her modesty had always recoiled from the idea of appearing before the world as an authoress; but her passion for travel at last overcame her reluctance, for it now occurred to her that she might make money enough by the sale of the book to defray the expenses of another continental tour; and before her start for Scotland she had asked William to write to Rogers to that effect. In his reply Rogers urged the retention of the copyright: 'Wherever', he wrote, 'there is *real merit* in a work, and you know my opinion of your Sister's, I think when *it can be done*, it is best to enter the Lottery oneself and not sell the ticket for little or nothing to the bookseller.'

> 'I cannot but be flattered', Dorothy answered,[1] 'by your thinking so well of my journal as to recommend (indirectly at least) that I should not part with all power over it, till its fortune has been tried. You will not be surprised, however, that I am not so hopeful; and that I am apprehensive that, after having encountered the unpleasantness of coming before the public, I might not be assisted in attaining my object. I have, then, to ask whether a middle course be not possible, that is, whether your favourable opinion, confirmed perhaps by some other good judges, might not induce a bookseller to give a certain sum for the right to publish a given number of copies. In fact, I find it next to impossible to make up my mind to sacrifice my privacy for a certainty *less* than two hundred pounds—a sum which would effectually aid me in accomplishing the ramble I so much, and I hope not unwisely, wish for. . . .
>
> 'If you knew how much it has cost me to settle the affair of this proposed publication in my mind, as far as I have now done, I am sure you would deem me sufficiently excused for having so long delayed answering your most obliging letter. I have still to add, that if there be a prospect that any bookseller will undertake the publication, I will immediately prepare a corrected copy to be sent to you, and I shall trust to your kindness for taking the trouble to look over it, and to mark whatever passages you may think too trivial for publication, or in any other respect much amiss.'

Dorothy set herself forthwith to revise her manuscript for

[1] D. W. to Samuel Rogers, Jan. 3, 1823.

press, and a copy is extant which incorporates her alterations.[1] But nothing came of it. We can only suppose that Rogers was unable to find a publisher ready to accept Dorothy's terms. Fifteen years later, when her health had already given way, the matter was raised again. William hoped that the business of 'taking it through the press' might act 'as a profitable stirring of her mind'[2] and in order to share her work he set about correcting and enlarging his poems on Burns which were to be included in it, but after much hesitation he decided that she was not equal to the task; he was, moreover, acutely sensitive to the painful nature of her illness, and felt that there 'would be some indelicacy in drawing public attention to her in her present melancholy state'. The *Journal* never saw the light till 1874.

Of the year 1823, which was spent quietly at Rydal, Dorothy only records one 'rememberable day', when she drove up Mardale with William and walked home over the head of Long Sleddale, and so to Kentmere, Troutbeck, and Low Wood. But a letter from Dora written to her friend Elizabeth Crump in November gives another and very characteristic glimpse of her: 'My aunt has caught a severe cold which still hangs about her and is accompanied by a very troublesome cough which shakes her to pieces. We are all sure it was brought on by a *tremendous* walk she took with my father over the mountains, but she wont hear that this was the case.'

In the next year (1824) Dorothy was again upon her travels. After a few days at Oxford, where John was now an undergraduate, she reached London in the last week of March, and put up for a month, together with William and Dora, at Tom Monkhouse's. A few days were given to the little Quillinans at Lee Priory, May was divided between Cambridge and Playford: in June she was back at home.

A letter to Tom's brother, John, tells of all her doings in London.[3] She went to the British Museum with the Beaumonts and with Crabb Robinson, visited Mrs. Hoare at Hampstead, and saw as much as possible of the Lambs. On one morning, she says, 'I breakfasted with my admirer, as Dora calls him, Mr Rogers, and his sister', another day she visited old

[1] *V.* Appendix, p. 409.
[2] W. W. to H. C. R., Dec. 15, 1837.
[3] D. W. to John Monkhouse, Apr. 16, 1824.

Miss Hindson, who had been one of her mother's bridesmaids and more than fifty years before had dressed for her her first doll, and she was surprised to see her 'move with as much activity as many young ones'. And of course she did not neglect the latest public exhibitions. 'Though often thwarted by showery and pinched by cold weather, we have', she says, 'seen the first of all sights, the Diorama', where the Swiss giantess, then the talk of London, was on show; another day Crabb Robinson took them all to see the Mexican curiosities in Piccadilly—'the modern very amusing and the live Mexican not the least interesting object—Mr R. talked Spanish with him. The *antient* curiosities for which you pay another shilling are but a collection of ugly monstrous things—thence to the Panorama of Pompeii, where we were all much delighted—looked at Somerset House and paid our toll over Waterloo Bridge, for the sake of the prospect.'

More interesting to Dorothy than the Swiss giantess or the Mexican Exhibition was the preaching of Edward Irving, the eloquent Scotch divine who had come to the little chapel at Hatton Gardens two years before, and taken London by storm. Irving had already become not only a fashionable craze, but a noted figure in intellectual society, well known to Carlyle and Coleridge, Sir George Beaumont and Crabb Robinson. In the previous summer Tom Monkhouse, who had in a measure fallen under Irving's spell, had sent to Rydal a copy of the much discussed *Orations*, in which Irving had launched an impassioned attack upon Southey and Byron for the impiety of their *Visions of Judgment*. Dorothy, though she recognized him as 'a man of no common talents', had not been much impressed. Topical sermons, 'bringing living characters (as authors especially) into notice in a place of public worship' offended her sense of religious propriety, whilst she was outraged at seeing Southey 'coupled with the Blasphemer Lord Byron'. Still more repugnant to her was Irving's florid rhetoric. 'His description', she said,[1] 'of the joys of Heaven is, to me *worse* than Methodist rant.' But she was eager to probe for herself the secret of his popularity, and when she had met him and heard him preach, she summed up with admirable shrewdness of judgement his weakness and his strength.

[1] D. W. to Thomas Monkhouse, Aug. 20, 1823.

'His person is very fine in my opinion and his action often graceful—though often far otherwise—his voice fine—reading excellent, and, while he keeps his feelings under, nothing can be finer than his manner of preaching—but it is grievous to see him wasting his powers—as he does in the latter part (especially) of his discourses—the more grievous as it is plain he must sink under such exertions while yet a young man. When I say *wasting* his powers you must understand that I mean that with less effort the effect on his hearers would be more beneficial. He wholly wants taste and judgment—but one essential I give him full credit for—*sincerity*—without which no preaching that would address the feelings can be efficacious.'

Her enjoyment of London was seriously affected by her distress at the failing health of her kind host. It was clear to her that Tom Monkhouse was breaking up under the stress of some mysterious ailment, and only a month or two later he was found to be in a galloping consumption. In the autumn he joined William, Mary, and Sara in a visit to Hindwell, and, says Dorothy, 'my brother and sister were heartstruck at the first sight of him'.[1] Sara, who was deeply attached to her cousin, has related how a gloom fell upon them all, which William alone could dispel. 'The poet', wrote Sara, 'was the life of the party, doing always his utmost to keep up our spirits, which he always does, God bless him, where there is real necessity for his exertions.'[2] 'My brother's company', wrote Dorothy, 'was an especial comfort to him.'[3] From Hindwell the devoted Sara took her cousin to Torquay—Mrs. Monkhouse was a poor lackadaisical creature quite unfit for the duties of a nurse—and thence to Clifton, where he died in the following January.

His death was a heavy blow to a wide circle. Before the end came Dorothy had written to Crabb Robinson,[3] 'What a loss the Lambs no less than you must feel this winter of the chearful resting place and never-failing cordial welcome by Tom Monkhouse's fireside': her devotion to him has been evident from the story of the last four years. Of the men who loved her brother he had been, since the defection of Coleridge, her closest friend, the cheeriest and most generous of comrades, and never, like Coleridge, the source of pain as well as joy. But she struggled

[1] D. W. to John Kenyon, Oct. 4, 1824.
[2] S. H. to E. Q., Oct. 24, 1824.
[3] D. W. to H. C. R., Dec. 13, 1824.

against her grief. 'Why', she wrote to Crabb,[1] 'should I dwell on regrets for a loss which Time can never repair to us? We feel it daily—though so far distant from the house which he inhabited, that was a hospitable home ever ready for us . . . he had been a fortunate and happy man, and was deeply attached to family and friends.' Her sorrow drew her closer to those who, as she knew, shared it with her. 'A few days ago my brother had a most interesting letter from Charles Lamb. He feels Thomas Monkhouse's death just as I thought he would feel it. Oh that I could flatter myself that this release from the necessity of remaining in, or near London would ever bring us the happiness of seeing them here—and above all, of having them stationary near us for a few months—a whole winter—or a whole summer! This I fear can never be.'[1] The happy tidings had just reached her that Lamb had been superannuated from the India House. 'I could fancy him', wrote Dorothy to John Monkhouse, 'with almost boyish glee beginning life again—then follows a sigh and a sad thought—but I will not go on in this strain.'

Experience had taught her the folly of nursing her griefs, instead of dwelling rather upon the joys that still remained. And this lesson she strove to impress upon others. To a convalescent friend who was a prey to melancholy broodings she wrote about the same time:[2] 'I wish you could see how pretty the chapel looks from my bedroom window and how charming the prospect. It would chear your spirits, which I am grieved to find so drooping. Why not rouse yourself? Why lament for the past? Rather you should rejoice at your escape, for which I know you are thankful.' It was thus that she had learned to face life herself.

After a year of much wandering the Wordsworths were content to be at Rydal during the summer of 1825. To Robert Jones, who had intended to visit them, Dorothy wrote in October: 'we really were not sorry that you did not arrive in the course of last summer, for you would have had no *quiet* enjoyment, and you are not made for *bustling* pleasures. We never in our lives had so many visitors. The newspapers (for I suppose newspapers are not excluded from the Vale of Meditation) will have announced to you the names of some of them, Mr

[1] D. W. to H. C. R., Apr. 12, 1825.
[2] D. W. to Elizabeth Crump, summer 1825.

Canning, Sir Walter Scott etc., etc., but if we had kept a private register of the names of others of less note you would really have been astonished at their number.' In the previous May Dorothy had written to Scott asking him to settle an amusing dispute she had with William about a visit to Miss Seward, 'the Swan of Lichfield', when they were living at Coleorton twenty years back. Dorothy was confident that Scott had been with them; and this William denied, though he distinctly remembered taking Scott as far as Lichfield on his journey home. Scott replied that as far as he remembered, though they went with him for a stage or two of his journey, he had reached Lichfield alone. 'It is a singular illustration', he wrote,[1] 'of the uncertainty of human testimony that of three individuals certainly not of the class through whose mind incidents pass most lightly two should have contradictory recollections with respect to such a fact, and the third should be unable to speak with any confidence or certainty.' He went on to send them a warm invitation to visit him at Abbotsford. 'I wish your brother and Mrs Wordsworth and you would think of our blue hills once more . . . no human beings would I like to see so much under my roof.' But it was Scott's part to visit them: in the early summer he was in Ireland, and on his return he passed through the Lake country.

The arrival of Scott and Canning in the district was the occasion for general festivity; Scott spoke afterwards of his tour there as 'one ovation'. Wilson, now a Professor at Edinburgh, had come to Elleray to welcome Scott, Canning was staying with a Mr. Bolton, a resident at Storrs on Windermere, and Lockhart tells[2] how at Mr. Bolton's a large company, including Wordsworth, had been assembled to do honour to the guests.

> 'The weather was as Elysian as the scenery. There were brilliant cavalcades through the woods in the mornings, and delicious boatings on the Lake by moonlight; and the last day "the Admiral of the Lake" presided over one of the most splendid regattas that ever enlivened Windermere. Perhaps there were not fewer than fifty barges following in the Professor's radiant procession, when it paused at the point of Storrs to admit into the place of honour the vessel that carried kind and happy Mr Bolton and his guests. The bards of the Lakes led the cheers that hailed Scott and

[1] Scott to D. W., May or June, 1825. [2] Lockhart, *Life of Scott*, chap. lxiii.

Canning; and music and sunshine, flags, streamers, and gay dresses, the merry hum of voices, and the rapid splashing of innumerable oars, made up a dazzling mixture of sensations as the flotilla wound its way among the richly foliaged islands, and along bays and promontories peopled with enthusiastic spectators.'

From Windermere the party came on to Rydal Mount; William and Dora took them over to see Southey, and the day after Dorothy joined the party in an expedition over the Kirkstone to Airy Force and Lyulph's Tower and to pay a visit to the Marshall's. From Hallsteads the party went on to Lowther Castle. It was a real pleasure to William and Dorothy to have Scott once more in their midst. But if Lockhart delighted in the homage paid everywhere to his father-in-law he did not share Scott's enjoyment of his old friend's society, and in letters[1] to his wife held up to contempt the company assembled at Rydal to do him honour. Wordsworth struck him as 'proud and pompous and absurdly arrogant', though, he said, 'he is well where he ought to be, would he only drop a little of his airs and his preaching above all'. He resented the way in which the poet spouted his own verses *en route* to Keswick: the breakfast party at Rydal Mount he dismissed as vulgar, 'little Quillinan, the heavy dragoon, the only genteelish figure', and he reports how when they returned from Keswick in the evening 'there was a great party of abominables to stare at Sir Walter'. On Dorothy his only comment was that she was 'as yellow as a duck's foot'.

Dorothy was, indeed, ageing in body if not in spirit: yet upon a less jaundiced observer, who saw her first during this summer, she had made a very different impression: 'I dread growing old,' wrote Maria Jane Jewsbury[2] to Dora, 'it is a gradual death; if I could age like your aunt Wordsworth, and unite green vigour with grey maturity, it were well; but who is like her?'[3]

Early in May Maria Jane Jewsbury had introduced herself to Wordsworth by dedicating to him her first miscellany of prose and verse, and accompanying the volume with a letter expressing 'the most genuine sentiments of respectful admiration';

[1] *V.* Scott, *Familiar Letters*, ed. Douglas, 1894, vol. ii, 340–3.

[2] The elder sister of Geraldine Jewsbury who was later to be the friend of Jane Welsh Carlyle. A selection of her Essays, with a charming introductory biography, has been edited by E. Gillett, Oxford University Press, 1932.

[3] Maria Jane Jewsbury to Dora W., Oct. 8, 1825.

emboldened by the kindness of his reply she lost no time in presenting herself at Rydal Mount. The vivacious charm of her personality quickly won all hearts; before the end of the month she was a guest in their house, a close friend of Dora's, and taking long rides through the country whilst the poet walked by the side of her pony. Two months later, when the family moved for a few weeks to Kent's Bank, that Dora might have the benefit of sea air and bathing, Miss Jewsbury was invited to join the party. Dorothy remained at home, only spending one day at Kent's Bank, but she had already seen enough of her to share Dora's enthusiasm. In her diary under May 23 we read 'struck with Miss Jewsbury'. And in the following February, when she was again upon her travels, she stopped three or four days at Miss Jewsbury's home in Manchester. 'I was even more pleased with her at home than abroad', she wrote. 'Her talents are extraordinary, and she is admirable as a daughter and a sister and has, besides, many valuable friends.' To Miss Jewsbury's vivid pen we owe some of the most delightful pictures of Dorothy as she was in her last active years.

Reference has just been made to a diary kept by Dorothy in these years. When she had begun to keep it we cannot tell, but eleven shabby little notebooks still preserve for us entries covering the period from December 1824 to 1833. This diary has little of the character of the Alfoxden or Grasmere Journals. At times, indeed, when she is away from home, it blossoms out into something of a journal, but for the most part it consists of the briefest entries, scrawled in a careless, often illegible, hand, recording the weather, the comings and goings of the family and their guests, sometimes a book she has been reading,[1] details of her health and that of the different members of the household, and in the last years much about her own painful symptoms. The nature of the entries is wholly capricious; events which we know to have been of vital concern to her are barely alluded to—sometimes omitted: only rarely does she make the diary the repository of her feelings, or the vehicle for transmitting to us her impression of life's comedy. But here and there passages occur that reveal the delicate artist or the shrewd observer of human absurdity:

[1] It is interesting to note that through 1824–5 she was reading Dante, often a canto a day, and later Tasso.

'July 8. 1825. reach Newby Bridge about 8. After tea strolled up and down river—the dark figure of an Angler standing on the slippery slope of the Weir, that with its whiteness brought out the lower part of the man's figure. Could not see the pipe in his mouth, but discovered he was smoking by a thin volume of vapour in the air which was faintly reflected in the still water above the Weir.

'Sept 5. 1826. fair mild morning—walk to Mrs Troughton's sale at Weobley Parsonage. Bells ringing for new vicar—very discordant with the melancholy appearance of strangers gathered together and furniture spread on the lawn. Mrs Lomax admired Paradise Lost—wished she could buy one—had never heard of Paradise Regained. Her young friend observed it was "very entertaining, very pretty."

'Sept 6. 1826. Party from village cross fields to coach—a Lady about 50 minces, smiles, and makes a fuss about a place inside for a fat companion much older than herself—broad and dressy; entrusts her with a serious charge to the coachman and guard to take care of her to Worcester, it being the first time the Lady had ever travelled in a mail.'

XIX

BRINSOP. THE ISLE OF MAN. WHITWICK. BREAKDOWN OF HEALTH

1826–1834 (aet. 54–63)

THE two entries which brought the last chapter to a close are from the diary of 1826. In that year Dorothy was separated from her brother for a longer time than ever before since she had joined him at Racedown. She left home in February, contemplating no more than a three months' parting; for he had promised to join her in May at Robert Jones's parsonage in the Vale of Clwyd,[1] and they had planned to ascend Snowdon together, that she might relive with him one more of his great poetic experiences.[2] But a general election supervened, in which he felt bound to take an active part; and electioneering was almost the only taste of William's which Dorothy did not share: its bustle and turmoil were hateful to her, whereas, as Sara wrote, 'he enjoyed the sport', though he paid afterwards for his exertions in a serious recurrence of eye trouble. So she yielded readily to the entreaties of her friends to prolong her stay with them, and did not reach home till November.

The greater part of her time was spent with the Hutchinsons at Brinsop Court, whither they had moved from Hindwell in the previous year. She broke her journey for a few days at the Jewsburys' in Manchester:

> 'from Manchester', she tells Crabb Robinson,[3] 'I came by way of Worcester and the delightful hills of Malvern to Hereford, where I was met by Mrs Wordsworth's sister. Brinsop Court is six miles from Hereford—the country rich and the climate good—far less rain than we have in Westmorland, but as I have always said our compensations do much more than make amends—our dry roads, where, after the heaviest shower, one can walk with comfort, and above all our mountains and lakes which are just as beautiful, just as interesting, in winter as in summer. Brinsop Court is, however, even now, no chearless spot, and flowers in the hedges and blossoms in the numerous orchards will soon make it gay. Our fireside is enlivened by four fine well-managed children and chearful

[1] W. W. to Robert Jones, May 18, 1826.

[2] *V. Prelude* (1805), xiii.

[3] D. W. to H. C. R., Feb. 25, 1826.

friends, and Mrs Hutchinson is one of the most pleasing and excellent of women.'

Dorothy threw herself with zest into the family life at Brinsop. It was a joy to her to be again among children; with Mary Hutchinson and Joanna she was always happy, and her old friend John Monkhouse, now nearly blind but as cheerful and vigorous as ever, who was still farming at Stow, some ten miles off, was often upon the scenes. Brinsop Court was charmingly situated; as at Hindwell there was a small lake in front of the house—'swans floating before me', she noted in her diary, 'and 32 cattle feeding like one[1] on the slope opposite my window'. There were delightful walks in the neighbourhood, and when she wished to go farther afield the farm cart or the gig was ready to convey her. In April she made a little tour down her beloved Wye Valley, in May she spent ten days with Joanna at Gwerndyffnant, a small farmstead three miles south of Hindwell which Tom Hutchinson still retained. Joanna had a special love for this quiet place, and would often make her escape there for a little rest from the exacting company of nephews and nieces. Then for a week in June Joanna took her to Worcester, where they stayed with Lady Beaumont's cousin, Miss Willes, saw much of the Cathedral society and roamed the Malvern Hills; in July she attended the race meetings at Kington and Hereford, and passed another ten days at Gwerndyffnant, for three of which the Hutchinson children were of the party. The 'frolic games', 'the mirth and revelry' of this little holiday she afterwards celebrated in some irregular stanzas;[2] we could wish that she had chosen to describe it in her more vivid prose.

Early in September she left Brinsop for Leamington to visit Miss Jewsbury, who was there recruiting her health after a bad illness. Travelling by way of Worcester she spent a night or two with Miss Willes, and again enjoyed a long day upon the Malvern Hills. At Leamington she astonished her hostess by her inexhaustible passion for sightseeing:

'Your aunt left us on Friday', wrote Jane Jewsbury to Dora on October 2. 'She did, I hope, receive pleasure from her visit: no thanks to me, for I was invisible nearly the whole of every day,

[1] Cf. 'The Cock is crowing', *Oxf. W.*, p. 190.

[2] The stanzas will be found in *Poems* of Wordsworth, ed. Knight, viii. 284–9. The holiday is there dated *May* 1826, but it took place in July.

but Mentor and Mr Burra and she, in a yellow gig and brown Bobby travelled and saw—"words are wanting to say what"—You will hear and you will see, for she has got some pictures. She is a real darling—the exemplification of an old age as serene and bright and lovely as a Lapland night! Kenilworth she knows by heart, stick and stone—Warwick she has absolutely digested, St Mary's Chapel and Guy's Cliff included—Stratford and Charlecote she swallowed whole—and bye bits of rides and sights went down between times.'

She returned to Rydal by way of Coleorton and Liverpool, and reached home on November 4; she had been absent nine months.

On a walk to Grasmere, some ten days later, she called in at Dove Cottage, to which the De Quincey family had now returned from Fox Ghyll. De Quincey was away in Edinburgh, and she found his wife lonely, and so worried about the uncertainty of his plans that she undertook to write to him on her behalf. It was a delicate task, for she might easily lay herself open to a charge of impertinent interference: since his marriage and his subjection to the pleasures and pains of opium, De Quincey had become estranged from the Wordsworths, and they had seen little of him. But Dorothy had still a warm place for him in her heart, and her letter was a model of friendliness, tact, and common sense.

Nov. 16. 1826.

My dear Sir,

A letter of good tidings respecting Mrs De Quincey and your Family cannot, I am sure, be unwelcome; and besides, she assures me that you will be glad to hear of my safe return to Rydal after nine months' absence. I called at your cottage yesterday, having first seen your Son William at the head of the schoolboys; as it might seem a leader of their noon-tide games, and Horace among the tribe—both as healthy-looking as the best, and William very much grown. Margaret was in the kitchen preparing to follow her Brothers to school, and I was pleased to see her also looking stout and well, and much grown. Mrs De Quincey was seated by the fire above stairs with her Baby on her knee. She rose and received me chearfully, as a person in perfect health, and does indeed seem to have had an extraordinary recovery; and as little suffering as could be expected. The Babe looks as if it would thrive, and is what we call a nice Child,—neither big nor little.

Mrs De Quincey seemed on the whole in very good spirits; but, with something of sadness in her manner, she told me you were not likely very soon to be at home. She then said that you had at present some literary employments at Edinburgh; and had, besides, had an offer (or something to this effect) of a permanent engagement, the nature of which she did not know; but that you hesitated about accepting it, as it might necessitate you to settle in Edinburgh. To this I replied "why not settle there for the time at least that this engagement lasts? Lodgings are cheap in Edinburgh, and provisions and coals not dear". Of these facts I had some weeks' experience four years ago. I then added that it was my firm opinion that you could never regularly keep up to your engagements at a distance from the press; and, said I, "pray tell him so when you write". She replied, "Do write yourself". Now I could not refuse to give her pleasure by so doing, especially being assured that my letter would not be wholly worthless to you, having such agreeable news to send of your Family. The little cottage and everything seemed comfortable.

I do not presume to take the liberty of advising the acceptance of this engagement, or of that—only I would venture to request you well to consider the many impediments to literary employments to be regularly carried on in limited time, at a distance from the press, in a small house, and in perfect solitude. You must well know that it is a true and faithful concern for your interests and those of your Family that prompts me to call your attention to this point; and, if you think that I am mistaken, you will not, I am sure, take it ill that I have thus freely expressed my opinion.

It gave me great pleasure to hear of your good health and spirits, and you, I am sure, will be glad to have good accounts of all our Family except poor Dora, who has been very ill indeed—dangerously ill; but now, thank God, she is gaining ground, I hope daily. . . . My brother's eyes are literally quite well. This surely is as great a blessing, and I hope we are sufficiently thankful for it. He reads aloud to us by candlelight, and uses the pen for himself. . . .

I cannot express how happy I am to find myself at home again after so long an absence, though my time has been passed agreeably, and my health been excellent. I have had many long walks since my return, and am more than ever charmed with our rocks and mountains. Rich autumnal tints, with an intermixture of green ones, still linger on the trees.

Make my respects to Mr and Mrs and Miss Wilson, and believe me, dear Sir,

Yours affectionately,
D. Wordsworth.

One o'clock Thursday. I have been at Grasmere, and again seen your wife. She desires me to say that she is particularly anxious to hear from you on her father's account.

In the following year (1827) Dorothy was again away from home, for three weeks with the Cooksons at Kendal, and from June to September with her many friends in Halifax. It added to her pleasure that her god-daughter, Julia Marshall, was also staying in the town, and with her she revisited many of the spots that she had frequented in girlhood with Julia's mother, Jane. And on some fine summer mornings, while the young people were still in their beds, she was out alone walking on the moors. She passed much of her time with the Fergusons; with Edward, especially, she renewed her friendship, and in the years to come, as Mrs. Rawson's health declined, it was on him that she relied for news of Halifax.[1] On September 3 she was at home, on the 5th she made one of a party of eighteen, among them the Southeys and her old acquaintance Bloomfield, now Bishop of Chester, who ascended Saddleback. But the walk was too much for her, and for once in a way she admits that she 'knocked up', though she adds in her diary that it was a 'charming day, all were delighted'.

For much of the succeeding winter Dorothy was left alone at Rydal in charge of her two nephews, John and Willy. John had just taken his degree at Oxford, and was soon to enter holy orders; Willy's fate was still undecided, and his aunts were not a little anxious about him. 'He has got the Army so strongly into his head', wrote Sara,[2] 'that I am *sure* there will be no turning him from it, and his poor Mother will be wretched when she finds this to be the case—for she has no idea that he will persist in opposition to his Father's and her wishes.' But, fortunately, by March Willy's army fever had abated, and his thoughts turned to business: it was decided that next winter he should go abroad to learn languages, but that in the meantime, as his health was still uncertain, he should be entrusted to the care of Henry and Joanna Hutchinson, who were now living in the Isle of Man. In the early summer of 1828 Rydal Mount was deserted: John, now in orders, had obtained the curacy of Whitwick near Coleorton, and his mother had gone there to

[1] *V.* D. W. to Mrs. Pollard, Apr. 12, 1834.
[2] S. H. to E. Q., Jan. 27, 1828.

settle him in; William and Dora were on a trip with Coleridge in Germany. 'Dora says they get on famously, but that Mr C. sometimes detains them with his fiddle faddling, and that he likes prosing to the folks better than exerting himself to see the face of the country, and that Father with his few half dozen words of German makes himself better understood than Mr C. with all his weight of German literature.'[1]

Dorothy joined Willy in the Isle of Man: an account of her visit there, with a record of her trip over the island, finds its place in her rough diary. It was never revised, and much of it takes the form of notes rather than finished narrative, but it shows the same zest for adventure, the same keen observation of the country and its inhabitants as her more elaborate records of tours in Scotland and on the Continent.

'*Thursday June 26th.* Called by Anne at ½ past 2, and breakfasted by kitchen fire—walked to the end of quiet Terrace, grey calm and warbling birds—Sad at thought of my voyage, cheered up only by the end of it—sate long at Morris' door—grey and still—coach full, and sour looks within, for I made a 5th. Won my way by civility and communicating information to a sort of gentleman fisher going to Wytheburn—English manners ungracious—he left us at Nag's Head without a bow or good wish. Morning still foggy—Wytheburn Cliffs and trees big and soft—stayed inside till an Inn beside Bassenthwaite, but only another lady in coach, so had a good view of the many cloudy summits and swelling breast-works of Skiddaw. . . .

'Beautiful approach to Whitehaven—comfortless Inn, but cheered by a Grasmere waiter, Backhouse's daughter, Mrs Hodgson, all kindness. Pretty streets often terminated prettily, a hill, a church, the sea, the Castle. Fine view of cliffs and stone quarry—pretty smokeless blue-roofed town, castle and trees—a foreign aspect. Embarked at 10—full moon—lighthouse—luminous sky. Moved away and saw nothing till a distant view of the Isle of Man—Hills cut off by clouds—again sick and below till near Douglas. Beautiful approach, harbour calm—wind fallen—Henry met me at the Inn. Surprized with gay shops and store houses. Comfortable breakfast with dear Joanna, who was overpowered with pleasure. . . .

'. . . Very fine walk after tea on the cliffs—sea calm and as if enclosed by hazy dark steeps. Fishes sporting near the rocks—a few sea-birds to chatter and wail, but mostly silent rocks. Two

[1] M. W. to E. Q., July 26, 1828.

very grand masses in a little bay—a pellucid rivulet of sea water between them—the Hills mostly covered with cropped gorse, a rich dark green. The moon rose large and dull, like an ill-cleaned brass plate—slowly surmounts the haze and sends over the calm sea a faint bright pillar.

'*Saturday June 28th.* Slept till ½ past 7. Breakfast at 9. Lovely morning. Douglas Market very busy. Women often with round hats, like the Welsh; and girls without shoes and stockings, though otherwise not ill-dressed—country people speak more Manx than English, the sound is not coarse or harsh.

'*Sunday 29th June.* Called in the post office lane at the postmaster's; narrow as an Italian street, and cool; and the house low, cool and old-fashioned, and cleanly; stairs worn down with much treading and everything reminding one of gentry life at Penrith 40 years back. Crowds inquiring for letters. . . . After tea walked with Joanna on the pier—a very gay and crowded scene; saw the steam packet depart for Liverpool. . . . For the first time I saw the Cumberland hills, but dimly. Sea very bright. Talked with an old sailor and tried his spectacles. Alone to the Douglas Head. Very fine walk on the turf tracks among the shorn gorse, bright green studded with pearls in bunches—the ladies bed-straw—the green sea-weed with the brown bed of the river produces a beautiful effect of colouring.

'*Monday 7th July.* Departed for Castletown at 10 minutes past 10. Hot but fine breeze. . . . The bay lovely on this sweet morning. High rocks. Hampton Cottage—Mrs Garstang, luscious with loves and dears: the sweet Mona, and sweet Fanny, and the darling cow that gave 8 lbs of butter. Afterwards poor cottages, now and then a large house and plantations—happily the larch does not thrive. High ground, narrow flowery lanes—wild sea view—low peninsula of Long Ness. Low water at Castle town—Drawbridge, river and castle, handsome strong fortress—soldiers pacing, sentinels, officers and music—groups of women in white caps listening—very like a town in French Flanders.

'*Tuesday 8th July.* Rose before 6—pleasant walk to Port Murray Kirk along the bay before breakfast. Port Murray, harbour for Manx fleet; very pretty green banks near the port, neat huts under those banks with flower gardens, fishing nets and sheep, really beautiful. To Port Iron over the heights—a fleet of near forty—sails and nets—in the circular rocky harbour. Thence cross the country past Christ Rushen, a white church standing low . . . peat stacks all over, and a few warm smoking huts—thatches secured by straw ropes—and the walls, in which was generally buried one window, cushioned all over with thyme in full blow, sedum and various other flowers. Called on Henry's friend beside the mountain gate; her house blinding with smoke. I sate in the doorway—she was affectionately glad to see Henry; shook hands and blessed us at parting; "God be with you and prosper you in your journey!" Descend—more cottages. Dolby Glen beautiful—stream and stone cottages, and gardens hedged with flowering elder and mallows as beautiful as geraniums in a greenhouse—trees very flourishing—close and hot, weary descent and ascent to a pothouse on the heights—no spirits, nothing but ale—but greedily I fixed my eyes on the potatoe pot ready for her husband's dinner. "Can I have some potatoes?" "Plenty" was her glad reply—but it was strange to her that I would not partake of the fish. She seemed quite contented and chearful. Fowls pecking about—a wry-necked lamb—and she produced a cuckow, full fledged with gaping yellow mouth—would have given it us, I doubt not, yet seemed greatly to prize it—boiled me two eggs, produced a pewter spoon from sugar pot unwashed—then sought her silver one—no bread—on great days makes tea. We paid her a shilling—"I know not what I must do for change" with a perplexed countenance, and what was her surprize and delight to hear it was all for herself! she insisted on our taking another pint. "We must have it", and she pledged Mr H. We shook hands at parting. She was astonished at my walking, but looking after us said. "That woman steps so light, she's made for walking." Glen Mary very romantic—steep and hot. . . . I too tired to seek the waterfall. Pretty, wide, populous vale, and hills well shaped near Peel; fine bridge and steep river banks. Town finely situated under mountain. Tea, and soon to bed, most thankful for rest.

'*Wednesday July 9th.* Rose refreshed—morning bright—all brisk now, and all the town busy. Yesterday the first of the herring fishery, and black baskets laden with silvery herrings are hauled through the town—herrings in the hand on sticks, and huge black fish dragged through the dust—sick at the sight and smell—cross the harbour to the Island Castle very grand and very wild with Cathedral tower, extensive ruins, and tombstones of recent date, several of shipwrecked men. . . . Turned out of road to Kirk Christ Lizaire, embowered in trees on the hill, and pretty house near. The whole country pleasant to Ramsey—steep red banks of river, the town close to the sea within a large bay, backed by a green mountain and glen—fine trees, with houses on the steep. . . . the cottage[1] all unsuspected till we reach a little opening where it

[1] Near Ramsey, where D. was to spend two nights.

lurks at the foot of a glen, under green steeps, a low thatched white dwelling, the grassy pleasure-plot adorned with flowers, and above it on one side a hanging garden, flowers, fruit, vegetables intermingled, and above all the orchard and forest trees. Kindly welcome from the hostess Mrs Brew and her friend; the one faded and sickly, yet bright and elegantly formed; the other a lively little stump, toothless in the underjaw—hardworked hands and arms, telling of all day labour in their little garden. A bewitching spot the Cottage. Peeps of the sea and up the glen, and a full view of the green steep; a little stream murmuring below. We sauntered in the garden, and I paced from path to path, picked ripe fruit, ran down to the sands, there paced—watched the ships and steam boats—in short was charmed with the beauty and novelty of the scene, the quiet rural glen, the chearful shore, the solemn sea. To bed before day was gone.

'*Friday July 11th* again sunny and delightful—this the sweetest morning place I ever housed in, warm, yet breezy, and so retired it tempts you to walk out half-dressed from the ground-floor bedroom. After dinner at 2 o'clock parted from my hospitable friend Mrs Brew . . . and waited ½ an hour on the road for the Carrier's cart in which the front place had been taken for me, a most pleasant conveyance—road smooth and a variety of delightful views all the way to Douglas—at first over very high ground, crossing frequent glens with rivulets, and trees thriving wherever scattered. We descend to Laxey, a village at the foot of a long glen headed by Snawfield Mountain—tempted by the cleanliness of a poor hut to enter it with my companion, a young Methodist, who exclaimed to the poor inmate: "How happy you are! Here you have everything, health and contentment!" "Nay", says she, "I have very little—I have only what I get by spinning, and that is but so much the hank and so much the pound." "Well! but there are good people to help you." "Good people are but scarce in this world—I do not get much in that way." "Well! but you have health, and that is the best of earthly blessings." "It *is* a great blessing, but I have nothing else." Now there was no reason why the young Methodist should conclude that this poor woman had any unusual share of health. She had no appearance of it, and must have been above 50 years of age. She had never been married, lived alone, and was one of 9 children, all now dead or dispersed. "After all" again exclaimed my friend "How sweet! here is everything for contentment", and so satisfied parted with these words, uttered in a soft piping tone, "Peace be with you! Think upon Jesus". "Aye," replied the poor woman, "That is the only thing. That is the best thing." I said little but noticing the extreme cleanliness of her poor hovel, divided between her and an aged neighbour, who was keeping her company, the few halfpence I had in my bag, which certainly seemed to give her more comfort than my friend's felicitations on her blessed condition.

'The road still pleasant through the pretty village of Kirk Conchall on the heights, that looks down on Douglas Bay. This was certainly one of the loveliest evenings ever seen; sea as still as a mirror reflecting the streaky sky!

'*Saturday July 19th.* Sate all afternoon with Joanna, sailed at 10 minutes before 12. The moon soon set. The night warm. Magnificent castle and mountain clouds over England. In the opposite quarter Mona light-house. And what a sunrise! More heavenly than any earthly sight. Mountains and sea, cliffs, and bright sunshine in bay—sunshine and shade.'

When Dorothy is at home again the entries in her diary shrink to their normal brevity, but they have a pathetic interest, for they record the last days in which she had strength as of old to roam the country-side. On August 7 she is 'on Fairfield—very fine views'; in September she passed a week at Hallsteads with William and 'only encountered two half-wet days'; and two days after her return is off to Keswick with Dr. Bell: on October 9 'Wm and I had a charming ramble on Loughrigg Fell. The weather', she adds, 'continued unusually fine and warm till my departure on Friday Nov. 7, 1828 with Wm in gig, Dora on pony; we parted below Elleray.'

Her objective was Whitwick, where she was to keep house for her nephew John during the winter; but a week on the way had been allotted to Maria Jewsbury at Manchester, who duly forwarded to Dora a lively account of aunt Wordsworth's tireless energy.

'She left us yesterday in excellent health and spirits with a most lovely day for her journey. I hope she enjoyed herself tolerably whilst here. I think you would smile if you knew all she did and saw. "Panting Time", that is myself, "toiled after her in vain". Churches, Museums, Factories, Shopping, Institutions, company at home and abroad—not that I attempted to compete with her—no, I merely lay in bed and legislated—provided relays of friends and carriages—and had the pleasure of knowing that my visitor was pleased and that she won all hearts before and round her. She is the very genius of popularity—an embodied spell—I should be jealous of her for a continuance—I should be dethroned upon my own sofa—amidst my own circle.' 'Do you know', she breaks out in a later letter, 'I call her, among other things, Logan's Cuckoo;

There is no winter in her year
No sorrow in her song.'

From Manchester to Whitwick was a two days' journey:

'*November 17th.* outside of Coach to Nottingham. (8 A.M.–9 P.M.) Darley Dale and Matlock enchanting—Bakewell a pretty village—like market town. Darley Church—"largest yew-tree in England" but not so vigorous as Lorton, nor so large in girth as the Borrowdale brethren.[1] Haddon Hall a venerable castle-like mansion. *Tuesday Nov. 18th.* sun rises out of gold—met Mr M.'s carriage at the Turn-pike. Lady B. to lunch at Mr M.'s—put in carriage—met John—much pleased to find myself within his lowly parsonage—chatted and worked till bed-time.'

With John she passed a winter of quiet happiness, helping him in his parish duties and rejoicing to find how seriously he had taken up his work, walking in Charnwood Forest, reading, visiting at Coleorton, which was only three miles off. Sir George Beaumont had died two years before, and a young Sir George, his distant cousin, reigned in his stead; but her old friend Lady Beaumont, though failing in health, was as affectionate as ever. The simple life at Whitwick parsonage had much in it to recall to her those distant, happy days spent with John's father at Dove Cottage. Before the end of March she had the extra joy of a visit from Willy, now on his way to Germany. Then, on one of the first days of April, she was suddenly struck down. 'Imprudent exposure during a long walk'[2] brought on a violent inflammation of the bowels. For twenty-four hours she lay in a raging fever, and all that time in torture. Her life was in imminent danger.

When the news reached Rydal, Mary and Dora were already in great distress about the state of William's eyes. The inflammation was worse than ever: whereas before it had only affected the lids, it had now moved to the eye itself, and any mental worry or occupation aggravated the trouble; for him to leave the house might result, they feared, in a total loss of sight: so it was decided that Mary should set out at once for Whitwick, whilst Dora tended her father.

[1] Cf. *Yew-trees*, *Oxf. W.*, p. 184.

[2] W. W. to H. C. R., Feb. 5, 1833.

WHITWICK PARSONAGE
from a pencil drawing by
DORA WORDSWORTH

Before Mary could report her safe arrival they were cheered by a 'letter from the dear invalid's dear self'.[1] She had been allowed to leave her bed, and wrote from the fire-side where she had been sitting for nearly three hours; and the next day a note came from Mary opening with the reassuring words, *all well as heart could wish*, but warning them that Dorothy had had a most narrow escape, and that for a long, long time she would require great care and watchfulness.

'What a shock it was to our poor hearts', wrote William[2] to Crabb Robinson a few weeks later. 'Were she to depart, the Phasis of my moon would be robbed to a degree that I have not the courage to think of. During her illness we often thought of your esteem of her goodness, and of your kindness to her on all occasions.' From this time forward, though her progress to health seemed rapid, he realized that her constitution was shattered, and his restless anxiety never slept. Dorothy herself, though fully aware of the danger through which she had passed, was for long inclined to take too sanguine a view of her condition, and all sense of self pity was lost in her joyful gratitude for the sympathy which met her on every hand.

> 'It drew tears from my eyes', she wrote to Crabb Robinson on May 2, 'to read of your affectionate anxiety concerning me. In fact it is the first time in my life of fifty six[3] years in which I have had a serious illness, therefore I have never before had an opportunity of knowing how much some distant Friends care about me—Friends abroad—Friends at home—all have been anxious . . . and more so, far more, I am sure, than I deserve; but I attribute much of this to my having been so remarkably strong and healthy, it came like a shock to everyone to be told of a dangerous illness

[1] Dora W. to E. Q., Apr. 11, 1829. For the next few years Dora's letters to E. Q. are a valuable source of information concerning Dorothy. Ever since the death of Mrs. Q. in 1822 they had been on terms of growing intimacy, but their correspondence proves conclusively that it was not till 1836–7 that each of them realized the feelings of the other to be more than friendship, and it was probably not till 1838–9 that E. Q. applied to W. W. for her hand in marriage. Knight's misdating of W. W.'s letter to Dora on the subject 1828 instead of ten years later (*v. Letters*, ii. 321) has given rise to the impression that W. W.'s opposition to the marriage was far more stubborn and protracted than it actually was. His reluctance at parting with his daughter in 1839 is less inexcusable than it would have been in 1828. Largely owing to the kind offices of Miss Fenwick, W. had withdrawn his objections by Feb. 1840, and they were married in 1841.

[2] W. W. to H. C. R., Apr. 26, 1829.

[3] She was really fifty-seven and a half.

having attacked me. I am now, through God's mercy, perfectly restored to health, and almost to strength; but quiet care—for a time at least, I am assured is necessary; and indeed my own frame admonishes me that it is. But for the sake of my kind friends I am bound to take care, and I promise them all—including you who will be far away from us, that I will be neither rash nor negligent. Indeed I never can forget what I suffered myself nor the anxiety of those around me. My nephew William was the tenderest nurse possible—It would have moved anybody's heart to see him. . . .'

A month later she expresses disappointment that 'her usual strength is so slow to return';[1] early in July, however, she was judged fit to move. She broke her journey North at Halifax, where, wrote Dora, 'she is gaining health daily, but as usual finds a more than plausible excuse for putting off her return.'[2] At Halifax, however, she was again seriously ill, this time with a complaint diagnosed as cholera morbitis.

On September 9 she was back at Rydal, 'thankful to be at home again. It is very pleasing', she wrote,[3] 'to observe the joy in every face at the sight of me, looking as they say, healthy and well. So indeed I am, but I find that I must not try my strength at all.' In November she was again confined to her bed and was forced to enact the invalid till April. Yet when her brother wrote to Lamb[4] in January of 'her dangerous illness—the effects of which are not yet got over' she protested in a postscript: 'His account of me is far too doleful. I am, I assure you, perfectly well; and it is only in order to become strong, as heretofore, that I confine myself mainly to the house; and yet, were I to trust my feelings merely, I would say that I am strong already.'

Her affection for the Lambs had lost none of its warmth:

'I do not ask you, Miss Lamb, to write, for I know you dislike the office; but dear Charles L., you whom I have known almost five-and-thirty years, I trust I do not in vain entreat you to let me have the eagerly desired letter at your earliest opportunity. . . . Tell us of all whom you know, in whom you know us also to be interested, but above all, be very minute in what regards your own dear selves, for there are no persons in the world, exclusive of members of our own family, of whom we think and talk so frequently, or

[1] Dora W. to E. Q., June 3, 1829.
[2] Dora W. to E. Q., July 20, 1829.
[3] D. W. to J. M., Sept. 15, 1829.
[4] W. W. and D. W. to C. and M. Lamb, Jan. 9 and 10, 1830.

with such delightful remembrances. Your removal from[1] London (though to my thought London is scarcely London without you) shall not prevent my seeing you both in your own cottage, if I live to go there again; but at present I have no plans leading me thither.

'Now that Mr Monkhouse is gone, we females have no absolute home there, and should we go it will probably be on our way to the Continent, or to the southern shores of England. Wishes I do now and then indulge of at least revisiting Switzerland, and again of crossing the Alps, and even strolling on to Rome. But there is a great change in my feelings respecting plans for the future. If we make any, I entertain them as an amusement perhaps for a short while, but never set my heart upon anything which is to be accomplished three months hence, and have no satisfaction whatever in *schemes*. When one has lived almost sixty years, one is satisfied with present enjoyment and thankful for it, without daring to count on what is to be done six months hence.

'My brother and sister are both in excellent health. In him there is no failure except the tendency to inflammation in his eyes, which disables him from reading much, or at all by candle light; and the use of his pen is irksome to him. However, he has a most competent and willing amanuensis in his daughter, who takes all labour from mother's and aged aunt's hands. His muscular powers are in no degree diminished. Indeed, I think he walks regularly more than ever, finding fresh air the best bracing to his weak eyes. He is still the crack skater on Rydal Lake, and, as to climbing of mountains, the hardiest and the youngest are yet hardly a match for him. In composition I can perceive no failure, and his imagination seems as vigorous as in youth; yet he shrinks from his great work, and both during the last and present winter has been employed in writing small poems. Do not suppose, my dear friend, that I write this boastingly. Far from it. It is in thankfulness for present blessings, yet always with a sense of the possibility that all will have a sudden check; and, if not so, the certainty that in the course of man's life but a few years of vigorous health and strength can be allotted to him. For this reason, my sister and I take every opportunity of pressing upon him the necessity of applying himself to his great work, and this he feels, resolves to do it, and again resolution fails. And now I almost fear habitually that it will be ever so.

'Miss Hutchinson and her sister Joanna are both with us. Miss H. is perfectly well, and Joanna very happy, though she may

[1] 'from' printed 'to' in K., but the sense requires 'from'. The Lambs were now living at Enfield.

always be considered an invalid. . . . She is an example for us all. With the better part of her property she purchased Columbian bonds at above 70, gets no interest, will not sell, consequently the cheapness of the little isle[1] tempted her thither on a visit, and she finds the air so suitable for her health, and everything else so much to her mind, that she will, in spite of our unwillingness to part with her, make it her home. As to her lost property, she never regrets it. She has so reduced her wants that she declares she is now richer than ever she was in her life, and so she is. . . . I believe you never saw Joanna, and it is a pity, for you would have loved her very much. She possesses all the good qualities of the Hutchinsons. My niece Dora is very active, and her father's helper at all times; and in domestic concerns she takes all the trouble from her mother and me.'

Other letters written during the year show that illness had not made her self-centred; her loving interest in her friends—the Southeys, the Coleridges, Miss Barker—was alive as ever.

'Miss Barker', she tells Mrs Clarkson,[2] 'wrote to me to inform us that she was going to be married to a young man of not more than thirty-five, desperately in love with her. . . . I hope it will come to nothing. We suspect the youth to have been a Boulogne swindler. I wrote my mind, counselled inquiries and settlements etc, perhaps not very palateable—as no notice has been taken of my letter. . . . We had some hopes of the Southeys becoming our neighbours; but they have renewed the lease of their present house, and really I am disinterested enough to be glad, as, though wishing to be near us, they dreaded a removal. . . . Edith is engaged to be married to a Mr Warter, now chaplain to the Embassy at Copenhagen. . . . Mrs Coleridge is the proudest and busiest of grandmothers—Sarah an excellent nurse, and her husband the most contented of men—if we may judge from his letters. Poor S.T.C. declining in body, but they tell us as vigorous as ever in mind. I am happy to think that William and he will meet together yet once again. Hartley goes on as usual—leaves his comfortable home about once in three months wandering about no one knows where,—sleeping in barns etc. etc. When you meet him smiles and talks away as if all were right—how busy he is—what he is writing for—this Annual or that Magazine—but alas! no money comes in—and his Friends through me, pay for his board etc. etc. This, however is a secret, so do not mention it.'

[1] i.e. the Isle of Man.

[2] D. W. to C. C., Apr. and Nov. 1830.

Dorothy had already spoken of

'Hartley's hopeless state. We had provided good lodgings for him. He had no one want, was liked by the people of the house, and for seven weeks was steady and industrious. Money came to repay him for his work, and what does he do? Instead of discharging his just debts, he pays a score off at a public house, and with eight sovereigns in his pocket takes off: is now wandering somewhere, and will go on wandering till some charitable person leads the vagrant home. We have only heard of his lodging at first at different inns—this no doubt while the money lasted—and since of his having been seen on the roads, and having lodged in this Barn and that. It has been my sad office to report to his poor mother of his doings, but my *late* reports have been of a chearing kind. I now dread the task that is before me. I shall not, however, write till he is again housed with the charitable Matron who is willing again to receive him. You will, perhaps, say, my dear friend, "Why do you not rouse the country, and send after him? or at least yourselves seek him out?" alas, we have done this so often without any good coming we are determined not to stir—but it is impossible not to be very much distressed and uneasy in mind, and especially for his Mother's sake. Of course you will not speak of what I have told you—though it is notorious enough in these parts.'

Nephew John had now left Whitwick for the living of Moresby, near Workington, and the family event of 1830 was his engagement and marriage to Isabella, daughter of Mr. Curwen of Workington Hall. The wedding took place upon October 11. Dorothy was not sorry to have an excuse for avoiding 'a bustle and ceremony which to say the best of it is but a melancholy pleasure', and her mind must have reverted to the homely simplicity of her brother's wedding; yet there is a touch of pride in the lively account of it which she sent to Playford:[1]

'Five carriages conveyed the parties to Church—servants perched outside—Mr Curwen and Dora and Isabella in the first carriage—postilions and servants wore favours. All Workington was abroad making a lane for the carriages to drive through—some on house-tops—all the windows crowded. The people shouted Hurra! Curwen for ever! and the two young brothers of the Bride outside her carriage kept off their hats smiling and bowing all the way.

[1] D. W. to C. C., Nov. 1830.

Not a tear shed at Church, or till they reached home, when, as Dora says "We all had a good cry". Fifty people sate down to breakfast. Then departed the Bride and Bridegroom for Scotland. By the bye I should have told you that on their way from Church they scattered silver among the people according to the family custom at W. Hall. Guns were fired and ships in the harbour hoisted their flags.'

All through this year (1830) and till the following December Dorothy's health was slowly mending. 'It seems to be decreed', she tells Crabb,[1] 'that I must stay at home, and surely it is no punishment to be confined to this beautiful spot . . . this mode of life has no effect whatever upon my spirits, and certainly it has agreed with my health.' The summer and autumn of 1831 were full of happiness for her. At the end of April little Rotha Quillinan came for a nine months' stay with them, in May Willy returned from Germany; John and Isabella paid them frequent visits, and they saw more company than ever.

'The summer', wrote William[2] to Kenyon, 'has been a brilliant one for sunshine and fair and calm weather, brilliant also for its unexampled gaiety . . . in short a fever of pleasure from morn to dewy eve, from dewy eve till break of day. Our youths and maidens, like Chaucer's squire, have "slept no more than doth the nightingale", and our old men have looked as bright as Tithonus when his withered cheek reflected the blushes of Aurora, upon her first declaration of her passion for him. In the room where I am now dictating, we had, three days ago, a dance,—forty beaux and belles, besides matrons, ancient spinsters, and grey beards—and to-morrow we are to muster for a venison feast. Why are you not here, either to enjoy or to philosophise upon this dissipation?'

Dorothy, if she had not the strength to take an active part in all the dissipation, was well enough to enter into its spirit. Nor was her company restricted to visitors at Rydal Mount, for though she seldom walked beyond the garden terrace, she had her pony chaise in which from time to time she called on friendly neighbours; and early in September she even ventured to leave home for ten days, and join John and Isabella at the Curwens' house on Belle Isle, Windermere. And then, in October, when William and Dora returned from a visit to Scott at Abbotsford, she had the joy of welcoming Robert Jones, 'the companion', as she

[1] D. W. to H. C. R., Apr. 22, 1830.

[2] Sept. 13, 1831.

reminded Mrs. Clarkson,[1] 'of my brother forty years ago over the Alps. He looks back to that journey as the golden and sunny spot in his life. It would delight you to hear the pair talk of their adventures. My brother active, lively, and almost as strong as ever on a mountain top; Jones fat and roundabout and rosy, and puffing and panting while he climbs the little hill from the road to our house. Never was there a more remarkable contrast; yet time seems to have strengthened the attachment of the native of Cambrian mountains to his Cumbrian friend.'

But this happy year ended sadly enough. In the week before Christmas Dorothy had a violent recurrence of internal inflammation, accompanied by acute pain and nausea, and this was followed by a swelling of the legs and ankles which, even when she was convalescent, deprived her almost entirely of the power of walking. The story of the next few years is one of repeated attacks of illness, from which she seemed, almost miraculously, to recover, only to be once more laid aside.

Thus on April 12 (1832) 'she is seated on the sofa, looking almost like herself again, trying to husband her strength for the meeting with her nephew Willy, who is expected this morning';[2] in May again she is ill, and again convalescent. The eager hope with which her ups and downs were followed by all the family shines out with a beautiful clarity in Dora's letter to Quillinan of May 25:

> 'I need only write what I hear Mother at this moment saying to convince you what happy people we are just now at Rydal Mount. "Jane, where are Miss W's bonnet and cloak?", and now I hear her going downstairs to sit upon the bench in the garden, and for the second time too. She was sadly overcome by the exertion the first time—but of course she was affected at once again finding herself in this lovely garden, which looked to all of us a thousand times more lovely than it ever looked before. I see her out of my window making her way by help of Mother's arm towards the Green Terrace. Father is very anxious that she should see the improvements that he has been making in that bit of ground, and I think they will accomplish it for she says "I am quite strong". I hope she will sometime let me send you an affecting poem which she has written on the pleasure she received from the first spring flowers that were carried up to her when confined to her sick room—the 3 last stanzas which I remember I will steal for you

[1] D. W. to C. C., Sept. 9, 1831. [2] Dora W. to E. Q., Apr. 12, 1832.

I felt a power unfelt before
Controlling weakness, langour, pain;
It bore me to the terrace walk;
I trod the hills again.

No prisoner in this lonely room
I *saw* the green banks of the Wye,
Recalling thy prophetic words,
Bard! Brother! Friend from infancy.

No need of motion or of strength
Or even the breathing air;
I thought of Nature's loveliest scenes
And with memory I was there.

you must excuse limping measure. Aunt cannot write regular metre.'

As Dorothy lay upon her sick bed one of her chief pleasures was the writing of verses. They have little intrinsic merit; their measure, as Dora says, is often limping, their expression flat, their thought somewhat commonplace; only rarely are they lit up by that alertness of vision and felicity of phrasing of which to the last her prose was capable. Yet they reflect a real part of her mind, chastened and subdued as it was by her prolonged suffering. Their prevalent tone is religious, suggesting the spiritual strength she drew from that simple orthodox piety which, during the last twenty years, had gradually superseded the natural piety of her youth—'the assurance of immortality', as she noted in her diary, 'strengthening as the body decays—feelings kept down repressed by exuberant health and strength'. Viewed in this light her physical weakness was to her an intimation of divine love, bringing no loss, but rather a stronger assurance of the abiding blessings of her life:

No prisoner am I on this couch,
My mind is free to roam,
And leisure, peace and loving friends
Are the best treasures of an earthly home.

Such gifts are mine, then why deplore
The feeble body's slow decay,
A warning mercifully sent
To fix my hope upon a surer stay?

And may I learn those precious gifts
Rightly to prize, and by their soothing power
All fickle murmuring thoughts repress
And fit my fluttering heart for the last hour.

'Loving friends', indeed, she had in plenty, and constant proof of their devotion. A small instance of this, which gave her special delight, was a gift of money which Jane and her sister-in-law, Mrs. Pollard, 'with a delicate kindness', began at this time to send her annually. 'So far', she wrote,[1] 'from being ashamed of receiving such a gift from *such* friends, I am proud of it. Already I have schemed for the supply of several small—*wants* I will not call them—but gratifications, such as I might otherwise have scrupled to indulge myself with.' And several letters written in the next years bear witness to the pleasure she gained from 'doing many a charitable deed', or from making little presents to her family and friends. Thus, when Willy was hesitating whether he could raise the money for a journey to Rydal, she wrote[2] to him 'Do not let the low state of your purse prevent your coming; I will admit of no excuse or reason except that of business, and as to the money I will help you with all you may want, and take it without scruple, as I have a little Fund of my own which enables me to give pleasure to the rich or comfort to the poor.'

The total neglect of her diary from December 1831 to the following October suggests that this was a period of great weakness: when she resumes it there are some pathetic entries:

'Oct 6th. Now at 1 o'clock have dined and am ready to go out, but the wind is cold and sky threatening. I must lie down to rest. I wished to go and lie on sofa to hear Wm read part of the poem on his own life, but had a melancholy pleasure in the sound of his voice—with now and then a word or two giving me the key to what was employing their thoughts.

'Nov. 15th with James[3] to Grasmere and by Church—overtook

[1] D. W. to J. M., Nov. 20, 1832.

[2] D. W. to W. W. (jun.), Jan. 2, 1834.

[3] James Dixon, for many years in the Wordsworths' employ, was a model servant and something of a character. Dorothy speaks of him as 'an industrious and simple-hearted serving man, who could do all sorts of little jobs', and describes his bow as 'the most exquisite sample of respectful simplicity'. For many years one of his chief duties was to take her for drives in the pony chaise, or wheel her about the garden in her chair; and it was he who, on Dora's death, innocently reproved his master for his over-indulgence in grief. He was devoted to them all and 'often spoke

an old man with crutches. His pace so slow we stopped some time to enable him to be in safety . . . in passing recognised the changed features of Robt Newton—Eye slow and dull, mouth sunken. Even from middle age as much altered as the child of 6 years grown into the man.

'Dec. 26th The Fiddlers went their round. Found me awake.'

It was at Robert Newton's cottage that Mrs. Clarkson had spent the summer of 1805; here, probably, that Dorothy had herself slept a night, nearly forty years before, when she first passed through Grasmere; and as she lay awake, listening to the fiddlers, she must have recalled that winter's evening long ago, when she heard the pattering of little feet on the stone floor at Dove Cottage, and Johnny would dance with no one but her.

A later entry has a pleasant glimpse into the future: 'Sunday 30th the wind at rest and sun shining to-day. Dr Arnold and his boys come in from Church. Their gladsome feet and voices very pleasant.'

Early in the next year (1833) she had another dangerous attack, worse than any since her first seizure. 'A week ago', wrote Dora on February 22, 'we little expected my dear aunt would look on this fair world again—Mr Carr thought with us that she had scarcely an hour to live'; and Dorothy herself referred afterwards to 'one fearful night', when 'Mr Carr left me because he could do no more for me, and my poor brother went to lie down on his bed, thinking he could not bear to see me die.'[1] But again she rallied. 'I wash her face', writes Dora, 'as she used to do mine 30 years ago. She is happy and contented and has only one regret, that she cannot read or even bear to be read to—she cannot gain new ideas and she knows she must lose old ones: she has written for me some very pretty stanzas.' Towards the end of April she was well enough to make one entry in her diary: 'Two glowing anemones and a snow white companion are in a pot on my window ledge, and two knots of primroses of the Alpine purple. Rooks busy—all the birds of

of himself as a favourite of fortune'. To H. C. R., who had a warm regard for him and used to send him an annual gift of a sovereign, he wrote in 1863: 'I am the only one of the famaly left. But I pay many little visits to the famaly in the Church yard at Grasmere and there I often reflect on the Many happy Years that I spent with them in life.' (*v.* H. C. R.'s *Diary*, ed. Sadler, 1872.)

[1] In an undated letter to Mrs. Hoare of Hampstead, but it seems to refer to this crisis in her illness.

sky and earth are singing and all is wrapped in happy brightness'; and in May William writes to Charles Lamb[1] that they had just been enjoying together his new volume, *The last essays of Elia*; at the close of his letter, after referring to her illness, he breaks out: 'In tenderness of heart I do not honestly believe she was ever exceeded by any of God's creatures. In loving-kindness she has no bounds. God bless her for ever and ever.'

Quillinan, hearing about this time from Dora that 'aunt is in great glee at the prospect of seeing her lover Mr Robinson' in July, replied in some alarm: 'I really had some fears that Crabb with the best intentions would talk her to death'; but after the visit Dora was able to reassure him:[2] 'Mr Robinson's 40 lawyer power has been of infinite service to our dear invalid, who is so much improved that we can scarcely believe our eyes when we see her hobbling along the upstairs passage as far as my mother's room.' An entry in Dorothy's diary runs: 'his company always pleasant when I was strong enough to listen—no need of effort on my part. Patiently would he sit by the hour, trying to entertain me. He was my prop in walking and even led me to my bedroom when tired—*would* have rubbed my feet and ankles, but this I *could* not consent to. It was my good brother's office twice in the day—if but once how he groaned and lamented.'

By September she seemed to have made up much of the ground lost by her attack at the opening of the year.

> 'She can read', wrote Dora,[3] 'write, work, talk and walk about her room without a stick—dress herself—and drives out every day—has been sitting for her portrait to a Mr Crosthwaite (a self-educated artist from Cockermouth). We did not expect much, but he has done wonders and delighted us all with an excellent likeness—and such a pretty picture. She is taken just as she is now, sitting in the large chair with paper-case on her knee and pen and ink on the table on one side and "little Miss Belle" on the other, looking so pert and funny.'[4]

But two months later she had another relapse, and all through the year 1834 she was visibly weaker. In a little note to Crabb

[1] W. W. to C. Lamb, May 17, 1833.

[2] Dora W. to E. Q., July 24, 1833.

[3] Dora W. to E. Q., Sept. 10, 1833.

[4] Looking to-day at this portrait, which is the only one of Dorothy that is known to survive, we can hardly avoid the feeling that the approval they gave it was influenced in part by the poverty of their expectations.

Robinson, written on July 24, she tells him what a great delight it would be if he would come again and drag her on the green terrace, 'for alas! my legs are of little use except in helping me to steer an enfeebled Body from one part of the room to the other. The longest walk I have attempted has been once round the Gravel Front of the House.'

The death of Coleridge in July, and of Lamb in December, severed two strong links with the past. The news of Coleridge must have revived many poignant memories, but he had long been no more than a memory to her, and she was herself too near to death to feel acutely any further sense of separation. Rather did the passage of life, and her own frailty, impress upon her more deeply than ever the folly of those who, with their best years still before them, throw away, wilfully or in sheer apathy, their golden opportunities. Of Sara Coleridge, who had a tendency to melancholy, she wrote: 'Her father's death rouzed her, but before that she had profited by my advice and plain speech, as I heard from both herself and others—and she now seems determined to be well, and God grant that she may, for it is a deplorable thing to see a young creature, who seems to have every wish of her heart gratified, give up to fanciful despondency.' And in the same spirit she addressed one of her god-daughters;[1] 'I send you a God-mother's blessing, with sincerest wishes that you may not waste the happy days of Youth. Make the most of them. They will never return, and if you do not profit by present advantages you will bitterly repent when it is too late.'

It was the inexhaustible resources of a past of which she had herself wasted no moment that made her own life, old and broken as she was, still precious to herself and to her friends.

[1] D. W. to Elizabeth Hutchinson, Sept. 14, 1834.

XX
POSTHUMOUS LIFE
1835–1855 (aet. 63–83)

THE year 1835 brought trouble on trouble to the household at Rydal Mount. In the early months Dora was seriously ill with inflammation of the spine, and had to spend her days upon the sofa; she lost her appetite completely, and appeared to be in rapid decline; a little later Sara, who for years had been the family sheet-anchor, was prostrated by an attack of lumbago which developed into acute rheumatic fever; Dorothy, it seemed, was dying. 'Aunt Dorothy', wrote Dora[1] on June 1, 'grows weaker and weaker, but so imperceptibly—at one time you might think she had not ten minutes to live, at another (she is) so bright and strong that you are almost cheated into a belief that she may be spared to you even for years. Dear Father keeps up his spirits most patiently, though at times I see his heart is well-nigh breaking, and when the blow comes I am sure he will meet it with resignation—how mercifully has this bitter blast been tempered to him!' As the month wore on Sara was thought to be turning the corner, whilst Dorothy sank rapidly, and for days was only kept alive by stimulants. But on the 27th Sara passed peacefully away: Dorothy began slowly to regain some physical strength; but as her body revived she lost control over her mind. 'Speaking of her faculties', writes William,[2] 'she told me that Miss Hutchinson's vanishing had been a sad *shattering* to them.'

Up to this time her brother's prophecy and dearest hope for Dorothy had been fulfilled. In her old age, as we have seen it reflected in her letters and her diary, through the eyes of old friends and new acquaintances, her thoughts and feelings had not died,[3] her spirit was bright and lovely as ever. With restless

[1] To E. Q., June 1, 1835. [2] W. W. to H. C. R., July 6, 1835.
[3] Cf. 'Dear child of Nature', ll. 13–18 (*Oxf. W.*, p. 218).

> Thy thoughts and feelings shall not die,
> Nor leave thee, when grey hairs are nigh,
> A melancholy slave;
> But an old age serene and bright,
> And lovely as a Lapland night,
> Shall lead thee to thy grave.

energy she had thrown herself into each fresh experience—whether it was the scenery of the Isle of Man, or the churches and factories of Manchester, or the society of men and women whom she met upon her travels; and in her five years of physical decline she had strained her powers to the utmost to take a full share in the 'goings-on' of those she loved. Since girlhood, the effort to maintain control over so full an emotional life, affections so tender and passionate, sensibilities so acute, had entailed a constant drain upon her nervous energy. It is characteristic of her highly-strung temperament that she should have remarked, years before, to Lady Beaumont,[1] 'Any strong emotion cures my diseases for a time, and if I am well as surely brings them on'; she was continually asking of her body more than it could safely give. For sixty-four years her physique, never robust, had bravely responded to the call: then the onset and successive shocks of a severe illness destroyed the delicate adjustment of mind and body; and Nature chose to preserve the worn-out physical frame by releasing it from the most exacting demands upon it. The will power, which resists and controls alike the wayward suggestions of fancy and the natural promptings of physical impulse, was taken from her. The body was saved at the expense of the mind.

The twenty years of posthumous life that followed only belong to the biography of Dorothy Wordsworth in so far as they reveal in fitful gleams something of what she once had been: the tale of her days of insensibility or mental vagary is more properly regarded as a part of the lives of those who suffered the greater torture of witnessing her wreck, and who, through the long years of hope and sorrow, repaid to her in full measure the love which she had lavished upon them.

> 'I fear you cannot read this letter', wrote William[2] to Crabb Robinson a fortnight after her collapse. 'My hand is shaking. I have had so much agitation to-day in attempting to quiet my poor sister, and from the necessity of refusing her things which would be improper for her.'

> 'Dear Dorothy is now asleep after having been half an hour in the garden', writes Mary[3]—'on going out she wept aloud like a baby, being overcome with the beauty around her, and asked to

[1] D. W. to Lady B., Oct. 7, 1804. [2] July 6, 1835.
[3] M. W. to J. M., May 7, 1836.

be taken to a certain border . . . at first was too overpowered to look at it . . . on a sudden she began to sing.'

'Do keep out of ear shot of Aunt W. when she is not comfortable', wrote Quillinan[1] to Dora. 'I think you ought to stop your ears.'

'She is exactly like a very *clever tyrannical* spoilt child (for she is acute and discriminating to a marvellous degree), yet she has intervals of mildness and is overcome by her old affections, and sometimes she is very languid and weeps—which is very afflicting.'[2]

'Distressing as her state is', writes Mary[3] again, 'more especially to those who know what she once was, it is a comfort to see that she is happy—that is that she has no distress or sorrow that oppresses her more than the transient sorrow of a spoilt child,—to such an one we can only liken her. Yet at times, if you can fix her attention, her intellect is as bright, and she will express an opinion when asked, with as much judgment, as in her best days—but alas these gleams are shortlived. Her restless feelings (which we attribute to something amiss going on in the head which she rubs perpetually) prevent her finding quiet from reading—nor will she often listen to it—she says she is too busy with her own feelings! And thus, my dear friend, she wears away the day. Her greatest discomforts proceed from habits that I cannot describe—it would be too painful for us both were I to attempt it.'

Yet in these 'restless feelings' there was often a terrible intensity of which Mary's statement gives no inkling. The fitful returns of her real self would have been less complete had they not at times brought with them a tragic sense of what she had lost; and in letters which she penned in her more lucid intervals, written with her old mastery of style, she plumbed depths of anguish never sounded in the most poignant sorrows of earlier days. Thus to Edward Ferguson, the companion of her girlhood at Halifax:

Rydal Mount, Sunday, October 8th, 1837.

My dear Cousin Edward,

A madman might as well attempt to relate the history of his own doings, and those of his fellows in confinement, as I to tell you one hundredth part of what I have felt, suffered, and done. Through God's mercy I am now calm and easy.

[1] Oct. 13, 1836.
[2] M. W. to Mary Anne Marshall, May 4, 1836.
[3] M. W. to C. C., 1837.

I have not seen Charles Lamb's book.[1] His sister survives—a solitary twig, patiently enduring the storm of life. In losing her brother she lost all—all but the remembrance of him, which chears her the day through.

May God bless you

Yours ever truly,

DOROTHY WORDSWORTH.

This is not the letter of one who has 'no distress or sorrow that oppresses her more than the transient sorrow of a spoilt child'; and this little note to Dora,[2] with its rhythmic reiteration, and its lilt of wild melancholy, is drawn from a depth of suffering which seems to transcend mere personal experience, and become a lyrical lament on the irony of all human things:

(1838)[3]

My dearest Dora,

They say I must write a letter—and what shall it be? news—news—I must seek for news—My own thoughts are a wilderness "not pierceable by power of any star"[4]—News then is my resting place—news! news! Poor Peggy Benson lies in Grasmere Churchyard beside her once beautiful Mother. Fanny Haigh is gone to a better world. My friend Mrs Rawson has ended her ninety and two years pilgimage—and *I* have fought and fretted and striven and am here beside the fire. The Doves behind me at the small window—the laburnum with its naked seedpods shivers before my window and the pine-trees rock from their base. More I cannot write, so farewell! and may God bless you and your kind good Friend Miss Fenwick[5] to whom I send love and all the best of wishes. yours evermore

DOROTHY WORDSWORTH.

But doubtless for the most part her state was such as Mary has described it; she could still draw pleasure from poetry, for which

[1] Lamb's book here referred to must have been *The Letters of C. L. with a Sketch of his Life*, ed. *by T. N. Talfourd*, Moxon, 2 vols., 1837.

[2] This letter is written in as firm and clear a hand as she wrote in her prime—a striking contrast to the wavering and childish scrawl usual in her last days.

[3] This letter may be dated by the facts that Mrs. Rawson had died in 1837, and Peggy Benson in Feb. 1838.

[4] Spenser, *F.Q.*, I. i. 7. 'Not perceable with power of any starre'. Dorothy here significantly recalls Spenser's vivid description of the forest of Error in which Una and the Red Cross Knight 'wander too and fro in wayes unknowne'.

[5] Miss Fenwick was largely responsible in reconciling Dora's father to her marriage with E. Q.

her memory seemed hardly to have failed; thus when her brother quoted a line from Dyer's *Grongar Hill* she astonished him by finishing the passage. She took a pathetic delight in making little rhymes of her own, and copying them out for her friends; and her childish petulance would often pass if she were asked to repeat some of her verses. Birds and flowers still gave her vivid pleasure. As in the days at Forncett a robin was a constant visitor to her bedroom; she would watch for hours its graceful movements, and 'its soft warblings', Mary tells us, were 'most delicious to her feelings'. In fine weather she would be wheeled into the garden. 'Thousands of Lake tourists', wrote[1] Harriet Martineau, 'must remember the locked garden gate when Miss Wordsworth was taking the air, and the garden chair going round and round the terrace, with the emaciated little woman in it, who occasionally called out to strangers, and amused them with her clever sayings.' But though she was closely guarded from the casual intruder, she still enjoyed the company of friendly neighbours, Quillinan and his daughters, Miss Fenwick, Mrs. Arnold, and Lady Richardson; and the annual visits of Crabb Robinson were as welcome to her as to her brother. On her better days even a stranger was allowed to see her. In 1849 Julia Wedgwood, great niece of that Tom Wedgwood who, as the friend of Coleridge, had visited Dove Cottage in 1802, called at Rydal Mount:

> 'I was waiting', she says,[2] 'at the door when her chaise drew up, bearing the little shrunken figure from her daily excursion, and I looked into those "wild eyes" which kept all their life and light though the mind had grown dim. There was no dimness in her interest when she heard my name. "From whom are you sprung?" she inquired eagerly. My father's name meant nothing to her, and his uncle's, alas! meant nothing then to me, but her allusion to the latter clothes him with a halo perhaps more vivid to my eyes because the vision is so absolutely untransferable.'

But if the mere name of Wedgwood, by its throw-back into the distant past, could thus rekindle something of her old fire, what wonder that she was most herself when William was at her side, with the same 'restless watchfulness, the tenderness that

[1] Obituary notice of M. W. in *Daily News*, republished in *Cor. of H.C.R. and the W.s*, ed. Morley, ii. 828.

[2] *The Personal Life of Josiah Wedgwood the Potter*, by Julia Wedgwood, p. 332.

never sleeps', as had won her heart in girlhood? For the past he evoked was no mere episode: it comprised all that was most precious in her life. In her worst fits of wayward passion he alone had the power to calm her. 'But', said Quillinan,[1] 'he, you know, *spoils* her, poor thing.' The secret of his spell over her lay deeper than that, deeper even than the love that bound them together; it had its roots in an affinity of mind and temper that had united them instinctively in childhood, and had been strengthened by years of intimate companionship. Like William in the intensity of her emotions, she had always been like him too in her power of drawing inspiration from 'hiding places ten years deep', in the habit, consciously and passionately cultivated, of flooding the present with a light that shone from the remotest past. Thus on Christmas Day 1805, even while she spoke of her recent years at Grasmere as the happiest in her life, 'my heart', she had said, 'flutters and aches, striving to recall to my mind the remembrance of some of the more thoughtless pleasures of former years'. And now that her intellect was dimmed, the power of evoking the past remained providentially with her, for the habit had become a second nature. Hence for William her mind was still the mansion, though ruined, of all lovely forms, her memory the dwelling place of all sweet sounds and harmonies. Together they relived the days long gone by, trudging again over the Quantock Hills or along the banks of the Wye, meeting again the radiant Coleridge as he burst in upon them at Racedown or at Alfoxden, sitting again by their half-kitchen half-parlour fire at Dove Cottage, when she made of her shoulder a pillow for the head of her beloved. The life thus shared was no less necessary to William than to Dorothy. And when, with the death of his passionately loved daughter, the last shattering blow fell upon him, the broken-hearted old man found his only consolation in unremitting attendance upon his sister; and Mary, though bowed by a grief as deep as his, stood aside with the sublime self-effacement that had become a habit of her soul. 'The only enjoyment he seems to feel', she wrote[2] simply, 'is in his attendance on her—her death would be to him a sad calamity.'

[1] E. Q. to H. C. R., Aug. 12, 1848.

[2] Quoted in letter, H. C. R. to Miss Fenwick, Jan. 15, 1849; *v.* also Miss F. to H. R. C., Aug. 12, 1847. Dora had died in July, 1847.

But his release came first. On April 23, 1850, when he lay dying, her faculties were restored to her as though by miracle. 'Miss Wordsworth', wrote Quillinan,[1] 'is as much herself as she ever was in her life, and has an almost absolute command of her own will! does not make noises; is not all self; thinks of the feelings of others (Mrs Wordsworth's for example); is tenderly anxious about her brother, and in short, but for age and bodily infirmity, is almost *the* Miss Wordsworth we knew in past days. Whether this will last, or be the sign that she will not long survive her brother is beyond us.'

On his death she sank once more into insensibility. Even now there were momentary glimpses of her former self, she would still repeat her verses in the old sweet voice, and the mention of William would rouse her from lethargy; 'while all other affections seem to be dried up', we are told,[2] 'her love for her brother is as fresh as ever'. But Mary, who still watched over her with a loving tenderness, noticed that while she was less excitable, she grew at the same time more indifferent to byegone events. On January 25, 1855 the end came.

For four more years Mary lived on, almost the last of her generation.[3] Of those three friends whose lives had been so inextricably intertwined she, in truth, was the only one who was fitted to stand alone. With emotions less turbulent and passionate, with an imagination less urgent, her mental and spiritual vigour had suffered no decay; and though she, too, of necessity, lived much in the past, she was sustained by a fuller confidence in the future. Before her simple, unquestioning faith William's 'trembling fears, that friends disjoined by death should meet no more', had often stood rebuked. Misgivings, he had confessed,

> Misgivings, hard to vanquish or control,
> Mix with the day, and cross the hour of rest;
> While all the future, for thy purer soul,
> With "sober certainties" of love is blest;[4]

[1] E. Q. to H. R. C., Apr. 23, 1850.

[2] Miss Bronson to Mrs. Reed, May 26, 1854.

[3] Lady Beaumont had died in 1829, Joanna H. in 1843, Christopher W. in 1846, Mary Lamb and Jane Marshall in 1847, Thomas H. in 1849, Mrs. Clarkson and Miss Fenwick in 1856, Mary H. in 1858. Of M. W.'s brothers George alone survived her: he died in 1864.

[4] 'O dearer far', &c. (*Oxf. W.*, p. 112). The poem was probably inspired by grief at the approaching death of his friend, Thomas Monkhouse.

and, indeed, when Dora died, the truth of his confession was pathetically proved.[1] But Mary, fortified by the 'sober certainties of love', met each successive blow of fate with a calm courage, and regaining her tranquil cheerfulness, grew steadily to a greater beauty and amplitude of spirit. To her ninetieth year, though now deaf and almost blind, she kept that serene temper in which, through half a century, husband and sister had increasingly found comfort and support; so that one who met her in her latest years[2] could speak of her as 'the most lovely image of old age that I have ever seen in woman'. Her old age was, in truth, the crown and consummation of her life.

Dorothy, like William, though even more tragically, had long outlived herself. Hence, when the thought of her breaks in upon us—'like a flash of light', it is not her last days, despite their pathos, that we remember, but rather what she was in early womanhood—the frank impulsive child of nature, the companion of waterfalls and mountain breezes, with her eager delight in birds and flowers and all common things; the 'exquisite sister' who recalled a wayward poet to his vocation, giving him eyes and ears;

> A heart, the fountain of sweet tears;
> And love, and thought, and joy;[3]

and who, by her passionate devotion, won from him the noblest tribute that friend ever paid to friend:

> She who dwells with me, whom I have loved
> With such communion that no place on earth
> Can ever be a solitude to me.[4]

[1] For W. W.'s uncontrollable grief at Dora's death, *v.* H. C. R. to T. R., Dec. 23, 1847, and to Miss F., Dec. 24, 1847, Jan. 10, and 24, 1848.

[2] Miss Bronson to Mrs. Reed, May 18, 1854.

[3] 'The Sparrow's Nest' (*Oxf. W.*, p. 79).

[4] *Poems on the Naming of Places*, iii (*Oxf. W.*, p. 148).

APPENDIXES

ABRIDGED TABLE SHOWING THE CONNEXIONS HUTCHINSON, COOKSON,

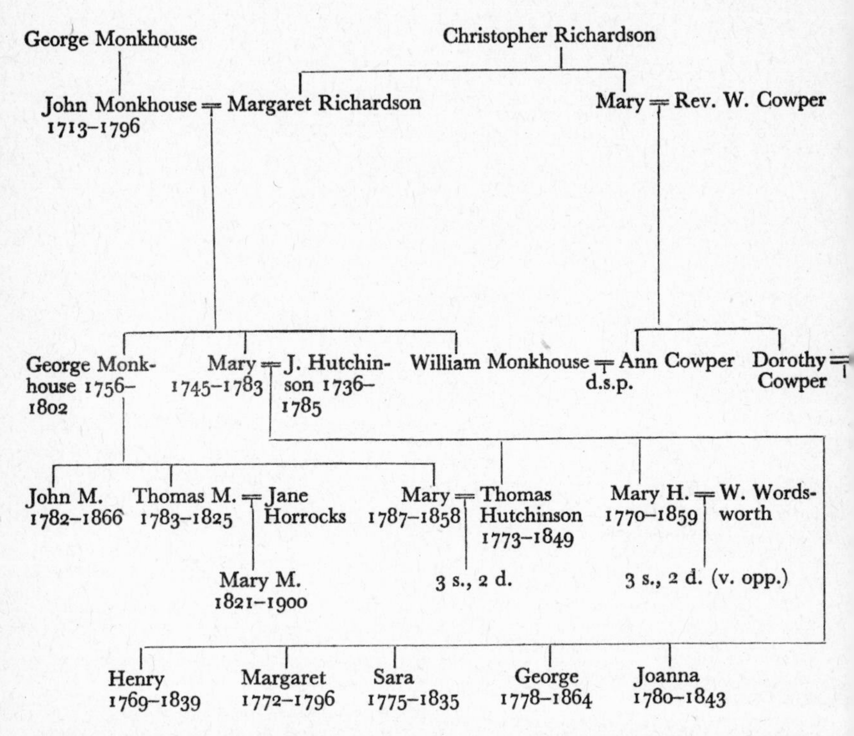

N.B. It will be noticed that William Monkhouse, uncle of Mary Hutchinson, and William Cookson, uncle of Dorothy Wordsworth, married two sisters, Ann and Dorothy Cowper, William Monkhouse and Ann Cowper being already first cousins.

Subsequently Thomas Hutchinson, brother of Mrs. Wordsworth, married Mary Monkhouse, his first cousin.

BETWEEN THE FAMILIES OF MONKHOUSE,
AND WORDSWORTH

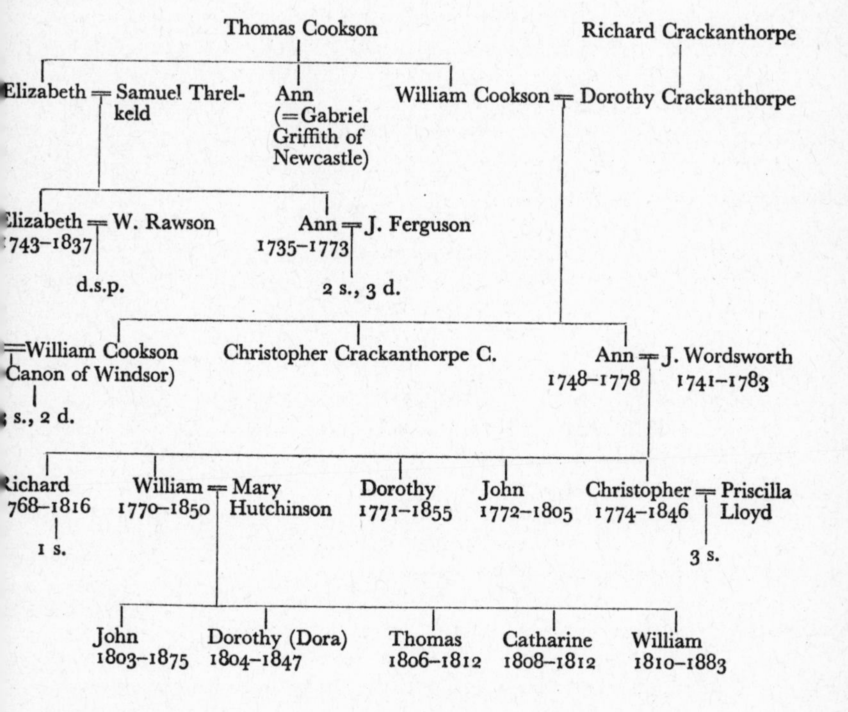

APPENDIX II

RECOLLECTIONS OF A TOUR IN SCOTLAND

THE importance of Dorothy Wordsworth's *Recollections of a Tour in Scotland*, as the best known and most carefully composed of her writings, and the only one that has been published *in extenso*, justifies a fuller account of its composition and history than could well have found a place in the main body of this book. There are at present known to me four complete manuscripts, which I shall call A, B, C, and D, and two printed texts.

MS. A, made by Mrs. Clarkson between early September and November 1, 1805, has already been partly described on p. 195. It occupies two quarto volumes, written on one side of the paper. The three parts into which it is divided are separated by two blank sheets: Part I goes down to the entry for August 25 (11 days): Part II gives the entries for August 26–September 5 (11 days); Part III September 6–25 (20 days). As Dorothy's copy from which Mrs. Clarkson transcribed is no longer traceable this MS. represents the first version of the work. Its title runs: Recollections / of a / Tour in Scotland / by / D. Wordsworth / Addressed to her Friends.

Notes inserted in this MS. give detailed information of the dates at which the different parts of the *Recollections* had been composed. Beginning soon after her return from Scotland in September 1803, Dorothy worked on steadily into December; but on December 20 she was interrupted by the arrival of Coleridge to pay them a farewell visit on his way to Malta. She had then brought down her record to the entry for September 2. She resumed work on February 2, but a few days later she laid it aside in order to make a copy of William's poems for Coleridge to take abroad with him; and though she took it up again towards the end of March (*v.* letter to S.T.C., March 29, quoted p. 178) she seems to have found it difficult to get back again into the mood of composition, for after the entry made under the date September 5, there follow in the MS. these two notes:

> 'Now on Saturday June 23rd 1804 I resume my work after a long pause—I have been ten days in Solitude, namely since last thursday sen'night, and now having finished my sewing, written letters etc, I shall endeavour to recollect the latter part of our journey. I feel I shall often be deceived—A long time and many thoughts have passed between, and also, except a few places or tracts of country, as, for instance, Edinburgh, the Tweed the Tiviot and the Esk, the character of the places was less distinguishable, one place more resembling another, and differing less from

what we had seen in England than the space between Loch Lomond and Tyndrum.'

But apparently nothing was done, except possibly the scribbling of a few rough notes, for the MS. continues:

'So far the 23rd of June—It is now the 23rd of July and I take the pen more heartless even than before, for my recollections must needs be fainter and fainter. The little incidents of our journey are many of them forgotten, or will now hardly seem worth recording, such as this day's good or bad dinner, a kind welcome, gentle or sour looks from the landlady, etc. etc.'

But again nothing was written, and it was not till nearly a year later that she resumed her task, urged on by William, who thought rightly that if she could be prevailed upon to undertake it, it would prove some distraction to her from her grief at the loss of her brother John, who had been drowned in the previous February (*v.* p. 193). On April 11, 1805, she began Part III, thus:

'I am setting about a task which however free and happy the state of my mind had been, I could not have performed well at this distance of time, but now, I do not know that I shall be able to go on with it at all—I will strive, however, to do the best I can, setting before myself a different object from that which I have hitherto aimed at, which was to omit no incident, however trifling, and to describe the face of the country so minutely that you should, where the objects were the most interesting, feel as if you had been with us. I shall now only attempt to give you an idea of those scenes which pleased us most,[1] dropping the incidents of the ordinary days, of which many have slipped from my memory; and others which remain it would be difficult and often painful to me to endeavour to draw out and disentangle from my other thoughts. I the less regret my inability to do more, because in describing a great part of what we saw from the time we left Kenmore my work would be little more than repeating what I had said before, or where it was not so, a longer time was necessary to enable us to bear away what was most interesting than we could afford to give.'

At the end of the MS. is added the note:

'Finished copying this Journal May 31st 1805 in the Moss hut at the top of the Orchard. D.W.'

A few days later Dorothy added to her first copy her brother's poem *Stepping Westward*; for it is incorporated in the A text with the following note:

[1] It will be noted that Part III (Sept. 6–25) is much less detailed than Parts I and II.

'The poem (which I now transcribe) was written this day while W. and I and little Dorothy were walking in the green field, where we are used to walk, beside the Rothay. June 3rd 1805.'

MS. B is Dorothy's own second copy, written in the clear, beautiful handwriting in which she had just transcribed *The Prelude*. It is a quarto volume, written on both sides of the paper and divided, like MS. A, into three Parts, but numbered continuously. On the last page is the note: 'This transcript finished Friday February 21st 1806. D.W.' It must have been begun some time after November 1, 1805, when Mrs. Clarkson had completed her transcript and returned the original, and there is good reason to suppose that it is almost entirely the work of the months of January and February 1806 (*v. infra*). In the main, MS. B follows A, but, as she copied, Dorothy added some passages of importance and introduced a large number of minor changes. Other changes which, to judge by the ink and the writing, were probably made soon afterwards, appear in the MS. as corrections.

A complete collation of the two texts would be both tedious and unnecessary, but the general character of the changes introduced into MS. B is worth noting and illustrating, for they were obviously made with the intention of rendering the style less casual and informal. Thus the phrase 'By the bye' is three times cut out, 'I daresay' altered to 'I believe', 'out-of-the-way' to 'lonely', 'seemed' continually to 'appeared', 'guessed' to 'conjectured', and 'about' to 'respecting' or 'concerning'; whilst the adverb 'very', which in A is far too often prefixed to the adjective, is frequently removed. Other changes in the direction of a more literary style are not always for the better: thus 'dead to the enormous vices of Hatfield' becomes 'utterly insensible of the enormity of H.'s offences'; 'struck me with a sort of stupid wonder', 'struck me with astonishment'; 'a beech in the prime glory of its manhood', 'a beech in the full glory of complete and perfect growth'; 'I thought less of the Trossachs', 'I was less occupied by the remembrance of the T.s'; 'How late it was', 'How far the evening was advanced'; 'it was nearly dark', 'the twilight was far advanced'; 'close to the water', 'on the brink of the lake'; 'shut up', 'confined'; 'mistaken', 'erroneous'; 'place', 'region'; 'virtues', 'excellent qualities'; 'lie', 'untruth'.

One must also regret the loss of a few little personal touches, of which, when Dorothy is the writer, we can hardly have too many. Thus in describing the stunted trees on the road from Longtown (Aug. 17) she had written in A: 'growing irregularly, they reminded me of the Hartz forest near Goslar and I was pleased; besides Wm had spoken to me two years before of the pleasure he had received from the hether plant in that very spot'; and in telling how, in the churchyard at Gretna Green, the graves of married women were inscribed, she had added 'as for instance, Mary Hutchinson spouse of W.W. *in* Grasmere, instead of *of*'. So we are told in A that the bookseller who accompanied them to the churchyard at Dumfries was the man 'of whom I had bought some little books for Johnny', and similarly that the cup given her by the kind landlady at Loch Etive, but afterwards lost, she had hoped to bring home 'for Johnny'. And details of her health on the journey given in A are sometimes toned down and sometimes dropped. After the terrifying experience on Loch Etive, when their horse nearly wrecked the boat, she tells how despite their hunger they were glad to pay off the men and depart, 'though I was not well and needed refreshment' (B), which is tame by the side of the version in A, 'though I was faint in my stomach and had a violent headache'.

But the additions made to MS. B amply compensate for the losses. It was in recopying that Dorothy added to the entry for August 18 the passage which begins with a reference to Drayton and ends with four stanzas addressed by her brother to the Sons of Burns; that she added to September 3 the apt quotation of William's poem *Brook and road*; to September 8 the reference to the battle of Killiecrankie; to September 12 the poem on *Rob Roy*, to September 13 *The Solitary Reaper*. The first appearance in MS. B of three poems of William's enables us to date them with a closer accuracy than has before been possible. In the *Oxford Wordsworth* the four stanzas *To the Sons of Burns* are attributed to 1803, *Rob Roy's Grave* to between September 1803 and April 1805, and *The Solitary Reaper*[1] to 'between 1803 and 1805'. But we now know that they must all have been composed between June 1805 and February 1806, for if they had been written before May 31, 1805, they would certainly have found their place in MS. A.

MS. B was the copy used by Principal Shairp for his edition of 1874. That he used the actual copy, and not a transcript from it, is proved by his quotation, in his Introduction, of a note which Dorothy added on re-reading it in 1832 (*v.* p. 268), after which date no transcription of it is likely to have been made. Shairp makes a few modifications of the punctuation, corrects the reference to the *Haymarket* in Edinburgh to the *Grassmarket*, and improves the spelling of some of the place-names,[2] whilst he prudently puts dashes in place

[1] *The Solitary Reaper* can be dated still more accurately by the letter to Lady Beaumont of Nov. 29 (*v.* p. 200) where it is quoted, obviously as a quite recent composition.

[2] This was often necessary; *cf.* D.W. to Lady B., Dec. 1806: 'do not wonder if you or Sir George should detect some inaccuracies, often misspelt and even

of the name of the churlish landowner of Fascally. He is guilty of very few errors of transcription, but he substitutes, for Dorothy's division of her book into three parts, a division into weeks.

Professor Knight (*Journals of D.W.*, 2 vols., 1897, republished in one vol., 1924) printed from Shairp, only making some changes in punctuation, and without reference to any MSS. He states, indeed (p. xi), that he has seen the transcript made by Dorothy for Mrs. Clarkson, by which we must suppose him to mean Mrs. Clarkson's transcript from Dorothy's MS., already described as A, but it is clear that he made no use of it, for he remarks (ii. 78): 'It is difficult to know what the Author meant by the First Second and Third Parts of her Journal: as it is divided into separate "Weeks" throughout'; this, as we have seen, was first done by Shairp, and has no MS. authority. Knight also faithfully reproduces all Shairp's misprints. I give here the most noticeable of these, as readers may be glad to correct their own copies:

station (S. 60; K. i. 215) *for* situation
one single horse (S. 77; K. i. 230) *for* our single horse
steps of the main shore (S. 100; K. i. 251) *for* steeps of the main shore
quit it again with the morning light (S. 165; K. ii. 47) *for* greet, etc.
Lickburn (S. 260; K. ii. 138) *for* Sockburn.

The note in K. ii. 34 'not very probable' is attributed by K. to Shairp, but it is really Dorothy's own note which S. (p. 139) had omitted to acknowledge.

MS. C is in the exquisite handwriting of Sara Hutchinson, filling 206 quarto pages, and written on both sides of the paper. It is preceded by 4 pages of Contents, and has 6 blank pages between Parts I and II and 4 (2 cut out) between Parts II and III. On the title-page is written 'S. T. Coleridge. Oct. 24th, 1806'. It will be remembered that Sunday October 26 was the day on which W., M., and D.W., together with S.H., first met Coleridge after his return from Malta (*v.* pp. 208–9). This copy was therefore prepared for Coleridge during his absence, and is the one referred to by D.W. in her letter to C.C. of March 2, 1806: 'We have been engaged in making copies of W.'s poems, and I also in re-copying my Journal[1] in a fair hand to be bequeathed to my Niece and namesake. These works are finished, and also Sara's copy for Coleridge' (i.e. Sara's

miscalled, for I never looked into a book, and only bore in mind my own remembrance of the sounds as they were pronounced to us.'

[1] i.e. MS. B. As Dorothy survived her 'niece and namesake' it came into the hands of her nephew John, who, suitably enough, handed it on to her 'namesake' of the next generation. On the flyleaf of the MS. is the inscription 'Dora Wordsworth from her aff^te father, J. Wordsworth. Nov. 1st 1866.'

copy of the poems, including *The Prelude*, and of the Journal; *v.* my edition of *The Prelude*, 1805, p. xvi).

MS. C represents a stage in the development of the text intermediary between A and B. It contains most of the passages which Dorothy added to B, but not the corrections and verbal alterations which she introduced into the B text. The most natural explanation of this would be that when, on November 1, 1805, Mrs. Clarkson returned Dorothy's MS. of the *Recollections*, both she and Sara were already hard at work making copies of William's poems (*v. The Prelude*, p. xvi, cited above); and that, as both could not copy at the same time from the same MS., Dorothy, after adding the new passages to the Journal, handed it over to Sara, and addressed herself to the poems. Then, when Sara had copied the Journal, Dorothy, who had now finished the poems, took over her Journal and, as she wrote MS. B, made the verbal changes already referred to. For Sara would hardly have copied A, if B had been in existence.

MS. D is the copy made in 1822–3, when the book was being prepared for the press (*v.* pp. 360–2). Some corrections may have been made to the MS. in 1832, when the idea of publication was again raised, but it is not likely that much was done at that time. This MS. is written on quarto sheets (with watermark 1820) roughly stitched together into four booklets. No. 1 goes down to the end of the entry August 25, and is in D.W.'s handwriting, No. 2, in a hand at present unidentifiable, to the middle of the September 1 entry; No. 3, the first 20 pages in the writing of John Carter and the rest in D.W.'s, takes the Journal down to Sunday September 4 inclusive: No. 4 completes the whole. It is in D.W.'s hand, but with the inserted poems in the unknown writing of No. 2. The numbering of the pages is meant to be continuous, but 209 was misread and is followed by 300, and similarly 429 is followed by 500. This copy differs widely from previous MSS.; it is much corrected, and in places new versions are stuck with wafers over the older text. We can hardly be too grateful that the proposals for the publication of the book fell through, and that Shairp did not have access to MS. D; for in preparing her work for the press Dorothy submitted it to far too drastic a revision. It still remains a delightful book, but in her desire to make it, as she thought, more suitable for the general public, she removed from it many of its most charming intimate touches, whilst at the same time she 'wrote it up', giving it here and there a pomposity of phrasing which ill befits the Dorothy we know. Like her brother, she tended in later life to fall back on a more conventional and Latinized vocabulary. This is the late version of the first day's travel:

'On Monday the 15th August 1803, I left Keswick with two

companions—our vehicle a jaunting-car, of the kind which is jestingly called an Irish *vis-à-vis*, the Parties sitting back to back. We chose it for the convenience of alighting at will, in the rough and mountainous region through which we were about to wander. On quitting the Vale of Keswick, passed on our right hand, the well-known druidical circle, and, soon after, the village of Threlkeld, where formerly stood one of the Mansions of Sir Launcelot Threlkeld, in a domain which he was proud of for being so well stocked with Tenantry to follow him to the wars. Here also he protected his Son-in-law, Lord Clifford, when the Youth was obliged to hide himself in Shepherd's Garb to avoid the power of the revengeful Yorkists.—Crossed, in travelling under Saddleback (formerly called Blencathara) several ravines almost choked up in places with rubbish brought down by the waters from the mountain-side and spread upon the road and adjoining fields. These formidable inundations are principally caused by the bursting of thunder-clouds; and Blencathara (allow me to give the mountain its ancient appellation) shews in a remarkable degree with what perseverance the fountains of the sky are wearing away the bodies of these giants of earth. At no very great elevation from the road, though entirely hidden from it, on the side of this mountain, lies a pool or small Tarn of singularly melancholy appearance. It is enclosed by circular rocks very steep and on one side rising to a great height, and you might fancy that the pool had filled up the crater of a volcano, a notion one is disposed to encourage as Blencathara has more appearance of having undergone the action of fire than any of his brethren.—Beyond the 5th mile-stone, turned off from the Penrith road. Passed the foot of Grisdale and Mosedale, both pastoral vallies, narrow, and soon terminating in the mountains—green—with scattered trees and houses, and each a clear brook. Travelled at the base of Carrock Fell, covered with loose stones to a considerable height, and very rocky above. The aspect of the whole recalled that characteristic and laboriously moving verse of Dyer

"Huge Bredan's stony summit once I climbed".

Had time allowed, we should have been inclined to ascend this mountain, to visit some vestiges of antiquity of which writers give but a confused account, agreeing, however, that the work must have been of a very remote age. Heaps of stones (some of the stones being of enormous size) are said to be scattered over a large area upon the summit. In what form the architecture had arranged those stones cannot be even conjectured; but the country people believe in the tradition that some of those heaps are the remains of a church without troubling themselves with a question what sort of building such masses would compose or with a doubt whether the worship was different from that of their own days. Reached Hesket Newmarket and in the evening walked to Caldbeck Falls,[1] a pleasing spot in which to breathe out a summer's day—lime-stone rocks—hanging trees—pools and water-breaks—caves and caldrons, which have been honoured with fairy names, and no doubt continue, in the fancy of the neighbourhood, to resound with fairy revels.'

This first entry shows, indeed, much more than the average amount of alteration, but the changes introduced into it are typical of the general character of the revision. I give a few others culled here and there from the MS., in order to illustrate the unfortunate effect on a modest natural writer of the delusion that in addressing the great public something more 'literary' than her wont is expected of her: 'this might be owing to our having come', 'we might be indebted for this pleasing association, partly to our having come'; (the rock at Dumbarton) 'is not grand but curiously wild', 'has more of strange and curious wildness than of grandeur'; 'the point where we had set off', 'the point where we had commenced our circuit'; (the houses at Dumbarton have) 'a tradish look', 'a tradish exterior (may I be allowed the expression?)'; 'business of the house', 'everyday petty disturbances'; 'we were unwilling to leave this sweet spot', 'we reluctantly wheeled away from the scene'; 'I seem to myself to wake up', 'my mind seems to be roused and awakened'; 'such a cruel woman', 'a woman who appeared to be destitute of common humanity'; the dirty house which was 'quite Hottentotish', 'no cleaner than the dwelling of a Hottentot'; the girl whose hair was 'fastened up with a comb', 'becomingly braided'; and 'I would willingly have given twenty pounds to', 'happy should I have been to'. Similarly 'showed us up' is altered to 'conducted us', 'walked on' to 'proceeded', 'close' to 'adjoining', 'hunted out' to 'set ourselves to discover', 'building' to 'edifice', 'lesser beauties' to 'minuter attractions', 'in a hurry' to 'impatient', 'disgusted with' to 'did not please our taste'; 'called out' to 'exclaimed', and 'works of God' to 'works of the Creator'.

Naturally enough, when the audience for whom she destined her Journal was widened, she severely reduced its *personalia*. Familiar details, which a few intimate friends might welcome, appeared to her wholly unsuited for the world at large. Authors in her day were for the most part reticent of their own and their friends' private

[1] The spot is called the *Howk*—a word commonly used in the North of England, as a verb, which signifies to scoop or hollow out. (*note* by D. W.)

lives; she had herself an abnormal shrinking from publicity, and she was anxious, too, in speaking of her fellow-travellers, men already famous and the subject of an irritating and at times malicious gossip, not to overstep what she held to be the bounds of a proper decorum. Accordingly, William and Coleridge are often referred to simply as 'my companions', William's awkwardness in unharnessing the horse is cut out, 'poor C. being unwell' becomes 'our companion, not in strong health', and many references to his ailments are omitted, as well as the account of how they divided their purse with him at parting, and how, when he had left hem, their 'thoughts were full of him'. So, too, the name of Scott, who added so largely to the pleasure of the last week of their tour, is never mentioned; he is spoken of simply as 'our friend', and inevitably many delightful details of the time they spent with him—such as their arrival at his house before he was up, their extravagant indulgence in a bottle of wine in his honour, and his recitation to them of his new poem, *The Lay of the Last Minstrel* find no place. Of herself, also, Dorothy is less communicative; if she tells that she tried in vain to buy a silver thimble at Dumfries, she omits the fact that she actually bought a halfpenny brass one, and the world was not to know of occasional headaches, stiffness, or fatigue, or how at the inn she lay stretched at her ease upon the carriage cushions and three chairs. Other passages, not so intimate in character, yet seemed, as they had been recorded in MS. B, to be unsuited to the printed page. Her account of the churlish landowner at Fascally, whose name, as we have seen, Shairp concealed behind a dash, she omitted altogether, and her description of the landlady at Luss,—'the most cruel and hateful-looking woman I ever saw. She was overgrown with fat, and was sitting with her feet and legs in a tub of water for the dropsy,—probably brought on by whisky-drinking. The sympathy which I felt and expressed for her, on seeing her in this wretched condition—for her legs were swollen as thick as millposts—seemed to produce no effect', is toned down into a rendering in which charity prevails over vividness and vivacity: 'She was sitting with her feet in a tub of warm water; and I soon learned from her that she used the warm water as a relief for the dropsy, and her extreme bulk might have been caused by that grievous malady. The sympathy I felt and expressed on seeing her in that wretched condition seemed to produce no effect in changing her resolution, nor did it in the least humanize her countenance, which has left upon me an impression to this day which I would gladly get rid of.'

In the entry under August 15, already quoted, it will have been noticed that in place of the reference to their jibbing horse she has substituted such historical or legendary information as a literary guide-book is expected to supply: with the same desire to impart information rather than simply to give utterance to her own immediate impressions, she made other additions to her narrative. Of Bothwell Bridge she tells (Aug. 22) that it is 'memorable for the discomfiture of the Convenanters by the Duke of Monmouth, who shewed on that occasion, if we may credit Burnet, a clemency which was ill relished by Charles and his Brother'; and of Stirling Castle (Sept. 14) that it is 'so famous in Scottish History—the overlooker of many a bloody Battle—and with the Field of Bannockburn lying almost at its base. Stirling Castle, was, in latter times, a favorite residence of some of the kings of Scotland on account of its delightful situation, and the salubrity, as it was supposed, of the air; but being almost at a central point between the two coasts, it must be exposed to tremendous storms from the meeting of winds that blow from both quarters'. To her account of Roslin Chapel (Sept. 17) she adds in 1822: 'One of the pillars of this beautiful little Gothic edifice is singularly elaborate, a twisted column, of which they tell a story at Roslin, that the master builder slew his apprentice, who performed the work, through envy in being surpassed by him in his own art'. But her additions have sometimes a biographical interest. In speaking of her impressions of Glencoe (Sept. 3) she added in 1822:

> 'Shall I be forgiven when I add, that we were but little affected by recollections, on the spot, of the barbarous massacre of Glen Coe?—which William the third neglected to punish, and by so doing, left an indelible stain upon his memory. One reads and thinks with indignation and sorrow of similar events: but here, in presence of such sublime objects, intimating the power of the creator to confer durability in what manner he chuses, yet affording undeniable evidences of the revolutions to which this planet has been subject, the mind sinks under the pressure of time;—the crimes and sufferings of individuals, or of this or that generation are lost in a feeling of the great mystery of decay and renovation, of life, and of death.'

In the same way she added to her account of their stay at Killin (Sept. 5):

> 'I hardly know why we did not go to visit the turf, which is said to cover the grave of Fingal:—The tradition is in unison with the romantic character of the mountainous recesses at the head of Loch Tay, and probably we did not expect to have our faith strengthened by seeing with our own eyes (what we had been told) that there was no *visible* monument on the spot: besides, the

situation of the village is so very interesting that we were satisfied after our walk along the banks of the silent stream with strolling about and lingering not two hundred yards from the houses.'

And after the description of her arrival at Langholm (Sept. 23) MS. D goes on:

'After sunset we bent our course up the vale—poetic ground! for Mickle, the translator of *The Lusiad*, was born at L. and has celebrated several of the brooks tributary to the Esk. We thought of him, and with the more interest, evening being the time in which his fancy seems most to have delighted. My companion repeated with pleasure some of his verses—the beautiful description of evening and the approach of night, in the beginning of his elegy on the death of his Brother, and that exquisitely musical stanza at the opening of his Poem of Sir Martyn.

Awake, ye west winds, through the lovely dale
And Fancy to thy faery bower betake etc,

nor could we forget that other equally appropriate, and still more beautiful stanza,

Now bright behind the Cambrian mountains hoar etc.—'

This entry of Dorothy's is valuable as bearing conclusive evidence of her brother's intimate knowledge and appreciation of a poetry which he is commonly held to have ignorantly despised.

There are at least two additions, in her reflective manner, which give welcome pictures of the working of her mind. After speaking (Aug. 20) of the little boy, alone with his sheep, who 'had in his appearance a solemnity which recalled to our remembrance the old man before seen in the cornfield' she goes on:

'Such a Boy, thought I, *he* once was; and such an old man will this child become; and how much have they now in common!—dress—occupation—mode of life—grave movement of body and of mind!—So begins, here, and so ends human life; and the intermediate space might seem to have so little variety that the whole presents itself to meditation with the simplicity of a circle.'

And after describing (Sept. 8) how the Duke of Atholl's gardener, with conscious pride, escorted them into the room in which the cascade of Bran was reflected in innumerable mirrors upon the ceiling and the walls, she adds:

'We both laughed heartily, which no doubt the gardener considered as high commendation, and probably he would have been well satisfied if we had cast but a slight regard upon the living waters of the Bran, or regarded them as merely illustrative of the skill and taste of the contriver of this, to us, ludicrous exhibition:

but we soon fixed our eyes only on the breezy dinning cataract—the fretted stones, overhanging crags, and pendant, or stately trees—yet such is the injurious effect of this conceited interposition of artifice, that, grand as are the accompaniments of that mountain torrent, my recollections are very indistinct except of the first overcoming sensation of oddness and surprize; and this, I believe from repeated experience, is the universal effect of obtrusive attempts to illustrate or adorn nature in places such as this, where submissiveness to her power seems to be the only legitimate homage.'

Despite the general inferiority of MS. D to the text with which we are already familiar, the passages which I have quoted are well worth the recovery.

APPENDIX III

EXTRACTS FROM LETTERS OF MARY WORDSWORTH RELATIVE TO THE DEATH AND BURIAL OF DOROTHY WORDSWORTH

I

Mary W. to Mrs. Thos. Hutchinson.

Dearest [Mary][1]

Our remaining Sister[.] [Yesterday?] at 20 minutes past 5 o'c (too late for post) [?] Our dear Sister was released after her prolonged but *fitful* suffering & some few hours of peaceful & anx[ious] waiting. The 2 Johns 2 Wms the [?] Mr C[2] James & myself present at *the Close.* Wm has just brought & read me your welcome letter. You are with me in *heart* & that is all I wish for; here we are fairly [?] & you are best where you are; I do not mean to venture to Grasmere. No one will be asked to go but Mr H. 2 Godsons & Benson & W. Smith. The Wordsworths[3] may come. John is gone off poor fellow, missed the coach, & a snow storm came on—the two sons walking part of the way with him to [?] where he joins the Coach which waits there two hours. The Boys will be with me till after the funeral which takes place on Wednesday at 12 o'c. John felt it necessary to go to his duty & his domestics. . . . He will return next Tuesday. Wm can stay & is all in all to me. I shall get Mrs Dorothy Harrison to come & sit with me while all the H.s attend the funeral—& all others will be at liberty to do so if the weather & their inclinations lead them—so beloved Sister, nieces & dear John all be quite free from any anxiety about me.

Willy does not go to Sed. till about the 4 or 6th of Feb, so I [?] [?] likely be alone independent of my good neighbours—& milder weather will bring you & the little Mary to comfort & cheer me when the birds begin to sing.

God bless & preserve you all
Lovingly yours. M.W.

1 o'c Friday mg. 26th Jan.
The Cooksons are kindness itself.

[1] The omissions and occasional incoherence of this letter seem to be due to M. W.'s rapidly failing eyesight. It is much blotted and some of the gaps are due to an undetected absence of ink from the pen.

[2] i.e. John Carter, *v.* p. 280; for James, *v.* p. 389.

[3] The Wordsworths, i.e. Dr. Christopher, Canon of Westminster, and his wife.

II

Mary W. to Mrs. Christopher Wordsworth.

Rydal Mt Febry 7th 1855.

This being a bright morning, I feel a desire to tell you & dear Chris.r with my own Pen, that notwithstanding the void that must henceforth remain at my heart, I shall ever feel thankful for the Almighty's goodness for having spared me to be the Solitary Lingerer, rather than the beloved Sufferer now laid at rest & whose restless Spirit I humbly trust is now among the Blessed in the bosom of her heavenly Father.

Last Wednesday the Remains were laid under the Thorn in the South East corner of the Church Yard by the side of the Grave of her loved Companion my Sister, who after a very short illness died in 1835—& up to the very *day*, I may almost say, of her departure—it seemed to be a doubtful case which of the pair would be the first to occupy that chosen Spot.—20 years, all but 3 Months has your dear Aunt been the Survivor. . . .

Trusting that you are all as well as, during this very severe weather, can be expected, & with dear love, I am dearest Susan believe me to be your affec Aunt

M. WORDSWORTH.

INDEX

PRINTED IN GREAT BRITAIN AT THE UNIVERSITY PRESS, OXFORD
BY JOHN JOHNSON, PRINTER TO THE UNIVERSITY